Prof. Dr. phil. Harald Müllich studierte Romanistik, Anglistik und Germanistik und promovierte in Angewandter Sprachwissenschaft. Nach dem zweiten Staatsexamen unterrichtete er zunächst an bayerischen Gymnasien, bevor er zum Professor für Wirtschaftssprachen und interkulturelle Kommunikation an die *Hochschule München* (Fakultät für Betriebswirtschaft) berufen wurde. Er lehrt außerdem *Wirtschafts- und Kulturgeschichte* an der *Munich Business School* und gibt Vorlesungen in Bachelor-, Master- und MBA-Programmen an ausländischen Hochschulen in und außerhalb Europas. Durch internationale Projekte und Einsätze ist er mit volks- und betriebswirtschaftlichen Zusammenhängen gut vertraut und kennt den unternehmerischen Alltag. Auf der Grundlage seiner didaktischen Erfahrungen in Schulen, Hochschulen und Weiterbildung, in der Lehrerbildung, der eigenen Entwicklung von Lernmaterial und der Mitwirkung bei der Weiterentwicklung von Studiengängen sowie von Lehr- und Lernmethoden und von spezifischen Modulen ist er seit vielen Jahren Autor und Co-Autor von Lehrwerken und Arbeitsbüchern.

Harald Müllich

Business and Grammar

*Grammar Rules and Exercises
with Business English*

Arbeitsbuch zum Selbstlernen
mit Lösungen

Bibliografische Information der Deutschen Nationalbibliothek:
Die Deutsche Nationalbibliothekverzeichnet diese Publikation
in der Deutschen Nationalbibliografie; detaillierte bibliografische
Daten sind im Internet über http//dnb.dnb.de abrufbar.

© 2016 Harald Müllich
Herstellung und Verlag:
BoD – Books on Demand, Norderstedt

ISBN: 978-3-7412-9064-0

INHALT

Vorwort 6

Benutzungshinweise 7

Abkürzungen / Abbreviations 10

Grammatikregeln und –übungen im wirtschaftlichen Kontext 11

Adverbs (ch. 1): Vorgedanken 12
  Level 1: Theory 16 – Practice 18
  Level 2: Theory 20 – Practice 22
  Level 3: Theory 24 – Practice 26
  Level 4: Theory 30 – Practice 34

Past Tenses (ch. 2): Vorgedanken 40
  Level 1: Theory 42 – Practice 46
  Level 2: Theory 48 – Practice 50
  Level 3: Theory 54 – Practice 58
  Level 4: Theory 66 – Practice 70

Modal Auxiliaries (ch. 3): Vorgedanken 76
  Level 1: Theory 78 – Practice 84
  Level 2: Theory 86 – Practice 90
  Level 3: Theory 94 – Practice 96

Reported Speech (ch. 4): Vorgedanken 104
  Level 1: Theory 106 – Practice 108
  Level 2: Theory 110 – Practice 114
  Level 3: Theory 120 – Practice 124

Passive Voice (ch. 5): Vorgedanken 136
  Level 1: Theory 138 – Practice 140
  Level 2: Theory 144 – Practice 146

***If*-Clauses (ch. 6)**: Vorgedanken 152
  Level 1: Theory 154 – Practice 156
  Level 2: Theory 160 – Practice 162
  Level 3: Theory 166 – Practice 168

Mixed Tenses (ch. 7): Vorgedanken 172
  Level 1: Theory 174 – Practice 178
  Level 2: Theory 186 – Practice 188
  Level 3: Theory 196 – Practice 200

Vocabulary English – German 208

Vokabular Deutsch – Englisch 235

Glossar (grammatikalische Begriffe) / Glossary 262

Diagnose-Test: Aufgaben 269 Lösungen 278

Lösungen und Übersetzungsvorschläge 283

Vorwort

Dieses Arbeitsbuch entstand über mehrere Jahre hinweg aus der Unterrichtsarbeit mit Studierenden der Betriebswirtschaftslehre in Wirtschaftsenglisch-Vorlesungen, Übungen und aus den Klausurerfahrungen bezüglich typischer Fehler in der englischen Grammatik, Struktur und Fachterminologie.

Gedankt sei allen Studierenden, die durch ihr Feedback zu einzelnen Übungen, Übungszyklen und Kapiteln die konkrete Ausgestaltung des Arbeitsbuches unterstützt haben. Zu danken ist insbesondere dem Studierenden Martin Leibold, der durch seine feinsinnigen systematischen Analysen und Rückmeldungen aus Sicht eines Lernenden zur didaktischen Konzeption beigetragen hat.

Ganz besonderer Dank gebührt Frau Sheila Scott, die die gesamte Arbeit mit ihrer muttersprachlichen Kompetenz begleitet hat. Ihre unermüdlichen Anmerkungen, Kommentare und Vorschläge waren besonders hilfreich in didaktischer Hinsicht und in puncto Idiomatik und Natürlichkeit englischsprachiger Formulierungen.

All dies diente der Zielsetzung dieser Arbeit, ein Lern- und Übungsbuch vorzulegen, das Grammatikthemen behandelt, welche typischerweise strukturelle Probleme für Lernende darstellen, und das zugleich Regeln und Übungen (Theorie und Praxis) im Kontext wirtschaftsenglischer Fachterminologie und Strukturen bietet.

I also thank *the Economist* for its inspiring texts and vocabulary, which prompted contexts and examples.

Benutzungshinweise

Englisch ist als *Lingua Franca* der globalen *Business Community* unverzichtbares Kommunikationsmittel für Führungskräfte. Dazu ist *allgemeine* englische Sprachkompetenz erforderlich, aber auch die Beherrschung *wirtschaftsenglischer Begriffe und Strukturen* sowie typischer *Sprachgepflogenheiten in der Geschäftskommunikation* und -korrespondenz.

Korrekte Grammatik ist dabei nicht eine reine Frage der Ästhetik, *nice to have*, sondern ein absolutes *Muss*. Sie ist Voraussetzung für erfolgreiche Verständigung; Analysen von Missverständnissen lassen sich häufig auf (z.T. weit zurückliegende) Grammatik-, Strukturoder Formulierungsfehler in früheren Phasen des Kommunikationsstranges zurückverfolgen, d.h. grammatikalische Korrektheit in Verbindung mit korrekten fachsprachlichen Begriffen ist für erfolgreiche Verständigung in den unterschiedlichen Kommunikationskanälen, internationale Zusammenarbeit und geschäftlichen Erfolg entscheidend.

Nicht zu unterschätzen sind auch Effekte auf der Metaebene. Schlechte Sprachbeherrschung, fehlerhafte oder irreführende Grammatik, das Unvermögen, sich richtig, klar, verständlich und auf angemessenem Sprachniveau auszudrücken und zu argumentieren, können durchaus die Glaubwürdigkeit und Autorität sowie das Vertrauen in die Kompetenz einer Führungskraft untergraben. Kleinere Abweichungen von formal korrekter Grammatik werden hingegen auch von Muttersprachlern toleriert, können sogar durch die absichtlich untypische Form (Grammatik) und Lexik (Wortschatz) bestimmte Wirkungen erzielen. Dazu ist allerdings virtuose Sprachbeherrschung erforderlich. Lernenden (ohne *near-native* Sprachkompetenz) ist daher davon abzuraten.

Auf der anderen Seite bedeutet es, dass nicht jede grammatikalische Feinheit und komplexe Ausnahme unbedingt erforderlich ist. Wenn Lernende eine sichere Beherrschung der Gesamtsystematik weitgehend erreicht haben und damit die meisten gängigen (fach-) sprachlichen Situationen gut beherrschen, mag es empfehlenswert sein, sich nicht auf jede feine Verästelung grammatikalischer Phänomene, d.h. Sonderregeln und Ausnahmen, einzulassen, um die Gesamtsystematik nicht durch völlige Unübersichtlichkeit wieder zu gefährden. Dies wurde bei der Auswahl der Aspekte, des Komplexitätsgrades und des Aufbaus dieses Arbeitsbuchs in der Weise berücksichtigt, dass die einzelnen Kapitel grundlegender Grammatikthemen in verschiedene Anspruchsniveaus, *Levels*, aufgegliedert sind, diese wiederum in grammatikalische Regeln (*theory*) und praktisches Übungsmaterial (*practice*).

Das Arbeitsbuch versucht einerseits, die Grammatikkapitel relativ umfassend abzubilden, andererseits nicht über alle Maßen zu verkomplizieren, und v.a. konkrete Hilfestellung zur Problemlösung sowie pragmatische Umsetzungstipps zu geben. Generell sollte der höchste Level im Zweifelsfall lieber ‚geopfert', d.h. ignoriert werden, wenn die Gefahr besteht, dass z.b. aufgrund der schwierigen Top-20 % (oder weniger) perfekter Beherrschung die 80 % genereller grammatikalischer Richtigkeit wieder auf der Strecke bleiben.

Dieses (Selbst-)Lern- und Arbeitsbuch orientiert sich also an den Bedürfnissen von Geschäftsleuten, die **korrektes *Business English*** benötigen; der Mehrwert besteht in der systematischen Ausrichtung auf typische **Grammatik**fragen, eingebettet **in (betriebs- und volks-)wirtschaftliche Kontexte mit** entsprechendem relevantem **Fachvokabular**. Das Arbeitsbuch eignet sich daher als **Selbstlernmaterial zum gleichzeitigen Wortschatz- und Grammatiklernen** für Berufstätige wie für Lernende (normalerweise mit Deutsch als Ausgangssprache) an Universitäten, Hochschulen für Angewandte Wissenschaften, Business Schools, VHS, FOS, BOS, Gymnasien, weiterführenden Bildungseinrichtungen und ergänzend zu In-house-Trainings in Unternehmen.

Das Lern- und Übungsbuch bietet eine Auswahl an Kapiteln, die sich im Wesentlichen um Verben drehen, bzw. um das *Verb* (als grammatikalische Kategorie). In gewisser Weise gliedert sich das Adverb hier an (Latein: beim/zum Verb) - auch wenn Adverbien natürlich nicht nur auf Verben bezogen verwendet werden.

Prinzipiell können die Kapitel – je nach Bedarf – auch in anderer Reihenfolge genutzt werden. Allerdings sollten die einzelnen *Levels* sinnvollerweise in der vorgegebenen aufsteigenden Progressionslinie abgearbeitet werden. Dabei kann zum Beispiel ein einfacher Level (etwa L 1, Bildung von bestimmten Formen) komplett ausgelassen oder nur kurz gesichtet werden, wenn hier bereits die entsprechende Verwendungssicherheit vorhanden ist. Bei der Bearbeitung der Übungen (*practice*) ist es zweckmäßig, immer wieder zu den Regeln (*theory*) zurückzugehen und die Aufgaben und Lösungen mit den Grundmustern rückzukoppeln, um den Lernerfolg dauerhaft zu sichern. Demgegenüber ist ein ständiges Hin- und Herspringen in den Übungen und Anspruchsniveaus nicht empfehlenswert, da auf diese Weise die Architektur der progressiv aufbauenden Abfolge der Regeln und Übungen nicht zum Tragen kommt. Damit könnte ein kontinuierlicher Lernerfolgspfad empfindlich gestört werden. Die Reihenfolge der Kapitel 1-7 folgt einem roten Faden, der in der komplexen Zusammenschau der „Mixed Tenses" (Kap. 7) auf dem höchsten Komplexitätsniveau (im Zusammenwirken von Effekten der vorangegangen

Grammatikaspekte wie Modalverben, *If*-Sätze, indirekte Rede, Vergangenheitszeiten) kulminiert.

Es ist auch sinnvoll, große Abschnitte nicht auf einmal abzuarbeiten, sondern eher in kleinen Häppchen voranzuschreiten, d.h. in Portionen, die der individuellen Auffassungsgabe und dem bereits erreichten Sprachniveau des lernenden Benutzers entsprechen. Dabei sollen die kurzen Texte und Übungen nach Möglichkeit nicht nur Aha-Effekte und Erfolgserlebnisse vermitteln, sondern durchaus auch Spaß machen.

Das **Arbeitsbuch** ist **für das Selbstlernen** konzipiert, daher werden Lösungen, Übersetzungsempfehlungen und Erklärungen geboten. Diese können nicht völlig umfassend sein, da es häufig viele Variationen und alternative Möglichkeiten gibt. In vielen Fällen sind Erklärungen beigefügt, zum besseren Verständnis, warum eine Möglichkeit richtig, eine andere (z.B. häufige oder typische Fehlerquelle) falsch ist.

Der **Wortschatz** findet sich in alphabetischer Reihenfolge sowohl Englisch-Deutsch als auch Deutsch-Englisch nach den Theorie- und Praxiskapiteln. Ganz am Ende des Lern- und Arbeitsbuches steht ein **Diagnosetest** mit Lösungen, anhand dessen sich individuell ermitteln lässt, wie es mit dem eigenen Lernniveau steht (d.h. welcher *Level* jeweils mehr oder weniger erreicht ist) und welche Grammatikaspekte besser und welche unzulänglich beherrscht werden. Zusätzlich besteht die Möglichkeit, durch Zuordnung der erzielten Punktzahl zu Qualitätsstufen, die dem angelsächsischen Benotungssystem nachempfunden sind, eine Gesamtnote der eigenen Leistung im Diagnosetest festzustellen.

Abkürzungen / Abbreviations
(deutsch / englisch)

Adj. / adj.	Adjektiv / adjective (e.g.: *cheap*)
Adv. / adv.	Adverb / adverb (e.g.: *cheaply*)
AE	amerikanisches Englisch / American English (e.g.: *labor*)
Asp. / asp.	Aspekt / aspect (e.g. *Simple Form* vs. *Progressive Form*)
BE	britisches Englisch / British English (e.g.: *labour*)
ugs. / coll.	umgangssprachlich / colloquial; informal (e.g.: *He went bust – Er ging pleite.*)
Konj. / conj.	Konjunktion, Bindewort / conjunction (e.g.: *während / while*)
etw.	*etwas*
Fig. / fig.	figurativ, bildlich, im übertragenen Sinn / figurative (e.g.: *to shed a company division – eine Unternehmenssparte abstoßen*; vgl. [wörtlich]: *to shed leaves – Blätter abwerfen*)
inv.	unveränderlich(e Form) / invariable (e.g.: *used to*)
jmd.	*jemand*
jmdm.	*jemandem*
jmdn.	*jemanden*
N. / n.	Nomen, Substantiv, Hauptwort / noun (e.g.: *Unternehmen / company*)
P.	Prädikat, ‚Satzaussage' (e.g.: *Er investiert.*)
Pl. / pl.	Plural, Mehrzahl / plural (e.g.: *Aktien / shares*)
pp	Partizip Perfekt, Partizip der Vergangenheit / past participle
Präp. / prep.	Präposition, Verhältniswort / preposition (e.g.: *während / during*)
Sg. / sg.	Singular, Einzahl / singular (e.g.: *Aktie / share*)
sth.	something
so.	someone
t	Tempus, (grammatische) Zeit(form) / tense (e.g.: *Past Tense*)
V. / v.	Verb, Tätigkeitswort / verb (e.g.: *kaufen / [to] buy*)
vi	intransitives Verb / intransitive verb (verb without a direct object; e.g.: *fallen / to fall*)
vt	transitives Verb / transitive verb (verb + direct object; e.g.: *[Aktien] kaufen / to buy [shares]*)
vs.	*versus* (gegenüber, im Gegensatz zu) / *versus* (e.g.: *Simple* vs. *Progressive [Forms]*)

Symbole / symbols

°	Wort davor in der Übersetzung weglassen (e.g.: *Wir müssen erst einmal° … - We first have to …*)
>	wird zu (e.g.: *cheap > cheaply – adj. > adv.*)
≈	*agency (advertising ≈): advertising agency*

theory & practice

Grammatikregeln und – übungen

im wirtschaftlichen Kontext

- § tenses
- § adverbs
- § if ...

Intro   Vorgedanken

ADVERBS
Adverbien / Umstandswörter

Wozu denn Adverbien? Wozu der Umstand?
Was ist das überhaupt?

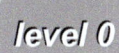 *level 0*

> Dann müsste es aber eigentlich auch * *fastly* * heißen, oder? Hab' ich aber noch nie gehört!

> He did it really * fastly *!
> (2 x *Adverb*)

* falsche (nicht existente) Form!

> He did it really fast. (2 x *Adverb*)
> oder:
> He did it really quickly.
> (2 'normale' *Adverbien*)

> Stop, stop, stop!!! Ganz falsch! Die Form <u>*fast*</u> ist <u>unregelmäßig</u> – * *fastly* gibt es nicht! *Fast* ist auch gleichzeitig Adverb.

> Ist das bei *hard* auch so? Aber es gibt doch auch *hardly*! Geht beides?

> My colleague hardly worked.
> He worked hard.

> My colleague worked hard. (*Adverb*)
> ▶ Mein Kollege arbeitete hart.
> My colleague hardly worked. (*Adverb*)
> ▶ Mein Kollege arbeitete kaum.
> (*Adverb mit anderer Bedeutung!*)
> This is hard work! This work is hard.
> (*Adjektiv!*)

> Es gibt beides, aber mit unterschiedlicher – fast entgegengesetzter – Bedeutung. Wieder eine Ausnahme – sorry!

> Komplettes Chaos! Andersherum funktioniert's ähnlich – oder?

> My plan is not good.
> My boss is not well.

> My plan is not good. (*Adjektiv*)
> ▶ Mein Plan ist nicht gut.
> My boss is not well. (*Adjektiv!*)
> ▶ Mein Chef ist nicht gesund.
> Aber ('normal'): He works well.
> Er arbeitet gut. (*Adverb*)
> (*Adverb mit anderer Bedeutung!*)

> Hier wird well als Adjektiv benutzt – und hat prompt eine andere Bedeutung!

Intro   Vorgedanken

> Ok, ok. Aber:
> Wie ist es denn nun normalerweise?
> Was sind Adverbien eigentlich?

He is often absent-minded.
She is very ambitious.
Our boss spoke loudly.
He argued vehemently.
It is a really good job.
Sadly he resigned.

> Es gibt Wörter und Formen, die sind von vornherein Adverbien und werden nicht verändert.
> Aber man kann aus Adjektiven Adverbien machen, meistens indem man *-ly* anhängt. So einfach ist das.

> Aha! ... Jetzt wirkt's wieder ganz einfach. Aber wann und wozu braucht man diese Formen?

The angry (a) customer complained heavily (1) and regularly (1). But he always stayed calm (b).
The applicant was extremely (2) nervous. She needed the job really (3) quickly (4). Luckily (5) she got it quickly (6).

> Adverbien heißen auch Umstands-wörter – nicht, weil sie Umstände machen, sondern weil sie Begleitumstände angeben, oder die Art und Weise, wie etwas geschieht oder wie schön, wie oft, wie stark etwas ist.

> Adverbien stehen also bei Adjektiven (2), bei Verben (1 & 4), bei anderen Adverbien (3) und können sich auf ganze Sätze beziehen (5 & 6).
> Adjektive bezeichnen Eigenschaften und stehen bei Substantiven (a) oder in Verbindung mit sein, bleiben (b), werden u.ä.

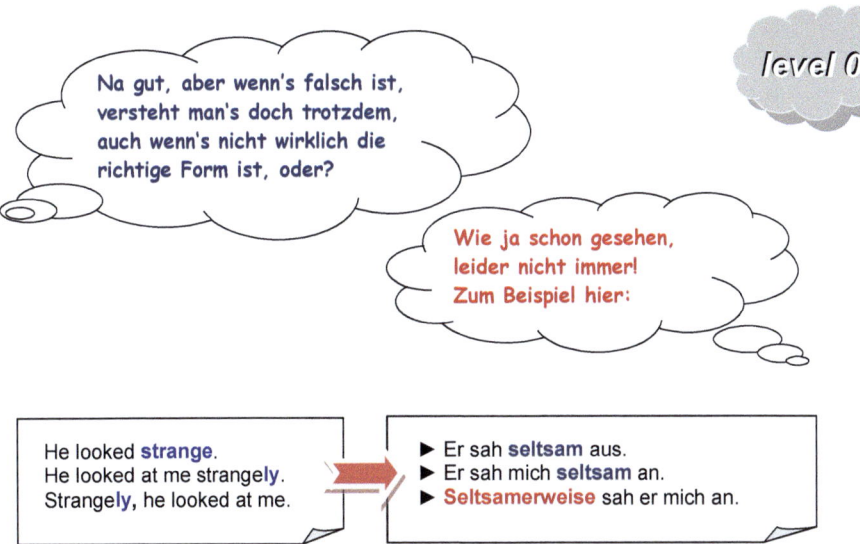

Merkbox:

Adverbien und **Adjektive** haben im Deutschen **oft die gleiche Form**, sind aber – grammatikalisch gesehen – unterschiedliche Wortarten. Im Englischen haben sie daher fast immer auch unterschiedliche Formen, v.a. die Endung *–ly*.
Zudem gibt es **Wörter, die nur als Adverbien vorkommen** und außerdem noch einige (häufige) **Ausnahmen**.

Adverbien bezeichnen, **wie** etwas zu verstehen ist, d.h. einen Umstand, eine Art und Weise, eine Modalität, eine graduelle Abstufung u.ä. ...
- **wie** schön oder effizient (**beim Adjektiv**) etwas oder jemand ist:
z.B.: *sehr schön*: *very beautiful* oder *unglaublich effizient*: *incredibly efficient*
- **mit welcher Frequenz** oder **wie** jemand etwas tut (beim Verb):
z.B.: Er kam *immer* (Häufigkeit) *pünktlich* zu Besprechungen: *He always came punctually to meetings* - oder sogar: Er kam immer extrem pünktlich: *He always came extremely punctually*. (Hier stehen zwei Adverbien hintereinander! Das Adverb *extremely* steht **bei** einem anderen **Adverb**, nämlich *punctually*, dieses gehört **zum Verb** ... *kam pünktlich*).

Adjektive (**Eigenschaftswörter**) bezeichnen eine **Eigenschaft** (wie jemand oder etwas ist), sie stehen demnach vor allem beim **Substantiv**:
- *Wir haben funktionale Büromöbel bestellt*: *We have ordered functional office furniture*.
Die Eigenschaft wird häufig durch *sein*, *to be*, ausgedrückt, steht also häufig in Verbindung mit einer Form des Verbs *sein* (*to be*), welches eine **Eigenschaft** zuschreibt:
- *Die Büromöbel sind funktional*: *The office furniture is functional*.
Ähnliche Verben haben dieselbe Funktion: *bleiben* (*remain, stay*), *finden* (*find*), auch *aussehen* (*look*), *riechen* (*smell*) u.ä.:
- *Die Streikenden blieben friedlich*: *The strikers remained peaceful*. oder:
- *Gewerkschaftsvertreter fanden den Vorschlag inakzeptabel*:
  Union representatives found the proposal unacceptable.

ADVERBS

nicely	happily	easily	regularly	fast
early	narrowly	hardly	here	quite
pretty	subtly	far	daily	well
very	fully	dramatically	extremely	
weekly	late	often	badly	visibly	only

Adverbien (Umstandswörter) sind im Deutschen oft nicht von Adjektiven (Eigenschaftswörtern) zu unterscheiden. Im Englischen muss differenziert werden, da Verwendung und Form unterschiedlich sind. Nicht alle Adverbien werden mit –ly gebildet, indem sie von Adjektiven abgeleitet werden (No. 2). Es gibt auch Wörter, die immer nur Adverbien sind (No. 1), Wörter, die beides (No. 3) sein können - mit (a) und ohne (b) Bedeutungsunterschied - und unregelmäßige Bildungen/Formen (z.B. well, in a friendly way).

1. primary adverbs
   (ursprüngliche Adverbien):

   Some adverbs are **not derived from adjectives**:
   now, soon, yet, still, already, now, then, today;
   rather, very, quite, too;
   here, there, up, down;
   ...

Tasks:

a, Find the *primary* adverbs in the box. *(level 1)*
b, Find the words (in the box) that are used in the same form and with the *same meaning* as *adjective and adverb*. *(level 2)*
c, Find the words (in the box) which are used as *adjectives and adverbs* (without changing their form), with *different meanings*. *(level 3)*

2. adverbs derived from adjectives (and participles)
(abgeleitete Adverbien):

Formation (Bildung):

Adverbs can be **formed from (most) adjectives**, by adding *-ly*.

a, regular formation (regelmäßige Bildung):
quickly, finally, slowly, immediately, badly, ...
also: extremely, gravely, sincerely, ...
but: full > fully
but: true > truly, due > duly; whole > wholly

b, *Consonant* + le > ly,
possible > possibly; capable > capably;
gentle > gently, subtle > subtly

c, -ic > -ically , ical > ically
logical > logically, fantastic > fantastically
ironic > ironically, ironical > ironically
economic > economically,
economical > economically
historic > historically,
historical > historically
but: public > publicly

d, y > i
easy > easily, happy > happily,
angry > angrily; gay > gaily, dry > drily, ...
but: shyly

Watch out:

usually no adverb from some adjectives:

lonely, lively, lovely, likely, friendly, elderly, costly, sickly, cowardly ...

adverbial use:
in a friendly way,
in a lovely manner,
in a cowardly fashion

e, good > well *(adv.)* = *gut*
Note: well (*adj.*!) = *gesund*

f, Present Participle > adverb
smiling > smilingly, knowing > knowingly

Past Participle > adverb
decided > decidedly, admitted > admittedly

advice: Do not use yourself!
(restricted and tricky application)
(Hände weg, da nicht völlig frei verwendbar!)

Merkbox:

❖ Manche Wörter sind von vornherein (ursprüngliche) Adverbien und ändern daher ihre Form nicht.

❖ Adjektive können zu Adverbien werden, indem sie abgeleitet werden, indem sie die Endung *-ly* annehmen. Dabei gibt es einige Besonderheiten, und zwar bei Adjektiven, die auf *-le, -ic / ical* und *-y*, bzw. auf *-ly* enden.

❖ Hände weg von Partizipien!

❖ Das Adverb zu *good* (*well*) ist eine Ausnahme. Das Adjektiv *well* hat eine andere Bedeutung (*gesund*).

A Translate the following statements, concentrating on the underlined (primary) adverbs.

1. Da die Fabrik <u>zu</u> alt ist, wird sie <u>bald</u> stillgelegt werden.
   _____

2. Wir werden unseren neuen Sommerkatalog <u>schon</u> <u>morgen</u> verschicken.
   _____

3. Haben Sie unseren Stand auf der Messe <u>schon</u> besucht?
   _____

4. Wir warten <u>noch</u> auf Ihr Angebot!
   _____

5. Wir haben <u>hier</u> <u>schon</u> eine Menge Handys verkauft.
   _____

6. Diese Marke ist <u>sogar</u> in China beliebt.

B The ideal candidate - Use the attributes below to make statements.

1. ... speaks Chinese ____*fluently*____.
2. ... plans things _____.
3. ... acts _____.
4. ... arrives _____.
5. ... listens _____.
6. ... understands _____.
7. ... doesn't criticize _____.
8. ... doesn't make decisions too_____.
9. ... doesn't answer _____.

- fluent
- thorough
- wise
- punctual
- patient
- immediate
- public
- hasty
- cynical or dry

C Rephrase the following statements, using derived adverbs.

1. Our recent sales increase has been *impressive*.
   Sales have increased _____.
2. The launch of our latest product has been *successful*.
   The product has been launched _____.
3. The CEO gave a *sincere* and *friendly* answer.
   The CEO answered _____.
4. There is an *easy* solution to the problem.
   The problem can be solved _____.

D **Translate the following statements, concentrating on the underlined (derived) adverbs.**

1. Die Arbeitslosigkeit ging im letzten Monat <u>leicht</u> zurück.

2. Der Vorstandsvorsitzende reagierte <u>extrem</u> <u>langsam</u> auf die Krise.

3. Sie könnten den Umsatz <u>leicht</u> steigern, wenn Sie Ihren Service <u>deutlich</u> verbessern würden.

4. Unsere Mitarbeiter sind <u>voll</u> engagiert und bekommen <u>regelmäßig</u> Leistungsprämien.

5. Denken Sie <u>logisch</u>: Es ist ein gutes Geschäft. Unterschreiben Sie <u>sofort</u>!

6. <u>Schließlich</u> gelang es ihm <u>bemerkenswert</u> <u>gut</u>, Marktanteile zu gewinnen.

7. Der Vorstandsvorsitzende beklagte sich <u>öffentlich</u> über Mobbing.

8. Unser Chef teilte uns <u>höflich</u> mit, daß die Fabrik geschlossen werden würde.

9. Viele Kunden verlangten <u>wütend</u> ihr Geld zurück.

10. Diese Erfolgsgeschichte ist <u>historisch</u> einmalig.

11. Der Mitarbeiter gab seinen Fehler <u>offen</u> zu und es tat ihm <u>sichtlich</u> leid.

12. Nun ist das Unternehmen <u>vollständig</u> ruiniert. Die Belegschaft ist <u>total</u> geschockt.

13. China braucht <u>dringend</u> Stahl und Öl, daher sucht die chinesische Regierung <u>intensiv</u> nach Partnern in Afrika.

14. Die neuen Modelle werden <u>wahrscheinlich</u> auf der Modemesse vorgestellt werden.

15. Die Aktienkurse sind in den letzten Wochen <u>dramatisch</u> in den Keller gegangen.

theory  adverbs

Wie kann man Adverbien von Adjektiven unterscheiden, wenn sie doch im Deutschen oft gleich aussehen? ... durch ihre grammatikalische Funktion und das Bezugswort.

Use (Gebrauch): adverb vs. adjective

Adjectives indicate **attributes** *(Eigenschaften)* **and go with ...**

- **nouns**

    e.g.: a *reasonable* strategy, *good* sales,   eine *vernünftige* Strategie, *guter* Absatz,
    naïve optimism, *strong* demand, ...   *naiver* Optimismus, *heftige* Nachfrage, ...

- **the verb** *to be* (*sein* / =) indicating **attributes**

    e.g.: This attempt **is** *hopeless*.   Dieser Versuch **ist** (=) *hoffnungslos*.
    Their quality **is** *excellent*.   Ihre Qualität **ist** (=) *ausgezeichnet*.

- **verbs** indicating lasting or future **attributes** (= / >),
such as *to remain* (=); *to become, to get, to turn* (>) ...

    e.g.: Inflation **remains** *dangerous*.   Die Inflation **bleibt** *gefährlich*.
    Customers **have become** *choosy*.   Die Kunden **sind** *wählerisch* **geworden**.

- **verbs** indicating attribution of **qualities**, such as
to find (s.o./sth. + adj.), to seem, to appear, ...

    e.g.: She **finds** her boss *self-righteous*.   Sie **findet** ihren Chef *selbstgerecht*.
    This location **seems** *ideal* (to me).   Dieser Standort **scheint** (mir) *ideal*.

- **verbs** indicating **perception** (*Verben der Wahrnehmung*), perceived attributes,
such as *to look, to taste, to smell, to feel, to sound*, ...

    e.g.: This strategy **sounds** *promising*.   Diese Strategie **klingt** *vielversprechend*.
    Your shop **looks** *beautiful*.   Ihre Laden **sieht** *schön* aus.

Distinguish (Unterscheide):
    She **looked** *sad (adj.)*.   Sie **sah** *traurig* **aus**.
    She **looked** *sadly (adv.)* at me.   Sie **sah** / **blickte** mich *traurig* **an**.

AE: In American English some short and frequent adjectives are also used without *–ly*, especially *real* - e.g.: That looks real good.

Hyphenated compound adjectives (zusammengesetzte Adjektive mit Bindestrich):

Distinguish (Unterscheide):
    new-born, easy-earned, high-flying   new**ly** married, new**ly** built, high**ly** paid
    much-travelled (BE), ready-made

Adverbs indicate manner, place, time, frequency, degree
(Art und Weise, Ort, Zeit, Maß, Häufigkeit) **and go with ...**

- **adjectives**
  e.g. *rather* positive, *too* good   *eher* positiv, *zu* gut
  relatively wealthy, *purely* theoretical, ...   *relativ* wohlhabend, *rein* theoretisch, ...
- **adverbs**
  e.g.: She earns her money *rather* easily.   Sie verdient ihr Geld *ziemlich / eher* leicht.
  He sold his furniture *incredibly* cheaply.   Er verkaufte seine Möbel *unglaublich* billig.
  The office was *really* poorly equipped.   Das Büro war *wirklich* armselig / dürftig ausgestattet.
- **verbs**
  e.g.: This client rings up *often / regularly*.   Dieser Kunde ruft *oft / regelmäßig* an.
  Our engineers work *conscientiously*.   Unsere Ingenieure arbeiten *gewissenhaft*.
  Our products are packaged *attractively*.   Unsere Produkte sind *attraktiv* verpackt.

Manche Wörter sind Adjektive und Adverbien, d.h. sie ändern ihre Form nicht:

3a, adverb = adjective

early, daily, weekly, monthly, yearly, quarterly ...
e.g.: He arrived **early** *(adv.)*. We had an **early** *(adj.)* dinner.
He came here **weekly** *(adv.)*. We resumed our **weekly** *(adj.)* meetings.

fast, far, leisurely, likely, little ...
e.g.: He works very **fast** *(adv.)*. He is a **fast** *(adj.)* eater.
We travelled **far** *(adv.)* and were **far** *(adj.)* away from home.
The street vendor walked **leisurely** *(adv.)*. He walked at a **leisurely** *(adj.)* pace.
Profits will most **likely** *(adv.)* have risen. It is very **likely** *(adj.)* that his business idea works *or:* His business idea is very **likely** *(adj.)* to work.
His business partner spoke **little** *(adv.)*. But they had **little** *(adj.)* time. *(wenig)*
Watch out: **little** as an **adjective** is *klein* with **countable nouns,** *wenig* with **non-countable nouns** – e.g.:
The executive answered the questions of a **little** (*adj.* - *klein*) group (*countable noun*) of selected journalists, but offered **little** (*adj.* - *wenig*) help (*non-countable noun*) when it was about delicate issues.
Distinguish: **little** (*wenig*) *vs.* **a little** (*ein wenig, ein bisschen*)

to sell / buy *sth.* cheap; to speak loud, to take *sth.* easy etc. *(feste Wendungen)*

Merkbox:

❖ Adjektive bezeichnen Eigenschaften und stehen daher beim Substantiv oder werden mit Verben wie *sein* (*to be*), *bleiben* (*to remain, to stay*), *werden* (*to become, to get*) kombiniert (als Zustand oder Zustandsänderung).

❖ Zugeschriebene Eigenschaften, etwa durch eigene Meinung (*I don't find it funny.*) oder Sinneswahrnehmung (*to smell good, to taste sweet, to sound nice* etc.) stehen ebenfalls in adjektivischer Form.

❖ Adverbien bezeichnen die Art und Weise, das Maß, Ort, Zeit etc. und beziehen sich auf Verben, Adjektive oder andere Adverbien (*wortbezogene Adverbien*).
❖ Einige Wörter werden unverändert, also in gleicher Form und mit gleicher Bedeutung als Adjektive und als Adverbien gebraucht.

practice — adverbs

E Adjective or adverb? Complete.

1. Mr Wang works for a Chinese company with _____ partners. Meanwhile, the bulk of his business is _____. *(international)*
2. Wages have increased _____ over the last few years, but employees are sick of _____ pay rises. *(modest)*
3. Our company scores _____ low in ratings; I still think the quality of our service is far from being _____. *(embarrassing)*
4. This is an _____ task. We can _____ cope with it. *(easy)*
5. Your plan sounds quite _____, but we will have to carry it out _____, too. *(good)*
6. Working conditions in sweatshops are _____. My company refuses to cooperate with suppliers that treat their workers _____, even if this could help cut costs. *(inhumane)*
7. We will design our website _____. We want it to look _____ from the web presence of all our competitors. *(different)*
8. Even if your offer seems very _____, it isn't the most _____ offer we have received so far. *(attractive)*
9. The company changed its name ten years ago. But most people _____ continue to use the old one, as they find it clear and _____. *(simple)*
10. Last year many customers reacted _____ and sent _____ e-mails. But only few remained _____ for long. *(furious)*

F An unusual fashion store - fill in.

1. As we entered the market _____, we benefited from the _____ mover advantage.
2. *Misfits* is by _____ the most spectacular fashion store; we are _____ ahead of our competitors.
3. We will report to you _____.
4. The logistics industry has changed _____.
5. The supply chain changes almost _____.
6. Please read our _____ newsletter.
7. Always be _____ to customers!
8. Never treat a customer _____.

1. early
2. far
3. quarterly
4. dramatic
5. annual
6. weekly
7. friendly
8. unfriendly

G   The European Community: integration and expansion.   *level 2*
Insert the appropriate forms.

(1)_____ many people were (2)_____ about the (3)_____ created European Economic Community. But (4)_____ the Community gained momentum and became (5)_____ to other European countries. Even (6)_____ (7)_____ Britons felt the need to join the (8)_____ trading bloc quite (9)_____.
(10)_____ the European Community grew (11)_____ and expanded (12)_____ beyond its (13)_____ borders.
In 2004 ten (14)_____ members (15)_____ celebrated their accession to the EU. When Bulgaria and Romania were (16)_____ allowed in on Jan.1st, 2007, some economists were (17)_____ concerned and issued warnings. An even more (18)_____ issue is the membership of Turkey, which seems (19)_____ determined to join the EU. Some politicians find the country too (20)_____ (21)_____ and (22)_____, others fear the (23)_____ impact. A (24)_____ decision is (25)_____ needed: Europe will (26)_____ have to speak out (27)_____ and say where it ends.

1. initial	2. sceptical	3. new	4. gradual
5. irresistible	6. former	7. critical	8. prosperous
9. early	10. consequent	11. fast	12. far
13. original	14. new	15. enthusiastic	16. surprising
17. deep	18. controversial	19. firm	20. different
21. cultural	22. religious	23. demographic	24. final
25. bad	26. inevitable	27. clear	

H   Translate the following statements, concentrating on the underlined (derived) adverbs.

1. Ihre neuen Bürostühle sehen modern und bequem aus. Könnten Sie uns sofort ein paar

_____

Muster zusenden? Wenn die Wirtschaftslage stabil bleibt, können wir unsere Verkaufs-

_____

zahlen sicher verdoppeln. Das wäre auch für Sie vorteilhaft.

_____

2. Produktpiraterie verursacht global enormen wirtschaftlichen Schaden. Da Imitate

_____

zunehmend absolut echt aussehen, wird es immer schwieriger, geistiges Eigentum wirkungs-

_____

voll zu schützen. Hersteller und Nachahmer arbeiten fast gleich schnell und professionell.

_____

theory   adverbs

Manche Wörter haben als Adjektiv und Adverb dieselbe Form, als (abgeleitetes) Adverb mit –ly können sie eine andere Bedeutung haben.

3b, adverb (-ly) → **different meaning** from adjective:

hard (*hart, schwer*)   vs.   hardly (*kaum*)
   e.g.: He worked **hard**.   He **hardly** worked.
      Er arbeitete *schwer / hart*.   Er arbeitete *kaum*.

near (*nahe*)   vs.   nearly (*fast*)
   e.g.: He was **near** the exit.   He was **nearly** 50.
      Er war **nahe** dem Ausgang.   Er war **fast** 50.

fair (*fair, gerecht*)   vs.   fairly (*ziemlich*)
   e.g.: This isn't **fair**.   This is *fairly* reasonable.
      Das ist nicht **fair**.   Das ist *ziemlich* vernünftig.

      but: We want to be treated **fairly**.
           Wir wollen **fair** behandelt werden.

late (*spät*)   vs.   lately (*in letzter Zeit*)
   e.g.: You are **late** again!   I haven't met him **lately**.
      Sie sind wieder **spät** dran.   Ich habe ihn **in letzter Zeit** nicht getroffen.

Note:
   late + *noun* = *verstorben* !
   e.g.: My **late** uncle was very rich.
      Mein **verstorbener** Onkel war sehr reich.

short   vs.   shortly (*in Kürze / vor kurzem*)
   e.g.: The transition phase was **short**.   The shipment will arrive **shortly**.
      Die Übergangsphase war **kurz**.   Die Lieferung wird **in Kürze** eintreffen.

      He died **shortly (kurz)** after the deal.

      "Can you sum up **briefly**?" he said **shortly**.
      „Können Sie **kurz** zusammenfassen?" sagte er **kurz / schroff**.

high, low, deep   vs.   highly, lowly, deeply (*fig.*)
   e.g.: The aircraft flew **high / low** (*adv.*).   He thought **highly** (*adv.*) of her.
      Das Flugzeug flog **hoch / tief**.   Er hielt viel von ihr.
   Prices are **high**. (*adj.*)
      Die Preise sind hoch.
   Still waters run **deep** (*adv.*).   The boss was **deeply** impressed. (*adv.*)
      Stille Wasser sind / gründen tief.   Der Chef war tief beeindruckt.

warm, cold   vs.   warmly, coldly (*fig., emotional*)
   e.g.: This spring is quite **warm**.   The boss welcomed us **warmly**.
      Dieser Herbst ist recht **warm**.   Der Chef begrüßte uns **herzlich**.

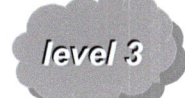

Manche Adverbien beziehen sich auf bestimmte Wörter, andere auf die Satzaussage im Ganzen.

adjunct *(wortbezogen)* vs. disjunct *(satzbezogen)*:

Adverbs that refer to **words** (adjectives, adverbs, verbs) are called **adjuncts**.

e.g.: This outcome is **hardly** imaginable.   Dieser Ausgang ist **kaum** vorstellbar.

He ran his business **quite** badly.   Er führte sein Geschäft **recht** schlecht.

We **quickly** gained market leadership.   Wir erlangten **rasch** Marktführerschaft.

Adverbs that refer to a **whole sentence** or statement are called **disjuncts**.

e.g.: **Unfortunately,** the bank went bust.   *Unglücklicherweise / Leider* ...

Surprisingly, the housing bubble did not burst.   *Überraschenderweise*...

Strangely (enough), everybody bought the new version.   *Seltsamerweise* ....

Financially, the project was a mess.   *Finanziell (gesehen)* ...

Adjuncts and disjuncts in context:

A company spokesman admitted **reluctantly** that the crisis was **unexpectedly** serious.

Politically, the merger had been more than welcome, **economically,** it was a real disaster.

Analysts had warned **unusually** clearly that corporate philosophies were **hardly** compatible.

Merkbox:

❖ **Adverbien** können sich **auf Verben, Adjektive, Adverbien beziehen**, also wortbezogen (*adjuncts*) sein, oder auch auf eine ganze Aussage, einen ganzen Satz, also satzbezogen (*disjuncts*). Manchmal werden satzbezogene Adverbien (*disjuncts*) am Satzanfang durch Komma abgetrennt, im Deutschen wird häufig *-weise* angehängt oder ein andere Wendung benutzt (*... gesehen* u.ä.).

❖ **Vorsicht:** Einige Adverbien können eine andere Bedeutung oder Bedeutungsnuancen haben als die adjektivischen Formen!

practice adverbs

I   **Adjective or adverb? Fill in the correct form.**

Business News

1. Rental costs have been rocketing _____ (late). Although shopkeepers have been trying _____ (hard) to attract more customers by staying open longer, most of them have _____ (hard) increased sales; about 40 % may have to give up _____ (short) although they have been working very _____ (hard) to find new strategies. The surviving majority may still find it _____ (hard) to make ends meet in the long run; so new ideas are _____ (bad) needed and may still come too _____ (late).

2. The board had _____ (hard) announced the merger when the share price rose _____ (high) above former levels. Now many employees are afraid of being laid off _____ (cold-hearted) in the new management's pursuit of synergies and cost savings. It is _____ (wide) known that mergers are _____ (common) followed by job cuts. _____ (unsurprising) _____ (near) all shareholders are happy about the _____ (current) development. Union representatives, however, are _____ (fair) worried and _____ (understandable) demand job guarantees.

3. Again, a famous bank is _____ (near) bankruptcy. _____ (repeated) the government has been _____ (literal) forced to bail out banks to prevent a _____ (dangerous) domino effect throughout financial services. _____ (fortunate) this seems to be the end of a series of collapses that have shaken financial markets _____ (late). Economists _____ (large) agree that the sector now seems _____ (sufficient) consolidated and _____ (near) its _____ (usual) stability.

4. _____ (strange) enough, there were _____ (sudden) blackouts again last month. Electricity providers reacted _____ (pretty) _____ (late) and found it _____ (hard) to fix the problem. They _____ (angry) blamed regulators for imposing too _____ (low) price caps. Companies _____ (prompt) announced they would sue energy providers for damages _____ (short).

K Shortage of skilled labour looming

Fill in the correct forms.

(1)_____ politicians are (2)_____ worried about unemployment figures. (3)_____ unemployment is a (4)_____ nightmare: (5)_____ it may deter voters, (6)_____ it may put the economy at risk. (7)_____, however, there is another (8)_____ problem: a (9)_____ shortage of skilled labour, with companies (10)_____ finding enough people to keep their business running. Earlier on, experts had (11)_____ warned almost (12)_____, but their warnings were (13)_____ ignored. Now, rather (14)_____, politicians realize that they have to act (15)_____ in order to push education levels (16)_____ enough. (17)_____ a lot of time has already been lost and it will be (18)_____ (19)_____ to catch up.

1. traditional	2. chief	3. growing	4. permanent	5. political	6. economic
7. increasing	8. unfamiliar	9. acute	10. hard	11. already	12. monthly
13. general	14. late	15. fast	16. high	17. sad	18. pretty
19. hard					

L Translate the CEO's words.

Liebe Kollegen,   *Dear colleagues,*

bis vor kurzem glaubten wir alle, dass Korruption ein Problem der Dritten Welt sei.

___

Leider sind wir nun mit einem unangenehmen Fall in unserer eigenen Firma konfrontiert,

___

ironischerweise in unserer Antikorruptionsabteilung. Und möglicherweise sind wir nicht weit

___

von einem Verbraucherboykott entfernt (= weg), nachdem lokale Zeitungen kürzlich genaue

___

Einzelheiten veröffentlicht haben. Wir werden den Fall gewissenhaft prüfen und uns streng

___

an unsere Unternehmensregeln halten. Unsere Null-Toleranz-Politik habe ich bereits

___

öffentlich unterstrichen. Nun müssen wir mit Kommentaren äußerst vorsichtig sein, damit

___

wir die öffentliche Debatte nicht unabsichtlich am Leben halten. Zugegebenermaßen war die

___

Lage vorübergehend kritisch.

___

practice   adverbs

M   Company News - Translate.

1. Bald werden noch mehr billige chinesische Autos mit europäischen Marken in Europa konkurrieren. Paradoxerweise haben die Chinesen von Allianzen mit europäischen Autoherstellern und Zulieferern profitiert. Diese massive technologische Unterstützung hat den Chinesen geholfen, relativ schnell konkurrenzfähige Fahrzeuge für den europäischen Markt zu entwickeln. Die Kunden werden bald neue Autos mit unvertrauten Namen und ungewöhnlichem Aussehen, aber ungewöhnlich niedrigem Preis entdecken. Der Autokauf (= *das Autokaufen*) bleibt weitgehend emotional. Daher können die Kunden durch rein rationale Argumente kaum überzeugt (*to persuade*) werden.

2. Viele Geschäftsleute haben Billigflüge mit wenig Service bereitwillig akzeptiert. Selbst große Fluggesellschaften mit traditionell gutem Service und relativ hohen Ticket-Preisen sind zunehmend gezwungen, Billigflüge anzubieten. Das ist genau das Problem, nach Meinung einiger Experten. Sie befürchten, dass technische Überprüfungen nicht mehr zuverlässig und sorgfältig durchgeführt werden könnten. Die Fluggesellschaften betonen, dass es „absolut keinen Kompromiss bezüglich der technischen Sicherheit" gebe. Reisende werden auch in Zukunft ihre Flüge sparsam planen können, besonders wenn sie wöchentlich oder monatlich dieselben Hin- und Rückflüge buchen.

3. Der Elektronikkonzern ist mit den neuesten Absatzzahlen in der Eurozone *level 3*

völlig unzufrieden und bereitet aktuell eine Werbekampagne mit Sonderangeboten vor.

„Unsere vierteljährlichen Ergebnisse sind in der EU vergleichsweise schlecht, obwohl die

Nachfrage deutlich gestiegen ist," gab ein Firmensprecher gestern öffentlich zu.

Mit diesen Worten kritisierte er indirekt die Politik des früheren Vorstandsvorsitzenden, der

nach der ungewöhnlich turbulenten Hauptversammlung unerwartet zurückgetreten war.

„Der verstorbene Sohn des Unternehmensgründers wäre schrecklich wütend," fügte er

überraschend hinzu.

4. Wirtschaftlich gesehen sieht die Zukunft Australiens strahlend aus. Die geopolitische

Position im pazifischen Raum, die einst isoliert erschien, stärkt die australische Handels-

bilanz deutlich. Für viele Firmen ist das Land ‚dort drunten' für den Handel in Südostasien

außerordentlich wichtig geworden. Besonders Chinas unglaubliches Wirtschaftswachstum

hat Australien hoch attraktiv gemacht, da es westlichen Unternehmen vertraute Geschäfts-

gepflogenheiten bietet. Geographisch weit weg, erscheint das Land europäischen

Mentalitäten emotional und kulturell immer° noch relativ nahe.

5. Londons Bedeutung für das britische BIP hat in letzter Zeit eher zu- als abgenommen. Die

City ist ein beeindruckend nachhaltiger Wachstumsfaktor; das Land bleibt (*to stick to*) treu

bei seiner Währung, lehnt den Euro strikt ab und gewöhnt sich langsam an den *Brexit*.

theory — adverbs

Nicht nur Adjektive können gesteigert werden, sondern auch Adverbien, und zwar erfolgt die Steigerung der Adverbien nach ähnlichen Regeln wie bei Adjektiven.

Comparative and superlative forms of adverbs

Adverbs with one syllable (*einsilbige* Adverbien):
fast – fast**er** – fast**est** (schnell – schnell**er** – am schnell**sten**);
hard – hard**er** – hard**est** (z.B.: Dieses Team hat hart – härt**er** – am härt**esten** gearbeitet.)

und **early**:
early – earl**ier** – earl**iest** (früh – früh**er** – am früh**esten**)

Adverbs with two and more syllables (*mehrsilbige* Adverbien):
quickly – **more** quickly – most **quickly**; profitably – **more** profitably – **most** profitably
Note: *most* can also mean *very*: **most** grateful = höchst dankbar)

Irregular forms:

well – better – best; badly – worse – worst; late – later – last, **aber:** at the latest (spätestens);
much – more – most; little – less – least (wenig – weniger – am wenigsten);
far – further – furthest / far – farther – farthest (*for distance only*)
e.g.: Last, but not least … (*wörtlich:* Zuletzt, aber nicht am geringsten …)

Bei manchen Adverbien wird in informeller, bzw. Umgangssprache auch die Steigerung mit *–er* verwendet.
Compare: This is **more easily** said than done. / This is *easier* said than done. (*coll.*!)
    (Das ist leichter gesagt als getan.)
    We should repay the loan **more quickly** / *quicker*. (*coll.*!)

Für die Stellung von Adverbien gibt es gewisse Grundregeln. Allerdings wird in bestimmten Fällen davon abgewichen, z.B. bei mehrdeutigem Bezug, Häufung von Adverbien, zur Hervorhebung / Betonung, zur Bezugnahme (auf Vorheriges), zur Verlagerung der eigentlichen Hauptaussage u.ä.

Position of adverbs (Stellung der Adverbien)

Beim Einzelwort:

Adverbs **normally** come **before the adjective or adverb** they refer to.
Das Adverb steht normalerweise vor dem Einzelwort, zu dem es gehört.

e.g.: Her profit margin is **rather** / **comparatively** / **really** /… **small** (adj.).
    The CFO was **perfectly** right (adj.): the production costs were **too** high (adj.) / … were **far** too (adv.) high and **totally** unacceptable (adj.).
    The product launch went **quite** / **exceptionally** well (adv.).

The adverb *only* needs to be placed carefully, otherwise there may be ambiguity or misunderstandings (*Gefahr: unklare oder falsche Zuordnung*) – compare:
Only the boss was yesterday informed about the merger. *Nur der Chef …*
The boss was informed about the merger **only** (*erst*) yesterday … *erst gestern.*
The boss was **only informed** (*betont!*) about the merger, not consulted about it. *Der Chef wurde nur informiert …* (nicht gefragt, nicht einbezogen etc.)
The boss was informed **only** about the merger. … *nur über die Fusion* (nichts weiter).

Position of adverbs (Stellung der Adverbien)

Im Satz:
S P-O (Subjekt Prädikat/Verb–Objekt)
Im **Normalfall** darf **nichts zwischen Verb und Objekt** stehen:

(adv.) S (adv.) P-O (adv.)

e.g.: **The other day** (*neulich*), consultants **unexpectedly** arrived **early in the morning**.
Yesterday they **suddenly** interrogated all administrative assistants **in the canteen**.
Of course, this **immediately** caused fears among the executives **here**.
Increasingly the members of staff **really** feel unsure about their future **in the team**.
Probably the company is **greatly** overstaffed **in certain areas** and **urgently** needs to downsize **as soon as possible** in order to cut labour costs **dramatically this year still**.

In **einfachen Zeiten** (*Present, Past*) stehen kurze, nicht besonders hervorgehobene **Adverbien** der **Häufigkeit (*frequency*)** und des **Maßes (*degree*)**, allgemeine Zeitangaben (*always*, *rarely* etc.) und z.T. auch der **Art und Weise (*manner*)**, **VOR dem Verb** - aber **NACH *to be* als Hauptverb**, auch (mehrere Adverbien) in Kombination.

He (S) **simply** <u>rejected</u> (P/V.) every proposal (O₄ - [*direktes / Akkusativ-Objekt*]).
She (S) **quickly** <u>changed</u> (P/V.) her negotiation strategy (O₄).
They (S) **always** <u>complain</u> (P/V.) about low wages (*präpositionales Objekt*).
The CEO (S) **hardly ever** <u>leaves</u> (P/vi) before 8pm (*adverbial Zeitbestimmung*).
The CEO (S) <u>is</u> (P/V.) **always** late, while his assistant (S) <u>is</u> (P/V.) **almost always** on time.

In **zusammengesetzten Zeiten** und **bei Modalverben** stehen Adverbien gewöhnlich **nach dem ersten Hilfsverb** (außer *used to* [*inv.*] und *to have to*).

They *had* **almost** *accomplished* their tasks.
The workforce *has* **simply** *been* too slow.
They *have* **simply** *been working* too slowly.
They *will / can / should / ...* **easily** *catch up* tomorrow.
(They *will / can / should / ...* *catch up* **easily** tomorrow. - **easily** *betont!*)
The head of department *was* **slowly** *explaining* the new company policy, which *would* **probably** *cause* a new round of lay-offs.
But: They *really* <u>had to</u> accept the wage cut.

Aber: In **zusammengesetzten Zeiten** stehen Adverbien oft <u>VOR dem verneinten ersten Hilfsverb</u>.

He **probably** <u>couldn't</u> have stopped her from investing all her money at once.
The CEO **certainly** *did not* expect such a disastrous consumer reaction.
The workers **clearly** *did not* know about the planned job cuts.
(**But:** When they heard of them they *did not* go on strike **immediately**.
- *Das heißt: Sie streikten **nicht sofort**, vielleicht später; **sofort** ist **Kernaussage!***)

Im <u>Passiv</u> stehen **Adverbien der *Art und Weise*** (*manner*) gewöhnlich <u>vor dem</u> Hauptverb, d.h. vor dem <u>*Past Participle*</u>.

The project *had been* **thoroughly** <u>*planned*</u>.
The temporary workers *might have been* **badly** <u>*treated*</u>.
A business plan *should be* **properly** <u>*prepared*</u>.

theory   adverbs

Adverbien des **Ortes** (*place*), der **Zeit** (*time*) und der **Häufigkeit** (*frequency*) stehen gewöhnlich **nach dem Objekt**, **hinter dem Verb (ohne Objekt)** oder am **Ende des** Satzes oder **Satzteils**.

I found your business plan **there / yesterday / there yesterday**.
Our Japanese partners came (*vi*) **here**. They arrived **yesterday**.
The payment is due **tomorrow**.
When he worked in the City he came **here many times after work / in the evening**.
He **urgently** (*adv. – manner / degree*) needed information about the latest developments **at the Stock Exchange** (*place*) **several times** (*frequency*) **every day** (*time*).

Generell gilt: **Am Satzende** oder des Satzteils stehen längere, **hervorgehobene** und/oder für die Satzaussage **bedeutende Adverbien**.

The project had been planned **thoroughly**. (*Hauptaussage: gründlich!*)
The immigrant workers have been treated **badly**. (*betont: schlecht! behandelt*)
The manufacturer needed the licence **urgently**. (*Die Dringlichkeit ist das Wichtige hier!*)
vs. The manufacturer **urgently** needed the licence. (*Die Lizenz ist das Entscheidende!*)
"In my experience, negotiations in Asia are very time-consuming – with the Chinese **in particular**." (*Das Wichtige in der Satzaussage ist, mit wem es ganz besonders so ist.*), oder "… - in particular with the Chinese." (*hervorgehobener, mit wem es besonders so ist*)

Am Satzanfang stehen **adverbiale Bestimmungen** zur **Themenanknüpfung** an Vorheriges, **in enger Beziehung zum Vorherigen, kontrastierend**, gelegentlich zu **besonderer Betonung**; **auch, um eine Häufung am Satzende zu vermeiden.**

By the way, we must reconsider our negotiation strategy. (*Anknüpfung, bzw. Signal für Themenwechsel*)

On the contrary, we have to stick to it to be consistent and credible. (*Kontrast*)

Perhaps last year you didn't notice the problem **at such an early stage**. (*Anfang: Bezug / zeitliche Verortung der Aussage; Ende: Hauptaspekt - in einer so frühen Phase*)

Quite obviously the company owner needed fresh money in his competitive market segment. (*Hervorhebung der Offensichtlichkeit*)

On the first day of his business trip, the sales manager **only** had a lot of small talk with low-ranking staff **here and there**, **in different offices**, **the whole afternoon**. (*Häufung von adverbialen Bestimmungen; zeitliche Einordung als Auftakt*)

Towards the end of his stay, quite late in his opinion, the CEO met all the decision-makers **again and again on several days in a row**. (*Häufung*)

Understandably, (*disjunct*) the new CEO met with a lot of resistance **at first**. **But gradually** more and more employees realized that while new ideas did **indeed** mean change, they could make the company more profitable **in the long run** – and sustainable, **too**.

Split Infinitive: In seltenen Fällen kann ein **Adverb** zwischen *to* und dem Verb stehen, z.B. um falschen Bezug zu vermeiden – *to finally succeed* …

Inversion (Umstellung von Subjekt und Verb) - Sie erfolgt,

...wenn **negative oder einschränkende Adverbien** zur Betonung **am Satzanfang** stehen.

Never had his business *been* more lucrative.	vs. His business had never been …
Seldom were his speculations more successful.	vs. His speculations were seldom …
Hardly ever did the CEO *listen* to his lawyers.	vs. The CEO hardly ever listened …

… wenn **bestimmte Adverbien am Satzanfang** stehen (und das Subjekt kein Pronomen ist): **in**, **out**, **up**, **down**, **round**, **over**, **back**, **forward** *etc.*

In came (V) the CEO (S).	vs. In he came, (*personal pronoun*.)
Up jumped (V) two strikers (S).	vs. Up they jumped.
Out / Back went the burglar.	vs. Out / Back he went.

Mixed adverbs and adverbial phrases in context:

Not so long ago *[Zeitbezug, Intro]*, German car brands **desperately** *[manner]* wanted to diversify, expand and build **truly** *[wortbezogen auf folgendes Adj.]* global car brands **faster / more quickly / quicker** (*coll.*) than their competitors *[einzig mögliche Stellung]*. **However** *[Kontrast]*, **quickly** *[wortbezogen auf forged]* forged alliances or overseas mergers were **often** *[nach to be]* unsuccessful / **often** *[verneintes Hilfsverb]* did *not* work out. **Not quite unexpectedly** *[disjunct]*, some of the mergers failed **dramatically** *[betont; vs. unbetont: dramatically failed]* so that the boards **finally** *had to* admit *[vor* to have to*]* defeat to prevent higher losses and, **maybe**, *[Einschub und nur auf den folgenden Satzteil bezogen]* serious damage to the brand image **worldwide** *[place]*. **Never** had *[Inversion nach neg. / verneinendem Adverb]* company boards feared that they could **ever really** *[nach modalem Hilfsverb]* fail **completely**, **across the board** *[hervorgehoben als wichtiger Bestandteil der Satzaussage]*. **By contrast** *[Kontrast]*, Renault's merger with Nissan **surprisingly** *[manner; normale unbetonte Stellung]* showed that **even rather** *[zwei wortbezogene Adverbien]* pronounced differences in company cultures could **somehow** *[nach Modalverb]* be bridged **successfully** *[für die Kernaussage wichtig]* – if the top management got everything **right** *[Sinn: alles richtig machen, daher nicht rightly]*. Many see it **rightly** *[zu Recht]* as the merit of **only** *[wortbezogen]* one person, Mr Ghosn, who was **then** *[nach to be]* in charge of the ailing Japanese company. Experienced **interculturally** *[manner]*, he **stoically** and **stubbornly** *[manner]* turned the merger into an **almost** unprecedented success story, which **later** *[unbetont, beiläufig; sonst am Satzende]* earned him the position of Renault's and Nissan's CEO, even if, **untypically** *[betont am Satzteilanfang]*, he had not graduated from a French elite school and was not **really** *[im Passiv vor pp]* supported by the French government.

Merkbox:

> ❖ Adverbien können sich auf Verben, Adjektive, Adverbien beziehen, also wortbezogen (*adjuncts*) sein, oder auch auf eine ganze Aussage, einen ganzen Satz, also satzbezogen (*disjuncts*) sein. Gewöhnlich werden satzbezogene Adverbien (*disjuncts*) am Satzanfang durch Komma abgetrennt, im Deutschen wird häufig *-weise* angehängt oder ein andere Wendung benutzt (*... gesehen* u.ä.).
>
> ❖ Die Stellung von Adverbien und adverbialen Bestimmungen im Satz hat Einfluss auf die Bedeutung. Oft wird die Stellung davon bestimmt, ob Adverbien betont sind oder nicht, also beiläufig, oder worauf sie sich genau beziehen.
>
> Es gibt gewisse Grundregeln für die normale Stellung von Adverbien bei zusammengesetzten Zeiten, temporalen und modalen Hilfsverben, bei verneinten Hilfsverben und dem Passiv (natürlich mit Ausnahmen).
>
> ❖ Bestimmte adverbiale Bestimmungen erfordern Inversion (Umstellung).

N *Well, better, best* – Fill in the appropriate forms of the adverbs (from the adjectives in brackets), using comparative and superlative forms where required.

"As I was afraid of losing my job, I worked (1) _____ and _____ (hard), starting (2) _____ (early) than my colleagues and often going home even (3) _____ (late) than the cleaners, (4) _____ (absolute) exhausted. It may (5) _____ (good) be that others worked (6) _____ (fast) than me, but hardly as (7) _____ (conscientious) or as (8) _____ (efficient) as me. I reacted (9) _____ (early) to new trends than the whole marketing department and was (10) _____ (easy) the first to come up with a (11) _____ (true) innovative advertising approach focusing (12) _____ (precise) on the expectations of our target group. Maybe I was the one who performed (13) _____ (good), but probably I didn't make my presence felt (14) _____ (clear) enough. Others staged their modest success (15) _____ (self-confident) than I did and did (16) _____ (noticeable) (17) _____ (good) in their careers than me. They were promoted (18) _____ (fast) and (19) _____ (far) up the ranks than me. In the end, my boss told me (20) _____ (grateful) that he knew (21) _____ (perfect) (22) _____ (good) that of all the employees, I had served the company (23) _____ (loyal) – but, I thought to myself, probably also (24) _____ (naïve) of all. Even those who had worked much (25) _____ (bad) than me earned only (26) _____ (marginal) (27) _____ (little) than me. (28) _____ (regrettable), our agency was taken over by a competitor, who fired the whole marketing team. Maybe I should have seen that coming much (29) _____ (early), but afterwards you always know (30) _____ (good). At (31) _____ (little) I should have analyzed my situation (32) _____ (realistic) than I did, but when you feel very (33) _____ (strong) about your job it is difficult to look at it (34) _____ (objective) and (35) _____ (rational). Maintaining a distance is (36) _____ (easy) said than done. If you want my advice: Rely (37) _____ (firm) on your judgement and, (38) _____ (much) of all, avoid wishful thinking."

O What is the right position?

Right or wrong? Strike out the adverbs which are in a wrong position in the sentence and indicate with an asterisk (*) where they should normally be placed (*normale Stellung, ohne Betonung*).

e.g.: The discounter quickly was taken over by a competitor. It had badly been run.
The discounter ~~quickly~~ was * taken over by a competitor. It had ~~badly~~ been * run.

1. The company could have easily gained more market share in China.
2. The foreign delegation didn't simply want to strike a deal at that time.
3. It really was obvious that the government official expected a bribe.
4. The product launch has carefully been planned.
5. Our market entry in India had been terribly delayed several times.
6. They send normally a letter of credit.
7. We soon would send out a reminder.
8. We have to still cut costs.
9. Our application for the licence is being still examined by the authorities.
10. The pharma group accepted readily the deal.
11. The consignment safely arrived.
12. Since the incident, we have repeatedly changed suppliers.
13. Our suppliers yet don't understand what we really need.

P What is the difference? – Make it clear by explaining it in German.

1. a, The goods were, astonishingly, in good shape.
   b, The goods were in astonishingly good shape.
   c, Astonishingly, the goods were in good shape.

2. a, Only regular customers were granted discounts last month.
   b, Regular customers were only granted discounts last month.
   c, Regular customers were granted only discounts last month.
   d, Regular customers were granted discounts only last month.

3. a, Actually, the luxury brand gets its products from low-wage countries.
   b, The luxury brand actuallly gets its products from low-wage countries.

4. a, Surprisingly, the share price remained stable after the scandal.
   b, The share price remained surprisingly stable after the scandal.

5. a, The CEO deeply regretted his statements.
   b, The CEO regretted his statements deeply.

6. a, Sadly, the CEO handed in his resignation.
   b, The CEO sadly handed in his resignation.

7. a, She complained repeatedly that products had been faked.
   b, She complained that products had been faked repeatedly.

8. a, The negotiator sat quietly in his chair and waited for an answer.
   b, The negotiator quietly sat in his chair and waited for an answer.
   c, Quietly the negotiator sat in his chair and waited for an answer.
   d, The negotiator sat in his chair quietly and waited for an answer.

practice   adverbs

Q   Housing and mortgages in the USA
(inspired by and adapted from "Housing in America" in *The Economist*, , Aug. 20ᵗʰ 2016, p. 10)

Where does it all belong? What are the possible positions of the adverbs and adverbial expressions indicated in the box, in this order (in dieser Reihenfolge)? Write them into the sentences; mark normal (n) positions and emphasized positions (e), like in the example (a).

a, The most dramatic moment of the global financial crisis of the late 2000s was the collapse of Lehman Brothers on September 15ᵗʰ 2008. **Clearly (e)** the most dramatic moment …. was **by far (n)** the collapse …. **By far (e)** the most dramatic moment … was **clearly (n)** the collapse …	a, clearly; by far
b, The drama had become inevitable two years earlier. _____	b, but; already
c, In order to make enough profits to satisfy their shareholders, banks have cut costs and introduced new administration charges. _____ _____	c, meanwhile; again; significantly; completely
d, US banks are despised, they are in reasonable shape: _____ _____	d, still; widely; but; now
e, capitalised and profitable. _____	e, highly; fairly
f, The problem is that in the USA the banks are part of the game. _____	f, only
g, There is a second, independent structure outside the mortgage system, which is capitalised. _____	g, highly; very badly
h, This parallel system is profitable and nationalised. _____	h, barely; largely
i, It is linked to the global financial system and represents the biggest concentration of risk to be found anywhere. _____	i, still; closely; probably
k, It remains dangerous. _____	k, altogether; fundamentally

R Self-driving lorries
(Inspired by and adapted from "A long haul" in *The Economist*, Aug. 20th 2016, p. 51)

Use the German words in the box (in the given order): Translate them into English and find adequate positions for them in the text, in their correct forms as adjectives and adverbs, as required by the context.

a, Carmakers and tech firms have been dominating the headlines, in the race to develop autonomous vehicles.	a, *in jüngster Zeit*; *klar*; *heftig*; *so bald wie möglich*
b, A range of firms have been working on lorries.	b, *(eine) ganz(e) Reihe*); *sehr intensiv*; *fahrerlos*
c, Fears that steering wheels will disappear seem exaggerated.	c, *jedoch*; *völlig*; *irgendwann bald*; *weitgehend*
d, What employees in the road haulage (Straßentransport) industry fear is the risk of losing their jobs to lorries that can do without drivers.	d, *aber*; *wirklich*; *am meisten*; *neu*; *automatisch*; *leicht*
e, Systems are being designed for motorways ... than for small roads.	e, *im Allgemeinen*; *(die) meisten*; *autonom*; *aktuell*; *eher*
f, Drivers will continue to be necessary – until innovation makes humans redundant.	f, *höchstwahrscheinlich*; *zumindest kurzfristig*; *weitere*; *völlig*
g, Self-driving lorries may attract drivers to this job and require other skills.	g, *auf der anderen Seite*; *neu*; *hart*; *besser bezahlt*
h, Road haulage in rich countries is an old-fashioned business, dominated by small firms, which means that such lorries will not be ready before 2030.	h, *ziemlich*; *hauptsächlich*; *voll autonom*; *sicherlich*;

S   India's cow business
(inspired by and adapted from "Cowboys and Indians" in *The Economist*, Aug. 20th 2016, p. 40)

a, Use the German words in brackets to fill in the gaps with correct English equivalents (mind the forms: adjectives, adverbs, comparatives, superlatives).

India is home to (1) _____ (*etwa*) 200m cows and more than 100m water buffaloes. It is (2) _____ (*weit, weithin*) known that cows are sacred for the Hindu population. So the distinction is (3) _____ (*absolut*) crucial. The beef sold is (4) _____ (*fast*) all buffalo; in past scandals, beef also came from street cows and was (5) _____ (*falsch*) labelled. (6) _____ (*überraschenderweise*), India now rivals Brazil and Australia as the world's biggest exporter of beef. Even (7) _____, (*noch überraschender*) many Indians (8) _____ (*glücklich*) earn money from cows in (9) _____ (*ganz*) different ways. Some Indians in the 'cow business' (10) _____ (*einfach*) run (11) _____ (*wohltätig / English:* charitable) funded retirement homes for ageing cows, others find it (12) _____ (*klüger / English:* wise) to demand a few rupees *[Indian currency]* from passing Hindus for providing their cows with 'snacks', a (13) _____ (*bequem / English:* convenient) way to please the gods and to earn money - (14) even _____ (*bequemer*). Dalits, members of the (15) _____ (*niedrig, Superlativ*) caste, (16) _____ (*traditionell*) dispose of dead cows, thus providing a service which is (17) _____ (*rein*) (18) _____ (*religiös*) motivated and (19) _____ (*völlig*) free for society, while others make money (20) _____ (*leichter*), by (21) _____ (*einfach*) demanding protection money from cattle breeders (22) _____ (*bedacht / English:* keen) to go about their business without the risk of getting (23) _____ (*brutal*) lynched by an infuriated mob.

b, Translate into English.

1. Vor einem Monat wurden einige *Dalits*, früher als *Unberührbare* bezeichnet (= *genannt*), plötzlich von einer Gruppe von religiösen Fanatikern (*fanatics*) angegriffen, die fälschlicherweise glaubten, die *Dalits* hätten eine Kuh getötet.

_____

_____

2. Nie zuvor hatte der indische Geschäftsmann ernsthaft daran gedacht, mit Kühen Geld zu verdienen. Später begann er jedoch, zunehmend Milch zu verkaufen.

_____

_____

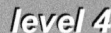

T Business problems – Translate.

1. Strategisch folgte die Entscheidung des Möbelkonzerns, die Produktnamen besser an die einzelnen Märkte anzupassen, einem weltweiten Trend. Marketingexperten sehen in diesem Fall besonders hohe Risiken für die Markenidentität, die durch diese unerwartete Maßnahme deutlich verändert werden könnte. Völlig unterschiedliche Produktpaletten könnten die Gewinnspannen drastisch verringern, was die Dinge noch schlimmer machen würde.

2. Der Geschäftsführer beabsichtigte sicherlich nicht, öffentlich zu verkünden, dass die Expansion nach Indien nicht so schnell stattfinden würde. Doch ein Journalist hatte am Flughafen zufällig (= *to happen to*) ein Telefongespräch belauscht (= *to overhear*) und machte die vertrauliche Information umgehend öffentlich.

3. Lebhaft (= *vivid*) erklärte der Leiter der Entwicklungsabteilung Einzelheiten des neu entwickelten Produktes. Während er wild gestikulierte (*to gesticulate*), fragte ein Vertreter der Verkaufsabteilung kritisch, ob es für das Produkt eigentlich echte Nachfrage gebe.

4. Offenbar war das abgelaufene Geschäftsjahr für die Versicherungsbranche außergewöhnlich schwierig gewesen. Ein Branchenvertreter versuchte schüchtern, die Verluste logisch zu erklären: „Die Naturkatastrophen werden definitiv nahezu biblisch (*biblical*) in Regionen, die dem Klimawandel extrem ausgesetzt (*exposed to*) sind. Selten haben wir so viele Überflutungen und Brände erlebt wie in den letzten Monaten."

5. Tief bewegt blieb der Direktor minutenlang sitzen, ungewöhnlich schweigsam, bevor er lächelnd von seinem Stuhl aufstand. Er sah erleichtert aus und dankte seiner Belegschaft aufrichtig. Die Firma hatte sich besser und früher als erwartet von der schweren Krise erholt.

Intro   Vorgedanken

PAST TENSES
Vergangenheitsformen

Wozu denn verschiedene Zeiten in der Vergangenheit?
Vorbei ist vorbei - oder?

Warum so viele Zeitformen?
Vorbei ist vorbei! Eine
würde doch auch reichen!

Ich **habe** den Preis **gezahlt**.
I **have paid** the price.
I **have been paying** ...?
I **paid** the price.
I **was paying** ...?
I **had paid** / **been paying** ...?

Naja, im englischen Zeitsystem werden Zeitebenen nicht nur nach *tense*, sondern auch nach *aspect* unterschieden, je nachdem, ob etwas eine einfache (*simple*) Tatsache oder Handlung ist, abgeschlossen (*perfect*) oder im Verlauf (*progressive*) ...

Oft ist alles vergangen und es war vorher auch schon was passiert. Dann braucht man eine Vergangenheit und eine zweite, länger zurückliegende!

Als er seine Aktien verkaufen **wollte**, **war** der Aktienkurs **abgestürzt**.
▶ When he **wanted** to sell his shares, the share price **had crashed**.

Na gut, dann läuft das wenigstens wie im Deutschen. Oder?

Er **wollte** seine Aktien verkaufen.
He **wanted** to sell his shares.
Aber der Aktienkurs **war abgestürzt**.
The share price **had crashed**.

Our boss **had** not **expected** so many complaints.
▶ Unser Chef **hatte** nicht so viele Beschwerden **erwartet**.

Naja, das Past Perfect steht schon meistens für die 3. Vergangenheit im Deutschen. Das stimmt.

level 0

He **checked** the invoice twice.
→ *zu dem Zeitpunkt, damals*
He **has checked** the invoice twice.
→ *insgesamt bis jetzt*

Aber **Past Tense** und **Present Perfect** haben ganz unterschiedliche Bedeutungen. Hier kann man nicht einfach 1 : 1 übersetzen.

Aber wenn's bis jetzt andauert, muss doch die <u>Verlaufsform</u> (*progressive form*) stehen, oder nicht?

The CEO **has been talking** to the shareholders *for* five hours.

▶ Der Vorstandsvorsitzende **spricht** (!) *seit* fünf Stunden zu den Aktionären.

Hier schon - in diesem Fall steht im Deutschen sogar die Gegenwart! Es ist ein Vorgang, der im Verlauf von der Vergangenheit bis in die Gegenwart reicht.

I **have drafted** my business plan.
→ *Jetzt steht der Entwurf.*
I **have been drafting** my business plan.
→ *Damit war ich beschäftigt, vielleicht ist er noch gar nicht fertig.*
I **have written** *five* pages.
→ *Ergebnis mit Anzahl (quantifiziert)*

Auch die Simple Form des Present Perfect reicht bis zur Gegenwart – und weiter, z.B. als Zustand oder Ergebnis.

Merkbox:

Zeit (im Alltag) ist nicht gleich *Tense* (= grammatikalische Zeitform!).

Auch wenn die Stufen der englischen **Vergangenheitszeiten** dem deutschen System grundsätzlich ähnlich scheinen, ist die **Verwendung** von *Past Tense* und *Present Perfect* in der **Bedeutung** ganz **anders**; sie folgt immerhin gewissen **Regeln**, differenziert die **Zeitebenen** in der Aussage aber **anders**.

Die **Unterschiede** zwischen *Simple Form* und *Progressive Form* (*aspect*) **kommen** gewissermaßen **hinzu**. Damit gibt es praktisch jew. **zwei Formen** in derselben ‚Zeit'. *Present Perfect Progressive* wird im Deutschen sogar oft als **Präsens** (Gegenwart) wiedergegeben. Aber auch die *Simple Form* des *Present Perfect* dauert bis jetzt an, bzw. hat einen **Bezug zur Gegenwart** (in einer Abfolge-Serie oder dem Ergebnis).

 *theory*

PAST TENSES
(overview & forms)

For months the CEO <u>has been</u> under attack from shareholders. When the company <u>went</u> public two years ago, profits <u>seemed</u> to start rocketing, while investors <u>were buying</u> shares like mad. But all those hopes <u>have not been fulfilled</u> so far.

Before the IPO, the company <u>had</u> always <u>recorded</u> modest, but stable sales figures, largely due to its reputation as a traditional family business. Most of the time, it <u>had been doing</u> rather well. The head of the company, a genuine father figure, <u>had</u> always <u>given</u> higher priority to long-term development than to short-term gains.

Since the IPO some of the best employees <u>have left</u> the company, others <u>have been thinking</u> about leaving. Only few <u>are</u> really <u>enjoying</u> the new work environment. Now the company <u>is</u> in search of a new philosophy, as it <u>has</u> apparently <u>lost</u> its familiar sense of identity.

Tasks (see the text in the box above):

a, Identify the **tenses and forms** used. *(level 1)*
b, Find out and explain signals (**signal words**) that help decide on the appropriate tense in English. *(levels 2 & 3)*
c, Explain the **use** of the English tenses (look at the chart on the next page). *(level 4)*

Es gibt einen Unterschied zwischen der Zeit (**time**) in der Alltagswirklichkeit und den grammatischen Zeitebenen und –formen (**tense** & **aspect**), also den **formalen Ausdrucksmöglichkeiten** in der Sprache!

time   <--> tense:
(Realzeit <--> grammat. Zeitform)

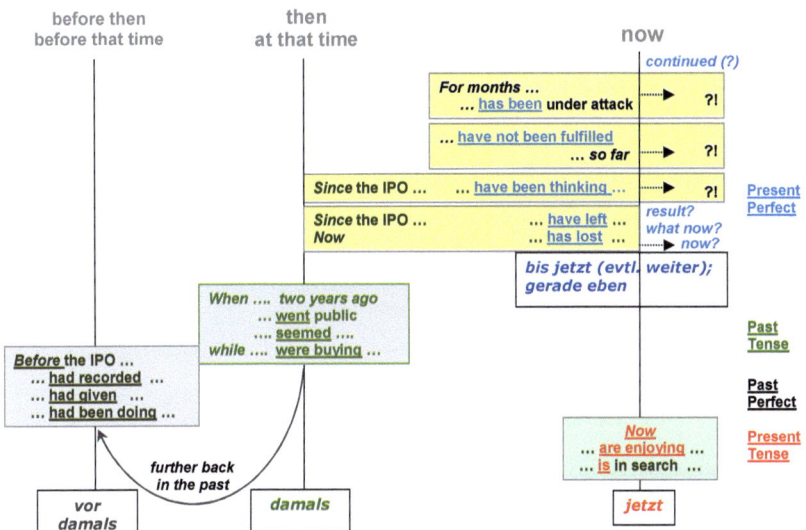

Merkbox:

Zeiten (in der Realität) und sprachliche, <u>grammatikalische Zeitformen</u> sind <u>nicht identisch</u>. Im Englischen sind sie im Gebrauch sehr stark vom **Bewußtsein** des **Sprechers** abhängig und stehen **in einem wechselseitigen Verhältnis zueinander**.

Wie der **Begriff** bereits sagt, beinhaltet das *Present Perfect* (im Bewußtsein des Sprechers) sowohl **Vollendetes (Perfect), Vollzogenes, Vergangenes** als auch **Gegenwärtiges (***Present***), Gegenwartsbezug – oder** etwas aus der Vergangenheit **Andauerndes**. Daher stehen sich *Present* und *Present Perfect* nahe, sind sozusagen **Partner-Zeiten**, die oft im Wechselspiel miteinander gebraucht werden.

Past und *Past Perfect* **korrespondieren** mindestens ebenso **eng** miteinander, wechseln sich ab, sind oft nur **im gegenseitigen Verhältnis** sinnvoll, da sie **zwei** aufeinander bezogene näher und entfernter liegende <u>Zeitebenen</u> in der Vergangenheit (<u>Vergangenheit</u> und <u>Vorvergangenheit</u>), also **zwei unterschiedliche Vergangenheitsebenen** bezeichnen.

 **past tenses**

Forms:
active voice (Aktiv)

Present Perfect:

Simple: have / has + past participle(-ed or irregular)
e.g.: The consultants **have** *already* **suggested** a change of strategy.
She **has** *just* **sold** her business.

Progressive: have / has + been + present participle(-ing)
e.g.: The employees **have been working** hard *in the last few weeks*.
She **has been trying** to sell her business *for several months*.

Past:

Simple: verb+-ed* or irregular past form
e.g.: The CEO **suggested** a change of strategy *yesterday*.
She **sold** her business *last week*.

* • *consonant* + **y** > ied: *carried, hurried,* ...; *vowel* + **y** = **y** : ob**ey**ed, st**ay**ed,...
• final -e is dropped: manag**e** > manag**ed**, charg**e** > charg**ed**, ...
• last consonant (l *[BE]*, g, p, b, t, d) doubled after short stressed syllable:
travelled (*BE*), lagged, robbed, shipped, skidded, fitted ...

Progressive: was / were + present participle(-ing)
e.g.: *Last week* the employees **were working** particularly hard.
She **was** desperately **trying** to sell her business *last month*.

Past Perfect:

Simple: had + past participle(-ed or irregular)
e.g.: The CEO **had suggested** a change of strategy (*before*).
She **had sold** the company *before the break-even point*.

Progressive: had + been + present participle(-ing)
e.g.: The employees **had been working** very hard (*before*).
She **had been trying** to sell her business (*before*).

Merkbox:

Für die **Bildung** gilt allgemein: **Present Perfect** und **Past Perfect** sind **zusammengesetzte Zeiten**, d.h. sie werden mit Hilfe eines temporalen **Hilfsverb**s + Partizip der Vergangenheit (*Past Participle*) gebildet. *Present Perfect*: have / has + pp   *Past Perfect*: had + pp *Progressive*:   have / has + been + -ing   had + been + -ing Das *Past Tense* hingegen ist eine sog. ‚einfache' Zeit, die ohne Hilfsverb auskommt, wobei das **Verb selbst verändert** wird, durch Anhängen von **-ed** oder **unregelmäßige Formen**: *worked* oder *told etc*. **Vorsicht** bei Frageform und Verneinung: **kein -ed** am Verb, wenn vorher mit **did** umschrieben ist: ***Did* you hand in** your business plan last week? - No, I **did not hand** it in in time.

Manche Formen (des Passivs) sind so kompliziert, dass sie kaum verwendet werden.

Forms:

passive voice (Passiv)

Present Perfect:

Simple: have / has + been past participle(-ed or irregular)
e.g.: All these strategies have already been tested.
Her business hasn't been sold yet.

[
Progressive: have / has + been + being + past participle(-ed or irregular)
e.g.: These strategies have been being applied slavishly *up to now* without doing any good.
The office block has been being built *for ages*. It will never be finished!

Not recommended! Avoid!
Note: Native speakers may use the forms with *getting* instead of *being*: The office block has been getting built ...
]

Simple Past:

was / were + verb+-ed or irregular past form
e.g.: All these strategies were tested *last year*.
Her business was sold *last week*.

Progressive: was / were + being + past participle(-ed or irregular)
e.g.: *While* the strategies were still being tested *last week*, the board had already ditched them.
She was still being urged by banks to sell her business when a friend offered to bail her out *last month*.

Past Perfect:

Simple: had + been + past participle(-ed or irregular)
e.g.: A change of strategy had been suggested many times *before*.
The company had been sold *before*.

[
Progressive: had + been + being + past participle (-ed or irregular)
e.g.: The strategies had been being tested....
She had been being urged to sell her business...

*Not recommended! **Avoid!***
]

Merkbox:

Im **Passiv** wird in den **zusammengesetzten Zeiten** in der Regel die **Verlaufsform** (mit *being*) **kaum gebraucht** (eher mit *getting*), da sie viel **zu schwerfällig** ist. **Wichtig:** Nicht verwechseln oder mischen - Konfusion vermeiden zwischen Passiv und Verlaufsform: **Passiv:** *to be + -ed* / unreg. Form   *Progressive Form*: *to be + -ing*   e.g.: *The factory was (being) pulled down...   They were pulling down the factory...*

practice

past tenses

A   Put the following text into the past.
(Present Tense > Past Tense; Past & Present Perfect > Past Perfect)

Liu **has** ten chat windows open on his laptop simultaneously, dealing with all kinds of

questions and requests from overseas branches. He **is trying** to obtain the latest sales

figures from Hong Kong when his mobile phone **rings**. He **has been expecting** a call from

San Diego, but the number shown on the display **isn't** American. He **feels** annoyed and

doesn't answer the call. He always **gets** calls from people he **has** never **met**. Teams **are**

made up of employees who **live** in all parts of the world and who **are told** to contact

each other directly so that no time or opportunity **is lost**, whether they **know** each other or

not. ... While Liu **is closing** the chat windows one by one, he suddenly **remembers** that he

was asked to forward the latest draft of the new website to Bangalore for the Indian team to

adjust it to local tastes - as far as possible - without diluting the global brand image.

Hardly **has** Liu **started** to look for the file on his laptop, when a message **arrives** on his

mobile phone - from India. They **have been waiting** for the draft and **become** impatient.

While the file **is being transmitted**, Liu **decides** that he **needs** something to eat before the

next meeting. He **has been asked** to explain the company's expansion plans. The

presentation **is** ready but some data **need** to be updated again. That**'s** it. Liu **opens** his

laptop again and **has forgotten** all about his hunger - for the moment.

B Offshoring and downsizing
Choose suitable verbs from the box to fill in the blanks.

> to move   to sell off   to expect   to begin   to trim
> to be   to announce   to hope   to worry   to become
> to look up   to come   to take over

Many simple tasks _____ (Present Perfect Simple, Passive) offshore or _____ (Present Perfect Simple, Passive) by machines. This trend _____ (Present Perfect Progressive) the entire workforce for some time now. Payrolls _____ (Present Perfect Simple, Passive) by 30 per cent in the meantime. Some parts of the company which _____ (Past Perfect Simple) totally unprofitable _____ (Past Simple Passive) months ago. Some employees _____ (Past Perfect Progressive) all those measures before they _____ (Past Simple, Passive) by the board, but when they actually _____ (Past Simple), everybody _____ (Past Simple) still shocked. Against their better judgement, employees _____ (Past Perfect Progressive) job cuts could be avoided. With underperforming company divisions gone profits _____ to increase (Past Simple) almost instantly. Since then things _____ (Present Perfect Progressive) again.

C Textile Industry in Africa - Translate the following sentences.

1. Als die EU Einfuhrbeschränkungen für Textilien aus Asien verhängte *(Past Simple)*, _____

   verlagerten *(Past Simple)* chinesische Unternehmen ihre Produktion nach Afrika.
   _____

2. In Nigeria wurden Textilfabriken gebaut. Sie schufen neue Arbeitsplätze. *(Past Simple)*
   _____

3. Das Land hatte bereits billige Kleidung hergestellt. *(Past Perfect Progressive)*
   _____

4. Seit neue Importquoten verhängt wurden *(Past Simple, Passive)*, schließen die neuen
   _____

   Fabriken eine nach der anderen *(Present Perfect Progressive)*.
   _____

#

Viele verwenden automatisch immer die Verlaufsform im Present Perfect, „weil es ja noch nicht abgeschlossen ist". Das ist zu pauschal und so nicht korrekt. Oft ist zwar beides möglich, Simple oder Progressive Form, aber nicht immer! Und: Es gibt Regeln und Signale!

Present Perfect (Simple & Progressive)

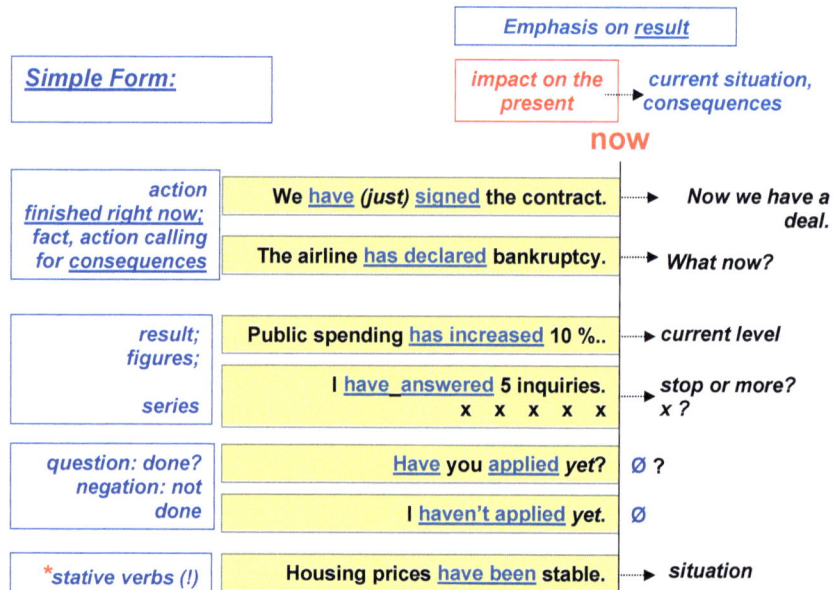

Characteristics:

- actions just finished or not quite finished yet;
- situations or actions, events going on until now (and maybe further);
- series of actions (continued) until now (and maybe further)
- with certain verbs, often called 'stative': to be, to remain, to think, ...
  (expressing situations, opinions, attitudes etc.)

  e.g.: Unemployment has remained high.
  Inflation has been low.

Stative verbs bezeichnen einen Zustand und haben (in dieser Verwendung) keinen Verlauf, also **keine Verlaufsform** *(progressive form)*.

Note the difference between stative use and use as an action verb:

| I *have* always *thought of* the threat of a hostile takeover. | vs. | I *have been thinking of* a hostile takeover. |
| Ich habe immer *an* die Gefahr einer feindlichen Übernahme *gedacht*. | | Ich habe *über* eine feindliche Übernahme *nachgedacht*. *(echter Denk-Vorgang)* |

level 2

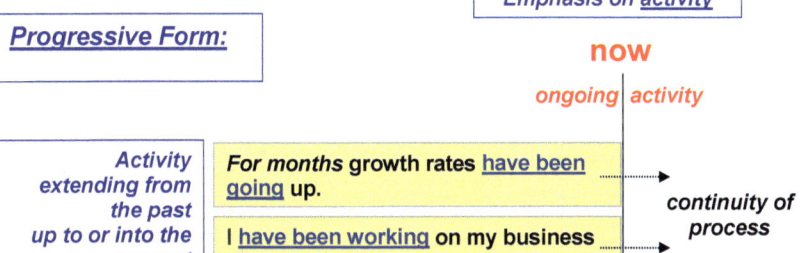

Progressive Form:

Emphasis on <u>activity</u>

now
ongoing activity

Activity extending from the past up to or into the present

For months growth rates <u>have been going</u> up.

I <u>have been working</u> on my business plan *all day long*.

continuity of process

<u>Signal Words</u> (simple & progressive):

until now, till now, so far, as yet, (up) to the present; ... yet? not ... yet;

in / over the last few days, weeks, months, years, decades, centuries; ...

 **Watch out:**

German   English
Present > Present Perfect   with *since (seit) ..., for ..., (recently)*

For several weeks, interest rates **have been rising** again.
Seit einigen Wochen **steigen** die Zinsen wieder.

Since the introduction of the euro, consumers **have been complaining** about rising prices.
Seit der Einführung des Euro **beklagen sich** die Verbraucher über steigende Preise.

Recently, the number of mergers **has been declining**.
In der jüngsten Zeit nimmt die Zahl der Fusionen **ab**.

 Distinguish:

Profits **have been rising** since last year.   (emphasis on the activity!)
Profits **have risen** by 30 per cent since last year.   (emphasis on the result!)

Merkbox:

Das **Present Perfect** bezeichnet Vorgänge, Handlungen, Situationen u.ä., die **in der Vergangenheit anfangen** und entweder **bis an die Gegenwart heran- oder in sie hineinreichen**. Das **Entscheidende** ist die **Betrachtungsweise** im Bewußtsein des Sprechers. Eindeutige **Signalwörter** machen den Gebrauch des **Present Perfect** zwingend. Ohne explizite zeitliche Zuordnung spricht viel für ein ‚überhaupt' oder ‚bisher', also das **Present Perfect**. **Aufschluß** gibt der weitere **Kontext** (auch implizit).

Achtung: Das dt. **Präsens** wird in Kombination **mit bestimmten Signalwörtern** (s. o.) im Englischen durch das **Present Perfect** wiedergegeben (v.a. mit *for*, *since*, *recently* etc.)

Im **AE** wird häufiger als im BE das **Past Tense** verwendet (auch nach *just, recently, lately, ...*), wenn der Vorgang an sich im Bewußtsein des Sprechers abgeschlossen ist.

Die **Progressive Form** betont den **Prozess**, die **Kontinuität** der Handlung, die **Aktivität** als solche. Die **Simple Form** legt den Fokus auf **Ergebnis** (v.a. auch in **Zahlen** oder der **Anzahl** der Male, Versuche u.ä.), **Konsequenzen, Auswirkung**, z.B. die sich ergebende **aktuelle** (evtl. neue) **Lage**.

practice — past tenses

D **Interview with an expert in 2010**
Present Perfect: Simple or Progressive?

1 reach
2 work
3 experience
4 be
5 get
6 go on
7 lose
8 struggle
9 try
10 bail out
11 be saved
12 succeed

What do you think of the property market? In your opinion, (1) _____ prices _____ a peak?

I (2) _____ as a real estate agent for more than 25 years, but I (3) _____ never _____ such a bubble! Of course, there (4) _____ always _____ the usual cyclical ups and downs, but this time speculation (5) _____ totally out of hand.

What (6) _____?

People who were talked into unaffordable loans (7) _____ their homes. Recently even banks (8) _____ with bankruptcy.

What about the role of the government?

Since the beginning of the crisis the government (9) _____ to stabilize the economy; it (10) _____ even _____ several banks. The system (11) _____ for now, I suppose.

Let's hope we (12) _____ now!

E   **Delays in delivery? - *Present of Present Perfect?***

Choose suitable verbs from the box to fill in the blanks.

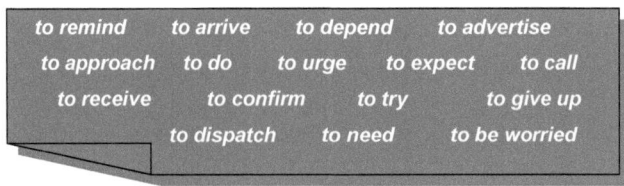

to remind   to arrive   to depend   to advertise
to approach   to do   to urge   to expect   to call
to receive   to confirm   to try   to give up
to dispatch   to need   to be worried

Dear Mr McCauley

With reference to our discussions at the trade fair two months ago we (1) _____ you of your promise to supply us with the latest fashion wear "promptly".

The summer season (2) _____ fast and, apart from the few samples you sent us weeks ago, we still (3) _____ nothing at all! We now (4) _____ the consignment urgently!

The head of your sales department, Mr Slough, (5) _____ the delivery time several times. For three days I (6) _____ to call you at the office and on your mobile phone, but so far without any success. And you (7) _____ not _____ me back so far.

If you (8) _____ not _____ the ordered products yet, we (9) _____ _____ you to send them by express freight immediately. If the goods (10) _____ not _____ at our premises by the end of next week, we will have no other choice but to cancel all orders.

As we (11) _____ your shirts and trousers in our commercials already we still (12) _____ to get them into our stores in time. As you can see, we (13) _____ not _____ hope, but we (14) _____ seriously _____ now.

Our season's sales (15) _____ on this order – and so (16) _____ our business partnership!

Please reply immediately or call us.

Kind regards

practice — past tenses

F Supply chains then and now

Put the verbs into the present or present perfect (active or passive) as required.

1. In the 17th century keeping perishable goods fresh during long voyages was difficult. Today flowers (1) _____ (to fly) over from Kenya to London overnight and (2) _____ (to be) for sale when department stores (3) _____ (to open) in the morning.

2. Before standardized containers were used, the loading and unloading of ships used to take a long time and required an army of workers. Nowadays major ports (4) _____ (to implement) automatic systems operated and monitored by a minimum of staff. Unskilled labour (5) _____ largely _____ (to make redundant) and processes (6) _____ (to become) much faster.

3. In the past, some cargoes were lost in transit. Today, with the help of GPS, the positions of vessels and freight trains (7) _____ (to indicate) in real time.

4. Until not very long ago, companies had to carry a lot of stock in warehouses. In the meantime, many companies (8) _____ (to cut down) stock to a strict minimum, relying on just-in-time delivery. As a result, however, they (9) _____ (to affect) much more easily by disruptions of the supply chain. Some of them (10) _____ (to downsize) continuously without realizing the pitfalls - sudden parts shortages which (11) _____ (may) bring assembly lines to a halt.

5. For centuries, vessels had to sail around the American continent to get from one coast to the other, from the Pacific to the Atlantic Ocean and back. Since the opening of the Panama Canal in the early 20th century, ever larger container ships (12) _____ (to use) that shipping-lane as a shortcut. As the Canal (13) _____ (to become) too small for the many XXL container ships, Panama (14) _____ (to decide) to widen it. Work (15) _____ (to start) already!

6. Unfortunately, India (16) _____ (to fail) to develop its infrastructure over the last few decades. About one third of food usually (17) _____ (to rot) on its way to the consumers.

G   **Developments and trends - *Translate*.**

1. Seit der Übernahme von Nissan durch Renault entwickelt der japanische Autohersteller kontinuierlich neue Modelle, um wieder eine attraktive Modellpalette anbieten zu können.

   _____
   _____
   _____

2. Der Handy-Hersteller fällt seit Jahren hinter Konkurrenten zurück. Bis jetzt hat er es noch nicht geschafft, die neuen Trends zu nutzen, um wieder Marktanteile zu gewinnen.

   _____
   _____
   _____

3. Die Fluggesellschaft kämpft erneut mit gestiegenen Treibstoffkosten. Seit Monaten macht sie Verluste und verliert Passagiere. Bis jetzt ist dies das schlechteste Jahr in ihrer Geschichte. Zur Zeit lockt sie Reisende mit Sonderangeboten, um Einnahmen zu generieren.

   _____
   _____
   _____

4. Die Luxusmarke ist immer noch Nummer 1 auf dem chinesischen Markt. Seit ihrem Markteintritt schafft sie es, den Absatz trotz billiger Nachahmungen beständig zu steigern. Einige andere ausländische Hersteller haben inzwischen aufgegeben.

   _____
   _____

5. Der Energiemarkt verändert sich im Augenblick dramatisch. Während einige Firmen an ihren alten Strategien festhalten, suchen andere neue Energiequellen.

   _____
   _____

6. Elektronikerzeugnisse werden seit Jahren immer billiger, während die Verbraucher für Obst und Gemüse ständig mehr bezahlen müssen. Kennen Sie die Gründe dafür°?

   _____
   _____

theory — past tenses

Past & Past Perfect:

Past Tense und Past Perfect stehen in einer logischen Zeitbeziehung und Abhängigkeit voneinander. Bestimmte Signale (Adverbien, Präpositionen etc.) helfen bei der Zuordnung.

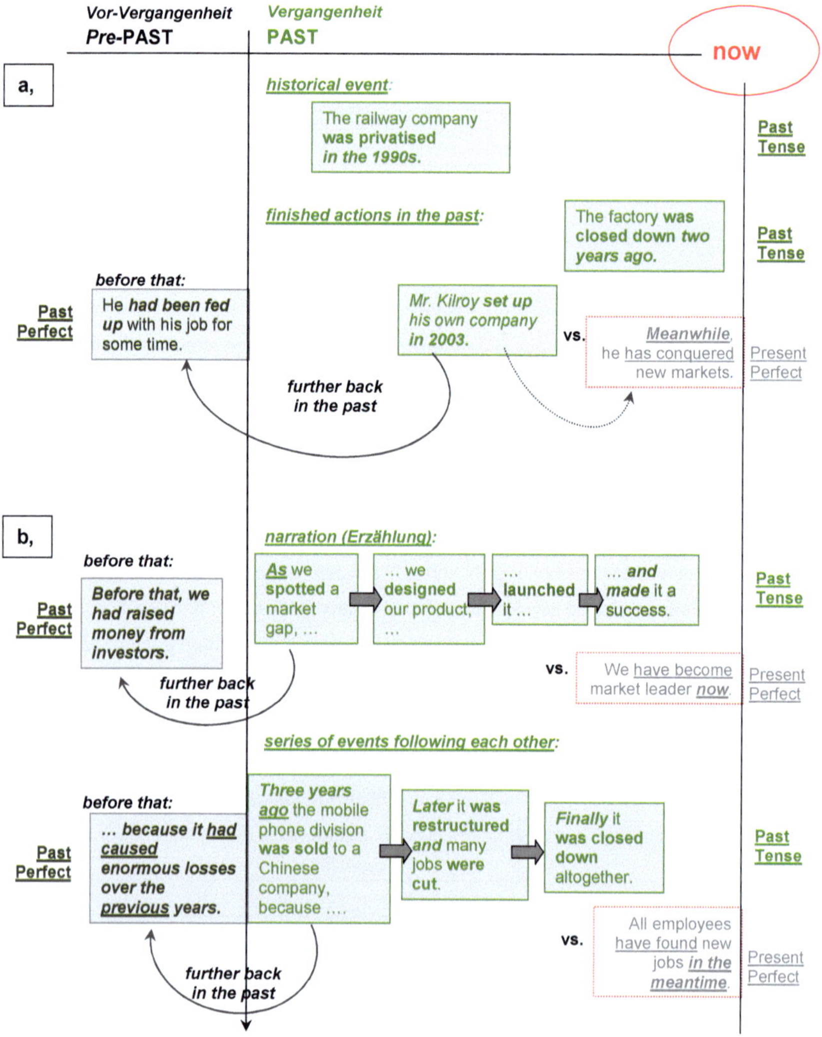

	Vor-Vergangenheit Pre-PAST	Vergangenheit PAST		now
a,		*historical event:* The railway company **was privatised** in the 1990s.		Past Tense
		finished actions in the past: The factory **was closed down** two years ago.		Past Tense
Past Perfect	*before that:* He **had been fed up** with his job for some time.	Mr. Kilroy **set up** his own company in 2003.	vs. *Meanwhile*, he has conquered new markets.	Present Perfect
		further back in the past		
b,		*narration (Erzählung):* **As** we **spotted** a market gap, ... → ... **we designed** our product, ... → ... **launched** it ... → ... **and made** it a success.		Past Tense
Past Perfect	*before that:* **Before that,** we **had raised** money from investors.		vs. We have become market leader *now*.	Present Perfect
	further back in the past			
		series of events following each other: **Three years ago** the mobile phone division **was sold** to a Chinese company, because .... → **Later** it **was restructured and** many jobs **were cut.** → **Finally** it **was closed down** altogether.		Past Tense
Past Perfect	*before that:* ... because **it had caused** enormous losses over the *previous* years.		vs. All employees have found new jobs *in the meantime*.	Present Perfect
	further back in the past			

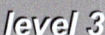

Past:

a, historical events happening at a fixed period of time in the past;
finished actions, events etc., usually pegged to a specific (period of) time
(with time adverbs etc.) and clearly perceived as over (in the speaker's mind);

	x	•	*(einzelnes Ereignis)*
	then	now	

b, the usual tense for narration & series of actions following one another

	x x x x	•	*(Handlungskette)*
	then	now	

Signal words:

yesterday, **last** night, **last** week, **last** month, **last** year, **last** century, ...;

the other day, on that day, at that time, in those days, during that period, ...;

five years / some time / long /... **ago**;

when (*dt.: als*)..., first, then, next, after that, finally / eventually, ...

Past Perfect:

Past actions, event etc. **before another past** moment or period

often **in combination with** verbs in the **Past Tense**

a,   x ←further back→ x   •   *(einzelnes Ereignis)*
before   then   now

b,   (x) x ←further back→ x x x x   •   *(Handlungskette)*
before   then   now

	some time **ago + Past**	**vs.**	*some time* **before + Past Perfect**
!	The bank *collapsed* two weeks **ago**. Die Bank *brach* **vor** zwei Wochen zusammen.		It *had* often *had* problems **before** [adverb!]. Sie *hatte* (auch schon) **vorher** oft Probleme *gehabt*.

≠ **before** + n. / verb: **before** [prep.!] *the collapse* / **before** [conjunction!] *it collapsed*

Das **Past** bezieht sich auf **abgeschlossene Vorgänge, Handlungen, Situationen** in der **Vergangenheit**. Im Bewußtsein des Sprechers gibt es **keine Verbindung zur Gegenwart**, es sei denn den **Gegensatz**, daß es **jetzt nicht mehr so** ist.
In der Regel gibt es Signale, implizit im Kontext oder explizit als **Signalwörter**, die das Geschehen in der Vergangenheit verankern: *last quarter, last month, a few days ago* etc.
Das **Past Perfect** geht einen Schritt weiter zurück in die Vergangenheit, in die ,**Vor-vergangenheit'**, und gibt Auskunft über **Dinge, die (bereits) vorher geschehen** oder abgeschlossen waren.
Zeitraum + ago ➲ Past; Zeitraum + before ➲ Past Perfect! (jew. **nachgestellt!**)

theory   past tenses

Past Tense: Simple vs. Progressive

Besonders im Past Tense gibt es eine ganze **Liste mit Verwendungsweisen der Verlaufsform**. **Blockiert** werden diese Mechanismen z.T. **durch die** sog. '**statischen**' **Verben**.

Progressive: Simple:

a, <u>background</u> to story, narration, action, series of actions etc.; description, explanation etc.
(Wie war die Situation ?)
situation:

story, narration, action, series of action(s), events ...
(Was geschah dann / daraufhin ?)
action(s), things happening (then):

   x   x   x   x

Cars **were rolling** off the assembly-line, workers **were smiling** into the cameras

... when the CEO **took** the microphone and **presented** the long-awaited new model.
When he **was asked** about the disastrous results of the latest crash test, all smiles *suddenly* **froze**.

b, <u>activity in progress</u>
(Was lief gerade ab? Was war schon?)

<u>new activity</u> interrupting or taking place
(Was geschah dann? Was kam dazwischen?)

———————————————▶   x

While the new financial director **was checking** the figures, ...

the screen suddenly **went** black.

c, <u>parallel activities in progress</u>   vs.   <u>actions completed in parallel</u>
(Was lief gleichzeitig ab?)   *(Was wurde gleichzeitig erledigt?)*

———————————————▶   x
———————————————▶   x

While Jim **was deal**ing with complaints, I **was answering** inquiries.

Jim **dealt** with complaints while I **answered** inquiries.

d, <u>(unfinished) activity</u>, occupation   vs.   <u>(completed) action</u>

———————————————▶   x

What **was** your boss **doing**?
Was **machte** dein Chef (***gerade***)?
(= Womit war dein Chef beschäftigt?)

What **did** your boss **do**?
Was **machte** dein Chef (***daraufhin***)?
(= Was war seine Reaktion?)

Progressive: Simple:

e, Ø   **stative verbs:**
                                                to be, to remain; to have; to seem, to appear; to think;...
                                                Sales **were** / **remained** stagnant last year.
                                                Growth **seemed** to be picking up.

but:
as a real activity (different meaning!):

We **were thinking** about it.   vs.   We **thought** it **was** a good strategy.
Wir **dachten** darüber **nach**.   Wir dachten, es sei eine gute Strategie.

as a temporary (!) activity:

We **were having** a lot of problems.   vs.   We **had** a lot of problems.
Wir hatten gerade Probleme.   Wir hatten eine Menge Probleme.
[ausnahmsweise; vorübergehend])

f, Ø   **habits, customary things in the past:**
                                                used to + inf. ('pflegte(n)' zu + inf.)
                                                (früher immer [- heute nicht mehr])
                                                We **used to** be ahead of our competitors.
                                                Wir waren unserer Konkurrenz voraus. *[früher]*

!   Watch out: used to + inf.: only Past Tense *(inv. - unveränderliche Form)*
    ≠   to be used to + -ing (all tenses!): etwas gewohnt sein

    ≠   CEOs in Europe **used to** [*inv.!*] *be* paid much less than in the U.S.
                Today CEOs **are used to** *getting* top compensation world wide.

                Früher erhielten Vorstände in Europa viel weniger als in den USA.
                Heute **sind** Vorstände **gewohnt**, weltweit Top-Gehälter zu bekommen.

Past Perfect: Simple & Progressive

Progressive: Simple:

activity in progress from before into past **action finished** before past.

⎯⎯⎯⎯⎯⎯→ x   •   ⎯⎯⎯⎯⎯⎯⎯→• x
in progress before then   now   **finished before** then   now

We **had been negotiating** for two hours   We **had** (*just*) **sold** all our shares
(... when the offer was withdrawn).   (... when the share price plunged).

Merkbox:

Das **Simple Past** bezeichnet einzelne oder aufeinanderfolgende **(abgeschlossene) Handlungen**, ist die typische Erzählzeit (**Was geschah [darauf]?**).
Das **Past Progressive** betont die **Aktivität als solche**, gibt die Art der **Beschäftigung** (ohne Ergebnis) an, die **Hintergrundssituation, erklärt, beschreibt**.
Ein *Past Progressive* wird im Kontext oft durch ein *Simple Past* ‚unterbrochen'.

Im **Past Perfect** bezeichnet die **Progressive** Form eine **bis zur vergangenen Handlung andauernde Aktivität**, die *Simple* Form eine **(vorher) abgeschlossene**.

practice — past tenses

H **Company strategies - choices made, trends missed or followed**
Use the Past Perfect and the Past Tense (both Simple and Progressive) to make statements.

e.g.:

> pay too much → end up making losses

→ Last year, the company <u>ended up making losses</u>, as it <u>had paid too much</u> for the acquisition of its smaller rival.

1. ignore market trends → be forced to sell off

   → The company _____ its mobile phone division, because it _____ for years.

2. sign → go bankrupt and lose

   → Many house owners who _____ everything _____ unaffordable loan agreements.

3. leave, already → collapse

   → By the time the whole market _____ investors _____ _____ the country.

4. wait → take effect

   → Two years ago the new law finally _____. Retailers _____ impatiently for that to happen.

5. be flooded → impose

   → Before the government _____ high import tariffs the market _____ with cheap products from low-wage countries.

I The car industry
Past or Past Perfect? Simple or Progressive? – Complete.

1. Many people believe that M. Ghosn became the CEO of Renault because he _____ (to rescue) Nissan before that. When he _____ (to announce) his plans to take a minority stake in AvtoVaz in order to get a foothold in the Russian market, some employees _____ (to be) afraid the strategic decision he _____ (to make) despite all criticism would not be successful this time. The situation in the old factory _____ (not to seem) very positive; but after a few months even those journalists who _____ (to write) critical comments before _____ (to have) to admit that the strategy _____ (to begin) to pay off - the Logan _____ (to develop, slowly) into a best-selling model. But some still _____ (to wonder) if that initial success _____ (to go) to last.

2. In the wake of the failed merger of Daimler and Chrysler Mr Schrempp was taken to court because he _____ (to promise) a "merger of equals". Hardly _____ the two car producers _____ (to merge), when Chrysler's CEO, Bob Eaton, _____ (to be ousted). Chrysler _____ (to keep) making heavy losses so that Daimler-Chrysler eventually _____ (to split up) again. But by then the German company _____ (to lose) a lot of money. According to some analysts Daimler _____ (to pay) too much for Chrysler in the first place and _____ (to underestimate, massively) internal problems.

3. When BMW _____ (to announce) the deal with Rover some British politicians _____ (to be) outraged, while the Rover workforce _____ (to welcome) the merger, hoping that Rover would be made competitive with the help of Bavarian knowhow. As we know, things _____ (not to work out) that way and BMW _____ (to give up) in the end. But by then, the whole British car industry _____ (to be sold out)!

4. Some time ago, while Toyota _____ (to suffer) from quality problems, the Japanese brand _____ (to be hit) by the economic crisis, on top of that. Apparently, the board _____ (to fail) to increase spending on R & D in good time. By that time, Korean carmakers _____ (to become, already) serious competitors.

K   Markets and industries – *Translate.*

1. Marktforschung zufolge stieg der Bierkonsum in China im Jahr 2000 um ca. 5 %.

   Einige Jahre später versuchte Foster's, auf dem chinesischen Markt Fuß zu fassen.

   Der australische Konzern hatte bereits vor 2000 eine teure Brauerei in China gebaut,

   sich aber aufgrund hoher Verluste vom chinesischen Markt zurückgezogen.

   Offenbar hatten die Australier die falsche Markteintrittsstrategie gewählt.

2. Anfang 2012 verstaatlichte Argentinien seine Ölindustrie. Obwohl viele Aktionäre

   überrascht waren, hatte die argentinische Regierung diesen Schritt offenbar schon

   lange erwogen. Sie folgte dem Beispiel anderer lateinamerikanischer Länder.

   Venezuela hatte seine Ölindustrie einige Jahre zuvor ebenfalls verstaatlicht.

3. Im Jahr 2011 schaffte es die Lobby der indischen Einzelhändler, ein neues Gesetz zu

   verhindern, das ausländischen Einzelhandelsketten den indischen Markt öffnen sollte.

   Carrefour und andere Unternehmen beklagten sich umgehend über die

   „Unzuverlässigkeit" der indischen Regierung. Schließlich hatten sie auf die Zusagen

   der Politiker vertraut und eine Menge Geld investiert.

4. In den frühen 1990er Jahren gingen die Immobilienpreise in München leicht zurück.

   Zwischen 1972 und 1990 waren sie drastisch gestiegen.

L   Euroland – joy and fear - *Translate*.

level 3

1. Wann wurde der Euro eingeführt?

2. Am 1. Januar 2002 hoben die Europäer zum ersten Mal Euroscheine an Automaten ab. Viele hatten ungeduldig auf diesen Moment gewartet und feierten ihn die ganze Nacht.

3. Hatten die Deutschen nicht ihre D-Mark geliebt? Warum haben sie ihre starke Währung so leicht aufgegeben?

4. Viele hatten bis zur letzten Minute heftig gegen die Einführung des Euro gekämpft. Andere hatten einfach den Politikern vertraut.

5. Waren nicht Konvergenzkriterien festgelegt worden, die die Stabilität des Euro garantierten?

6. Die Regeln wurden gleich zu Beginn der Währungsunion nicht von allen Ländern eingehalten. Als Griechenland fast pleiteging, wurde klar, dass das Land jahrelang betrogen hatte.

practice   past tenses

M Last month's motor show
a, Complete using Past or Past Perfect, Simple or Progressive, active or passive.

Last month, car manufacturers proudly _____ (1)
the new models their engineers _____ (2)
for many months. Some brands _____ (3)
with slightly modified popular models, others _____ (4)
a few gadgets, others _____ (5) old models with new
designs in line with the results their surveys _____, (6)
while others _____ (7) a full range of totally new
models. But all brands _____ (8) to reveal
spectacular innovation.
The biggest surprise _____ (9) from an Asian
company: they _____ (10) a model that
_____ (11) very badly in various crash tests
before, claiming that all problems _____ (12)
by their engineers in the meantime. Some incredulous visitors
_____ (13) to find out for themselves what
_____ (14) for the better, but
_____ (15) after a while.

to present
to work on
to come up
to add
to offer
to yield
to display
to claim

to come
to re-launch
to do
to solve
to try, desperately
to change
to give up

b, Complete using Simple Past or Past progressive, active or passive.

not to look
to be
to wait, still

to repair
to run
to want
to threaten
not to ban
to be

On the day before the opening of the motor show it
_____ (16) as if everything would
be ready in time. Some exhibitors _____ (17)
seriously worried, as they _____ (18)
for their latest model to be delivered. In one hall the roof was
still _____ (19), in another the
construction of the stands _____ (20)
far behind schedule. Suddenly, a company _____ (21)
to get a different stand, another _____ (22) to
leave if a Chinese rival _____ (23) from the
show with its star model which, allegedly, _____ (24)
"an imitation".

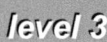

N   The old factory
*Use the verbs in brackets to complete the text (Past & Past Perfect).
Watch out, in particular, for Progressive vs. Simple Past.*

Last week a team of French managers was sent to Russia to inspect the factory that (1) _____ (to be acquired) from an ailing ex-communist company.
On their arrival, the Russian director (2) _____ (to express) his disappointment about the fact that the factory (3) _____ (to be sold) to "a foreign company", but he also (4) _____ (to point out) his hopes for the future.
He then (5) _____ (to take) the management team to the factory floor, where work (6) _____ (to be) in progress: Cars (7) _____ (to be assembled), workers (8) _____ (to solder) and (9) _____ (to weld), robot arms (10) _____ (to lift) car bodies up.
When the workers (11) _____ (to notice) the group of managers and their director, who (12) _____ (to walk) around the factory floor, they (13) _____ (to stop) working for a second and (14) _____ (to look up) in curiosity. The French managers (15) _____ (to seem) to sense the workers' mixed feelings; they (16) _____ (to respond) to anxious looks with reassuring smiles.
The factory (17) _____ (to be) clearly over-staffed, but no decision (18) _____ (to be made) at that point about the future of the workforce. A lot (19) _____ (to remain) to be done to make production profitable again. The workforce (20) _____ (to know) about the situation as they (21) _____ (to discuss) possible scenarios with their representatives before the takeover.
When the shift (22) _____ (to be finished) the inspectors (23) _____ (to examine, still) the equipment and the director, who (24) _____ (to sweat) from the heat and his worries, (25) _____ (to answer, still) questions.

past tenses

O   Online news - *Translate*.

1. Der Aktienkurs des Unternehmens hatte gerade ein neues Rekordhoch erreicht,

   _____

   als der Vorstandsvorsitzende massive technische Probleme in der Produktion

   _____

   einräumte. Sofort ging der Aktienkurs in den Keller.

   _____

2. Niemand hatte den Zusammenbruch des Konzerns vorhergesehen.

   Als der Geschäftsführer Konkurs anmeldete, gerieten viele Investoren in Panik.

   _____

   Sie hatten offenbar die strukturellen Schwächen nicht gesehen und versuchten nun

   _____

   verzweifelt, so viel Geld wie möglich zu retten. Aber für viele war es zu spät.

3. Während der Politiker zum Mikrophon trat, um die Messe zu eröffnen, ging das Licht

   _____

   plötzlich aus. Arbeiter hatten mal wieder ein Kabel durchgeschnitten. Stromausfälle

   _____

   waren auch während früherer Messen immer wieder aufgetreten und hatte Fragen

   _____

   über die Professionalität der Organisatoren aufgeworfen.

4. Während eine Werbekampagne ein umweltfreundliches Image des Konzerns

   _____

   zu schaffen versuchte, flossen viele Liter Öl aus einer leckenden Pipeline. Sie war im

   _____

   Bürgerkrieg beschädigt worden und verseuchte nun die wenigen fruchtbaren Felder.

   _____

5. Obwohl der Bericht vor Wochen fertiggestellt worden war, wurde er nicht gedruckt.

   _____

P **Work-life balance?**
Used to do (pflegte zu tun / tat früher immer) or
(be) used to doing (gewohnt zu tun)?
Complete.

"I remember very well: In the past, workers used to (1) _____
(stay) in the same company all their lives. It used to (2) _____ (be)
their 'family'. They were used to (3) _____ (get) regular pay
rises and they used to (4) _____ (take) pride in their brand.
In the meantime, however, many employees have got used to (5) _____
(change) jobs frequently in order to improve their salaries or to avoid getting laid off.
Many have become used to (6) _____ (work) overtime to cope with the
increasing workload. Others have got used to (7) _____ (survive)
on temporary jobs. If past generations used to (8) _____ (worry)
about work-life balance, people today are used to (9) _____
(worry) about job security. It seems that working life used to (10) _____
(be) less of a permanent battle."

Q **Niche players** – *Translate.*

Mit seinen Nischenprodukten hatte der Firmengründer einst (*used to*) ein weltweites

_____

Monopol. Er war es gewohnt, aus allen Kontinenten Aufträge zu erhalten und keine

_____

direkten Konkurrenten zu haben. Selbst in Krisenzeiten blieb die Nachfrage lebhaft.

_____

China schien der lukrativste Markt zu werden; daher erwog er bereits, die gesamte

_____

Fertigung nach Chongqing auszulagern, als ein chinesisches Unternehmen eine

_____

fast identische Produktpalette auf den Markt brachte. Diese Gefahr war ihm nicht

_____

bewusst gewesen. Er war es gewohnt gewesen, auf seine Patente zu vertrauen.

_____

theory   past tenses

Compare:

Air Munich **is** another example of the tough competition between airlines. **When** it **was established** *ten years ago*, everything **looked** very promising. **Before** *the creation of AM*, market research **had indicated** a genuine market niche and banks **had** readily **granted** generous loans. **By** the end of the start-up phase *AM* **had built up** a solid customer base, and **until** the arrival of foreign no-frills airlines the success story **continued**. *In the meantime*, however, the airline **has been** (!) **running up** heavy losses *for some time* and is struggling to survive. It **has had** (!) serious problems with the reliability of its flights *for the last few weeks*, *since* the departure of its chief engineer. *Recently*, some aircraft **were** even **grounded** after safety checks. *Yesterday* newspapers **announced** the takeover of Air Munich by *Franconian Airlines*. *Now AM* **has** at least **managed** to survive, but it **has lost** its independence.	*Air Munich* **ist** ein weiteres Beispiel für den harten Wettbewerb zwischen den Fluggesellschaften. **Als** sie *vor zehn Jahren* **gegründet wurde**, **sah** alles sehr vielversprechend aus. *Vor der Gründung* **hatte** Marktforschung eine echte Marktlücke **aufgezeigt** und Banken **hatten** bereitwillig großzügige Kredite **gewährt**. **Bis** zum Ende der Aufbauphase **hatte** *AM* einen soliden Kundenstamm **aufgebaut**, und **bis** zur Ankunft ausländischer Billigfluglinien **setzte sich** die Erfolgsgeschichte **fort**. Inzwischen jedoch **macht** (!) die Fluggesellschaft *seit einiger Zeit* schwere Verluste und kämpft um ihr Überleben. Sie **hat** (!) *in den letzten Wochen*, *seit dem Weggang* ihres Chefingenieurs, ernsthafte Probleme mit der Verläßlichkeit ihrer Flüge. *Unlängst* **blieben** sogar einige Flugzeuge nach Sicherheitsüberprüfungen am Boden. *Gestern* **kündigten** Zeitungen die Übernahme von *Air Munich* durch *Franconian Arlines* an. *Nun* **hat** es *AM* wenigstens **geschafft** zu überleben, **hat** aber die Unabhängigkeit **verloren**.

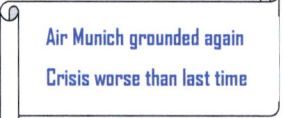

Air Munich grounded again

Crisis worse than last time

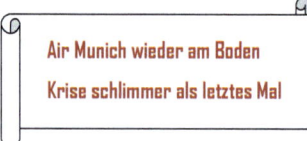

Air Munich wieder am Boden

Krise schlimmer als letztes Mal

Tasks (comparing the texts in the boxes above):

a, Identify the *tenses* and *aspects* (simple / progressive) used.
b, Compare and explain the use of the English and German tenses.
c, Find out and explain signals (signal words) that help decide about the appropriate tense in English.
d, What is tricky about the use of the Present in the German version?

*Besondere Probleme bereitet die **Unterscheidung zwischen** den einzelnen englischen **Vergangenheitszeiten** (sogar der Gegensatz zum deutschen Präsens, **weil dies nicht dem deutschen Zeiten-System entspricht**. **Signale** (temporale Adverbien, Präpositionen, Konjunktionen) spielen hier eine **wichtige Rolle** für die Früherkennung.*

level 4

Examples:

a Wir **warten** *seit zwei Monaten* auf die Lieferung. Nun müssen wir den Auftrag stornieren.
We **have been waiting** for the shipment *for two months*. Now we have to cancel the order.
──────────────────────────────────→ STOP

b **Haben** Sie unser Angebot *schon* **erhalten**?
Have you **received** our offer *yet*?
──────────────────────────────────→ ?

c **Haben** Sie *bereits* in der Marketing-Abteilung **gearbeitet**?
Have you *already* **worked** in the marketing department?
──────────────────────────────────→ ?
Ich **habe** *während meines ersten Praktikums* in der Marketing-Abteilung **gearbeitet**.
I **worked** in the marketing department *during my first internship*.
●────────────────────●

d My colleague **was** marketing director in Shanghai *for two years*.
Mein Kollege **war** *für zwei Jahre* (*zwei Jahre lang*) Marketing-Leiter in Shanghai.
●────────────────────●

I **have been** sales director in Cape Town *for two years*.
Ich **bin** *seit zwei Jahren* Verkaufsleiter in Kapstadt.
──────────────────────────────────→ ....

e I **had worked** for the company *for 25 years when* they **laid** me **off**.
Ich **hatte** *25 Jahre lang* für das Unternehmen **gearbeitet**, *als* sie mich **entliessen**.
──────────────────────────────────→ x

f **Haben** Sie *in letzter Zeit* eine Lohnerhöhung **erhalten**?
Have you **had** any wage increase *lately / recently*?
──────────────────────────────────→ ?
Kürzlich **hielt** ich in China einen Vortrag über Wirtschaftsethik.
Recently I **gave** a talk in China about business ethics.
        x

g They **manufactured** faked designer T-shirts in this factory *until last* weekend.
Sie **fertigten** *bis letztes Wochenende* gefälschte Designer-T-Shirts in dieser Fabrik.
────────────────●

By the time the inspectors arrived they **had removed** all fakes.
Bis die Inspektoren kamen, **hatten** sie alle Imitate **beseitigt**.
──────────────────→ x

 **past tenses**

in the last (few) years / months / weeks / ...

In the last <u>few</u> years Indian companies have been buying up
companies abroad. *(up to now!)*   *present perfect*

In den letzten Jahren haben indische Unternehmen Firmen im Ausland
aufgekauft. *(bis jetzt)*

In the last years *before his death*, the oil magnate (had) repeatedly donated
large sums of money. *(time over!)*   *past / past perfect*

In den letzten Jahren *vor seinem Tod* spendete / hatte ... gespendet der Ölmagnat
große Geldbeträge. *(bis zu seinem Tod ⊃ Zeitraum zu Ende)*

> **Watch out:**
>
> | last **time** | = letztes **Mal** |
> |---|---|
> | **recently** | = in der letzten **Zeit** |
> | for some **time** | = seit einiger **Zeit** |

German 'bis':

till / until:
Hong Kong was British **till / until** it **was handed** back to China in 1997.   *(conjunction)*
Hong Kong **was** the West's main gateway to China **till / until 1997.**   *(preposition)*

by:
By 2000 Shanghai **had become** a gateway to China too.   *(preposition)*

till / until vs. by:

They kept adapting the design **till / until** it was finally accepted.
Das Design wurde ständig angepasst, **bis** es schließlich akzeptiert wurde.

                                            ● *Ende des Vorgangs*
    Vorgang

They had got a foothold in the market **by** 2005.
Sie hatten **bis** 2005 auf dem Markt Fuß gefasst.

Entstehung, Vorgeschichte ... 'fertig' ⊃ *ab 2005: Situation eingetreten*

The brand was well known **until / till** 1990.
                                    all the time before 1990 *no more after 1990*
Die Marke war bis 1990 sehr bekannt.
                      (*Sie war es die ganze Zeit bis 1990,* | *danach nicht mehr.*)

The brand was well known **by** 1990.
                               had slowly become known 1990 *definitely known after 1990*
Die Marke war bis 1990 sehr bekannt.
(Sie wurde allmählich bekannt, 1990 Vorgang abgeschlossen, ab dann bekannt.)

recently / lately

The Fed *has issued* a number of reports **lately**.　　|x x x x|　　*period / series not finished*
Die Fed *hat* **in jüngster Zeit** eine Reihe von Berichten *herausgegeben*.

I *haven't heard* of this brand **recently**.　　|x x x x|　　*period / series not finished*
Ich *habe* **in letzter Zeit** nichts von dieser Marke *gehört*.

Recently, our consultant *had* an appointment with
a senior economist from the ECB.　　　　　　　　x　　*action over*
Kürzlich *hatte* unser Berater einen Termin mit
einem hochrangigen Volkswirt von der EZB.

recently and *lately* are **not reliable signal words**: the tense depends on whether the action or event is over or whether the period of time still continues into the present.

for vs. *since*:

We **have been discussing** the strategy **for** five hours, **since** 2 p.m.
Wir **diskutieren** die Strategie *(nun schon)* **seit** fünf Stunden, **seit** 2 Uhr Nachmittag.

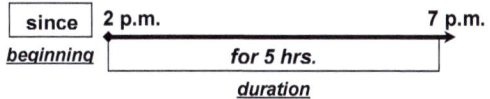

Watch out:

! I **have worked / been working** in this factory **for** 10 years. *(seit 10 Jahren, bis jetzt)*
I **worked** in that factory **for** 10 years. *(10 Jahre lang, jetzt nicht mehr)*

Note also:　the **different functions & meanings** of *since*

preposition:　**Since** *the introduction of the euro*, consumers have been complaining.
　　　　　　　Seit *der Einführung des Euro* beklagen sich die Verbraucher.

conjunction:　**Since** the currency ***was devalued***, exports have been booming.
　　　　　　　Seitdem die Währung ***abgewertet wurde***, boomen die Exporte.
　　　　　　　(beginning)

　　　　　　　Since Chinese cities ***are*** heavily polluted, public health is at risk.
　　　　　　　Da (ja) die chinesischen Städte unter starker Umweltverschmutzung
　　　　　　　leiden, ist die öffentliche Gesundheit in Gefahr. *(reason)*

Merkbox:

> Bei **von der Gegenwart aus gesehen**en und bis ins Jetzt andauernden Zeitabschnitten steht im Englischen gewöhnlich **zusätzlich *few***: *in the last **few** years, months, weeks, days* zusätzlich, im Deutschen i.d.R. unübersetzt.
> Die deutsche Präposition *bis* hat **unterschiedliche Bedeutungen**, die im Englischen durch **by** oder durch *till / until* wiedergegeben werden.
> ***Since* & *for* sind als Signalwörter tückisch**, weil sie auch in anderen Zeitgefügen (z.B. mit dem *Past* & *Past Perfect*) vorkommen können. Eindeutig sind sie, **wenn** sie **im Deutschen zusammen mit dem Präsens** verwendet werden. Dann steht **im Englischen Present Perfect**.
> Bei *recently* & *lately* sind die **Signale** ebenfalls **nicht eindeutig**. Die Zeitform hängt davon ab, ob es sich um einen abgeschlossenen Vorgang handelt (*Past*) oder um einen noch andauernden Zeitabschnitt (*Present Perfect*).

practice — past tenses

R   A job interview
Use the appropriate Past Tenses to complete the dialogue.

Ms Browne, you (1) _____ last year, too. Before that you (2) _____ us your application three times already. Altogether we (3) _____ _____ five applications from you so far. Why are you so keen to work with us?

1 *to apply*
2 *to send*
3 *to receive*

Well, you (4) _____ among the first companies to join the UN Global Compact in 2000/2001 and (5) _____ your sustainability standards ever since. For several years now you (6) _____ _____ the most employee-friendly company of your industry. And on top of that you (7) _____ market leader now. To me, you are the ideal employer.

4 *to be*
5 *to enhance*
6 *to consider (passive!)*
7 *to become*

But we are very demanding, too. What ethics courses (8) _____ you _____ at university? What international experience (9) _____ you _____ since graduation? (10) _____ you ever _____ and _____ for a longer period of time abroad?

8 *to attend*
9 *to gain*
10 *to live and work*

During my studies I (11) _____ in an exchange and (12) _____ a second degree in France. When I (13) _____ to work for a Sino-British joint venture I (14) _____ an internship in Hong Kong already.

11 *to take part*
12 *to obtain*
13 *to start*
14 *to do*

Would you like to work there again?

In fact, I (15) _____ to return there since I _____.

15 *to try*
16 *to leave*

S **Companies and careers**
Since or *for*? – *Complete.*

1. "_____ this company was set up in 2008 it has been growing at dazzling speed. _____ the last two years it has continuously been expanding across Asia and Africa. _____ the new CEO took over it has tripled its revenues. And _____ then it has regained and successfully defended its market leadership at home. It will be thriving _____ a long time to come!"

2. "I joined this company to write my thesis - and stayed on after my graduation _____ fifteen years! _____ last year, however, I have developed a taste for a new challenge. I now feel I shouldn't go on working like this _____ the next fifteen years."

3. "The influence of the UN Global Compact has been growing steadily _____ 2000, when it was set up. At the beginning, _____ several years, it was struggling for recognition. But _____ the rules were tightened a few years later it has been gaining ground. It will probably define global ethics _____ years to come.

T **Hong Kong**
By or *till / until*? - *Complete.*

_____ 1997 Hong Kong was a British crown colony. Then it was handed back to the People's Republic of China. Some of its inhabitants had obtained a British passport _____ then, because they did not trust the special status which was to be granted to Hong Kong for another 50 years, _____ 2047.

U **Go public or not?**
Ago or *before*? – *Complete.*

A month _____, five days _____ the retail chain's IPO, top executives were arrested for fraud. Sales figures plummeted _____ company representatives were able to comment. Quickly, the IPO was called off "until further notice". The company would not go public until all accusations were cleared up! Remember: A few years _____ another retail chain did not cancel its IPO despite a scandal. The share price lost half its value _____ the closing of the stock exchange!

practice — past tenses

V **Headlines –** *Make full statements.*
Mind the tenses and fill in appropriate time adverbs:
ago, before, since, for, till/until, by.

Animal testing stopped

1. The pharmaceutical company _____ all animal testing two days _____ due to a consumer boycott which had been going on _____ weeks.

| *Bankruptcy declared?* |
Debt piled up

2. The company _____ not _____ bankruptcy yet, but it _____ up too much debt _____ last year, when it was restructured.

Truck drivers on strike

3. _____ several days now, many truck drivers _____ on strike for better working conditions and higher pay. The strike is to continue at least _____ the end of this week, unless an agreement is reached _____ then.

Import tariffs lifted

4. Two weeks _____ the government _____ all import tariffs it had imposed on imported cars only a month _____ that. The domestic market has to be deregulated _____ the beginning of next year, when the country is to join the WTO.

Inflation rate on the rise

5. While the inflation rate _____ only marginally last year and _____ not _____ _____ two years before that, it _____ again quite significantly _____ January this year.

Train services disrupted

6. Train services _____ _____ 2 hours yesterday.

W   Dotcoms under attack - *Translate*.

Haben Sie gehört? Viele Internetfirmen kooperieren seit Jahren mit Regierungen und Geheimdiensten!

Vor seinem Börsengang stand mein soziales Netzwerk für Freiheit und Bürgerrechte. Das dauerte nur, bis sein Gründer den Wert der gesammelten Daten in Gewinne ummünzen konnte. Dann war sein Idealismus weg!

Ich las gerade die Allgemeinen Geschäftsbedingungen, als eine Nachrichtensendung im Fernsehen über den Skandal zu berichten begann.

Ich hatte darüber schon vorher in einer Zeitung gelesen. Seitdem benutze ich das Netzwerk viel weniger. Und ich habe meine Daten gelöscht.

Das Internet vergisst nie! Unternehmen, deren Webseiten Sie regelmäßig besucht haben, kennen Ihr Profil seit langem.

Ich habe nie Fotos hochgeladen und nie meine echte Identität enthüllt. Ich war schon vor Jahren misstrauisch.

practice past tenses

X **Statements from newspaper articles**

a, Take the following notes and the time adverbs on the right and write down statements in full sentences. Use Past Tenses.

(1) Ölpreise explodieren
_____

since the 1980s

(2) Kapitalismus zunehmend kritisiert
_____

in recent years

(3) England von der spanischen Armada bedroht
_____

until 1566

(4) Eine Menge Erfindungen in diesem Land
_____

lately

(5) Demonstrationen enden im Chaos
_____

last time

(6) Deutschland weitgehend wieder aufgebaut
_____

by the 1960s

(7) Messe kein so großer Erfolg
_____

for years now

(8) Deng Xiao Ping öffnet China
_____

decades ago

b, **Continue.**

seit Maos Tod

vor 2008

in letzter Zeit

vom 2. Weltkrieg bis 1990

1914 / bis 2008 / Jahrzehnte vorher

(9) China total gewandelt
_____

(10) Finanzbranche völlig außer Kontrolle
_____

(11) Immer mehr Zeitarbeiter
_____

(12) Deutschland geteilt
_____

(13) Panamakanal eröffnet / mehr als 800 000 Schiffe durchgefahren / Suezkanal eröffnet
_____

Y   **Rise and fall**

Translate.

1. Diese Firma wurde vor fünf Jahren von Jonathan Seagull gegründet. Er hatte eine sicherere Methode erfunden, Daten auf einem PC zu schützen und wollte sie selbst verkaufen. Zunächst steigerte das kleine Unternehmen seinen Absatz sehr schnell, die Zahl der Abonnenten schoss fünf Jahre lang in die Höhe – bis ein Datenskandal die Glaubwürdigkeit der Software ruinierte. Der Kundenstamm schrumpfte rapide und bis zum Ende desselben Jahres war die Firma pleite.

2. Der chinesische Technologiekonzern erobert seit zwei Jahrzehnten einen ausländischen Markt nach dem anderen. Er war ursprünglich als Gemeinschaftsunternehmen mit einem deutschen Unternehmen geschaffen worden und wurde bis 1988 als Symbol für erfolgreiche internationale Zusammenarbeit gesehen. In jenem Jahr beendete China die Partnerschaft und machte daraus einen Staatsbetrieb. Bis zum Jahr 2000 operierten der deutsche und der chinesische Konzern auf getrennten Märkten. Seit der Privatisierung des chinesischen Konzerns konkurrieren die beiden Technologieriesen weltweit miteinander. Aufgrund des aktuellen Absatzrückgangs musste der deutsche Konzern inzwischen 2000 Mitarbeiter entlassen.

3. Seit den 1990er Jahren kämpft Japan mit hohen Staatsschulden und Deflation.

Intro

Vorgedanken

MODAL AUXILIARIES
Modale Hilfsverben

Was ist das genau? Wo ist das Problem?

> Was sind denn <u>modale</u> Hilfsverben? Gibt's noch andere?

> Klar! Es gibt temporale und modale Hilfsverben. Die ersten benutzt man zur Bildung der zusammengesetzten Zeiten, die modalen Hilfsverben drücken eine ‚Modalität' (Art und Weise) aus, d.h. das <u>Verhältnis des Sprechers zur Aussage, Realität, Realisierung.</u>

Temporal:
The CEO has resigned.
The country will soon join the WTO.

Modal:
The company cannot clear its debts.
We must cut our workforce.

> Wo liegt das Problem? Die sind doch ganz einfach. Ist doch egal, ob sie temporal oder modal sind, oder?

The boss has cut jobs.
▶ Der Chef hat Stellen gestrichen.

The boss has to cut jobs.
▶ Der Chef muss Stellen streichen.

The boss has had to cut jobs.
▶ Der Chef hat Stellen streichen müssen.

> Nicht wirklich, denn die Strukturen sind anders – und v.a. die Bedeutung. Die ist bei Verwechslung oder Vermischung nicht klar oder sogar falsch.

> Und: temporale und modale Verwendung können in Kombination auftreten!

level 0

> Hm, ok. Dann sollte man wohl eher die einfachen nehmen, wie *can, must, should* usw.

We can increase our sales.
We have been able to increase our sales.
Will we be able to increase our sales?

> Die gibt es aber nur in der Gegenwart, denn es sind sog. unvollständige Hilfsverben. In anderen Zeiten braucht man sog. ‚Ersatzformen'.

> Wenn die in allen Zeiten gehen, dann nimmt man halt immer die ‚Ersatzformen' – oder?

I cannot buy the patent.
(Fähigkeit & Moral etc.! → vage)
I am not able to buy the patent.
(nicht in der Lage, z.B. finanziell)
I am not allowed to buy it.
(darf nicht, z.B. rechtlich)
He cannot have bought it.
(Es ist kaum möglich, undenkbar.)

> Keine gute Idee! Die ‚Ersatzformen' sind meist spezifischer, daher muss man dann in der Gegenwart, wo beide Formen möglich sind, nach der genauen Sinn-Nuance unterscheiden. Auch gibt es Variationen und Kombinationen, die eine ganz andere – übertragene – Bedeutung haben.

Merkbox:

Um Fehler mit den Formen und Strukturen zu vermeiden, sind temporale und modale Hilfsverben zu unterscheiden, da ihre Anwendungen und Bedeutungen unterschiedlich sind. Bei Vermischung der Strukturen ergibt sich u.U. falscher - oder kein - Sinn. Die unterschiedlichen Verwendungsweisen können verwirren!

Unvollständige Hilfsverben haben nur Gegenwartsformen, daher muss bei anderen Zeiten auf sog. ‚Ersatzformen' ausgewichen werden. Diese haben allerdings i.d.R. spezifischere, ‚engere' Bedeutungen. Daher: Vorsicht in der Gegenwart, wo unvollständiges Hilfsverb und Ersatzform konkurrieren!

Bestimmte Kombinationen aus unvollständigem Hilfsverb und zusammengesetzten Zeiten haben andere, übertragene, Bedeutungen.

theory

MODAL AUXILIARIES

Compare:

Due to the cold winter a backlog of orders **has** built up, which **is to** be reduced now. Many construction firms **have had to** work extra hours for the last few weeks in order to catch up – with orders and revenues.	Aufgrund des kalten Winters **hat** sich ein Rückstau an Aufträgen aufgebaut, der nun ab**zu**bauen **ist**. Viele Baufirmen **müssen** seit einigen Wochen Überstunden machen, um aufzuholen – bei den Aufträgen und den Einnahmen.
The backlog, however, **might** actually turn out to be helpful rather than problematic, since order intake decreased significantly last month after the government **had cut** its budget for public projects. In particular, SME's **could** be severely hit by the cut; so they **should** get ready for hard times.	Der Rückstau **könnte** sich indessen eher als hilfreich denn als problematisch erweisen, da der Auftragseingang letzten Monat deutlich zurückging, nachdem die Regierung die Haushaltsmittel für öffentliche Aufträge gekürzt **hatte**. Insbesondere KMUs **könnten** von der Kürzung schwer getroffen werden; daher **sollten** sie sich auf schwere Zeiten einstellen.
But in the current economic situation nobody **can** really predict what **will** come next – an economic recovery or another recession.	Aber in der aktuellen Wirtschaftslage **kann** niemand wirklich vorhersagen, was als nächstes kommen **wird**: eine wirtschaftliche Erholung oder eine weitere Rezession.

Tasks:

a, Distinguish between *temporal* and *modal auxiliaries* in the box. *(level 1)*
b, Identify the *tenses*. *(level 1)*
c, Distinguish between 'incomplete' (*unvollständige*) modal auxiliaries (without any infinitive, such as can, may etc.) and inflected (*in allen Zeiten konjugierbare*) forms (such as to be to, to have to etc.). *(level 2-3)*
d, Distinguish between the *different meanings / uses*. *(level 3)*

78

*Zunächst sehen wir uns die Formen der **temporalen Hilfsverben**, also jene zur **Bildung der Zeiten** (inkl. **Verlaufsform** und **Passiv**) an.*

1. temporal auxiliaries: forms

a, used to form compound tenses (zusammengesetzte Zeiten):

have/has, had; (shall)/will; would

Present Perfect:	The company has declared bankruptcy.
	Politicians have rejected any rescue plan using public funds.
Past Perfect:	The first two rescue plans had not worked out.
Future I:	How will the government help the workforce?
Future II:	When will all of them have got a new job?
Conditional I:	Would a private investor's rescue plan still be possible?
Conditional II:	Would another strategy have worked better?

b, used to form Progressive forms (Verlaufsformen): *to be + -ing*

Present Tense:	The young start-up is struggling.
Past Tense:	The young start-up was struggling last year.
Present Perfect:	The young start-up has been struggling for some time.
Past perfect:	The young start-up had been struggling too long.
Future I	The young start-up will be struggling in weeks to come.
Future II:	The start-up will have been struggling hard by then.
Conditional I:	The young start-up would be struggling by now.
Conditional II:	The start-up would have been struggling a lot more if ….

c, used to form the Passive Voice (Passiv): *to be + past participle*

Present Tense:	Consumers are (being) deceived.
Past Tense:	Customers were (being) robbed while waiting.
Present Perfect:	Consumers have been deceived for a long time.
Past perfect:	The regulator had been lied to.
Future I	Tax payers' money will be spent.
Future II:	Alternatives will have been dismissed.
Conditional I:	Other options would be examined more closely.
Conditional II:	Another company would have been wiped out immediately.

d, used to form questions, negation and emphasis: *to do + infinitive*

The EU commission does not intervene. / Don't consumers ever mind?
Why did the CEO lie to the commission? – He did not! - Oh yes, he did lie!

modal auxiliaries

Nun zu den Modalverben:

2. <u>modal</u> auxiliaries: forms and frequent substitutes in other tenses

a, 'incomplete' forms:
   no infinitive, uninflected,
   ('unvollständiges' Hilfsverb;
   kein Infinitiv, ,starre' Form)

b, inflected forms:
   all tenses
   (in allen Zeiten verwendbar;
   ,gebeugte', also konjugierte Formen)

We **can** start producing right away.

Could the government bail out the bank?

Will the entrepreneur **be able to** reach all the objectives?

"In that case we **would be able to** grant you a quantity discount."

The investor **has not been able to** raise enough money yet.   *etc.*

To be able to + infinitive can replace *can,* in the sense of *imstande / in der Lage sein*. However, *can* is used in various senses, often generally and diffusely.

Distinguish:

Can you help me with my business plan?   ***Are you able to*** help me?
Kannst du mir ... helfen?   **Bist** du **in der Lage**, mir ... zu helfen?

In the **Present Tense**, where both forms co-exist, *to be able* is used to specifically emphasize the **ability**.

He said we could boost profits that way. (here also: ... we *would be able to* ...)

The bank turned her request down before she *could* prove her credit worthiness.

Could is chiefly understood as a **Conditional,** but in **Reported Speech** and in complex temporal sentences, following the logic of the **sequence of tenses,** *could* is also used as a form of the **Past Tense.**

Could is also used in the **Past** to describe a *repeated or general ability* as opposed to a single event **and** generally **in negative statements**:

When he was young, he could swim very well. *(in general)*
Before he lost consciousness, the injured climber **was able to** tell the paramedics his name. *(specific situation)*
The CEO couldn't remember what he had said before the AGM.

level 1

| **may / might** | *dürfen* | to be allowed to |

"*May* I join your group?" (***Darf ich*** …)   Was I allowed to join?
"Yes, you *may*."   Had they been allowed to join before?
"No, you *may not*."   Will I be allowed to join?
"*Might* I attend the meeting?" (***Dürfte ich*** …?)   Would I be allowed to attend?   *etc.*

In the sense of ***dürfen***, *may* and *might* are typically used in questions and subsequent answers. In other structures these two forms clash with another frequent use / meaning.

Advice: Do not use *may* / *might* in the sense of ***dürfen*** outside questions!

| ***shall / should*** | *sollen* | (to be to) |

"*Shall* we get rid of non-core activities?"   (We *are to* get rid of non-core activities.)
"They *shall* wait in front of the factory gate."   (They *are to* wait in front of the gate.)
The level of debt *should* be reduced.   (The level of debt *is to* be reduced.)
"You *should* do market research first."   (The start-up *was to* pay a fine.)

Similarly to *may* and *might*, (as ***dürfen***), *shall* is often used in **questions** or (sometimes) **formal instructions.**

Advice: Do not use *shall* in the sense of *sollen* outside questions!

By contrast, *should* is very frequently used for **advice** or (polite) **instructions**.

To be to is **no real substitute** because its meaning is much stronger, more like a strict external **obligation**, such as "hatte zu bezahlen", "sind zu unterlassen" or even „müssen loswerden" etc.
Also, *to be to* has **further meanings**. Therefore, it is **not really an equivalent**.
(See level 3)

   modal auxiliaries

"We **must** expand to Russia." They **had to** pay higher wages.
The company **must** increase prices. They **will have to** increase prices.
We **must** employ temporary workers. We **have had to** employ temps.
We **must** pay damages. It was our fault.* We **had to** pay damages due to a court ruling.* etc.

Generally, **to have to** + *infinitive* is used in all tenses to express an **obligation** (***müssen***).

* In the Present Tense, where both forms exist (***must*** and ***to have to***), ***must*** is often used to express a **subjective** feeling or sense of obligation while ***to have to*** rather tends to express an **external obligation** (e.g. due to a law, a regulation, a court ruling or another kind of external authority).

e.g.: We ***must*** do business together.   We ***have to*** file for bankruptcy.
(I feel very strongly about it.)   (The law requires it.)

We ***mustn't*** cut our workforce.   We ***are not allowed to*** cut our
(I firmly believe it would be wrong.)   workforce due to an agreement with the
                                             union. *(external or formal requirement)*

Our shop in Saudi Arabia ***mustn't*** sell   Our shop has not been allowed to sell
alcohol. *(We do not want it.)*   alcohol for years. *(... by law)*

Mustn't is the direct opposite of *must*, i.e. an **obligation not to** do something or a **negative obligation** (***nicht dürfen***)! In this sense, ***not to be allowed to*** is used to replace ***mustn't*** in other tenses.

However, **like *must***, frequently ***mustn't*** is used in a **wider, more diffuse sense**. Also, as ***mustn't*** is very strong, native speakers often prefer ***shouldn't***.

<u>Watch out</u>: Do not mix up with ***nicht müssen*** *(see below)*.

level 1

needn't | **nicht müssen** | **not to have to**

We *needn't* restructure our business.

Our head office *needn't* be relocated to Birmingham.

The goods *needn't* be sent by express freight.

Our workers *needn't* work overtime.

We **don't have to** restructure our business.

Our head office **doesn't have to** be to relocated to Birmingham.

The goods **didn't have to** be sent by express freight. *(… and were not!)*

Our workers **haven't had to** work overtime for ages.

The usual modal auxiliary to express a lack of obligation or necessity is *needn't*.

In other tenses **don't / doesn't / didn't have to** (or also: **need to**) are commonly used.

<u>Watch out</u>: Both structures are *nicht müssen / nicht brauchen* in German!

Zusammenfassung der Probleme mit den modalen Hilfsverben:

Das <u>erste Problem</u> ist, dass <u>Modalverben</u> häufig '<u>unvollständig</u>' sind, also nicht in allen Zeiten verwendet werden können; für die anderen Zeiten sind sog. <u>Ersatzformen</u> erforderlich.

Das <u>zweite Problem</u> ist, dass <u>Ersatzformen</u> in den Zeiten (Present, Past, Conditional), in denen auch die unvollständigen Modalverbformen vorkommen, <u>spezifischere Bedeutungsnuancen</u> haben.

Das <u>dritte Problem</u> ist, dass die <u>Formen</u> mancher <u>modal</u>er Ersatzformen den Formen <u>temporal</u>er Hilfsverben <u>ähneln</u> (to have - to have to; to be - to be to) <u>und</u> auch noch <u>in Verbindung miteinander verwendet</u> werden.

Ein <u>viertes Problem</u>: <u>Unvollständige Modalverben</u> haben z.T. <u>in verschiedenen Strukturen unterschiedliche Bedeutungen</u>.

Merkbox:

> Temporale Hilfsverben dienen zur Bildung der zusammengesetzten Zeiten, der Verlaufsform und des Passivs.
>
> Modale Hilfsverben fügen der Aussage sozusagen eine Modalität, eine 'Bedingtheit' (*müssen, sollen, können* etc.) hinzu.
>
> Temporale und modale Hilfsverben können kombiniert werden.
> Einige (sehr häufige) modale Hilfsverben (*must* etc.) gibt es nur in einer (starren) Form (ohne Infinitiv); d.h. in zusammengesetzten Zeiten müssen Ersatzformen benutzt werden.
>
> Diese Ersatzformen sind nicht 1 : 1 verwendbar, da es je nach Struktur und Kontext Bedeutungsunterschiede gibt.

 **modal auxiliaries**

A Reforms needed

Add a modality to the following statements by using appropriate forms of the modal verbs (stated in English or in German) in the tenses indicated in brackets.

e.g.: Full data protection ___couldn't___ (nicht können / Cond. I) be guaranteed.

As the economy of the socialist country was in deep trouble, reforms _____ _____ (1 *müssen* / Past) be undertaken. Of course, they _____ (2 *müssen* / Conditional I) be 'socialist' reforms. Some improvements _____ _____ (3 *need* / Past) be made in order to calm the ordinary people. Small businesses _____ already _____ (4 *dürfen* / Past Perfect) operate on a profit basis, but they (5 *nicht dürfen* / Past) _____ grow into medium-sized ones; also they _____ (6 *nicht können* / Past) get big enough loans from state banks. A common complaint was: "We _____ (7 *need* / Present) invest. Without money we _____ (8 *nicht können* / Present). grow. The government _____ (9 *sollen* / Cond. I) subsidize us. We _____ (10 *nicht dürfen* / Present) pile up too many debts." According to the government, the private sector _____ (11 *nicht müssen* / Past) be afraid of new tax raises.

B Excerpts from political speeches. – Translate.

1 Seit einigen Jahren *kann* die Polizei mehr Ladendiebe festnehmen.

2 Künftig *wird* der Discounter Gewerkschaften akzeptieren *müssen*.

3 Ohne staatliche Hilfe *hätte* die Fluggesellschaft nicht überleben *können*.

4 Seit Jahren *darf* Walmart in Indien (offiziell) als Großhändler tätig sein.

5 Die Firma *musste* niemanden entlassen, da sie die Schulden hatte tilgen *können*.

6 Banken *dürfen* sich nicht länger auf staatliche Rettung verlassen *können*.

C   **Bankruptcy of a city – *Translate*.**

level 1

Letzte Woche konnte die alte Industriestadt ihre Rechnungen nicht mehr bezahlen und musste Konkurs anmelden.

(1) *Last week* _____

(2) _____

(2) Hätte sie nicht rechtzeitig ausgelöst (= *to bail out*) werden können? Kann die Regierung überredet werden, die Schulden zu übernehmen? Sie muss das einfach tun!

(3) Nein, sie darf das nicht tun! Die Steuerzahler mussten schon so oft für Inkompetenz und Korruption bezahlen.

(3) _____

(4) _____

(4) Darf ich widersprechen? Die Steuerzahler werden ohnehin zahlen müssen. Die Regierung sollte sofort handeln.

(5) Ist sie dazu in der Lage? Darf sie das? Muss sie sich nicht heraushalten?

(5) _____

(6) _____

Mit Regierungsunterstützung hätte die Stadt die öffentlichen Dienstleistungen nicht kürzen müssen.

theory   modal auxiliaries

modal auxiliaries: structures & meanings - overview

*Bei der Auswahl der **Ersatzformen** muss die **Bedeutung** genauer **differenziert** werden!*

a, 'incomplete' forms and their meanings:

can / could	to be able to	*(ability)* [1]
	to be allowed to	*(permission)* [2]
Can't / couldn't ....?	Why not ...?	*(suggestion)* [3]
can't	mustn't	*(neg. obligation)* [4]

"You can('t) / could(n't) easily increase your market share." [1]

▶ „Sie können / könnten Ihren Marktanteil (nicht) leicht erhöhen." [1]

"*Can / Could* our employees go home earlier today?" [2]

▶ „Können / Könnten unsere Mitarbeiter heute früher nach Hause (gehen)?" [2]

"Can('t) / could(n't) we open our store earlier?" [3/2/1]

▶ „Können / Könnten wir unseren Laden (nicht) früher aufmachen?" [3/2/1]

"You can('t) (= mustn't) kick him out! He will never find a job again." [4]

▶ „Sie können (= *dürfen*) ihn nicht rauswerfen! Er findet nie wieder eine Arbeit." [4]

As shown in the third example, meanings can overlap; the **predominant meaning** usually becomes clear from the **context**!

Advice: As *can* is used very similarly to German *können*, with its different shades of meaning, you shouldn't think too much about it. **Use it like in German.**

| may / might | it is possible ... | *(possibility)* [5] |
| | to be allowed to | *(permission)* [6] |

The new strategy may / might pay off quickly. [5]

▶ Die neue Strategie mag / kann / könnte sich rasch auszahlen. [5]

He may be an excellent financial expert, but he is a bad team-player. [5]

▶ Er mag (ja) ein ausgezeichneter Finanzexperte sein, aber er ist nicht teamfähig. [5]

"May / Might I suggest another procedure?" [6] *(see level 1)*

▶ „Darf / Dürfte ich ein anderes Verfahren vorschlagen?" [6]

Just for your understanding – rather avoid using it yourself:

Will	usually	*(typical habit)* [7a]
	all the same	*(obstinate action)* [8a]
	future	*(temporal auxiliary)*
would	used to + *inf.*	*(Past habit)* [7b]
	insisted on+ -ing	*(Past obstinate insistence)* [8b]
	Conditional	*(temporal auxiliary)*

Note: In these meanings the short forms (`ll & 'd) are not used!

"A greedy investment banker **will** never let an opportunity slip to make easy money." [7a]

▶ „Ein gieriger Investment Banker **wird** sich nie eine Gelegenheit, leichtes Geld zu machen, entgehen lassen." [7a]

"If the executive **will** leave his mobile phone at home, it is not surprising that he loses business, because he can never be reached." [8a]

▶ „Wenn der ältere Vertreter sein Handy *(etwa: ‚mutwillig')* zu Hause lässt, ist es nicht überraschend, dass er Aufträge verliert, weil er nie erreichbar ist." [8a]

Customers **would** queue for hours to be among the first to get the new model. [7b]
= Customers **used to** queue for hours …

▶ Die Kunden standen *gewöhnlich / immer Schlange*, um unter den ersten zu sein, die das neue Modell bekamen. [7b]

"He **would** buy the shares though we warned him that their price would soon plunge." [8b]

▶ „Er kaufte die Aktien (**eigensinnig**)*, obwohl wir ihn davor warnten, dass der Wert bald in den Keller gehen würde." [8b]

* Im Deutschen entfällt häufig jede Übersetzung, da sie zu stark wäre.

used to	**would** *(see above)* *(past habit)* [9 = 7b]

The short opening hours **used to** be a nuisance for customers.

▶ Die kurzen Öffnungszeiten waren **(früher immer)** ein Ärgernis für unsere Kunden.

*Note: Here you cannot use **would**, as it is a discontinued 'habit' – opening hours are longer now.*

Watch out: **Do not mix up** with **to be used** (or: **accustomed**) to do**ing** (!) sth. – which can be inflected, i.e. used in all tenses (**= gewohnt sein zu …**) **or avoid using it** yourself altogether.

theory   modal auxiliaries

Unvollständige Hilfsverben dienen u.a. dazu, verschiedene **Wahrscheinlichkeitsstufen** auszudrücken. Um Verwirrung zu vermeiden, ist dabei auf **Struktur und Kontext** zu achten!

b, deductions / assumptions *(Folgerungen, Mutmaßungen, Annahmen)*:

| can / could – may / might | It is (not) possible that .. *(possibility)* [10] |
| may / might not | possibly ... *not* (neg. possibility) [11] |

This unusual business model **may / can** actually work. [10a]
▶ Dieses ungewöhnliche Geschäftsmodell **mag / kann** tatsächlich funktionieren. [10a]
The robust SUV **could have** been sold in rural areas. [10b]
▶ Der robuste SUV **hätte** in ländlichen Gebieten verkauft werden **können**. [10b]
Consumers **may (not)** accept higher prices now. [11]
▶ Jetzt akzeptieren die Verbraucher höhere Preise **vielleicht (nicht)**. [11]
Consumers **might (not)** accept higher prices now. [11]
▶ Jetzt **könnten** die Verbraucher höhere Preise **(vielleicht) (nicht)** akzeptieren. [11]
Consumers **may (not)** have accepted higher prices. [11]
▶ Die Verbraucher haben höhere Preise **vielleicht (nicht)** akzeptiert. [11]
Consumers **might (not)** have accepted higher prices now. [11]
▶ Die Verbraucher hätten höhere Preise **(vielleicht) (nicht)** akzeptiert. [11]

Possible Combinations:

may / might (not) + *present or past infinitive*
can / could + *present infinitive*

<u>Watch out</u>: **can't** + *present or past infinitive is the opposite of* **must** as below.

| can't | It is impossible that ... *(impossibility)* [12] |

Such an advertising campaign **can't have (had)** any effect. [12]
▶ Eine solche Werbekampagne **kann** keine Wirkung **(gehabt) haben**. [12]

| must | It is most likely that *(probability)* [13] |

The advertising campaign **must have (had)** a positive effect. [13]
▶ Die Werbekampagne **muss** (eine) positive Wirkung **(gehabt) haben**. [13]
The goods **must have been damaged** in transit. [13]
▶ Die Waren **müssen** beim Transport **beschädigt worden sein**. [13]

Assumptions: different levels of probability

degree of probability

high	Our design **must** win the award! The machine **must** have leaked / been leaking.	*for sure*
	The truck **will** be there by now. Our truck **will** have reached your premises by now.	*very likely*
	The shipment **should** arrive by Friday. *Note: should is rather not used when the assumption is unpleasant for the speaker (e.g.: ~~The shipment should get damaged in transit again~~. [… dürfte beim Transport wieder beschädigt werden.])*	*likely*
	The spare parts **could** be here in time.	*perhaps*
low	The shipment **may / might** arrive by Friday.	*possibly / little chance*

Wahrscheinlichkeitsgrad

German **equivalents** should not be taken as set in stone, they depend on the context, formulations **are relative**.
(Deutsche Entsprechungen flexibel und kontextgerecht anpassen; Sie sollten dem Abstufungsgrad - in Relation - entsprechen.)

hoch	Unser Design **muss** die Auszeichnung gewinnen! Die Maschine **muss** ein Leck gehabt haben.	*ganz sicher*
	Unser Lkw **wird** wohl inzwischen dort sein. Unser Lkw **wird** wohl inzwischen bei Ihnen angelangt sein.	*sehr wahrscheinlich*
	Die Lieferung **dürfte (!) / sollte** bis Freitag eintreffen.	*wahrscheinlich*
	Die Ersatzteile **könnten** rechtzeitig hier sein.	*vielleicht*
niedrig	Die Lieferung **ist vielleicht / könnte vielleicht** bis Freitag eintreffen.	*möglich /geringe Chance*

Merkbox:

Rat: Bestimmte Verwendungen (von *will / would* sowie *used to*) meiden, andere (*can / could*) wie im Deutschen verwenden.

Einige (sehr häufige) Hilfsverben können den Wahrscheinlichkeitsgrad von Ereignissen ausdrücken (z.B. *must + present or past infinitive*).

Da die Anwendung bei subtilen Abweichungen leicht mit anderen Bedeutungen kollidieren und Verwirrung stiften kann, eher nicht aktiv benutzen.

practice — modal auxiliaries

D Old habits – *will* or *would* / *used to* or *to be used to*? Complete.

1 Whenever bargain hunters see a chance they _____ take it.

2 During the IT bubble in Silicon Valley in the 1990s clever ideas _____ turn into gold.

3 When the economic crisis hit Japan and workers were fired, some of them _____ (a) leave home in the morning and return in the evening pretending they were going to work as usual. The traditional Japanese 'salaryman' _____ (b) expect a safe life-long job and _____ (c) working overtime without extra pay.

4 A young Harvard graduate _____ expect to enjoy high status from the start.

E Assumptions

Make assumptions about past or present and future actions or events by using the modal verbs in the margin and the verbs indicated in brackets (active or passive / present or past infinitive - according to the meaning).

e.g.: We suggest using encryption software, since your data   may

__*may be spied on*__ (*to spy on*) otherwise.

Over to you:

1 Until last year the restaurant chain regularly paid protection money.
   It _____ (*to frighten*) by the mafia.   must

2 The company ignored safety standards, so it _____   could
   _____ (*to hold*) liable.

3 By the time we are ready to enter the Indian market, the government   should
   _____(*to pass*) the new law.

4 The aircraft left Kenya on time last night. So the flowers _____   will
   _____ (*to be*) in Heathrow Airport by now. They
   _____ (*to get*) into the shops just in time.   should

5 All these facts & figures were not available at the time. So the CFO   can't
   _____ (*to have*) them.

F   **Boards and unions**
Rephrase the following statements introducing elements of assumption, i.e. the modal auxiliaries indicated in the margin.

1   The head of department knew about the fraud.
    He _____ about it.   *must*

2   But he had no idea about the extent and the consequences.
    He _____ an idea about it, really.   *can't*

3   Our container ship has been hijacked. The navy knows it.
    Our container ship _____ (a).   *must*
    The navy _____ it (b).   *should*

4   Due to videos released on Youtube, the fire in our Asian factory is
    a problem for our image at home. It _____ a problem.   *could*

5   Customers have seen it (a) and boycott (b) our textiles. They   *may*
    _____ (a) it and _____   *might*
    _____ (b) us.

G   **Boards and unions**
Rephrase the following sentences replacing the expressions in italics by adequate modal verbs.

1   *Possibly* the unions are right after all.
    The unions _____.

2   **a,** *It is most likely* the consultants have alienated the workforce.
    The consultants _____ the workforce.

    b, *Perhaps* that explains their resistance to the merger.
    That _____ their resistance.

3   *There is a tiny chance* we get the contract.
    We _____ the contract.

4   The new distributor has *probably* doubled our sales in China by now.
    The new distributor _____ our sales in China by now.

practice   modal auxiliaries

H Discussing the competitive situation
Complete the statements and questions using adequate modal verbs.

Our fiercest competitors got the deal. They (1) _____ (*to know*) our offer. I (2) _____ (*to imagine*) any other explanation.

They (3) _____ (*to see*) it. It is totally impossible. We gave it straight to the authorities.

It is hard to imagine but they (4) _____ (*to bribe*) someone. Really, the authorities have strict anti-corruption rules. I think, it (5) _____ (*to be*) something else.

We'll never know, I suppose. But one day, it still (6) _____ (*to come out*) after all.

I Objections

Object and contradict by using adequate modal auxiliaries.

1. The tyre producer didn't know about the dangerous quality problems.
   But they (1) _____! Consumer organizations had published tests revealing all the problems.

2. The shipment arrived at customs yesterday, they say.
   But it _____ yesterday, it was only dispatched an hour ago.

3. Didn't we agree to cancel the order? The items are hopelessly outdated!
   But there is still keen demand for them from our regular customers! I have not cancelled the order. So another shipment is actually due and _____ (*to reach*) us soon.

K Translate.

1. *Früher (Use a modal auxiliary)* blieben deutsche Mitarbeiter ihr ganzes Leben (Pl.!) im

   selben Unternehmen, da sie es gewohnt waren, regelmäßige Lohnerhöhungen zu

   bekommen, während sie älter wurden.

2. „Könnten wir unsere Preise in Afrika nicht senken? Auf diese Weise könnten wir

   vielleicht unseren Marktanteil erhöhen."

3. „Nein, wir können keine Ausnahme machen! Wir würden unser Luxusimage

   verderben. Unsere Konkurrenten könnten unsere Marktnische erobern."

4. Das Land dürfte seine Schulden in zehn Jahren deutlich abgebaut haben.

   Die Sparmaßnahmen (*austerity measures*) wurden gestern beschlossen und werden

   bis Ende des Jahres bereits Wirkung gezeigt (*to have an impact*) haben.

5. Italien wertete früher (*verb!*) seine Währung ab, um im Tourismus wettbewerbsfähig

   zu bleiben. Mit dem Euro kann die Regierung dieses Instrument nicht mehr nutzen

   und muss andere wirtschaftliche Maßnahmen ergreifen.

L Which *would* is it? *Write down the correct sentence number.*

Our former employer was generous; we (1) **would** make a break whenever we felt tired.
Today competition is tougher. So you (2) **would** quickly lose your job if you did that.

would = Conditional: no. ____   **would** = past habit: no.: ____

theory   modal auxiliaries

*Besondere Wachsamkeit und Übung erfordern folgende typische und häufige **Fehlerquellen** und **Verwechslungsgefahren**.*

modal auxiliaries: potential problem areas

a, Distinguish: frequent sources of mistakes

You **needn't have repair**ed the fax machine. We have already ordered a new one.

▶ Sie **hätten** das Faxgerät **nicht** reparieren müssen / nicht zu reparieren **brauchen**. Wir haben bereits ein neues bestellt.   → *getan, aber unnötig*

We **didn't need / have to repair** the fax machine. We had bought a new one.

▶ **Wir mussten** das Faxgerät **nicht** reparieren / brauchten es nicht zu reparieren. Wir hatten ein neues gekauft.   → *nicht getan, da nicht nötig*

He **could have** sold his company. (But didn't.)

▶ Er **hätte** seine Firma verkaufen **können**.

→ *wäre möglich gewesen, aber nicht getan*

He **was able to** sell his company and rid himself of all debt.

▶ Er **konnte** seine Firma verkaufen und sich schuldenfrei machen.

→ *war dazu in der Lage, und getan*

The bank director **should have** appeared in court. (But didn't.)

▶ Der Bankdirektor **hätte** vor Gericht erscheinen **sollen**.

→ *tat es aber nicht*

The witness **was to** put his right hand on the bible and make an oath.

▶ Der Zeuge **sollte** seine rechte Hand auf die Bibel legen und schwören.

→ *wurde dazu angewiesen (und tat es oder tat es nicht)*

! Je nach Kontext kann der Sinn unterschiedlich sein: *(see below)*

to be to: (1) *… musste seine Hände auf die Bibel legen* or:

(3) *… sollte (später) seine rechte Hand auf die Bibel legen*

b, *sollen*

> shall

"**Shall** I set up my own business?" – „**Soll** ich meine eigene Firma gründen?"

! *Vorsicht bei **shall** ! Es wird im Englischen weniger verwendet als das dt. 'sollen'!*
Bei direkten Fragen in der 1. Person: ok; auch in eher formalen Kontexten;

→ *im normalen Aussagesatz:* **Hands off!**

level 3

should

Conditional (oder Past in Zeitenfolge und Ind. Rede) von **shall** - allerdings erheblich **häufige**r **verwendet** (see level 1 & 2)!

ought to

Für **should** kann auch meist **ought to** verwendet werden, mit einem kleinen Beigeschmack von **sollte 'eigentlich'.**

to be to + *infinitive*

1. **Impersonal** way of giving **instructions** (mostly with the third person); or: when used with you → **passing on** somebody else's instructions

    e.g.: No one is to go on a holiday before Christmas. Everyone is to work overtime.
    ▶ Keiner **geht / darf** vor Weihnachten in Urlaub gehen! Jeder **muss / hat** Überstunden **zu** machen.

2. Actions or events that are **planned** or scheduled

    e.g.: The new phone is to be presented in all stores at the same time.
    ▶ Das neue Smartphone soll in allen Läden zur selben Zeit präsentiert werden.
    In **headlines** to be is usually left out: "Whistleblower **to be** jailed"

3. **Prediction of events** in the distant future, usually **seen from the past**

    e.g.: At the AGM, the CEO was celebrated. Two months later he was to resign.
    ▶ Auf der Jahreshauptversammlung wurde der Vorstandschef gefeiert. Zwei Monate später sollte er zurücktreten.

to be said to   *(sagt man)*

The CEO is said to have resigned. - Der Vorstand **soll** zurückgetreten sein.

to be supposed to

He is supposed to be promoted today: - Er soll heute befördert werden.
Umgangssprachlich für: *He is to be promoted today. (man nimmt es an.)*

Merkbox:

Aufgrund der großen Ähnlichkeiten (Dt.-Englisch) werden viele Modalverben intuitiv richtig verwendet. Probleme bereiten v.a. *sollen, nicht müssen* und Strukturen mit Bedeutungsunterscheidung wie *needn't have + pp* u.ä.
Ergo: Auf die (wenigen) Problemzonen achten und Verwechslungen vermeiden.

practice  modal auxiliaries

M **Necessary or not?** - *Fill in needn't have or didn't need (or: have) to*

1. Due to declining sales the fast fashion chain cancelled all its orders. But they
(a) _____ (*to do*) that as the economy picked up again.
Luckily customers started to spend more money on clothes again and the retail chain
(b) _____ (*to close down*) any stores.

2. After tough negotiations, the chemical giant agreed to pay damages. So the victims of the accident _____ (*to take*) legal action.

3. The government _____ (*to impose*) high import tariffs on foreign cars – they had become unafforable anyway.

4. You _____ (*to change*) university; your new one isn't any better.

5. The regulator _____ (*to put*) a price cap on fares, as the railway company did not increase its ticket prices in the end.

N **Did you actually succeed?** - *Fill in could have or was/were able to*

1. To cut costs, production _____ (*to be*) outsourced to Pakistan, but was not. The domestic plant simply enhanced its capacity utilization.

2. Thanks to rising revenues in Asia the carmaker _____ (*to make up*) for the losses incurred in its home market.

3. During past recessions, VW (a) _____ (*to cut*) its workforce, but did not. The German concern got its employees to work fewer hours – and to accept less pay – in return for job guarantees. Unlike other car brands, VW (b) _____ (*to retain*) skilled workers in that way.

4. Mercedes launched specially designed trucks in India some time ago. The company (a) _____ (*to keep*) R & D costs low by using and adapting older models. Of course, the carmaker (b) _____ (*to develop*) completely new models for the Indian market, but that would have pushed prices too high to be competitive.

5. They _____ (*to oust*) their CEO, but they raised his compensation instead.

O   Choices: A (past) option or an accomplished fact? *Decide and complete.*

a,   Needn't have (+ pp)   or:
     didn't need / (have) to (+ inf.)

b,   Could have + pp   or:
     Was able to + inf.

Needn't have – didn't need to / could have – was able to

e.g.:   He (a) *needn't have* *worked* (to work) day and night.; his father left him a fortune. He (b) *could have* *concentrated* (to concentrate) on his education instead as he (a) *didn't need/have* *to earn* his living.

1   "You (a) _____ _____ (to buy) the expensive equipment. You (b) _____ _____ (to lease) it. That would have been much cheaper."

2   At first the strategy was very successful: The car company (b) _____ _____ (to enter) the Chinese market with the help of a joint venture partner. That way, it (a) _____ _____ (to build up) its own distribution network and saved a lot of money. Later, however, the technology was copied and similar-looking cars were launched by a Chinese company.
They (b) _____ _____ (to know). In those days such things happened all the time.

3   "The consultants (a) _____ _____ (to interview) the whole workforce again. They (b) _____ _____ (to use) a survey that had been conducted only a month before. But they didn't want to rely on other people's findings and started from scratch."

4   "I worked all night long to calculate the production costs – I (a) _____ [full verb 'work' not repeated]: We didn't get the licence. What a waste of time!" – "You (b) _____ (to apply) for the licence before doing all that work!"

5   The Norwegian government (a) _____ _____ (to raise) taxes since the state-run oil company generated high enough profits to fill the gaps. It (b) _____ even _____ _____ (pay off) its entire public debt. Other political leaders, like Chavez in Venzuela, (b) _____ _____ (to do) the same thing. But they had other priorities, and public debt kept growing.

practice   modal auxiliaries

P   Got everything wrong? – *Translate*.

1   „Die Jugendarbeitslosigkeit ist erneut gestiegen. Die Regierung hätte viel früher reagieren sollen. Dann hätten die Maßnahmen vielleicht Wirkung gehabt."

2   „Wir hätten keine neue Software implementieren müssen. Wir hätten unsere Mitarbeiter einfach besser ausbilden können."

3   „Die Immobilienpreise in unserer Gegend sind deutlich gefallen. Wir hätten keine Schulden machen müssen. Wir hätten einfach warten können."

4   „Da die Regierung vor einiger Zeit die Unternehmenssteuern gesenkt hat, brauchten wir unseren Hauptsitz nicht nach Irland verlegen, um Steuern zu sparen."

Q   Which *sollen*? – *Write down the letter for the sense sollen is used in.*
a, impersonal instruction   b, planned action   c, (past) prediction   d, 'man sagt'
e, advice, criticism   f, sequence of tenses (i.e.: shall in the past)

1   The company posted record earnings last year and hired new staff. However, most of the newly employed **were to** lose their job in the following recession. _____
2   Yesterday the factory owner **was to** appear in court as a witness. _____
3   The media group **is to** be sold. _____
4   The provider **should** go for quality, not for quantity. _____
5   The Indian asked the European agency what he **should** do against child labour. _____
6   For safety reasons, all employees **are to** wear helmets on the factory floor. _____
7   The bank director **should** have taken complaints more seriously. _____
8   The bank **ought to** inform its customers fully about the data leak. _____
9   The entrepreneur **is said to** be serving a long prison sentence. _____
10   The new CR report **is supposed to** be released today. _____
11   Despite complaints the whole team **was to** work on the project. _____

R *Translate into English.*

1 Er soll das Patent gestohlen haben.

_____

2 „Sollten wir nicht versuchen, mehr Kunden zu bekommen?"

_____

3 Jeder Arbeiter hat an dieser Maschine Handschuhe zu tragen.

_____

4 Die Fabrik brannte komplett nieder. Der Eigentümer soll verschwunden sein.

_____

5 Die Bahngesellschaft sollte eigentlich in diesem Jahr privatisiert werden.

_____

Soll der Börsengang verschoben werden?

_____

6 Die Firmenleitung hatte entschieden: Alle Büros sollten am nächsten Tag durchsucht

_____

werden. Doch die gestohlenen Dokumente sollten nie gefunden werden.

_____

S **Data protection ... and mixed modals - *Translate into English.***

(1) _____

> Der Datendiebstahl hat gezeigt, dass wir künftig mehr in Sicherheitssysteme investieren müssen.

(2) _____

_____

> Das hätten wir schon vor zehn Jahren tun sollen. Jetzt dürfen wir keine Zeit mehr verlieren.

(3) _____

_____

> Der Vorstand soll bereits eine externe Firma beauftragt haben. Er hätte **uns** fragen können.

 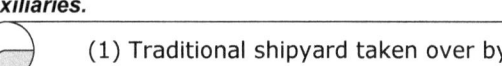

T Takeovers, mergers and acquisitions
Translate the following reports into English. Watch out for modal auxiliaries.

(1) Traditional shipyard taken over by Chinese group

Lange Zeit hatte sich die Werft mit innovativer Technik und erstklassiger Qualität gegen die asiatische Konkurrenz wehren können. Letztes Jahr musste sie aufgeben und wurde von einem chinesischen Konzern übernommen. Die Übernahme musste von den Aktionären gebilligt werden. Da sie online abstimmen durften, mussten sie nicht nach Hamburg reisen. Vielleicht (*modal auxiliary*) hätte die Werft mit staatlichen Subventionen überleben können. Aber der Staat hätte die Werft nicht subventionieren dürfen. Die EU-Kommission hätte Deutschland wegen unfairen Wettbewerbs verklagt. Seit Monaten müssen die Gewerkschaftsvertreter mit dem chinesischen Vorstand verhandeln, um Stellenabbau zu verhindern. Werden sie das erreichen (= *erzielen*) können?

(2) The fate of the European Monetary Union

Bevor EU-Länder der Euro-Zone beitreten durften, mussten sie die Konvergenzkriterien erfüllen. Seit der Einführung des Euro am 1. Januar 2002 mussten die Politiker immer wieder Länder retten, die die Kriterien bezüglich staatlicher Defizite nicht hatten einhalten können - oder wollen. Italien durfte den Euro einführen, obwohl es nur ein Jahr (statt zwei Jahre) Mitglied des Europäischen Währungssystems (EWS) gewesen war. Und dann ist da *(= gibt es)* Griechenland...
Was wird aus der Europäischen Währungsunion werden? Wird sie global als stabile Reservewährung dienen können? Oder wird man irgendwann in der Zukunft sagen müssen: „Es war einmal eine europäische Währung, die das Symbol der europäischen Union werden sollte. Aber daraus sollte nichts werden. *(= Das sollte nicht geschehen.)*"

practice

modal auxiliaries

(3) Industrial espionage

Mittelständische Unternehmen, deren Wettbewerbsfähigkeit von einem einzigen Patent abhängt, müssen ihr Knowhow schützen.
Sie dürfen nicht darauf vertrauen, dass sie immer Glück haben.
Welche Gefahren werden möglicherweise unterschätzt?
Wie können sich KMUs schützen? Sie müssen nicht in Panik geraten. Aber sie sollten ein wenig vorsichtiger sein.
‚Der chinesische Praktikant konnte kaum Deutsch sprechen; er kann es doch nicht gewesen sein, oder?' – ‚Er könnte es vielleicht schon gewesen sein.'
Daten könnten auch von einem Trojaner auf Ihren Rechnern an externe Computer übermittelt worden sein. Sie würden kaum etwas bemerkt haben. Sie müssen dringend ein professionelles Anti-Viren-Programm auf Ihrem System installieren.
Regelmäßige Aktualisierungen sind ein absolutes Muss.

U Ups and downs in entrepreneurship

Translate into English.

(1) _____

> Da ich keine Investoren finden konnte, musste ich meine Immobilie verkaufen, bevor ich genug Startkapital hatte, um mein Online-Geschäft allein aufzubauen.

(2) _____

> Hättest du nicht einfach einen Bankkredit bekommen können?

(3) _____

> Vielleicht hätte ich eine Bank von meiner Geschäftsidee überzeugen können. Aber ich sagte mir: „Ich darf nicht von Banken abhängig sein! Sie könnten meine Entscheidungen beeinflussen."

(4) _____

> Du hättest dich nicht allein auf Teppiche spezialisieren sollen.

> Vielleicht *(Verb)* hast du recht. Aber der Trend muss sich plötzlich gewandelt haben. Seit ein paar Wochen kann ich Zulieferer nicht mehr bezahlen. Ich werde Konkurs anmelden müssen.

> Du musst dir keine Sorgen machen. Du kannst als Gärtner für mich arbeiten.

Intro Vorgedanken

REPORTED SPEECH
Indirekte Rede

Wozu gibt es die überhaupt? Gibt es da Probleme?

> Wozu braucht man sowas wie eine indirekte Rede? Das kann man doch auch in direkter Rede sagen!

The Union has said there will be strikes. *or:*
The Union has announced strikes.

Workers claim wages are too low.
or: Workers find wages too low.

Our boss has told us we have to work harder. *or:*
He has told us to work harder.

> Sicher, kann man. Aber in Firmen-, Zeitungs- und anderen Berichten wird gern eine indirekte Wiedergabe von Aussagen bevorzugt. Einerseits ist das eine stilistische Frage, andererseits erlaubt es u.a. sinngemäße Wiedergabe, ohne Anspruch auf genauen Wortlaut.

> Na, gut. Was ist das Problem? Dann fallen eben die <u>Anführungszeichen</u> weg und werden <u>durch *that* ersetzt</u>.

The boss has said: "I will resign."
▶ The boss has said (that) **she** will resign.

She has said: „My plan is good."
▶ She has said (that) **her** plan is good.

The boss has said: "Work harder."
▶ The boss has told **us** to work harder.

> Ganz so einfach ist es nicht! Das *that* <u>kann wegfallen</u>. Aber zum Beispiel müssen die <u>Bezüge geändert</u> werden, z.B. Personal- und Possesssivpronomen. Und manchmal verwendet man dann auch <u>andere Strukturen</u>.

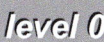
level 0

Das ist ja gerade noch zu schaffen! Wenn's weiter nichts ist!?

She said: "I will resign next year."
▶ She said (that) she **would** resign **the following** year.

She added: "I cannot stay here. The board has rejected my rescue plan."
▶ She added (that) she **could not** / **was not able to** stay **there** as the board **had** rejected **her** rescue plan.

Ist es aber! Im Deutschen hat man den Konjunktiv, um indirekte Rede auszudrücken, im Englischen muss man die Zeiten nach einem bestimmten Muster ‚verschieben', wenn das einleitende Verb in der Vergangenheit steht, sonst weiß man nicht, wann das war, ist, sein wird. Pronomina ändern sich natürlich auch!

Jetzt wird's aber kompliziert!

Yesterday the CEO said: "I must resign. I cannot stay here."
▶ She said she **must** resign, she could not stay **here**.
(gestern, aber immer noch gültig).
She said: „I can resign."
▶ She **offered to** resign.

! She said she **was** fed up.
 = She said: "I **am** (!) fed up!"

Dafür gibt es Regeln, z.B. den Tense Shift. ... Aber manchmal muss man nach dem Sinn, der Logik (im Kontext) entscheiden. Außerdem gibt es Besonderheiten, auch elegantere Möglichkeiten., Unterschiede in gesprochener und geschriebener Sprache.

Merkbox:

Die indirekte Rede im Englischen erfordert klare Bezüge (wer, wem, wen, wo, wann ...) und Genauigkeit bei Verwendung der Zeiten, da kein Konjunktiv verwendet werden kann als Signal, dass es sich um indirekte Rede handelt.

Wichtig ist der sog. *Tense Shift*, um klare Verhältnisse zu schaffen. Gefahr: Sonst liest es sich wie eine faktische Aussage (allerdings mit falschem Zeitbezug), nicht wie eine Wiedergabe einer Aussage. Es gibt etliche Besonderheiten aufgrund von Situation, Kontext und Sprachlogik.

REPORTED SPEECH

Compare:

The CEO of the big electronics group has been under enormous pressure for weeks. A month ago he **announced** that the target of a 12 % return on investment by the end of *the* next year **would have to be given up**. **Asked** *if* he **would resign** after the next board meeting *the following week* and *what* his next moves **were going to be**, he **said** he **was** convinced the supervisory board basically **supported** his strategy; after all, they **had called** him in and **(had)** repeatedly **praised** his decisions. After another crisis meeting of the board of supervisors he now **admits** that the situation **is** indeed critical and that he **will** not **stand** in the way if a change of strategy **is considered** to be necessary. But he still **insists** that the painful measures aiming at sustainable growth and profitability **have** already **started** to bear fruit.	Der Vorstandschef des großen Elektronikkonzerns steht seit Wochen unter enormem Druck. Vor einem Monat **kündigte** er an, dass das Ziel einer Rendite von 12 % bis Ende des nächsten Jahres **aufgegeben werden müsse**. Auf die Frage, ob er nach der nächsten Aufsichtsratssitzung *in der darauffolgenden Woche* zurücktreten **würde** und *was* seine nächsten Schritte **sein würden**, **sagte** er, er **sei** überzeugt, der Aufsichtsrat **unterstütze** seine Strategie grundsätzlich; schließlich **habe** er ihn ja **hereingeholt** und wiederholt seine Entscheidungen **gelobt**. Nach einer weiteren Krisensitzung des Aufsichtsrats **gesteht** der Vorstandschef nun ein, dass die Lage in der Tat kritisch **sei** und dass er nicht im Wege **stehen werde**, wenn ein Strategiewechsel für nötig **erachtet werde**. Aber er **beharrt** noch darauf, dass die schmerzhaften Maßnahmen, die auf nachhaltiges Wachstum und Rentabilität abzielen, bereits **begonnen haben**, Früchte zu tragen.

A month ago the CEO announced: "The target of a 12 % return on investment by the end of next year **will have to be given up**."
Press: "**Will you resign** after the board meeting next week? What are going to be your next moves?"
He said: "I **am convinced** the supervisory board basically **supports** my strategy; after all, they **called** me in and **have** repeatedly **praised** my decisions."
The CEO now admits: "The situation **is** indeed critical. I **will** not **stand** in the way if a change of strategy **is considered** to be necessary."
But he still insists: The painful measures aiming at sustainable growth and profitability **have** already **started** to bear fruit."

Tasks:

a, Distinguish the different mechanisms at work in *Reported Speech* in English and in German.
b, What happens to the verbs when converted from direct to indirect (or: reported) speech in English and what happens in German?
c, What causes the change in English? Always? To what extent?

106

In **direct speech** somebody's **exact words** are repeated in **inverted commas**.

e.g.: Union representatives keep asking: "Has a final decision been made?
How many workers are you going to lay off this time?"
Top managers regularly repeat: "*We are* doing *our* best to retain all skilled workers.
Please avoid drastic comments about *our* situation. Don't deter potential investors."

In **indirect (= reported) speech** no inverted commas are used. In order to avoid confusion about who says and does what, **personal and possessive pronouns** have to be **adapted or** even **replaced by** the **nouns** they stand for.

e.g.: Union representatives keep asking (top managers) **if** a final decision has been made and how many workers **they are** *(word order!)* going to lay off this time.
Top managers regularly repeat **(that) they are** *(word order!)* doing **their** best to retain all skilled workers and **ask** the union representatives **to** (please) **avoid** drastic comments on **their** situation and **not to deter** potential investors.

a, In **reported statements** (*Aussagesätzen*) **'that'** can be used, but is **often left out**.

> ! In longer text passages indirect speech may not always be recognized as such; statements may wrongly be taken as factual in several successive sentences without introductory verbs and without that.
> Watch out for other signals and the logic of the context.

b, In **indirect questions** there is **no question mark** and the **'normal' word order** is used: subject + verb, i.e. no inversion *(keine Fragestellung!)*.
If there is a question word it is used to introduce the indirect question.
If there is no question word, **if** (German: *ob*) is used.

c, **Indirect requests and orders** are expressed through the introductory verb (ask, tell, advise etc.) usually followed by the **infinitive + to**.

> ! The tense of the introductory verb is key!
> When it is in the present, present perfect or future, no change in tenses is required, from direct speech to reported speech.

Merkbox:

In indirekter Rede sind Pronomen sinngemäß anzupassen. Steht das einleitende Verb im *Present, Present Perfect* oder *Future* bleiben die Zeiten unverändert. Im Deutschen stehen häufig Formen des Konjunktivs. Vorsicht: Das ist oft eine Fehlerquelle bei der Übertragung ins Englische!

practice — reported speech

A   An old family business

a,   *Put the following statements and requests or instructions into reported speech. Watch the pronouns!*

1. The founder of the traditional family business often **tells** his children: "When I set up my first company the whole area had not been developed yet. The motorway hadn't been built and the delivery of goods took much longer. You are in a comfortable situation today. You don't need warehouses, as I have made the supply chain lean."

   The founder of the traditional family business often tells his children (that) when ____ set up _____ first company the whole area _____ yet. The motorway _____ and the delivery of goods _____ much longer. _____ _____ in a comfortable situation today. _____ _____ warehouses as _____ _____ the supply chain lean.

2. He **tells** them: „Be modest and patient. Don't go for quick profits, but plan for the long term. And, above all, don't ruin our business."

   He tells them _____ modest and patient and _____ for quick profits, but _____ for the long term and, above all, _____ _____ _____ business.

b,   *Put the following questions and answers into reported speech.*

3. On the occasion of the 30th anniversary of the company, a woman interviews its founder on the local radio station. She says: "We are very proud of your company and the employment opportunities you have created."

   She says (that) _____
   _____

4. Then she asks: "Was it difficult for you to get enough initial capital to set up your own business? Why did you do it on your own? How long did it take you to become profitable? Were you sure your business idea would work?"
   She asks _____
   _____

5. He tells her: "Read my autobiography. You can find all the answers there in detail."
   He tells her _____

B **French vineyard to be sold to Chinese actress**
Translate into English.

1
> Der Besitzer des Weinbergs sieht traurig aus und gesteht, er sei nicht glücklich über seine Entscheidung, seinen Weinberg an eine chinesische Schauspielerin zu verkaufen, aber er habe keine andere Wahl gehabt. Er mache seit Monaten Verluste, weil die Preise aufgrund der Konkurrenz aus Übersee zu niedrig seien. Er habe zu viele Schulden.

2
> Lokalpolitiker kritisieren seine Entscheidung öffentlich und fragen, ob er wisse, was es für die Region bedeutet, und warum er nicht mit Kollegen zusammenarbeite. Sie bitten ihn, seine Entscheidung zu überdenken und raten ihm, seinen Wein online zu verkaufen oder zu fusionieren.

3
> Die junge chinesische Schauspielerin sagt, es sei immer ihr Traum gewesen, in Frankreich zu leben, und weist darauf hin, dass französischer Wein in China immer beliebter werde. Sie fügt hinzu, dass sie plant, chinesische Angestellte auszubilden, die später in China Wein produzieren könnten.

Theory — reported speech

*Einige (**sinngemäße** oder **syntaktische**) Anpassungen müssen **immer** vorgenommen werden, ein besonderer Mechanismus (**tense shift / Zeitenverschiebung**) erfolgt, wenn das einleitende Verb in der Vergangenheit steht.*

A <u>Changes</u> **always** required when direct speech becomes reported speech:

1. **Personal and possessive pronouns** need to be adapted
   e.g.: He always says: "I have been in this department longer than anyone else."
   → He always says (that) he has been in this department longer than anyone else.

2. In **indirect questions** the **word order** needs to be adjusted
   (*keine Umstellung, keine Umschreibung mit to do*).
   e.g.: Customers will ask: "What service <u>can you</u> provide? <u>Do you have</u> a hotline?"
   → Customers will ask what services <u>we can</u> provide and if <u>we have</u> a hotline.

3. **Imperatives** (orders) are usually expressed with the help of an **infinitive + to**.
   e.g.: IT keeps telling us: "Update your software."
   → IT keeps telling us <u>to update</u> our software.

! <u>Distinguish</u>: introductory verb in the present or in the past:
Introductory verb in the <u>present</u>   → <u>no tense shift</u>
Introductory verb in the <u>past</u>   → <u>tense shift</u>
+ adjustment of demonstrative pronouns and adverbials of time and place

---

B <u>Additional changes</u> when the <u>introductory verb</u> is in the <u>past</u>

1. <u>tense shift</u>:

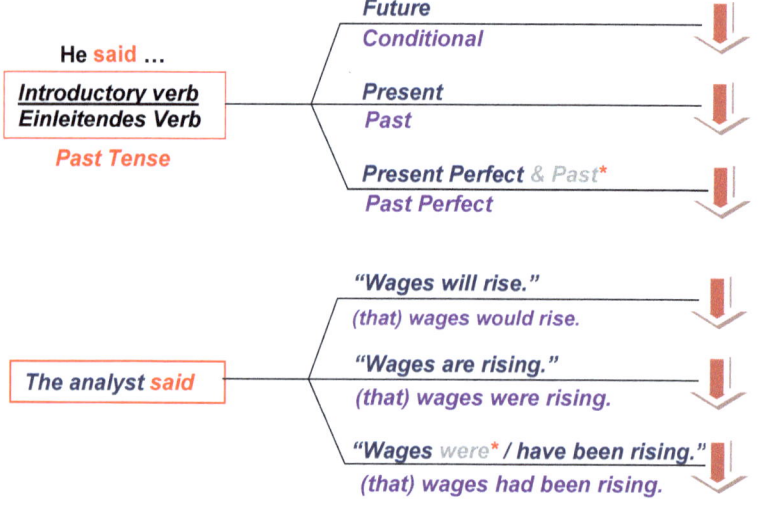

* While in <u>spoken English</u> the <u>past tense</u> is often left <u>unchanged</u> it is usually <u>changed to the past perfect in</u> written English with some exceptions *(see level 3)*.

*Im gesprochenen Englisch wird, wann immer ohne Missverständnisse möglich, das **Past** **beibehalten** und nicht zum Past Perfect.*

*Verben im **Conditional** (I & II) sowie im **Past Perfect** können **nicht** mehr weiter **verschoben** werden und werden **beibehalten**.*
Verlaufsform (Progressive) bleibt Verlaufsform, Einfache (Simple) Form bleibt einfache Form.

The tense shift after an introductory verb in the past cannot go further than Conditional I or II and the Past Perfect. So those tenses remain unchanged when direct speech becomes indirect speech.

e.g.:

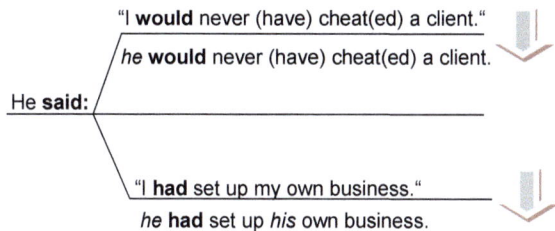

He said:
"I **would** never (have) cheat(ed) a client."
he **would** never (have) cheat(ed) a client.

"I **had** set up my own business."
he **had** set up *his* own business.

<u>Note</u>: Simple forms remain simple forms,
progressive forms remain progressive forms.

e.g.:

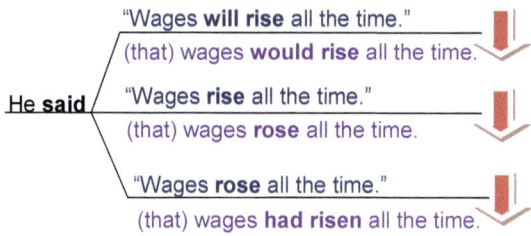

He said
"Wages **will rise** all the time."
(that) wages **would rise** all the time.
"Wages **rise** all the time."
(that) wages **rose** all the time.
"Wages **rose** all the time."
(that) wages **had risen** all the time.

and:

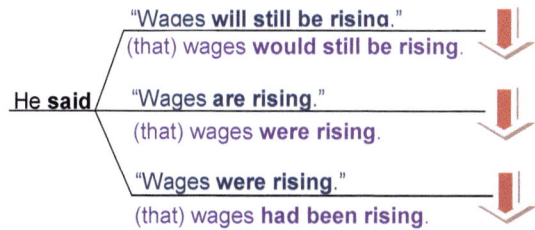

He said
"Wages **will still be rising**."
(that) wages **would still be rising**.
"Wages **are rising**."
(that) wages **were rising**.
"Wages **were rising**."
(that) wages **had been rising**.

Theory  reported speech

Compare:

English	vs	German
He **says** he **is** the owner.		Er sagt, er **ist** der Eigentümer.
		Er sagt, er **sei** der Eigentümer.
		Er sagt, er **wäre** der Eigentümer.
He **said** he **was** the owner		Er sagte, er **ist** der Eigentümer.
		Er sagte, er **sei** der Eigentümer.
		Er sagte, er **wäre** der Eigentümer.

He **says** he **has paid** the invoice.		Er sagt, er **hat** die Rechnung **bezahlt**.
		Er sagt, er **habe** die Rechnung **bezahlt**.
		Er sagt, er **hätte** die Rechnung **bezahlt**.
He **said** he **had paid** the invoice.		Er sagte, er **hat** die Rechnung **bezahlt**.
		Er sagte, er **habe** die Rechnung **bezahlt**.
		Er sagte, er **hätte** die Rechnung **bezahlt**.
		etc.

As you can see, the mechanisms of indirect (= reported) speech are very different between German and English; the German subjunctive (*Konjunktiv*) may make it rather difficult to identify the required tenses and forms of verbs in English.

> *Tipp:*
> *Zuerst die indirekte Rede (im Deutschen) in direkte Rede setzen (1), dann ins Englische übertragen (2) und danach (im Englischen) in die indirekte Rede setzen (3).*

z.B.: Er sagte, er würde gerade nach Russland expandieren.

 Schritt 1: Er sagte: „Ich expandiere gerade nach Russland."
 Schritt 2: He said: „I am expanding to Russia."
 Schritt 3: **He said he was expanding to Russia.**

> *Diese Methode kann man entweder von vornherein oder im Nachhinein – in Zweifelsfällen - zur Überprüfung der englischen indirekten Rede nutzen.*

2. Adjustment of demonstrative pronouns and adverbials of time and place:
(Remember: Only when the <u>introductory verb</u> is in the <u>past</u>!)

The analyst said	"**This** share will take off **tomorrow**."
	(that) **that** share would take off **the next day**.

The union claimed	"We are staying **here** until **next week**."
	(that) they were staying **there** until **the next / following week**.

The investor said	"I have financed **these** projects."
	(that) he had financed **those / the** projects.

direct   *indirect (= reported)*

Adverbs and adverbials of time change like this:

direct	indirect
today	that day
yesterday	the day before
the day before yesterday	two days before
tomorrow	the next/following day
the day after tomorrow	in two days' time
next week/month/year	the following week/month/year
last week/month/year	the previous week/month/year
a year ago etc.	a year before / the previous year.

this/these:

in time expressions: this/these	that (week) / (in) those (days)
otherwise: this/that; these/those	the (contract); the (contracts)
as pronouns: this/these	it/they, them
e.g.: *We'll discuss this tomorrow.*	*He said they would discuss it the following day.*

Merkbox:

Steht das **einleitende Verb im *Present, Present perfect oder Future*** bleiben die Zeiten unverändert. Meist jedoch steht das <u>einleitende Verb im *Past*</u>, dann greift normalerweise der sogenannte <u>*Tense shift*</u>, die <u>Zeitenverschiebung</u>.

Bei der Zeitenverschiebung wird der <u>*Aspect*</u>, d.h. *Simple Form* und *Progressive Form* <u>beibehalten</u>.

Im Deutschen gibt es diesen Zeitverschiebungsmechanismus nicht, hier stehen Verben meist im Konjunktiv, allerdings ‚flexibel' verwendet und daher eher irreführend für die korrekte Wiedergabe im Englischen.

<u>Tipp:</u> In direkte Rede umformen, ins Englische übertragen und gem. *Tense Shift* (Zeitenverschiebung) in die indirekte Rede setzen.

practice — reported speech

C **Made in Mexico** *(Based on: Fortune, July 22, 2013, p. S3-6.)*
   Put the following statements into reported speech.

1. Mr. Mancera, mayor of Mexico City: "We *are working* toward the concept of becoming a Smart City."

   In 2013, the mayor of Mexico City said (that) they _____ toward the concept of becoming a Smart City.

2. CEO Antonio Pedroza, Head of maltaCleyton: "*Our strategy centers have* the broadest portfolio in the animal-nutrition industry. *We have* two factories in Brazil, and *export* to Venezuela, Guatemala and even Cuba. In the area of animal nutrition, Mexico *is* secure due to several factors."

   Ceo Antonio Pedroza said (that) _____ the broadest portfolio in the animal-nutrition industry. _____ two factories in Brazil and _____ to Venezuela, Guatemala, and even Cuba. In the area of animal-nutrition, Mexico _____ secure due to several factors, he added.

3. Governor Rovirosa: "We *have* the capacity to attract companies like General Electric and Siemens. We *are moving* from a manufacturing state to a state of innovation and high technology."

   Governor Rovirosa said in 2013 (that) _____ the capacity to attract companies like General Electric and Siemens, and that _____ _____ from a manufacturing state to a state of innovation and high technology.

4. Commentator: "Querétaro, a Mexican state, *has witnessed* the largest amount of jobs development since 2009 and *is hailed* as the success story of NAFTA. It *has significantly increased* local supply."

   A commentator said (that) Querétaro _____ the largest amount of jobs development since 2009 and _____ as the success story of NAFTA. It _____ local supply.

114

D   Interview with the President of the ECB (in 2013)

Journalist: Mario Draghi:

1a, "Mr. Draghi, are you sure the euro crisis is over? Will the taxpayer be spared a heavy burden as some critics assume?"

1b, "I cannot give any guarantees; that would be foolish, but our measures have stabilized the euro."

2a, "How long will it be stable this time? So far, all the measures have been very short-lived."

2b, "Of course, a series of steps is needed, and this is what we've done. The euro will prevail."

3a, "What do you think of critics who would like to ditch the euro? Have you ever had any doubts?"

3b, "It is my duty to defend the euro. And this is what I will do. A few years ago the task was much easier. Be patient."

Put the above interview into reported speech.

1a, In an interview in 2013, Mr. Draghi was asked _____
_____ and _____
_____.

1b, He replied (that) _____
_____ but _____
_____ the euro.

2a, The journalist asked _____
So far _____.

2b, Draghi replied (that) a series of steps _____ of course,
and that _____ what _____. The euro
_____.

3a, The journalist asked Draghi _____
_____
and _____.

3b, Draghi replied (that) _____ to defend the euro. And
(that) _____. _____,
the task _____ much easier of course.
Then he told the journalist _____.

practice — reported speech

E   Wind of change at Siemens

a, *Rewrite the reported statements in direct speech in German (!),*
b, *then translate the direct speech into English and*
c, *finally, turn the direct speech into reported speech – or start with c and then check if everything is correct by doing a and b.*

1. Als der Aufsichtsrat von Siemens im Juli 2013 Löscher loswerden wollte, sagte der gefeuerte Vorstandschef, er werde gehen, aber Aufsichtsratsvorsitzender Cromme müsse auch zurücktreten. Sonst trete er gar nicht zurück, sondern würde in Übereinstimmung mit seinem Vertrag die nächsten vier Jahre bleiben.
2. Bereits zwei Tage später jedoch sagte Löscher der Presse, das Schicksal des Unternehmens sei wichtiger als die Interessen Einzelner.
3. Es wurde behauptet, dass die Entscheidung einstimmig gewesen und alles ganz schnell gegangen sei.
4. Der neue Vorstandschef Kaeser erklärte, er werde nicht versuchen, Siemens neu zu erfinden, denn das sei nicht nötig. Er wolle der Firma ihr Gleichgewicht zurückgeben.
5. Während Cromme sagte, Siemens habe unter Löschers Führung zwei der erfolgreichsten Jahre in der Unternehmensgeschichte erfahren, kritisierten Gewerkschaftsvertreter, Löscher habe auch durch seine Jobabbau-Politik Ängste erzeugt.

a,   *Transform into German direct speech:*

1. … sagte der gefeuerte Vorstandschef: „_____
   _____
   _____."

2. … sagte Löscher …: „Das Schicksal des Unternehmens _____
   _____"

3. Es wurde behauptet: „Die Entscheidung _____
   _____"

4. Kaeser erklärte: „_____ Siemens neu zu erfinden,
   denn _____. _____
   _____."

5. … Cromme sagte: „Siemens _____
   _____."

   Gewerkschaftsvertreter kritisierten: „Löscher _____
   _____."

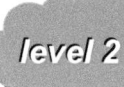

b, *Translate into English direct speech*

1. The ousted CEO said: "_____
   _____."

2. ... Löscher told the press: "_____
   _____."

3. It was claimed: "The decision _____
   And _____."

4. Kaeser declared: "_____
   _____
   _____."

5. ... Cromme said: "Under Löscher's leadership, Siemens _____
   _____."

   ... union representatives criticized: "Löscher _____
   _____."

c, *Now transform into reported speech:*

1. When the supervisory board of Siemens wanted to get rid of Löscher, the ousted CEO said (that) _____ but the chairman of the Supervisory Board _____. Otherwise _____
_____

2. Already two days later, however, Löscher told the press (that) the fate of the company _____

3. It was claimed (that) the decision _____
   and everything _____.

4. Kaeser declared (that) _____ to reinvent Siemens since _____. He added (that) _____ the company its balance back.

5. Whereas Cromme said (that) under Löscher's leadership Siemens _____
   _____ two of its most successful years in its history, Union representatives criticized (that) Löscher _____
   _____ policy of job cuts.

Anmerkung: *Diese Methode wirkt insgesamt vielleicht umständlich und zeitraubend, aber nach einiger Zeit dürfte sie schnell als gedankliche Routine umzusetzen sein.*

practice  reported speech

F Brief business news
Put the following statements into reported speech.

1. "The IPO has been postponed. It will be next year."
   ▶ The company boss announced (that) the IPO _____
   It _____.

2. "The investigation is to start the day after tomorrow. All witnesses will have been heard by the end of next week and the sentence can be expected early next year."
   ▶ The press reported (that) the investigation _____.
   All witnesses _____ and
   the sentence _____.

3. "Ten years ago we dominated the market, but since then we have had to compete with ever more players in the market. Luckily, we are market leader again this year."
   ▶ Before its sudden collapse last year, the IT company explained (that) _____
   _____ the market, but since
   _____ with ever more players in the
   market. Luckily _____ market leader again _____.

G 17 year-old to sell his software business for 1.2 bn dollars
At a press conference last month the young entrepreneur was faced with many questions – *Put into reported speech.*

1. "Why have you decided to sell your cash cow? Will you stay in the company?"
   A journalist asked _____ cash cow and
   _____ in the company.

2. "What other options did you consider before eventually accepting this offer? Did you expect to obtain such a horrendous price?"
   Another one wanted to know _____
   _____ and _____
   _____ to obtain such an astronomical price.

3. "What are your plans? Are you working on another project?"
   A third journalist asked _____,
   _____ on another project.

4. "Stop asking. Wait for a few answers first." The host asked the press _____
   asking and _____ for a few answers first.

H *Translate into English:*

1. Der Firmenboss teilte seinen Mitarbeitern mit, dass das Unternehmen mit seinem größten Konkurrenten fusionieren würde. Die Verhandlungen seien erfolgreich gewesen und die Fusion könne innerhalb der nächsten sechs Monate stattfinden.

_____
_____

2. Bereits vor fünf Monaten wurde der Belegschaft mitgeteilt, dass die Fabrik seit Jahren Verluste machte und die Bank nicht mehr bereit wäre, weitere Kredite zu gewähren. Unrentable Bereiche müssten abgestoßen werden. Der Firmenchef verhandle bereits mit Investoren, die Interesse gezeigt hätten.

_____
_____
_____

3. Im Sommer 2013 sagte James Galbraith, der Sohn des Ökonomen John Kenneth Galbraith, er verstehe nicht, warum Griechenland den staatlichen Energiekonzern verkaufen wolle, da die Branche fette Gewinne abwerfe und dem Staat langfristig hohe Einnahmen sichern würde. Für ihn sei dies ein Signal, dass die griechische Regierung nicht ernsthaft glaubte, sie wäre jemals in der Lage die Schuldenlast abzubauen. Er fügte hinzu, dass ihn dies nicht erstaune, da die alten Oligarchen ihren Einfluss nicht wirklich verloren hätten und sogar von der Krise profitierten und kontinuierlich ihren Reichtum *(= wealth)* vergrößerten, während die europäischen Steuerzahler ständig bezahlten. Er schloss, dies sei nicht nachhaltig und könne zu existentiellen Konflikten innerhalb der EU führen.

... Galbraith said _____ *why* _____
_____ *the state-owned energy group, as* _____
fat profits and _____ *high public revenues in the long term. For him,*
_____ *a signal that the Greek government* _____
_____ *it* _____ *to reduce the debt burden. He added that*
_____ *as the old oligarchs* _____
_____ *their influence and* _____ *from the*
crisis and _____ *their wealth while European*
tax payers _____. *He concluded* _____
_____ *sustainable and* _____ *existential conflicts*
within the EU.

Theory — reported speech

C Tense shift or not? *(introductory verb in the past)*:

Compare: The boss said: "The equipment **arrived** on Friday."

past tense

1. in **spoken** English

▶ The boss said (that) the equipment **arrived** on Friday.

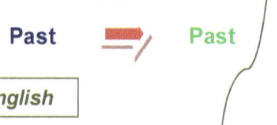
Past ➡ Past

2. in **written** English

▶ The boss said (that) the equipment **had arrived** on Friday.
Past ➡ Past Perfect

*Neben der Neigung des gesprochenen Englisch, das Past beizubehalten und nicht zum Past Perfect zu 'verschieben' gibt es Fälle, in denen das **Past aus logischen, bzw. Sinn-Gründen** auch im geschriebenen Englisch nicht zum **Past Perfect** werden kann, da **sonst** die **Zeitverhältnisse verfälscht** würden (d.h. es wäre dann vorzeitig, vorher geschehen). Daher (a & b):*

Exceptions: Past  Past *(also in written English)*

a, The past in **time clauses**:
 e.g.: The exhibitor said: "When we **built / were building** this stand curious competitors often **walked** by."

  ▶ The exhibitor said (that) when they built / were building the/that stand curious competitors often walked by.
  or: ... had often walked by.

  In the main clause the verb can either remain unchanged or be changed to the past perfect.

 Note: *Past progressive* does **not** change *to past perfect progressive* in practice **unless** it refers to a *completed action*.

 e.g.: Investor: "*I* **was considering** selling the company, but **have decided** not to."
  ▶ The investor said (that) he had been considering ..., but had decided not to.

 vs. Boss: "Whenever *I* **came** to the factory floor, workers **were standing** about."
  ▶ The boss said (that) whenever he came to ..., workers were standing (!) about.

b, A past tense referring to a **situation that still exists** when it is reported:
e.g.: CEO: "*We* decided not to relocate the factory because it was near the harbour."
▶ The CEO said (that) they **had decided** not to relocate the factory because it **was** near the harbour.   *[The factory is still near the harbour.]*

c, **would, should, ought (to), might, could, must, had better, used to**
→ **no change**:

e.g.: Sales manager: "You **should** emphasize ecological aspects because *we* **must** convince the new target group."
▶ The sales manager said (that) *they* **should** emphasize ecological aspects because *they* **must** convince the new target group.

Union leaders: "Before globalisation jobs **used to** be much safer."
▶ Union leaders claimed (that) before globalisation jobs **used to** be much safer.

Government advisor: "*We* **had better** reduce public debt first."
▶ A government advisor said (that) *they* **had better** reduce public debt first.

Do not forget: can ▶ **could, may** ▶ **might, will** ▶ **would, shall** ▶ **should**
    could, might, would, should: used as *Past Tense forms in reported speech*

d, Conditional sentences with **hypotheses** or **unlikely** assumptions
(if + past tense → Cond. I) → **no change:**

e.g.: CEO: "If labour costs **were** higher *we* **would** not **be** competitive."
▶ The CEO said (that) if labour costs **were** higher *they* **would** not be competitive.

Note: Of course a hypothesis about the past (**if +past perfect** → **Cond. II**) always remains **unchanged** anyway:

e.g.: CEO: "If labour costs **had been** higher *we* **would not have been** competitive."
▶ The CEO said (that) if labour costs had been higher *they* **would** not **have been** competitive.

Note: A 'realistic' condition(al clause), i.e. if + present → Future I, is changed according to the tense shift:

e.g.: CEO: "If labour costs **are** too high we **will not be** competitive."
▶ The CEO said (that) if labour costs **were** too high they **would not be** competitive.

Watch out for 'unrealistic' wishes:

e.g.: CEO: "*I* **wish** I **knew** future trends."
▶ The CEO said *he* **wished** he **knew** future trends.

Eine Sonderrolle nehmen auch **unvollständige Hilfsverben** *(c)* und **If-Sätze** *(patterns II & III)* mit Hypothesen *(d)* sowie die Struktur "*I wish*" („Ich wünschte") ein, die ebenfalls nicht ‚verschoben' werden (können).

121

Theory
reported speech

D Alternatives

1. **Questions** that are not really questions are often expressed differently

   a, Government official: "Shall I renew the licence?"
   ▶ He/She offered to renew the license.   `offer`

   or: He/She <u>asked</u> if he/she **should** renew the licence.
   (i.e.: if he/she wanted him/her to renew the licence
   – direct command)

   or: He/She <u>asked</u> if he/she **was to** renew the licence.
   (i.e.: if there was an external/neutral obligation to renew the licence
   – indirect command)

   b, Supplier: "Shouldn't we discuss quantities first?"
   ▶ The supplier suggested discussing quantities first.   `suggestion`

   or: The supplier wondered if they shouldn't discuss quantities first.

   CFO: "Shall I put our cash flow problems on the agenda?"
   ▶ The CFO suggested putting* their cash flow problems on the agenda."
   * Bei verschiedenem Subjekt: He (1) suggested they (2) should …

   or: The CFO <u>asked</u> if he/she **should / was to** put their cash flow problems on the agenda.

   c, Accountant: "Will you show me the latest estimates?"
   ▶ The accountant asked for the latest estimates.   `request`

   As it is not really a question, but an indirect request
   (Will you …?), an indirect question does not really make sense here.

2. **Commands, instructions etc.**

   d, (The) boss (said) to R & D: "Find a solution quickly."
   ▶ The boss told R & D to find a solution quickly.   `order`
   ▶ The boss instructed R & D to find a solution quickly.
   (Dt.: Der Chef wies die F & E-Abteilung an, schnell eine Lösung zu finden.)

   or: The boss told R & D (that) they **should** find a solution quickly.
   or: The boss told R & D (that) they **were to** find a solution quickly.
       (Dt.: Der Chef sagte der F & E-Abteilung, sie **solle/müsse** schnell eine Lösung finden.)

   The sales manager told his team: "Don't be too pushy."
   ▶ The sales manager told his team not to be too pushy.
       (Dt.: Der Verkaufsleiter sagte seinem Verkaufsteam, sie **sollten** Kunden nicht zu sehr drängen.)
   or: The sales manager warned his team not to be too pushy.
       (Dt.: Der Verkaufsleiter warnte sein Verkaufsteam davor, Kunden zu sehr zu drängen.)

   or: The sales manager told his team they **shouldn't** be too pushy.

Die Alternativen, Fragen, Befehle oder Vorschläge in der indirekten Rede auszudrücken, sind nicht nur eleganter, sondern oft auch einfacher.

"Will you stop pulling?"

"Can't I just sit here?"

"Can't we take a rest?"

"Leave me alone!"

"Couldn't you carry me?"

The little doggie is trying to ask / tell his human mistress ….

Merkbox:

Steht das einleitende Verb im *Past* bleibt in gesprochenem Englisch das *Past* meist unverändert bestehen (keine Zeitenverschiebung).

Auch in geschriebenem Englisch bleibt (nach einleitendem Verb im *Past*) das *Past* in einigen Fällen unverändert bestehen (keine Zeitenverschiebung), und zwar in Temporalsätzen, in Bedingungssätzen mit rein hypothetischen, irrealen, bzw. unwahrscheinlichen Annahmen (Bedingungen) und in Fällen, in denen Aussagen zum Zeitpunkt der Wiedergabe in indirekter Rede immer noch oder allgemein gültig oder im gleichen Zeitraum gelegen sind.

In indirekter Rede werden would, should, ought (to), might, could, must, had better, used to als *Past* unverändert beibehalten. (Außerhalb der indirekten Rede werden nur *could* [konnte], *used to* [für Gewohnheitszustand, bzw. –handlung] und *would* [für Gewohnheitshandlung] als *Past* verstanden!).

Statt der rein mechanischen Übertragung in die direkte Rede mit einem Verb des Sagens etc. wird oft – alternativ - eine der Logik folgende Formulierung gewählt: mit Verben des Anbietens, Vorschlagens, Bittens, Befehlens u.ä.

Da meist auch eine indirekte Frage oder Aussage möglich ist, empfiehlt es sich im Zweifelsfall, die direkte Rede schematisch in die indirekte Rede zu setzen. Auch ist (ohne ausreichende Information oder Kontext) aufgrund indirekter (oft höflicherer) Ausdrucksweisen im Englischen nicht immer eindeutig, ob es sich um eine Bitte, eine Anweisung, einen Ratschlag, bzw. eine Bitte um Rat oder eine echte Frage handelt.

practice — reported speech

I   **An employee about the end of job security**
Convert into reported speech - past or past perfect? (in written English)

1. The employee admitted (that) _____ _____ out work for two years when he _____ the job.

   "When I accepted the job I had been out of work for two years."

2. He added (that) he _____ _____ if they _____ _____ a temporary contract.

   "If they had offered me a temporary contract I wouldn't have signed."

3. He went on to say (that) he _____ _____ of looking for another job, but _____ to stay.

   "I was thinking of looking for another job, but have decided to stay."

4. Then he said (that) he _____ about _____ decision when the CEO _____ about a new strategy.

   "I had doubts about my decision when the CEO talked about a new strategy."

5. He continued to say (that) if the management _____ their employees' loyalty they _____ provide secure jobs.

   "If the management wanted their employees' loyalty they would have to provide secure jobs."

6. He also said (that) he _____ the CEO _____ the whole truth about his plans.

   "I wish the CEO told us the whole truth about his plans."

7. He concluded (that) _____ no clue about the real situation of the company until _____.

   "I had no idea about the real situation of the company until I was employed there."

K   A brewer's paradise
Complete the reported speech: past or past perfect? (in written English)

Journalists:

1a, "Mr. Erhard, your brewery was known as a local brand before you went to China. Why did you take the risk?"

2a, "Were you piling up losses when you took this step?"

3a, "What would you do if your joint venture with your Chinese partner failed? Could you survive without the huge Chinese market?"

Bavarian brewer:

1b, "Beer consumption was going down by 5 % per year in my local market, while Chinese brewers were selling 5 % more beer every year. What would you have done?"

2b, "I was not making losses at that point, but sales figures were going down continuously."

3b, "I probably could, but why should I withdraw from the Asian market? Indians would also take to Bavarian beer, for sure; I would go to India."

1a,   Journalists said to Mr. Erhard (that) _____ brewery _____ as a local brand before _____ to China. They wanted to know why _____ the risk.

1b,   The brewer replied (that) beer consumption _____ going down by 5 % per year in _____ local market, while Chinese brewers _____ 5 % more beer every year. He asked the journalists what _____ .

2a,   The journalists asked the brewer _____ losses when _____ step.

2b,   The brewer replied (that) he _____ making losses at that point but sales figures _____ going down continuously.

3a,   The journalists asked the brewer what _____ if his joint venture with the Chinese partner _____ , if he _____ without the huge Chinese market.

3b,   The brewer replied (that) he probably _____ but asked why he _____ from the Asian market, saying that Indians _____ Bavarian beer, for sure; he _____ to India.

 reported speech

L **A hotel in Marrakesh**
   Translate the reported statements of an entrepreneur building a hotel in Marrakesh (written English) – Be careful about tenses.

1. Der Hotelbesitzer berichtete, dass er ernsthaft in Erwägung zog, sein Hotel aufzugeben, als die Reservierungen während der Finanzkrise in den Keller gingen.

   _____
   _____

2. Schnell fügte er hinzu, er habe sich entscheiden, das nicht zu tun, als er einen Fernsehbericht über den Tourismus in Marokko sah, da es ein riesiges Potential für Hotels für europäische Gäste gebe.

   _____
   _____
   _____

3. Er sagte, er sei sofort nach Marrakesch geflogen und habe mit dem Bau eines Hotels für europäische Urlauber begonnen, da er hoffte, er könne bald seine Verluste ausgleichen, wenn das Hotel in Marokko schnell gebaut würde und er anfinge, dort Gewinne zu machen.

   _____
   _____
   _____

4. Er gab zu, er sei anfangs etwas zu optimistisch gewesen, aber schließlich habe er sein Hotel zuhause retten können.

   _____
   _____

5. Er sagte, er müsse der Reporterin für den Fernsehbericht danken; er wünschte, er könnte sich an ihren Namen erinnern.

   _____
   _____

6. Er lächelte und fügte hinzu, er sollte sie eigentlich einladen, eine Woche in seinem Hotel zu verbringen; das wäre vielleicht die beste Art, ihr zu danken.

   _____
   _____

M **Give and take in the office ...**
Put into reported speech in two ways.

e.g.: The accountant told his intern: "You should check all the figures carefully."
▶ The accountant told his intern to check all the figures carefully.
or: The accountant told his intern he should check all figures carefully.

1. Engineer: "Can't we emphasize the trendy design?"
   ▶ The engineer **suggested** _____ the trendy design.
   or: The engineer _____.

2. Assistant to her boss: "Shall I get you the file?"
   ▶ The assistant **offered** _____.
   or: The assistant _____.

3. CEO to his assistant: "Can you show me the minutes?"
   ▶ The CEO **asked** his assistant _____
   or: The CEO asked his assistant _____
   or: The CEO asked his assistant _____

4. Assistant to CEO: "Shall I fetch the product specification from your desk?"
   ▶ The assistant _____.
   or: The assistant asked the CEO _____ the product
   specification from _____ desk.

5. Employee to colleague: "Will you give me your support in the team?"
   ▶ The employee asked his colleague _____ in the team.
   or: The employee asked his colleague to _____
   in the team.

6. Retailer to supplier: "Shall we return the damaged goods?"
   ▶ The retailer wanted to know _____ return the damaged goods.
   or: The retailer wanted to know _____ return the damaged goods.

7. Investors: "Shall we acquire the ailing discounter?"
   ▶ The investor _____ to acquire the ailing discounter.
   or: The investor _____ acquiring the ailing discounter.
   or: The investor asked _____ acquire the ailing discounter.

8. Supplier: "Shall we send an advice note?"
   ▶ The supplier asked _____ an advice note.
   or: The supplier asked _____ an advice note.
   or: The supplier _____ to send an advice note.

practice   reported speech

N   **German managers abroad: German virtues – German weaknesses**
Put the following statements into reported speech.
Watch out for the tense of the introductory verb!

1. In 2013, an expert claimed: "While more than a third of top positions in Switzerland is held by Germans, few German top managers work in other countries."

   ▶ In 2013, an expert claimed while more than a third of top positions _____ _____ by Germans in Switzerland, few top managers _____ in other countries..

2. Another expert explained: ""Every country has its specific education system. National career paths often keep foreign candidates out. In France or the USA, for example, graduates have to come from one of the elite schools and universities, otherwise they don't stand a chance."

   ▶ Another expert explained (that) every country _____ its specific education system. National career paths often _____ foreign candidates out. In France and the USA, for example, graduates _____ to come from one of the elite schools and universities, otherwise they _____ stand a chance.

3. An experienced executive added: "Personal networks shouldn't be underestimated either. Qualifications alone are not enough to get a top position. Applicants need to know the right people and be part of the alumni of certain institutions."

   ▶ An experienced executive added (that) personal networks _____ _____ either. Qualifications alone _____ not enough to get a top position. Applicants _____ _____ part of the alumni of certain institutions.

4. Meanwhile experts say: "The situation is slowly improving. Companies are becoming more international and top executives have got used to spending much of their time abroad anyway. Still, German communication styles are often considered to be too direct, the German love of detail often appears to be an obsession."

   ▶ Meanwhile experts say (that) the situation _____.
   Companies _____ and top executives _____ much of their time abroad anyway.
   Still, German communication styles _____ to be too direct, the German love of detail often _____ to be an obsession.

N   continued: *level 3*

5. International head hunters still complain: „Germans are usually good engineers, but German managers lack flexibility and are not prepared to take risks. There could be a lot more Germans in top positions abroad if they were more flexible. They are usually believed to be punctual and diligent."
    ▶ International head hunters still complain (that) Germans _____ usually good engineers, but (that) German managers _____ flexibility and _____ willing enough to take risks. There _____ _____ a lot more Germans in top positions abroad if they _____ more flexible. They _____ _____ to be punctual and diligent.

6. They warn German managers: „You shouldn't leave the global stage to Anglo-Saxon executives or be afraid of speaking English." They tell them: "Be self-confident, learn about other corporate structures and understand foreign leadership styles. Then you will be very successful."
    ▶ They warn German managers _not_ _____ the global stage to Anglo-Saxon executives or _____ of speaking English. They tell _____ self-confident, _____ about other corporate structures and _____ foreign leadership styles. Then _____ very successful.

7. Last year, consultants reported: "German top executives who are successful in companies abroad usually worked for one of Germany's big global players before. Executives from medium-sized companies normally lose out, simply because they don't have the necessary international contacts."
    ▶ Last year, consultants reported (that) German top executives who _____ _____ in companies abroad _____ for one of Germany's big global players before. Executives from medium-sized companies normally_____, simply because _____ the necessary international contacts.

8. HR managers advise graduates: „Study and work abroad, build up an international network and don't shy away from risks when you receive an offer."
    ▶ HR managers advise graduates _____ abroad, _____ an international network and _____ from risks when _____ an offer.

practice — reported speech

0. Große Städte – Wachstumsmotoren oder Problemgebiete? – *Translate:* Big cities – engines of growth or problem areas?

1. Historiker betonen oft, dass Bildung und Fortschritt Hand in Hand mit dem Aufstieg der Städte gehen. Die Urbanisierung habe in griechischen und mittelalterlichen Städten zu Arbeitsteilung und Spezialisierung geführt, Kunst und Philosophie wären ohne städtische Strukturen kaum möglich gewesen.

2. Selbst kritische Ökonomen erkennen an, dass die reichen Städte der italienischen Renaissance die ‚Wissensindustrie' massiv gefördert haben, fügen aber hinzu, dass die frühe Industrierevolution in England eine neue soziale Schicht (*Klasse*) hervorgebracht und rasch zu Massenarmut geführt habe.

3. Bereits vor Jahren wiesen Wissenschaftler darauf hin, dass die demographische Entwicklung in armen Ländern zu Chaos in den Megacitys führen könne.

4. Soziologen warnten damals, überfüllte Städte könnten zu Bürgerkriegen führen.

5. Letztes Jahr sagte ein afrikanischer Politiker, Städte wie Lagos seien die neuen Zentren der Innovation, da die armen Menschen, die voller Hoffnung in die Städte geströmt seien, im täglichen Überlebenskampf Kreativität bräuchten.

O   continued:

level 3

6. Er fügte hinzu, Menschen in den reichen Ländern seien zu faul geworden und verließen sich zu sehr auf den Wohlfahrtsstaat. Das fördere Innovation nicht.

7. Autohersteller bestätigen, dass für sie die Schwellenländer wichtiger seien als die gesättigten Märkte in der Europäischen Union, da die entstehende Mittelschicht dort enorme Kaufkraft entwickle.

8. Während einer Pressekonferenz in der deutsch-chinesischen Handelskammer in Shanghai fragte ein Journalist, ob die chinesischen Städte nicht bereits zu viele Staus hätten, und kritisierte, dass der Smog bereits ernsthafte Gesundheitsprobleme verursache. Ein Vertreter der Autoindustrie antwortete, es sei Aufgabe der Politiker, nachhaltige volkswirtschaftliche und soziale Lösungen zu finden. Er bat die Journalisten, das Infomaterial zu lesen, bevor sie weitere Fragen stellten.

9. Der Bürgermeister hatte vor seiner Wahl versprochen, er werde die Unternehmenssteuern senken und die Stadt sicherer machen. Bevor er letztes Jahr erneut gewählt wurde, beklagte die Opposition, das organisierte Verbrechen habe ganze Stadtteile erobert und es sei praktisch unmöglich, Aufträge zu bekommen, ohne zu bestechen.

10. Die Stadtverwaltung kündigte letzte Woche an, Firmen dürften Wanderarbeiter von Januar an nicht mehr unter dem Mindestlohn bezahlen.

practice reported speech

P British banks
Translate into English:

1. Seit mehr als einem Jahrzehnt beklagen Verbraucherorganisationen, dass die britischen Banken viel zu hohe Gebühren und Zinsen für überzogene Konten berechnen. Bereits im Jahr 2000 fand eine Regulierungsbehörde heraus, dass die Banken exzessive Preise und Profite durchsetzen konnten, weil es keinen echten Wettbewerb gebe. Ein Sprecher sagte: „Genug ist genug. Wir brauchen dringend mehr Konkurrenz."

2. Ein ehemaliger Investment-Banker gab zu, dass in den folgenden Jahren nichts geschehen sei und dass Banken sogar die Steuerbehörde betrogen hätten. „Der Libor-Skandal hätte verhindert werden können," sagte er, aber es seien keine Maßnahmen ergriffen worden, um die Banken zu überwachen. Es werde sich auch nichts ändern, solange niemand bestraft würde.

3. Abgeordnete (= Mitglieder) des europäischen Parlaments behaupten, dass die britische Regierung alles getan hätte, um strengere Regeln zu verhindern. Sie sagen offen: „Die Steuerzahler zahlen weiterhin für die Exzesse der Banken, weil die britische Regierung ihre Finanzindustrie schützt."

4. Besorgte Ökonomen erklärten bereits vor der Finanzkrise, was getan werden müsse, und was schon falsch gelaufen sei. „Die EU muss handeln," forderten sie.

Q **Should mayors rule the world? – *Translate into German:***

1. Benjamin Barber argues that civilization was born in urban areas. They are "the public spheres where we announce ourselves as citizens" he adds.

2. He points out that more than half the world's population now lives in cities.

3. Mr Barber also states: „Democracy is in danger" and continues to argue that democracy was born in ancient cities and can therefore be reborn in the global *cosmopolis*.

4. At TEDGlobal 2013, Mr Barber expressed his conviction that mayors would therefore be the best rulers, since they were faced with daily problems and had to solve them, not only discuss them in theory.

5. Decades ago, some experts warned that cities might get out of hand if they became too big, especially in poor countries, while the demographic development in rich countries would make cities shrink.

6. A TV report pointed out a few years ago that the mayor of London had gained more influence, since the British capital accounted for one fifth of England's GDP and its wealth benefited poorer regions in the form of structural aid.

7. A former mayor of London demanded that London should be allowed to keep more of its money for itself as the infrastructure was badly underfunded. "We are paying for the whole of the country while London is faced with decay," he warned.

practice  reported speech

R **Before and after the election** – *Translate into English.*

1. Vor der Wahl beklagte die Partei, die Steuerlast sei zu hoch und müsse verringert werden. Es gebe kaum Anreiz für Arbeitslose, einen Job mit geringem Lohn anzunehmen. Die Regierung habe ihr Versprechen nicht gehalten. Anstatt eine Reform durchzuführen, habe sie die Situation verschlimmert.

2. Nach ihrem Sieg sagt diese Partei jetzt, in der aktuellen Wirtschaftslage sehe sie keine Möglichkeit, die Steuern zu senken. Alle öffentlichen Ausgaben seien überprüft worden, der Haushalt werde Ausgabenkürzungen erst in drei Jahren gestatten. Natürlich sei das die Schuld der früheren Regierung, da sie falsche strategische Entscheidungen getroffen habe.

3. Die Opposition hatte vor der Wahl versprochen, sie werde das Steuersystem radikal vereinfachen, da es ungerecht sei. Es müsse kaum Ausnahmen geben, wenn alle Subventionen abgeschafft (*to do away with*) würden. Dann wäre das Steuersystem einfach und gerecht (*fair*) und jeder Bürger könne seine Steuererklärung an einem halben Tag ausfüllen.

4. Jetzt ist sie Teil der Regierung und erklärt, es sei naiv zu glauben, in einer komplexen Volkswirtschaft könnte ein einfaches System fair sein. Schon vor Jahren hätten Experten das bewiesen. Das Finanzministerium werde dieser Erkenntnis folgen.

S   Before and after the election

Translate into German. Use conjunctive forms (Konjunktivformen).

1. During the election campaign the party complained that the middle-class was suffering from a heavy tax burden, while multinational companies had shifted their profits abroad and were contributing very little to the budget. If they were elected they would end what they called an unfair abuse of public funding. Big companies would be made to make their contributions to infrastructure and education, for example.

2. One day after the election politicians now maintain that international companies would simply leave the country, which would lead to massive job losses, if the government tried to get a bigger share of their profits. They now claim that the country's tax policy must not be changed, international regulations are needed to solve the problem, adding that that is what they have always tried to explain to the voters. They say they will put the issue on the agenda of the next EU summit.

3. Before the head of government resigned, the opposition leaders asked why entrepreneurs were not supported by tax breaks and other measures since the country badly needed more innovation. They claimed that the creation of start-ups had been stalled instead and told the government to change their policy.

4. The new Prime Minister now explains that genuine entrepreneurs must be able to survive without public money, otherwise their success will never be sustainable.

Intro

Vorgedanken

THE PASSIVE VOICE

Das Passiv braucht man doch gar nicht unbedingt –oder?

Man kann es doch umgehen und anders ausdrücken!

> Das Passiv braucht man doch gar nicht wirklich – man kann ja auch alles im Aktiv ausdrücken – ist ja viel leichter!

> The goods have been damaged in transit.
> ▶ Die Waren sind beim Transport beschädigt worden.
>
> He was fired after the strike.
> ▶ Er wurde nach dem Streik entlassen.

> Ja, klar. Oft geht das. Aber was ist, wenn man gar nicht weiß, wer etwas getan hat, oder man es nicht sagen will?

> Ja, gut. Aber dann ist das ja auch einfach. Man nimmt *to be + Partizip der Vergangenheit*. Das sind einfache Strukturen.

> While the goods were being unloaded, a worker was stung by a scorpion that had been hiding in a crate.
>
> The whistleblower had a heart attack while he was being interrogated.

> Stimmt – zumindest oft. Aber nicht immer. Wie geht das in der Verlaufsform? Da bringen viele die Strukturen durcheinander. Außerdem vergessen manche, dass der ‚Verursacher', derjenige, der die Handlung tut, mit der Präposition *by* ausgedrückt wird.

level 0

Aber da hat man ja zweimal hintereinander to be !?

So ist es! Einmal - konjugiert - für das Passiv; das zweite Mal *being* für die Verlaufsform.

Das kann ja in zusammengesetzten Zeiten sehr kompliziert werden!

He was granted exclusive rights. *or:*
Exclusive rights were granted to him.
▶ Ihm wurden Exklusivrechte gewährt.
The CEO was expected to resign.
▶ Es wurde erwartet, dass der Vorstandsvorsitzende zurücktrat.
This is what it is connected with.
▶ Damit ist es verknüpft.

Nicht wirklich, denn außer im Present und im Past wird die Verlaufsform im Passiv nicht verwendet - weil es einfach zu komplex - und häßlich - klingt. Aber es gibt Verwendungen, die viele nicht beherrschen, z.B. das persönliche Passiv oder auch die Stellung von Präpositionen.

Ok, ok …..

The textile brand is said to have been involved in corruption.
The board member cannot remember being held to account.

Das ist immer noch nicht ganz alles. Schwierig wird es vor allem in Verbindung mit anderen Strukturen …

Merkbox:

Das Passiv ist im Kern recht einfach: *to be* (in allen Zeiten) + *Past Participle*.
Der sog. ‚Agent' (‚Verursacher') wird mit *by* **angegeben.**

Die Verlaufsform (*to be* + *Partizip Präsens*, d.h. *to be* + *-ing*) darf man nicht mit dem Passiv (*to be* + *Partizip Perfekt*) verwechseln, es gibt aber die Verlaufsform des Passivs, also beides in Kombination, allerdings praktisch nur im *Present* & *Past*.

Schwierig kann es in Verbindung mit anderen Strukturen werden, wenn man den Überblick über die einzelnen Bestandteile verliert und alles vermischt, oder auch in Strukturen mit dem persönlichen Passiv (z.T. plus Infinitiv).

theory

THE PASSIVE VOICE

Compare:

Last week reports of alleged fraud were published by a business magazine. Since then offices have been searched, computers seized and witnesses interrogated. The CFO is reported to have disappeared, his computer is said to have been destroyed with all data lost.	Letzte Woche wurden von einem Wirtschaftsmagazin Berichte von mutmaßlichem Betrug veröffentlicht. Seitdem sind Büros durchsucht, Computer beschlagnahmt und Zeugen befragt worden. Es wird berichtet, dass der Finanzvorstand verschwunden ist, sein Computer soll zerstört worden wobei alle Daten verloren sind.
Who had the CFO been warned by? Who had he been helped by?	Von wem wurde der Finanzvorstand gewarnt? Von wem wurde ihm geholfen? (Besser: Wer hat ihm geholfen?)
Currently all email correspondence is being checked for evidence. The question is: Will anything be found? Can the other board members be convinced it is in their own interest to cooperate with the police?	Gegenwärtig wird sämtlicher E-Mail-Verkehr auf Beweise hin untersucht. Die Frage ist: Wird etwas gefunden werden? Können die übrigen Vorstandsmitglieder davon überzeugt werden, dass es in ihrem eigenen Interesse ist, mit der Polizei zusammenzuarbeiten? Können Sie dazu gebracht werden auszusagen?
Can they be made to testify?	
If the members of the board are granted impunity, they may remember having seen manipulated accounts or having heard of fraudulent practices.	Wenn den Vorstandsmitgliedern Straffreiheit gewährt wird, erinnern sie sich vielleicht daran, manipulierte Abrechnungen gesehen oder von betrügerischen Praktiken gehört zu haben.
Meanwhile, the company has been sued for damages, and the victims should get their money refunded.	Inzwischen ist das Unternehmen auf Schadensersatz verklagt worden und die Opfer sollten ihr Geld zurückerstattet bekommen.

Tasks:

a, Compare the English to the German version of the text.
b, Try to transform the English text into the active voice.
   Where and why is it not easy or even possible to do so?
c, Find out all the *personal passive* constructions.
d, Find out all the *Passive Progressive* constructions.
e, Explain the grammatical difference between "lost" and "convinced".

Forms: tenses & aspects - *Formenübersicht*

to be + past participle (pp)
= to be + -ed or to be + irregular pp
e.g.: *to be punished*   ---   *to be paid*

	Simple Form	Progressive Form
Present Tense:	The IPO is announced.	It is being announced.
Past Tense:	The IPO was announced.	It was being announced
Present Perfect:	The IPO has been announced	-----
Past Perfect:	The IPO had been announced	-----
Future I:	The IPO will be announced	-----
Future II:	The IPO will have been announced	-----
Conditional I:	The IPO would be announced	-----
Conditional II:	The IPO would have been announced	-----

FORMS: Infinitives - *Infinitvformen*

Present Infinitive   **Past Infinitive**

He seems to be bribed regularly.   He seems to have been bribed.

! **Watch out:** A lot is / remains to be done. ▶ Eine Menge *ist / bleibt* **zu tun**.

(Eine Menge **tut nichts**, sondern muss **getan werden** → *passivischer Sinn!*)

FORMS: Passive Gerund - *Gerund im Passiv*

They remember being hired and fired again and again.

Watch out: **action**   vs.   **result**
! to be beaten =   geschlagen werden *(oder:)*   geschlagen **sein**
  to get beaten = geschlagen werden   -----
                   Handlungspassiv   Zustandspassiv

Im Englischen kann das Passiv eine Handlung oder einen Zustand,
bzw. ein Ergebnis ausdrücken.
In bestimmten Fällen, v.a. im Present Tense und/oder bei statischen
Verben wird es automatisch als Zustand verstanden, außer der
'Verursacher' ist angegeben; häufig wird statt to be auch to get verwendet, um
klarzustellen, dass es um die Handlung, bzw. den Vorgang geht.
He is beaten.   He gets beaten.   He is beaten **by** a rival.
▶ Er **ist** geschlagen. Er **wird** geschlagen.   Er wird **von** einem
                                              Rivalen geschlagen.

Merkbox:

> Das Passiv wird in der Regel durch *to be + pp* gebildet. Die Verlaufsform wird im Passiv gewöhnlich nur im Present und im Past gebraucht.
>
> Das Passiv ist sowohl im Infinitiv der Gegenwart wie der Vergangenheit gebräuchlich; ebenso üblich ist das Passiv als Gerund.
>
> Grundsätzlich kann das Passiv als Handlung oder als Zustand verstanden werden. (Englisch: *to be* + *pp* – Im Deutschen gibt es dafür unterschiedliche Hilfsverben: *sein / werden*).

A   Transform the following sentences into the passive voice wherever it is possible. Leave the agent (by ...) out if possible.

a, While <u>they were updating</u> the anti-virus software the whole system broke down. What had to be done?

▶ While _____

_____

b, The police stopped the demonstrators at the factory gate.

▶ _____

c, The government had prevented the merger several times.

▶ _____

d, The mob has held up our delivery vans for hours now. When will the police stop them from rioting?

▶ _____

_____

e, The furniture store granted discounts of up to 20 per cent, before it had to declare bankruptcy.

▶ _____

_____

f, Currently we cannot access our premises because they are repairing a gas leak. When will they finish this job? A lot remains to be done.

▶ _____

_____

g, A competitor seems to have bribed our employee. The police have been questioning him for hours now. When will they release him?

▶ _____

_____

_____

h, If we produced pink washing-machines, would our customers buy them?

▶ _____

_____

B**Translate the underlined parts of the following text into German.**

Before we were able to enter the Russian market (1) many licences had to be obtained from the local authorities.

(1) _____

Regularly, (2) we were asked to pay bribes.

(2) _____

In the first few weeks (3) after our shops had been opened there were frequent blackouts (4) which seemed to have been caused by officials who thought we had not been 'generous' enough. But (5) we did not want to be blackmailed indefinitely and refused to pay.

(3) _____

(4) _____

(5) _____

(6) One of our executives was threatened by a gang.

(6) _____

They told him: "(7) You will get beaten up if we are not put on the payroll of your firm."

(7) "_____."

(8) I do not remember being blackmailed so massively, ever.

(8) _____.

After one year (9) we were defeated and closed all our outlets in Moscow.

(9) _____

If Russia wants more FDI (10) this has to be prevented. More foreign companies would set up business in Russia (11) if they were protected by the government.

(10) _____

(11) _____

It is not sufficient for companies (12) to be invited, (13) they should be supported in their fight against organised crime and corruption.

(12) _____ (13) _____

(14) Little seems to have been done to change the business environment and practices.

(14) _____

(15) Our staff in the CSR Department would have expected to be taken seriously when they asked for help, but (16) all their requests were ignored.

(15) _____

(16) _____

C   Stolen ideas – An entrepreneur talks about a bad experience.
    Translate the underlined passages into German.

"Ten years ago I flew to China to set up business in the Middle Kingdom.
(1) I had been contacted by the German Chamber of Commerce in Shanghai, who claimed (2) my newly developed environmentally friendly machine tool could be sold easily as there was high demand for it and (3) it was considered as unique. During my stay in China (4) I was asked many times by the press how it worked, but I told them (5) that had to be kept secret.
On my flight back to Munich (6) I was seated next to a Chinese woman from Tianjin, (7) who said she had been employed as an interpreter by a German insurance company and was on her way to start her job. (8) She seemed to be very well informed about technology (for a translator) and asked many questions, (9) which she wanted answered in detail. We had a long chat and (10) I felt flattered.
Six months later, (11) while our first production line was being built and right (12) before the advertising campaign was to be launched, I read an article in China Daily in which (13) a unique environmentally friendly machine tool was highly praised as (14) it was made in China. I looked at the illustration and (15) was shocked: (16) My technology had been imitated, (17) our chat had been recorded, (18) my business dreams were shattered – and (19) I was bust and felt cheated.

(1) _____
(2) _____
(3) _____
(4) _____
(5) _____
(6) _____
(7) _____
(8) _____
(9) _____
(10) _____
(11) _____
(12) _____
(13) _____
(14) _____
(15) _____ (16) _____
(17) _____
(18) _____
(19) _____

D Good or bad news? - *Translate into English.*

1. Auf der Jahreshauptversammlung wurde der Vorstandsvorsitzende kritisiert und gefragt, warum sein Gehalt verdoppelt worden sei. Während er von Reportern interviewt wurde, wurde er sogar von einem Aktionär ins Gesicht geschlagen.

2. Seit Monaten ist der Börsengang bekannt, aber bis jetzt sind noch keine Aktien ausgegeben worden. Wann wird das Unternehmen wirklich privatisiert werden?

3. Unser Logo hätte schon vor Jahren modernisiert werden sollen. Es wird von vielen als altmodisch betrachtet. Unsere Marke würde von jungen Kunden besser angenommen werden, wenn unser Image besser auf diese Zielgruppe zugeschnitten wäre.

4. Ein Teil unserer Produktpalette scheint von Firmen in Asien kopiert worden zu sein. Ich wäre überrascht, wenn die Imitate dort von den Behörden beschlagnahmt würden. Unsere Geschäftspartner müssen umgehend informiert werden.

5. Wie können Drogenkartelle in Lateinamerika wirkungsvoll bekämpft werden? Politiker scheinen ‚gekauft' worden zu sein; die Schlacht scheint verloren zu sein. Außerdem werden kontinuierlich Waffen ins Land geschmuggelt.

6. Seit Jahren wird die Eröffnung des neuen Flughafen immer wieder verschoben.

theory  passive

Personal Passive - *persönliches Passiv:* "Hier ~~werden Sie~~ wird Ihnen [!] geholfen."

active: Someone **gave** our competitor a hint.
             S   V   O₃   O₄

passive: A hint was given to our competitor (by someone).

personal passive: Our competitor was given a hint (by someone).

▶ Unserem (!) Konkurrenten wurde (von jemandem) ein Hinweis gegeben.

S = Subjekt (wer?)   V = Verben / Prädikat
O₃ = indirektes Objekt (wem?)   O₄ = direktes Objekt (wen?)

more examples (for personal passive):

The audience was shown a lengthy presentation. *(Den Zuhörern wurde ... gezeigt.)*
The employees were told to work overtime. *(Den Mitarbeitern wurde gesagt, sie sollten ...)*
The CEO was given a golden parachute. *(Dem Vorstand wurde ... gegeben.)*
She was helped by her boss. *(Ihr wurde geholfen ...)*

Infinitive constructions - *Infinitivkonstruktionen*
after: think, consider, know, believe, report, say etc.

It is expected that the director will resign. = The director is expected to resign (1b).
▶ Es wird erwartet, dass der ...   *oder:* Man erwartet, dass der ... zurücktritt.

It is reported that the CEO has cheated.   = The CEO is reported to have cheated (2c).
It was known that he had cancer.   = He was known to have cancer (1a).
It is believed that innovation is the key. = Innovation is believed to be (1a) the key.
It is said that he will quit soon.   = He is said to leave (1b) soon. (*Man sagt ...*)
It is supposed that taxes will be cut.   = Taxes are supposed to be cut (1b). (*sollen*)

Die zweite Variante (rechts) wird in der Regel als eleganter bevorzugt.
Häufig wird das Passiv im Englischen für das deutsche *man* benutzt.

1. Der Infinitiv der Gegenwart (z.B.: *to be promoted*) drückt aus, dass etwas zur **gleichen Zeit** (wie die Annahme, Erwartung etc.) oder später gilt
= *Gleichzeitigkeit (a) / Nachzeitigkeit (b)*

2. Der Infinitiv der Vergangenheit (z.B.: *to have been promoted*) drückt aus, dass etwas bereits **VOR** der Annahme, Erwartung, etc. geschehen ist.
= *Vorzeitigkeit (c)*

3. Oft ist auch der Infinitiv in der Verlaufsform möglich und üblich:

z.B.: He is said to be looking for a new job.
▶ Man sagt / Es heißt, *er sucht (gegenwärtig)* nach einer neuen Stelle.

Some migrant workers are reported to be protesting in the streets.
▶ Einige Wanderarbeiter sollen (Berichten zufolge) auf den Straßen *protestieren*.

You are supposed to be working on the project. (= You should be working ...)
also: You are supposed to have been working on the project.

  Watch out: *Certain <u>impersonal passive structures</u> in <u>German</u> ('es') are not used in the same sense in English! Therefore they have to be expressed differently.*

e.g.: "Jetzt wird verhandelt!" ▶ Now we'll (have to) negotiate.
„Erst wird gearbeitet, dann gefeiert." ▶ "First we'll work, then party."
"Es wurde viel gestritten." ▶ "They had / There were a lot of arguments."
"Es wird gern gekauft." ▶ It sells well.
"Das tut man nicht." ▶ "Don't do that." / "You should not do that."

lassen

to make somebody do sth *(veranlassen, zu etwas bringen)*
The boss **made** his team work longer. → The team **was made to** work longer.
 Passive: Infinitive **with to**
(also: He **got** his team **to** work longer. [*coll.*]   *no passive use!*)

(also: The boss **had** his team **work** longer.   *no passive use!*
(**Watch out:**   *no active form!*   He **had** his store cleaned. [*have + pp*]
 Er ließ seinen Laden reinigen.)

to let somebody do sth
The boss **let** his team **go** home earlier. → The team **was allowed to** go home earlier.
 (Active &) Passive: *Ersatzform*
  (The team **was let** go home earlier. *Unüblich!*)

Prepositions with passive verbs

The preposition indicating the **agent** is *by* Who was the invoice written **by**? **By** me.
 What was the failure caused **by**? **By** her.
The preposition indicating **materials** is *with* What was the room filled **with**? **With** dust.

The **preposition** usually remains **after the verb**. Our customers are well looked **after**.
 The case needs to be looked **into**.
 The plan must be thought **over** again.
 The idea has been talked **about** enough.

Merkbox:

Es gibt grundsätzlich zwei Arten, das Passiv zu bilden: Indem das direkte Objekt (O_4) zum Subjekt wird oder indem das indirekte Objekt (O_3) zum Subjekt des Passivsatzes wird. Dieses *persönliche Passiv* ist sehr gebräuchlich.

Das Passiv wird gern in unpersönlichen Ausdrücken verwendet, oft für das deutsche ‚man', vorzugsweise als persönliches Passiv (*He is expected to... / Von ihm / Es wird erwartet, dass er ...*). Andererseits sind typisch deutsche unpersönliche Wendungen im gleichen Sinn in Englisch nicht möglich.

Die Präpositionen, die zum Verb gehören, stehen i.d.R. nach dem Verb (*This problem must be taken care of instantly.*) Der Agent (‚Verursacher', ‚Täter', im Aktivsatz Subjekt) wird mit *by* angeschlossen.

practice **Passive**

E   *Transform the following sentences using personal passive forms.*

a, The licence was given to our fiercest competitor despite all our efforts.
   ▶ Our fiercest competitor _____
   _____

b, This year again, no dividend was paid to the shareholders.
   ▶ _____

c, Huge bonuses have been given to the whole team for their repeated success.
   ▶ _____

d, Most of the workers consider the pay rise that will be given to them as far too low. Also, due to the crisis a smaller Christmas bonus has been paid to them.
   ▶ _____
   _____

e, Before the latest prototype was shown to the journalists all cameras and smart phones had to be put into a box outside the showroom.
   ▶ _____
   _____

f, The government helped banks during the financial crisis. Now financial support would need to be given to the government by the banks. (2 x).
   ▶ _____
   _____

g, For a period of time, a monopoly of trade in India was granted to the East India Trading company by the British government.
   ▶ _____
   _____

h, If the manufacturer had given us exclusive rights we could have generated much higher revenues. The evidence has been shown to him many times – in vain. (2 x)
   ▶ _____
   _____

F   Transform the following sentences eliminating the impersonal construction with 'it'.

1. It is known that the company has made a bid for the IT division of its French rival.
   ▶ The company _____
   _____

2. For some time it has been believed that the solar project is a cash cow.
   ▶ For some time _____

3. It is expected that the retail chain will start an online shop soon.
   ▶ _____

4. It is said that the entrepreneur had lost a lot of money before he was successful.
   ▶ _____

5. It was thought that the politician had signed a secret agreement with an energy group.
   ▶ _____

G   Translate the following sentences into English in two different ways.

1. Es wird erwartet, dass die Zentralbank ein Rezept gegen die Deflation findet.
   ▶ _____
   ▶ _____

2. Dem Land wurde finanzielle Unterstützung gegeben, solange es Reformen gab.
   ▶ _____
   ▶ _____

3. Die Controlling-Abteilung soll den Betrug entdeckt haben.
   ▶ _____
   ▶ _____

4. Es wird berichtet, dass die Ölfirma inzwischen verstaatlicht wurde.
   ▶ _____
   ▶ _____

5. Gestern wurde berichtet, dass das Energieunternehmen bald wieder privatisiert würde.
   ▶ _____
   ▶ _____
   _____

practice — Passive

H *Translate the following sentences into German.*

1. Although the executive was offered another pay rise, he did not stay.

   ▶ _____

2. Domestic demand is expected to weaken, but not to collapse.

   ▶ _____

3. Before the project can be launched all the risks have to be evaluated. Many questions are still left° to be answered.

   ▶ _____

4. What else remains to be done? The investors have been given all relevant facts and figures already. Now they are supposed to decide within a week so that the project can be carried on.

   ▶ _____

5. Oman is said to have been modernized over the last few decades. Has tradition been traded in for wealth? In fact, the modernization has been helped by oil revenues.

   ▶ _____

6. Many immigrant workers are made to work in the sun without eating or drinking for hours. This is considered by human rights organisations to be a violation of human rights. It is criticized that the sports event is made possible by slave work.

   ▶ _____

7. The government is believed to be considering imposing import tariffs on used cars.

   ▶ _____

8. Our regular customers want to be looked after more intensively. We are expected to listen to their complaints and suggestions to improve the quality of our products.

   ▶ _____

9. The development is said to have been driven by greed.

   ▶ _____

I **Emerging economies, commodities and poverty**
Fill the gaps using the passive voice. Watch tenses!

Since oil (1) _____ (*to discover*) decades ago, the Persian Gulf region (2) _____ (*to change*) at dazzling speed: From a habitat of Nomads living in tents it (3) _____ (*to turn*) into one of the richest parts of the world, with a green strip of land that (4) _____ (*to create*) and (5) _____ (*to protect*) against the desert sand. Desalination plants (6) _____ (*to use*) for years to turn sea water into drinking water. All the modern achievements and the massive urbanisation (7) _____ (*to pay for*) by oil revenues – a development which (8) _____ (*not to be expected*) to last forever. Dubai (9) _____ (*to say*) to have speculated and (10) _____ (*to bail out*) by Abu Dhabi during the financial crisis in 2008. At that time, Dubai (11) _____ (*to blame*) for going against the rules of Islam according to which speculation and interest (12) _____ (*to forbid*). By now, the economies of the emirates (13) _____ (*to diversify*) in an attempt to reduce the dependence on oil. The area is (= *soll*) (14) _____ (*to turn*) into an international air hub, currently a tourism industry (15) _____ (*to develop*) as an additional source of income, with water sports facilities and skiing slopes in the sand. Around the world, Arabs (16) _____ (*to report*) to acquire real estate and buy shares in companies which (17) _____ (*to expect*) to prosper and yield the returns on investment that (18) _____ (*to need*) to fuel the UAE's economy in the future. Arab investments, however, (19) _____ (*not to want*) in every country, as some governments fear their domestic companies might (20) _____ (*to influence*) too much by Arabs and (21) _____ (*to make*) to serve foreign interests. China is a BRIC country that (22) _____ (*to plague*) by heavy pollution, a problem that still remains (23) _____ (*to solve*); China's industry badly needs (24) _____ (*to supply*) with enormous quantities of raw materials, which is why the country is seeking to secure supplies by signing cooperation agreements with African governments, for example. In the last few years, resource-rich Brazil, another BRIC country, (25) _____ (*to woo*) by China, too. India's development (26) _____ (*to hamper*) by rampant corruption for years. At present, Russia's economy (27) _____ (*to fuel*) by the export of natural gas.

practice   **Passive**

K   *Translate into English.*

1. In diesem Presseartikel wird darauf hingewiesen, dass man *(Passiv)* sich letztes Mal überhaupt nicht um die ausländischen Aktionäre gekümmert hat. Sie wurden vollständig ignoriert. Ihnen wurde nicht geholfen (= *Hilfe gegeben*), die Vorträge zu verstehen, ihnen wurde nicht einmal eine Übersetzung des Jahresberichts gegeben.

_____

_____

_____

_____

2. „Von wem war der Bericht übersetzt worden? Mit wem sollten wir uns treffen, um den Inhalt zu besprechen? Von wem musste der Bericht genehmigt werden? Es wurde erwartet, dass er in mehreren Sprachen veröffentlicht wird."

_____

_____

_____

3. „In der Graphik, die von Ihnen bei unserem letzten Treffen vorgelegt wurde, sind keine Kosteneinsparungspotentiale zu finden. Ich hätte erwartet, vor den Verhandlungen ein paar Alternativen angeboten zu bekommen."

_____

_____

_____

4. „Technische Fehler können nie völlig vermieden werden, das ist akzeptiert. Aber: Sind Sie auf die Verhandlungen vorbereitet? Unsere asiatischen Partner werden in diesem Augenblick im Hotel abgeholt; auf dem Weg hierher werden ihnen Bilder von den Prototypen gezeigt werden. Der Ausstellungsraum wird gerade dekoriert."

_____

_____

_____

_____

5. „Beim Geschäftsessen wurde uns Affenhirn serviert. Uns war nicht gesagt worden, wie man das isst. Es war offenbar als eine Geste der Gastfreundschaft zu verstehen."

_____

_____

_____

level 2

L *Translate the following statements and questions into English. Find appropriate ways of expressing them.*

„Was ist zu tun? Unsere Dienstleistungen müssen mehr auf die Bedürfnisse unserer Kunden zugeschnitten werden."

1."_____."

„Von wem wurde erwartet, dass er die Firma rettet? Uns war vor Jahren auch von niemandem geholfen worden."

2."_____."

„Die Schlacht ist verloren – der Krieg noch nicht! Es wurde gerade ein neues Übernahmeangebot gemacht."

3."_____."

„Uns wurde gerade die Lizenz erteilt (= gegeben) – Ab jetzt wird produziert und verkauft!"

4."_____."

„Erst wird die Fabrik inspiziert, dann wird mit den Mitarbeitern gesprochen."

5."_____."

„Die Ausgaben werden durch die rote Säule (= column) dargestellt. Wo sind die Einnahmen zu finden?"

6."_____."

„Die Kataloge sollten bis Montag abschickt werden. Die Broschüren sollten bereits verschickt sein!"

7."_____."

„Die Zahlen sind vor der Besprechung zu aktualisieren."

8."_____."

Intro — Vorgedanken

IF-CLAUSES
If-Sätze / Konditionalsätze

Gibt's da nicht bloß ein paar starre Strukturen, die man halt lernen muss?

> Eigentlich ist das doch ganz einfach, oder? Man nimmt *if* und *would* in drei Variationen – stimmt doch?

> Ja, es gibt drei Grundtypen, bzw. drei Grundmuster von If-Sätzen. Aber *would* darf nun wirklich nicht überall stehen – ganz besonders nicht im If-Satz selbst; wenn, dann steht es im Hauptsatz!

Pattern 2:
You would get a discount if you placed a major order..

Pattern 3:
You would have got a discount if you had placed a major order.

> Na also! Ist doch offenbar ganz einfach, wenn man dem Schema folgt. Und *would* ist auch immer dabei.

> Sehr oft, aber nicht immer, denn es gibt auch andere Strukturen, die man vielleicht übersieht, oder nicht als if-Sätze erkennt, weil sie völlig ohne *would* auskommen, zum Beispiel: „Wenn die Teile nicht rechtzeitig ankommen, stehen die Fertigungsbänder still."

If the parts do not arrive in time, the assembly-lines will stand still.
(Pattern 1)

Na gut, das ist dann die dritte Grundstruktur. Das war's dann aber doch!

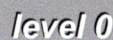

Das ist eigentlich das erste Grundmuster, denn es ist sozusagen ‚real', die beiden anderen Muster, 2 & 3, beziehen sich auf Hypothesen oder Irreales.

Kann man im If-Satz (if-clause) wirklich kein *would* nehmen – hab' ich schon gehört! Und im Deutschen heißt es doch auch oft *würde*!

If you *would* send us the sample promptly we would be grateful.
= *Wenn Sie das bitte tun wollen…*
If you *won't* refund the costs, we will have to sue you.
= *Wenn Sie sich weigern ….*

Im gesprochenen Englisch wird es manchmal auch von Muttersprachlern benutzt – obwohl es dann streng genommen eine ganz spezifische Bedeutung hat. In gepflegtem und im schriftlichen Geschäftsenglisch sollte man es nicht in dieser Weise benutzen. Im Deutschen ist es Konjunktiv!

Jetzt wird's dann doch komplizierter …

Tja, und das ist nicht alles – es gibt noch etliche Variationsmöglichkeiten, je nach Sinn und Logik!

Merkbox:

Am besten stützt man sich zunächst auf die drei Grundmuster (Pattern 1 – 3) und versucht diese drei Mechanismen zu verstehen. Vor allem sollte man vermeiden, im *If*-Satz ständig ‚*would*' zu verwenden.

Von den drei Grundmustern ausgehend, sollte man dann versuchen, die Logik im Kontext zu verstehen, um Grammatik und Sinn korrekt zu verbinden. Gerade weil es etliche Variationsmöglichkeiten – dem Sinn (aber auch der Grammatik!) folgend - gibt, ist es wichtig zu begreifen, was NICHT geht, bzw. was wann was heißt. Sonst sagt oder schreibt man etwas, das man nicht meint.

Es kann auch Spaß machen, die Bedeutungsnuancen virtuos zu nutzen!

theory

If-Clauses
(If-Sätze)

16-year-old Zach Simpson has become rich by selling his app to a big internet company. This is what he told the press the other day: "My dad kept telling me to concentrate on school and not to sit in front of my PC screen all day long. If I had done that I would not have developed my app and we would still be living in our small flat. I can only tell you, guys: 'If you have a talent for programming, go ahead, don't let anyone keep you from using your skills.' Maybe I would not have been so successful if my parents were rich and had sent me to one of those prestigious boarding schools. Should a big software company offer me a job right now, I would not hesitate a second and accept it - even if that meant that I would not finish school. But if everything goes as planned I will look for a job in programming only after my A-levels. Maybe I will set up my own business if I have not received a very good offer by then. In any case: If there are still unlimited opportunities they are to be found in IT. So don't think twice if you see a chance – take it!

Colours: level 1   level 2   level 3

Tasks (see the text in the box above):

a, Identify the *tenses and forms* used in the **if-clauses** and in the **main clauses**.
b, Find out the mechanisms, i.e. **combinations of if-clauses & main clauses**.
c, Try to **understand the logic** behind the patterns.
d, **Translate** the text into German.

*Die **drei Grundmuster** (patterns 1-3) sind die Basis der If-Sätze, sehr **häufig** und relativ leicht und mechanisch anzuwenden. Sie sollten sicher beherrscht werden!*

The most important standard structures are the following three patterns:

PAT 1 Probability **(in Latin: *Realis*) – *realistisch, realisierbar*:**
If we sell our patent we will be able to clear all debts.
▶ Wenn wir unser Patent verkaufen, können wir alle Schulden tilgen.
If + Present Tense → will-Future (main clause)

PAT 2 Improbability / Hypothesis **(in Latin: *Irrealis, gleichzeitig*) – unrealistisch oder hypothetisch *(gleiche Zeitebene)***
If we sold our patent we would be able to clear all debts.
▶ Wenn wir unser Patent verkaufen würden, könnten wir alle Schulden tilgen.
If + Past Tense → Conditional (main clause)

PAT 3 Impossibility / Hypothetical past action **(in Latin: *Irrealis, vorzeitig*) – unmöglich, da** vergangen, vorbei, nicht so geschehen *(Vergangenheits-Hypothese)*
If we had sold our patent we would have been able to clear all debts.
▶ Wenn wir unser Patent verkauft hätten, hätten wir alle Schulden tilgen können.
If + Past Perfect → Conditional II (main clause)

! Watch out:
No *will* or *would* in an *if*-clause (normally) !

Merkbox:

Die häufigsten *If-Sätze* kommen in drei Grundmustern vor: PATTERN 1 (durchaus) reale Annahmen,   PATTERN 2 unwahrscheinliche, bzw. hypothetische Annahmen, und   PATTERN 3 irreale Hypothesen über Vergangenes.   Im Deutschen steht bei den beiden hypothetischen Strukturen (PAT 2 + 3) der Konjunktiv im *If*-Satz.   In korrektem Englisch stehen *will* und *would* nicht im *If*-Satz (auch wenn dies im gesprochenen, v.a. amerikanischen, Englisch, mitunter geschieht); es gibt *if + will / would* in – eher seltenen - Sonderbedeutungen (s. Level 2).

practice

A   *Indicate the pattern of the if-clauses used in the sentences below. Then put the sentences into the other two basic patterns.*

a,   **If** the product launch **is delayed** our marketing director _____ (to be) ousted. (***PAT:*** ____)

  ▶ ***PAT*** ____: If the product launch _____ our marketing director _____ ousted.

  ▶ ***PAT*** ____: If the product launch _____ our marketing director _____ ousted.

b,   **If** the strike **had caused** a complete standstill of the assembly-lines, the board _____ (to sue) the union. (***PAT:*** ____)

  ▶ ***PAT*** ____: If the strike _____ a complete standstill of the assembly-lines, the board _____ the union.

  ▶ ***PAT*** ____: If the strike _____ a complete standstill of the assembly-lines, the board _____ the union.

c,   The merger _____ (not to take) place **if** the government **vetoed** it. (***PAT:*** ____)

  ▶ ***PAT*** ____: The merger _____ (not to take) place if the government _____ it.

  ▶ ***PAT*** ____: The merger _____ (not to take) place if the government _____ it.

d,   **If** the safety standards of the factory _____ (not to be improved) the authorities would have closed the plant down. (***PAT:*** ____)

  ▶ ***PAT*** ____: If the safety standards of the factory _____ the authorities _____ the whole plant down.

  ▶ ***PAT*** ____: If the safety standards of the factory _____ the authorities _____ the whole plant down.

e,   The retail chain would have to declare bankruptcy **if** the new major investor _____ (to refuse) to inject fresh money into it. (***PAT:*** ____)

  ▶ ***PAT*** ____: The retail chain _____ to declare bankruptcy if the new major investor _____ (to refuse) to inject fresh money into it.

  ▶ ***PAT*** ____: The retail chain _____ to declare bankruptcy if the new major investor _____ (to refuse) to inject fresh money into it.

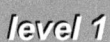

B **If ... - *Complete the following sentences choosing the appropriate tenses (basic patterns) for the verbs in brackets.***

The airline seems to be in a real dilemma: If it reduces the service on board to cut costs it (1) _____ (to lose) regular passengers, and revenues (2) _____ (to go down). If it (3) _____ (not to reduce) its overheads it will stay in the red. The situation would certainly be a lot better if the market (4) _____ (to be) less competitive. Also, the airline would be better off if fuel costs (5) _____ (to stop) rising. Some shareholders believe that the share price (6) _____ (not to plunge) if the board had not piled up so much debt by increasing the number of destinations too quickly. Others think the share price would have been stabilized or even increased if unprofitable routes (7) _____ (to be given up) in time. In any case, a solution is needed urgently. If the board (8) _____ (to fail) to take effective measures immediately it will be too late. Top executives have blamed the government, saying that the airline would not have been trapped like this if the skies (9) _____ (to be deregulated) more slowly. Their long-term strategy (10) _____ (to pay off) if they had had a little more time. It would also be better for the country if the airline (11) _____ (to stay) alive. They conclude: "If our traditional airline disappears foreign competitors (12) _____ (to jump in) and (13) _____ (to fill) the gap."

C **If ... - *Continue like above.***

1. "What do you think? Will our customers still buy our equipment if we (1) _____ (raise) our prices?"
2. "I think so – if we improve our quality substantially, they (2) _____ (to accept) higher prices. Wouldn't you be prepared to pay a little more if the quality and the service (3) _____ (to be enhanced)? I certainly (4) _____."
3. "If the wage agreements (5) _____ (to be) more modest last year, the company would not have run up so many losses; instead, they (6) _____ _____ (to recruit) new talent in order to boost innovation, as planned."
4. "If we had cut our marketing budget as suggested by the CFO the launch of our new online service (7) _____ (to work out). It would not be so popular now if we (8) _____ (to be) less present on the internet."
5. "What will happen if we (9) _____ (to cancel) our online support?"

practice — If-clauses

D What if …? - Discussing past and future strategies
*Complete the following sentences, using the verbs in brackets.
Watch out if the verb goes into the if-clause or the main clause!*

"I wonder what our competitors *will do* **if** we (1) _____ (to go) down-market."

"What (2) _____ (to happen) **if** we *don't*? **If** our biggest rival *had been* willing to form an alliance with us, we (3) _____ (to become) market leader by now."

"**If** we *were cooperating* with them, we (4) _____ (to have to) make compromises all the time."

"I believe that we (5) _____ (damage) our brand image **if** we *launch* a low-budget product range."

"**If** we (6) _____ (to do) that in Japan it *would be* ruinous, I agree."

"**If** we (7) _____ (not to do) that in China we would have been squeezed out of the market, I am sure of that!"

"Maybe. But **if** we (8) _____ (not to find) another marketing strategy soon we will be in serious trouble."

"I (9) _____ (to be) surprised **if** we did. We have discussed this again and again – to no avail."

"Wouldn't it be a good idea **if** we (10) _____ (to acquire) a local distributor?"

"It (11) _____ (to be) one – ten years ago! Now it's a bit late. **If** we (12) _____ (to accept) the offer of the then state-run monopolist, we would have got full government support."

"Be that as it may. **If** we don't find a solution quickly our revenues (13) _____ (to plummet)."

E Free movement of people …?
Translate into English using the three patterns of if-clauses.

1. "Viele qualifizierte Arbeitskräfte würden ihr Land nicht verlassen, wenn sie zuhause genug Geld verdienen würden. Wenn sich dieser Trend fortsetzt, gibt es bald einen massiven Mangel an Facharbeitern und Hochschulabsolventen."

   _____
   _____
   _____

2. "Wenn die vier Freiheiten des europäischen Binnenmarktes nicht im Januar 1993 in Kraft getreten wären, hätten viele junge Südeuropäer nicht die Möglichkeit gehabt, in anderen Ländern der EU Arbeit zu finden."

   _____
   _____
   _____

3. "Würdest du dein Land, deine Familie und deine Freunde verlassen, um in einem Land zu leben, dessen Sprache du nicht sprichst, wenn du keinen Job hättest?"

   _____
   _____
   _____

4. „Ich würde nicht zögern auszuwandern, zum Beispiel nach Australien, wenn ich dort bessere Berufsaussichten hätte. Würdest du das nicht tun, zumindest wenn du gut Englisch sprechen würdest?"

   _____
   _____
   _____

5. „Wenn die Regierung die Korruption wirkungsvoller bekämpft hätte, hätte sich die Wirtschaft viel besser entwickelt, das ist sicher. Wenn die EU-Kommission den Druck nicht erhöht, ändert sich daran° nichts."

   _____
   _____
   _____
   _____

6. Wenn der ‚Sozialtourismus' weiterhin zunimmt, muss die Regierung etwas tun."

   _____
   _____

theory   If-clauses

PAT 1 Probability – standard pattern (revision):

If you sell your patent you will be able to clear all debts.
▶ Wenn Sie Ihr Patent verkaufen, können Sie alle Schulden tilgen.

If + Present Tense → *will*-Future (main clause)

Variations in the main clause:

also possible: imperative in the main clause

If you sell your patent, clear all your debts with the money earned!
▶ Wenn Sie Ihr Patent verkaufen, tilgen Sie alle Schulden mit dem verdienten Geld.

or:

If you sell your patent, do not waste the money earned!
▶ Wenn Sie Ihr Patent verkaufen, vergeuden Sie das verdiente Geld nicht.

If + Present Tense → (pos. & neg.) imperative / 'Befehlsform' (main clause)

also: question in the present tense in the main clause

If you don't like your present job, why don't you try to change it?
▶ Wenn Ihnen Ihre gegenwärtige Arbeitsstelle nicht gefällt, warum versuchen Sie (dann) nicht, sie zu wechseln?

also: auxiliaries in the main clause

If he sells his patent, he should / must clear all his debts.
▶ Wenn er sein Patent verkauft, sollte / muss er alle seine Schulden tilgen.

If + Present Tense → should / must + infinitive (main clause)

or:

If he sells his patent, he can / may clear all his debts.
▶ Wenn er sein Patent verkauft, kann er alle Schulden tilgen / tilgt er vielleicht …

If + Present Tense → can / may + infinitive (main clause)

also, sometimes – when it is a natural law, general truth or habitual reaction

If the economy is overheated, low interest rates are toxic.
▶ Wenn die Wirtschaft überhitzt ist, sind niedrige Zinsen Gift.

If the interest rates are low, investment through borrowing is made easy.
▶ Wenn die Zinsen niedrig sind, fällt Investieren durch Kredite leicht.

If the interest rates are low, borrowing (usually) increases.
▶ Wenn die Zinsen niedrig sind, nimmt die Kreditaufnahme (gewöhnlich) zu.

(Der Hauptsatz gibt keine Folge an, er gibt eine generell gültige Erklärung.)

level 2

Die obigen Variationen des Grundmusters 1 sind logisch gut verständlich und leicht anwendbar. Daneben gibt es etwas schwieriger gelagerte Fälle von Variationen, zum einen die feste Wendung „would like", die auch im if-Satz beibehalten werden kann, zum anderen eine andere zeitliche Logik, die sich aus dem Sinn ergibt.

PAT 1 Variations in the if-clause:

You'll get a handout later if you'd like one (or: if you like).
▶ Sie bekommen später ein Handout, wenn Sie möchten (oder: mögen).

In der Bedeutung von *wollen, wünschen* kann *would like* im If-Satz stehen, allerdings nur, wenn eine Ergänzung (Objekt u.ä.) folgt.

also: instead of the present tense:

present perfect or present progressive in the if-clause

If you have finished that task I'll give you a new one.
▶ Wenn Sie mit der Aufgabe fertig sind [und zwar: jetzt], gebe ich Ihnen eine neue.

If you are considering joining us, I'll get everything ready straight away.
▶ Wenn Sie in Betracht ziehen [und zwar: jetzt im Augenblick] mitzumachen, mache ich gleich alles klar.

PAT 2 Improbability / Hypothesis – standard pattern (revision):

If we sold our patent we would be able to clear all debts.
▶ Wenn wir unser Patent verkaufen würden, könnten wir alle Schulden tilgen.

If + Past Tense → Conditional (main clause)

Variation in the main clause:

also: If + past → Past Tense in the main clause – gleichzeitig gültig, vergangen

If you knew his approach was wrong why didn't you tell him?
▶ Wenn du wusstest, dass sein Ansatz falsch war, warum sagtest du es ihm nicht?

Auch hier spielt der Sinn die Hauptrolle bei der ‚Abweichung' vom Standardmuster (PAT 2) – wenn (if) das eine war, wie es war, warum war dann das andere nicht soundso? (gleichzeitig, in der Vergangenheit, nicht als Hypothese!)

Merkbox:

In Grundmuster 1 gibt es einige Abweichungen, bzw. Variationsmöglichkeiten, je nach Logik. Es können im Hauptsatz – je nach Sinn – bisweilen Modalverben, (positive & negative) Imperative sowie Fragen stehen, u.U. sogar Present Tense (bei gleichzeitiger oder allgemeiner Gültigkeit).

Dem Sinn entsprechend kann in bestimmten Fällen im If-Satz Present Perfect oder Present Progressive erforderlich sein.

practice   If-clauses

F   **Indicate which of the following sentences are grammatically correct.**
    Put a cross in front of each possible/correct sentence.
    Note: There may be more than one - or no - correct sentence.

a, ○ If no publisher wants your manuscript, publish it yourself.
    ○ If your new book is rejected by all publishing houses you can publish it online.
    ○ If no one wants your manuscript you might consider having it printed at your own cost.
    ○ Your novel is really great! If no publisher wants it you should publish it yourself.
    ○ If your new book is rejected by all publishers, why don't you upload it for sale on your website?
    ○ What will you do if your publisher refuses to publish your next book?
    ○ If no one buys your book, don't despair. Try publishing it as an e-book.
    ○ If the bookshops did not display your latest novel it was because you did not give them any incentive to do so.
    ○ If you send an unsolicited manuscript to publishers they usually ignore it.
    ○ If you sent this manuscript to your publisher he will reject it.
    ○ If your publisher will reject your manuscript, you will send it to others.

b, ○ If you have already finished drafting your business plan I will read it right away.
    ○ If you had provided more detailed information the investors would have accepted your business idea.
    ○ The investors would certainly consider injecting money into your business idea if your business plan was more detailed.
    ○ Your business plan will be accepted by the bank if it was more detailed.
    ○ If the potential investors require a detailed business plan it is because they do not want to lose money.
    ○ You must raise your own funds or take a loan if no investor can be found for your project – it is a brilliant idea!
    ○ If the bank had really been willing to grant you the loan it had asked you to hand in a business plan.
    ○ Your business model might work if you would not have been so sloppy with the implementation.

c, ○ If you are sure they have cheated you sue them!
    ○ You sue them if they will cheat you.
    ○ You should change your suppliers if they are not reliable.
    ○ If you kick out an unreliable supplier the others will be more careful.
    ○ If you engage an NGO you may finally get rid of child labour in your supply chain.
    ○ If you do not inspect the factories in Bangladesh you can never be sure that safety regulations are respected.
    ○ Child labour must be avoided if you do not want to risk a consumer boycott.
    ○ If child labour will be discovered by the press, you have a problem!

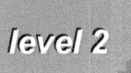

G   How to push up sales?
Complete the following sentences using will or the modal auxiliaries can, may, should, must according to logic and/or the indications in brackets. There may be more than one possibility.

If you feel you are not using your full market potential you (1) _____ *(urgent advice)* employ a marketing agency. Your current sales figures (2) _____ *(possibility)* go up if you advertise more frequently. But if you do not discuss your strategy with the agency you (3) _____ not be successful at all. If you find a distributor in Russia you (4) _____ *(advice)* seriously consider market entry there. You (5) _____ certainly not be able to grow if you get stuck in your home market. And what do you think (6) _____ happen if a foreign competitor challenges you at home?

H   Change of strategy? - *Complete the sentences below. Watch tenses.*

If online orders (1) _____ (to be) all the rage we must take our business online now! We cannot wait eternally if we (2) _____ (to want) to remain competitive. If we (3) _____ (to sell off) our mobile phone division we would earn enough money to invest in the development of computer games. We may quickly increase our market share if we (4) _____ (to boost) R & D. If you (5) _____ (to have) a better idea, come up with it now! It will be too late if we only (6) _____ (to wait) and do nothing. Actually, we could have concentrated on entertainment devices years ago if we (7) _____ (to have) the courage. By now we would be in a very comfortable market position if we (8) _____ (not to postpone) important decisions all the time. Why (9) _____ we _____ (to go) public if we need fresh capital? If we (10) _____ (to announce) an IPO tomorrow the business press would provide sufficient coverage to make it widely known. If we get one business magazine or TV programme to report on it, others (11) _____ (to follow) suit. In any case, we cannot sit around and do nothing if we (12) _____ (not to want) our sales to decline further. Handling software orders online can be a first step if we (13) _____ (to want) to prepare the IPO more carefully. But if we went on just discussing things without changing our strategy we (14) _____ (to miss) our last chance!

If-clauses

I **The real estate market and deflation** - *Translate into English.*

„Wenn die Zentralbank die Zinsen noch einmal senkt, gibt es bald eine Immobilienblase."

1. _____
_____
_____

2. _____
_____
_____
_____

„Wenn Investoren eine Deflation fürchten und der Zinssatz niedrig ist, kaufen sie eben° Immobilien. Das ist ganz normal."

„Aber wenn die Inflation nicht bald nach oben geht, verlieren viele Bürger ihre Ersparnisse."

3. _____
_____
_____

4. _____
_____
_____

„Wenn Sie meinen Rat wollen: Kaufen Sie Aktien oder Immobilien, wenn Sie Geld übrig haben."

„Wenn ich Geld hätte zu investieren, würde ich das tun."

5. _____
_____

6. _____
_____
_____

„Wenn die Immobilienpreise weiter in die Höhe schnellen, führt das bald zu einer gefährlichen Blase."

K   What if?
Translate into English.

1. Wenn die Geburtenrate in Japan nicht bald ansteigt, bricht das Rentensystem in einigen Jahren zusammen. Die Regierung könnte die Lage verbessern, wenn sie mehr junge Einwanderer ins Land ließe (= erlaubte).

2. „Warum verlagern Sie Ihre Produktion nicht nach Vietnam, wenn die Löhne in China so sehr gestiegen sind, dass Ihre Produktion dort nicht mehr rentabel ist?"

3. Die demographische Entwicklung in China wäre noch viel schlimmer, wenn die Regierung nicht vor ein paar Jahren die Ein-Kind-Politik aufgegeben hätte.

4. Wenn die Banken den Unternehmern nicht mehr Kredite gewähren, geht das Wirtschaftswachstum bald zurück. Die Regierung sollte ihre Wirtschaftspolitik überdenken, wenn sich nichts ändert.

5. Wenn der Geheimdienst von der systematischen Industriespionage wusste, warum informierte er nicht die Regierung? Viele Probleme hätten vermieden werden können, wenn die Unternehmen gewarnt worden wären. Was täten Sie, wenn Ihr Patent gestohlen würde? Wenn Sie ein Nischenprodukt haben, seien Sie vorsichtig!

6. Wenn Urheberrechte nicht ausreichend geschützt werden, gibt es weniger Anreize für Innovation. Wenn dies der Fall ist, muss die Regierung handeln!

theory — If-clauses

PATTERN 2 & **PATTERN 3** blended (according to time logic)

If + Past Tense → Conditional I (main clause)   PAT 2

If + Past Perfect → Conditional II (main clause)   PAT 3

e.g.:

If he did not have extraordinary gifts, he would never have made it.
▶ Wenn er nicht außergewöhnliche Begabungen hätte, hätte er es nie geschafft.
If + Past Tense → Conditional II (main clause)

If he had changed his job, he would not be depressed now because he let the opportunity slip.
▶ Wenn er seinen Job gewechselt hätte, wäre er jetzt nicht deprimiert, weil er die Gelegenheit versäumt hat.
If + Past Perfect → Conditional I (main clause)

Auxiliaries **can replace *would* in the main clauses of PAT 2 & PAT 3 again**,

e.g.: If ..., he could never have made it.
    If ..., he might not be depressed now ...

PAT 2 In pure hypotheses → *were* **can replace** *was*

If I were an oligarch, I would not go into exile. *(I am definitely not an oligarch)*
If there were any other option, I would do anything not to sell my business.
(Unfortunately there is not!)

PAT 2 *should* & *were to* **(never: *was*!) are sometimes used to express that something is** very unlikely **to happen:**

If the government should / were to [just in case] deregulate the market earlier, we would have to double our efforts.
▶ Wenn die Regierung den Markt früher deregulieren sollte [was eher unwahrscheinlich ist], müssten wir unsere Anstrengungen verdoppeln.

PAT 2 Inversion of *should* & *were to* & *other auxiliaries*

Instead of *if:* Inversion is often used - *Umstellung von Hilfsverb & Subjekt*):

If the government should / were to deregulate the market earlier .... →
Should the government deregulate the market earlier...   **or:**
Were the government to ....

Similarly in PAT 3 : Inversion of *had* (*Umstellung wie bei Frage*)

Had the inventor known how important his patent was for the industry, he would not have sold it so cheaply.

▶ Hätte der Erfinder gewusst, wie wichtig sein Patent für die Branche war, hätte er es nicht so billig verkauft.

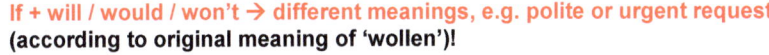

Watch out:

! **If + will / would / won't → different meanings, e.g. polite or urgent request (according to original meaning of 'wollen')!**

"If you *will* / *would* wait a moment I'll call the manager."

"If you would let me have an answer promptly I would be grateful."

(= be willing, would not mind ...)

"If he *won't* help us we'll ask somebody else." (= If he *refuses to*...)

▶ Wenn er uns nicht helfen *will*, ...

Bei den Grundmustern 2 & 3 gibt es (im Zusammenspiel) wieder einige (zeit-logische) Abweichungen, Anpassungen an den Sinn. Eine ‚Extrawurst' haben auch wieder Hilfsverben, in ihrer Anwendung – in Sinn, Form und Wortstellung.

Merkbox:

Es kann bei spezieller zeitlicher Logik zu einer 'Kreuzung' aus Grundmuster 2 & 3 kommen, je nach dem Sinn. Die üblichen modalen Hilfsverben (*might*, *could*) können – dem Sinn entsprechend – *would* ersetzen.
Bei irrealen Annahmen (e.g.: *If I were you*) steht immer *were*, nie *was* (*PAT 2*). Geringe Wahrscheinlichkeit kann durch *should* oder *were to* ausgedrückt werden. Häufig wird das *if* weggelassen und durch Inversion (Umstellung von Hilfsverb und Subjekt) ‚ersetzt' (*Should we fail ...*). Dies kann auch bei PAT 3 mit *had* erfolgen (*Had he known ...*).
Die Hilfsverben *will*, *would* & *won't* nehmen im *If*-Satz ihre ursprüngliche Bedeutung von *wollen* an, sind daher im Normalfall im *If*-Satz zu vermeiden.

practice   If-clauses

L   *Indicate which of the following sentences are grammatically correct.*
    Put a cross in front of each possible/correct sentence.
    Note: There may more than one - or no - correct sentence.

a, ○ If the car dealer would not have offered cheaper cars he had lost customers.
    ○ If the new model will not have lower petrol consumption it does not sell.
    ○ If the SUV did not have a rear camera it would be difficult for inexperienced drivers to park it.
    ○ If the fuel efficiency of the SUV had not been improved few Europeans would have bought the new model last year due to high petrol prices.
    ○ The new SUV would not sell well if it had not been made more economical.
    ○ If the car company does not spend more on R& D it may soon lag behind its competitors.
    ○ If the automotive group had not invested massively in new designs it might have lost even more market share.

b, ○ If the software company did not enjoy a near-monopoly it could not have imposed its third price increase in a row now.
    ○ If no new functions had been added to the standard software it would be hopelessly outdated by now.
    ○ The IT giant would have acquired the start-up if there would be no public protest against the acquisition.
    ○ The software company might have withdrawn from that market if the government had not clamped down on software piracy more severely.

M   *Rephrase the following sentences, leaving out "if" – if possible.*

1. If the immigrant workers should go on strike in Qatar, the stadium could not be completed in time.
_____
_____

2. If more migrant workers had committed suicide, the Chinese government would have had to intervene.
_____
_____

3. If the government were to decide against deregulation, all our plans would be thwarted.
_____
_____

4. If we had more market power, we could impose fairer prices.
_____

N Just in case ...
Translate the following sentences into English; leave out "if" where possible.

1. Sollte das Projekt von der Regierung nicht genehmigt (= *gebilligt*) werden, bräuchten wir dringend einen neuen Großauftrag.

   _____
   _____

2. Hätte unsere Forschungsabteilung besser gearbeitet, müssten wir nicht so hohen Schadensersatz zahlen.

   _____
   _____

3. Sollten wir die Fabrik schließen, falls sich die Berichte über schreckliche Arbeitsbedingungen als wahr erweisen?

   _____
   _____

4. Wäre das Produkt bereits letztes Jahr eingeführt worden, wären wir jetzt Marktführer.

   _____

5. Hätten wir bessere Beziehungen zur Regierung, müssten wir nicht so lange auf Lizenzen warten.

   _____
   _____

O What went wrong? - *Complete the sentences below. Watch tenses.*

If we publish the real sales figures our share price (1) _____ (to plunge) instantly. But can we 'embellish' our quarterly report if the press (2) _____ (to keep) a close eye on us all the time? If we had not permanently increased our product range we (3) _____ (can / to save) a lot of money and (4) _____ now _____ (to be) in a much better financial position. (5) _____ we _____ (to concentrate) on tablet PCs in time we would not be struggling now. If our operating system were still the most widely used, our customers (6) _____ (to stay) loyal until today.
(7) _____ (?) another disruptive technology emerge, that would be it. If we had gone into 3 D printing our prospects (8) _____ (to be) brilliant now.

If-clauses

P   The real estate market and deflation - Translate into German.

"If the boss won't pay us more for this dangerous job we will all go on strike."

1. _____

2. _____

"If you **will** [*special meaning!*] blackmail him you should not be surprised if he refuses."

"We would be obliged if you would stop criticizing us."

3. _____

4. _____

"If your negotiator were to get his way this company would not be competitive any longer."

Q   If things had developed differently ....
Complete the statements below using the words in the boxes.

a,   If the company had not paid ransom to the rebels
→ the executives (1) _____
→ the executives (2) _____
→ the executives (3) _____

1 not to be free
2 not to release
3 may / to kill

b,   If Nigeria had less corruption
→ the country (4) _____
→ the economy (5) _____

4 to be rich
5 to boom / earlier

c,   South Africa could be much better off
→ if corruption levels (6) _____
→ if it (7) _____
continuously from brain drain.

6 to be lower
7 to suffer from

R   Translate into English.

1. Wenn Mexiko die Drogenkartelle nicht besiegt, hört das Töten niemals auf. Vor allem dem Norden Mexikos wäre geholfen, wenn keine illegalen Waffen ins Land kämen.

2. Sollten die Spannungen in der Region zunehmen, könnte die Energie-Versorgungskette zusammenbrechen. Dies hätte ernste Folgen für die Wirtschaft der EU.

3. Wäre Öl in den USA nicht jahrzehntelang so billig gewesen, wären die Autohersteller viel früher gezwungen gewesen, Fahrzeuge mit niedrigerem Treibstoffverbrauch zu entwickeln. Dann wären sie heute wettbewerbsfähiger. *(ohne if)*

4. Wenn Sie mit uns absolut° *(mit dem Hilfsverb ausdrücken)* nicht zusammenarbeiten wollen, suchen wir einen anderen Partner. Das würde bedeuten, dass wir eine Allianz mit einem Ihrer Konkurrenten eingehen *(to form)* könnten. Wenn Sie unser Angebot bitte noch einmal prüfen wollten, wären wir sehr dankbar.

5. Wir würden Sie sofort einstellen, wenn Sie besser ausgebildet wären und Arabisch sprächen. Wenn in Ihrem Lebenslauf etwas fehlt, dann ist es Auslandserfahrung.

6. Wenn Sie das Anmeldungsformular schon ausgefüllt haben, dann warten Sie bitte hier. Wir können das Vorstellungsgespräch sofort beginnen, wenn Sie wollen.

Intro   Vorgedanken

MIXED TENSES
Sequence of Tenses
gemischte Zeiten / Zeitenfolge

Welche Zeit man braucht, hängt doch einfach davon ab, wann etwas passiert, oder?

> In einem Text ist doch klar, was Vergangenheit, Gegenwart oder Zukunft ist – Damit hat man dann ja die Zeiten – oder?

Our staff **has been** on strike *since last week*.
▶ Unsere Belegschaft **ist** *seit letzter Woche* im Streik.

"Ok, **I'll do** it."
▶ „Ok, ich **mach'** das."

> Im Prinzip: ja – im sprachlichen Zeitengefüge ist es aber komplizierter; die Zuordnung zu den Zeitformen ist in Englisch und Deutsch nicht gleich.

> Ja, klar. Dafür gibt's ja die Regeln mit dem Present Perfect vs. Past Tense, dem Future, die If-Sätze, indirekte Rede usw.

The train **leaves** at five.
"We **are having** a welcome party *tonight*."
"Where **are** you **going to** stay?"
"**I'll keep** you informed!"
"What **will** you **be doing** at this time next year, *when* the project *is finished*?"

> Stimmt – wenn mehrere Zeit(eben)en zusammenkommen, wird es allerdings schnell komplex und man muss sich erst mal durchfinden. Welche Zeitform, z.B. welche der (fünf) Möglichkeiten, Zukünftiges auszudrücken, ist gerade angebracht?

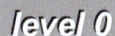

> Da muss man halt die Zeitenregeln anwenden.
> Ist ja nichts Neues.

> … und die Unterscheidung zwischen Simple Forms und Progressive Forms (die es im Deutschen ja gar nicht gibt).

> Klar.

He asked what we would do if the market was saturated.
▶ Er fragte, was wir tun würden, wenn der Markt gesättigt wäre / sei.

We will launch our new brand when / as soon as the new law takes effect.
▶ Wir führen unsere neue Marke ein, wenn / sobald das neue Gesetz in Kraft tritt.

When the gate opened we saw that the all the goods had been stolen.

> … und z.B. If-Sätze in der indirekten Rede oder auch die Verwendung von Zeiten nach temporalen Konjunktionen.

> Hm, ok, nachvollziehbar…..

> Gut! Dann gibt es da noch die unbestimmten Zeitformen (Partizipial-Sätze), die vom Kontext abhängen….

The ship was hijacked by the pirates while it was sailing along the Somalian coast. The captain had been warned but had done nothing, thinking his ship was too big to be captured.

Merkbox:

In einem Text kommen Zeiten normalerweise gemischt vor. Wichtig ist, was in der Wirklichkeit des Geschehens vorher oder nachher war (Situation) oder kam (Ereignis, Handlung); dies folgt sozusagen der ‚Zeit'-Logik. Daneben gibt es grammatikalische Mechanismen (z.B. If-Sätze oder indirekte Rede), eine Art grammatikalische Logik, die bestimmte Zeitformen (tenses) erfordert, die nicht gleichzusetzen sind mit der physikalischen Zeit (time).

Es gibt bestimmte Zeiten, die in Texten - logischerweise - häufig in Kombination vorkommen, aber je nach Zeitverhältnissen können im Prinzip alle Zeiten gemischt auftreten.

Daneben gibt es infinite Zeitformen (z.B. working, paid etc.), die selbst unbestimmt sind und erst im Kontext (Subjekt und konjugierte Verben) konkreter, bestimmter werden, im Zeit- und im logischen Bezug.

theory

MIXED TENSES

Compare:

A blueprint for structural reforms?	Eine Vorlage für Strukturreformen?
Japan's structural problems are still: a shrinking population, an exceedingly high national debt (more than 200 % of GDP), risk-averse companies and an inflexible labour market. It seems the problems have even been worsening since the big crisis in the 1990s, when the unthinkable happened: workers were laid off, some young graduates only got low-paid jobs as temporary workers, feeling useless and rejected. The government had failed to launch badly needed reforms, which became evident in the crisis, which triggered fears that had been unknown before among Japan's workforce. With unemployment rising, changes might have been easier to impose, but the chance was missed. While the central bank was dealing with deflation, even renowned companies that had been considered as pillars of stability were struggling, weakening Japan's economy even further. Does the current government have the courage to launch radical reforms now? Or will the Prime Minister shelve the blueprint he has been working on for months as soon as corporations, unions and bureaucrats unite against it?	Japans Strukturprobleme sind immer noch: eine schrumpfende Bevölkerung, eine ausufernd hohe Staatsschuld (mehr als 200 % des BIP), risikoscheue Unternehmen und ein unelastischer Arbeitsmarkt. Es scheint, die Probleme sind seit der Krise in den 1990er Jahren noch schlimmer geworden, als das Undenkbare geschah: Arbeiter wurden entlassen, manche junge Absolventen bekamen nur Niedriglohn-Jobs als Zeitarbeiter *und* fühlten sich (so) nutzlos und ausgestoßen. Die Regierung hatte es versäumt, dringend nötige Reformen einzuleiten, was in der Krise offenkundig wurde, *die* Ängste unter Japans Arbeitnehmern auslöste, welche vorher unbekannt gewesen waren. Bei steigender Arbeitslosigkeit wären Veränderungen vielleicht leichter durchzusetzen gewesen, aber die Chance wurde vertan. *Während* die Zentralbank mit der Deflation rang, hatten sogar renommierte Unternehmen zu kämpfen, die als Säulen der Stabilität betrachtet worden waren, *und* schwächten Japans Wirtschaft noch mehr. Hat die jetzige Regierung den Mut, nun radikale Reformen einzuleiten? Oder wird der Premierminister den Entwurf, an dem er *seit* Monaten arbeitet, auf Eis legen, *sobald* Unternehmen, Gewerkschaften und Bürokraten sich dagegen vereinen?

Tasks: *(Feel free to answer in German.)*

a, Compare the English to the German version of the text.
b, Where would you have made mistakes in the use of or in translating the tenses? Why?
c, Find out the temporal *mechanisms* / logic.
d, What can go wrong if inappropriate tenses are used? Give examples.
e, Spot infinite forms and define their tenses and senses in the context.

Sequence of tenses *(Zeitenfolge)*

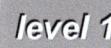
level 1

If the **sequence of tenses** is incorrect, the message is blurred, contradictory or simply wrong as far as tenses are concerned, i.e. it may not be clear what happened at the same time, before or after, or the timeframe may simply be misunderstood totally.

The problem arises especially in longer (con)texts and complex sentences with main clauses *(Hauptsätze)* and subordinate clauses *(Nebensätze)*.

e.g.: **main clause**   **subordinate clause**

      Everybody knows the stock market is volatile. *(same time / **gleichzeitig**)*
      Everybody knows the stock market was volatile. *(in the past / **vorzeitig**)*
      Everybody knows the stock market will be volatile. *(in future / **nachzeitig**)*

Also: Everybody knows the stock market has been volatile for months.
       Everybody knows the stock market had been volatile before the war broke out.
       Everybody knows the stock market would be volatile in any other situation.
       Everybody knows the stock market would have been volatile if the situation had been only a little different.

When the **main verb** is in the **Past** or **Past Perfect**, **verbs in subordinate clauses** cannot normally be **in the present** – similarly to the *tense shift* in Reported speech with an introductory verb in the past.

e.g.: **main clause**   **subordinate clause**

      Everybody knew the stock market was volatile. *(same time / **gleichzeitig**)*
      Everybody knew the stock market had been volatile. *(before that / **vorzeitig**)*
      Everybody knew the stock market would be volatile. *(after that / **nachzeitig**)*

Further examples:

Same time (gleichzeitig):

He sold his shares faster than we did. ◄► He sells his shares faster than we do.
He gave me the key because he trusted me. ◄► He gives me the key because he trusts me.
I worked so hard that I was always tired. ◄► I work so hard that I am always tired.
He had the tools that he needed. ◄► He has the tools that he needs.
They agreed as they had no choice. ◄► They agree when they have no choice.

Before (vorzeitig):

He handed the keys over to me as soon as I had signed the contract.
We saw that they had occupied the premises.
She bought the agency that she had always wanted.
The workers went back to work because the factory owner had accepted higher wages.
The union was aware that its members had made too many sacrifices already.

After (nachzeitig):

He sold his shares because he was sure that there would be a crash.
We knew that our debts would bring us to our knees sooner or later.
She bought the start-up, which would probably be worth ten times as much after the IPO.
She was afraid the merger might turn into a nightmare.
We accepted the offer as it would help to save jobs.

theory mixed tenses

Sequence of tenses (Zeitenfolge)

In a continuous text, two basic 'streams' of tenses can be identified:

a, Simple present, Present Progressive, Present Perfect and Future (I & II)

e.g.: The building-site is in a suburb as property prices are lower there and the infrastructure has been improved a lot over the last few years. Many companies are relocating from the city centre and this exodus will probably not come to an end soon as prices are still rising. Some experts predict that small retailers will not be able to afford a central location any longer unless they have paid off their own premises, and that most of them will have disappeared in twenty years.

b, Simple Past, Past progressive, Past perfect and Conditional (I & II)

e.g.: The building-site was in a suburb as property prices were lower there and the infrastructure had been improved a lot in the years before. Many companies were relocating from the city centre and that exodus would probably not come to an end soon as prices were still rising. Some experts predicted that small retailers would not be able to afford a central location any longer unless they had paid off their own premises, and that most of them would have disappeared twenty years later.

In real texts there may be **passages** in which one of the **'streams'** prevails, but the meaning and the time logic may require other tenses in between or a change to another stream *(see the text on the previous page)*.

If-clauses & Reported Speech

If-clauses follow their own rules, esp. the three basic patterns, and so does Reported Speech, esp. with the tense shift patterns when the introductory verb is in the past *(see the chapters on If-Clauses and Reported Speech)*

Watch out: **If-Clauses in Reported Speech**
(when the introductory verb is in the past):

The tense shift is only applied to the first basic pattern (*PAT 1*), the tenses in the other two patterns *PAT 2 & PAT 3* remain unchanged.

e.g.:
"I will outsource production if the labour costs keep going up."
▶ He *said* he would outsource production *if* the labour costs kept going up.

But:
"I would outsource production if the labour costs kept going up."
▶ He *said* he would outsource production *if* the labour costs kept going up.

And: "I would have outsourced production if the labour costs had kept going up."
▶ He *said* he would have outsourced production *if* the labour costs had kept going up.

Sequence of tenses (Zeitenfolge):
Progressive Forms (Verlaufsformen)

In principle, the **Progressive Forms follow the patterns and logic** of the **sequence of tenses** of the simple forms.

Same time (gleichzeitig):

He was working so hard that he was getting more and more exhausted.	◄►	He is working so hard that he is getting more and more exhausted.
She was using the tools she was familiar with.	◄►	She is using the tools she is familiar with.
The inspection took place while all the machines were running.	◄►	The inspection takes place while all the machines are running.

Before (vorzeitig):

We saw that our temps had been playing around with the fragile consignment.
She finally obtained the property rights she had been fighting for.

After (nachzeitig):

We knew she would be trying hard to undermine our strategy.
He gave up his business because he had understood he would be struggling forever.

In addition to this mechanism the aspects (i.e. *Progressive Forms & Simple Forms*) follow their usual patterns, of course.

e.g.:   While the CEO was making a speech, the workers attacked him.
While the CEO was making a speech, the workers were demonstrating.
The workers have been demonstrating since the CEO began his speech.   ***etc.***

*In der Realität treten **Zeiten in Texten gemischt** auf; stehen **in Relation zueinander** und bilden so ein **relatives Geflecht aus Zeitbezügen und Zeitebenen**. Hinzu kommen **die speziellen Regeln** für **indirekte Rede**, **Temporalsätze** (z.B. until), **If-Sätze**, **modale Hilfsverben** und **indefinite Satzteile** (Gerund, Partizip, Infinitiv). Das macht das Ganze recht **kompliziert**.*

Merkbox:

Die **Zeitenfolge** unterscheidet **Zeitebenen (in den Hauptverben, bzw. –sätzen)**, aus deren Perspektive **Gleichzeitigkeit, Vorzeitigkeit und Nachzeitigkeit** gesehen - und ausgedrückt - wird. **Falsche Zeitformen** (*tenses*) **führen zu falschen Zeitbezügen**, bzw. –zuordnungen.

Es lassen sich im Prinzip zwei Zeiten-**Ströme** identifizieren, bei denen **bestimmte Zeiten** zusammen jeweils eine Art **(logisches) System** bilden. Allerdings ist dies meist nur **passagenweise** der Fall, und auch dabei kann es immer wieder – je nach zeitlicher Logik – zum **Systemwechsel** kommen.

Die **Verlaufsformen** (*Progressive Forms*) in den verschiedenen Zeiten reihen sich **in dieses Zeitgefüge** ein.

Die ***If*-Sätze** und die **Indirekte Rede** haben ihre **eigenen Mechanismen und Muster**. **Nur ein** Grundmuster (**PAT 1**) der If-Sätze folgt der **Zeitenverschiebung**.

Mixed Tenses

A Complete the following text by putting the verbs in brackets into appropriate tenses.

America's crumbling infrastructure

For a country where everyone drives, the US (1) _____ (to have) bad roads. Three quarters of all spending on infrastructure generally (2) _____ (to take place) at the state and local level, and several states (3) _____ (to cut) their budgets significantly in recent years. As a result, many roads (4) _____ (to be) now in very bad repair, car drivers (5) _____ (to have) to put up with sudden potholes and bumpy roads for some time already. If the maintenance had been more systematic and the budgets (6) _____ (not to cut) so dramatically the infrastructure (7) _____ (not to deteriorate) so much. Bridges high above rivers (8) _____ (to be) also affected. Some of them (9) _____ (to look) a bit rickety – and (10) _____ (to pose) safety problems soon. Meanwhile, the issue (11) _____ (to extend) to airports too. They (12) _____ (to be funded) chiefly by passenger fees and (13) _____ (not to keep up) with the increasing air traffic over the last few decades. Denver Airport, the last big new airport that (14) _____ (to be opened) more than twenty years ago, (15) _____ (to become) too small now.

The US (16) _____ (to see) two great booms in spending on infrastructure in the past century, during the Great Depression, when important highways (17) _____ (to build), and in the 1950s and 60s, when most of the interstate highway system (18) _____ (to develop). Since then public spending (19) _____ (to decline) to appallingly low levels. When (20) _____ the situation _____ (to improve)?

B   The cost of doing nothing
Which of the suggested tenses below are appropriate?
Mark the letters with a circle. It is possible that more than one form is correct!

1. Since May 2014, business concerns about climate change ...
   a, have been growing   b, are growing   c, will grow   d, would grow

2. while public opinion in the US ...
   a, has not changed.   b, had not changed.   c, will not change.

3. If the oceans continue to rise at current rates, the sea level at New York City .... (by) 27-49 cm by 2050.
   a, would rise   b, has risen   c, will rise   d, will have risen

4. Studies have shown that, when the thermometer hits 37.8°C, labour productivity ....
   a, would fall.   b, has fallen.   c, fell.   d, falls.

5. In 2006 drought in South Dakota .... 10 % of the wheat crop.
   a, would have wiped out   b, will have wiped out   c, wiped out   d, has wiped out

6. Rising sea levels ....
   a, will affect future generations   b, might endanger whole coastal areas by 2050.
   c, are to be dealt with in time.   d, are causing concern in many countries.

7. Last year, experts said damage from storms ...
   a, has got worse   b, is getting worse
   c, had got worse   d, would get worse

8. They claimed that, if the right measures were taken right away, ...
   a, money could be saved in future.   b, money would have been saved.
   c, money had been saved   d, money will be saved.

9. They said the cost of doing nothing ...
   a, would be higher   b, was incalculable   c, could rocket

10. It is clear that climate change ...
    a, has already started   b, is taking place   c, will continue

11. Some years ago, some parts of Australia were flooded while other regions ...
    a, were suffering from a drought   b, had all dried up
    c, could have done with a little water   d, have been longing for rain.

   **Mixed Tenses**

C **Desertec – Solar energy from the Sahara for Europe**
   Translate the following sentences into English.

„Seit der Ölkrise in den 1970er Jahren ist klar, dass es Grenzen des Wachstums gibt, da uns die Rohstoffe ausgehen werden."

(1) _____

(2) _____

„Seit Jahren redet jeder von Nachhaltigkeit. Aber was ist getan worden? Haben wir eine Lösung?"

„Die EU finanziert zur Zeit ein Projekt in der Sahara, um Sonnenenergie zu nutzen. Es wurde rasch gestartet, als Investoren gefunden waren."

(3) _____

(4) _____

„Wird es genügend Energie für die europäische Industrie liefern? Wäre es nicht billiger, die Sonnenenergie in Spanien zu nutzen?"

„Die Kosten sind tatsächlich ein Problem. Während sie in den ersten Jahren nach oben gingen, zogen sich wichtige Investoren vom Projekt zurück."

(5) _____

D *Put the above dialogue into the Reported Speech. Use the following introductory verbs:*
The expert explained / said / replied ... (column on the left) **and**
The journalist asked ... (column on the right)

(1) The expert explained _____
_____
_____

(2) The journalist said _____
_____ and asked _____
_____

(3) The expert said _____
_____

(4) The journalist asked _____
_____
_____

(5) The expert replied _____
_____

E **Hong Kong - At the same time, before or after?**
Translate into German.

1. Before Hong Kong was returned to China the city had been a British crown colony. Since 1997 people have been worried about Beijing's influence.
_____
_____

2. In 2014 many inhabitants took part in a referendum in defence of Hong Kong's special status, which was evidently not fully recognized by Beijing. It was uncertain how the Chinese government would react.
_____
_____
_____
_____

practice   **Mixed Tenses**

F   Illegal immigration
Translate the following text into English
Watch the (sequence of) tenses.

Seit Jahren versuchen junge Afrikaner aus Ländern südlich der Sahara, die Wüste zu durchqueren und an die Küste zu gelangen. Ihr wahres Ziel ist Europa. Letztes Jahr kletterten wieder viele Menschen über den Zaun um Melilla, da sie gehört hatten, dass sie von der kleinen spanischen Enklave in Nordafrika nach Europa gebracht würden. Andere bezahlten für einen Platz in einem überfüllten Boot und erreichten Europa nicht. Italien bat die EU bereits mehrmals um Hilfe. Aber das Problem wird nicht gelöst werden, solange Afrika unter Armut und Kriegen leidet. Wird Europa wirklich zur Festung werden? Wäre es nicht in einigen EU-Ländern für die Bevölkerungsentwicklung gut, wenn mehr Menschen einwanderten?
Was geschieht, wenn es wirklich einen Mangel an Fachkräften gibt? Was werden die Unternehmen tun? Dann versuchen sie möglicherweise, junge Arbeitskräfte aus dem Ausland anzulocken, wie es in den 1950er und 60er Jahren, während des deutschen Wirtschaftswunders, der Fall war. Wäre es nicht besser, bereits jetzt junge Einwanderer auszubilden?

G **The ECB turning into a European Fed?**
Complete the following text with the verbs in brackets.
Be careful about the tenses and aspects (Simple vs. Progressive Forms)!

In the summer of 2014 the European Central Bank decided that meetings (1) _____ *(to hold / passive)* only every six weeks and that the minutes (2) _____ *(to publish / passive)* in the future. At the same time it (3) _____ *(to become)* clear that the central bank (4) _____ *(to continue)* to print money, a strategy that (5) _____ *(to criticize / passive)* fiercely already in the months before. Opinions about the right money policy (6) _____ *(to be)* divided then and (7) _____ (divided) now: while some economists (8) _____ *(to fight)* for stricter budget control even now, because they firmly (9) _____ *(to believe)* that otherwise money supply (10) _____ *(to get)* totally out of hand, others (11) _____ *(to keep)* arguing that the policy of cheap money (12) _____ *(to be)* the only remedy against deflation. Mario Draghi (13) _____ *(to attack / passive)* repeatedly in the previous months. "This policy (14) _____ *(to be)* very successful over the last few months so why should it (15) _____ *(to change / passive)?"* - some experts said. Others (16) still _____ *(to remain)* critical; in their opinion, speculators (17) _____ *(to strike)* again some time, because the problem (18) _____ *(not to solve / passive)* yet. While some (19) _____ *(to worry)* others (20) _____ *(to celebrate)*. "This (21) _____ _____ *(to fuel)* speculation in the long run! In the end, the pockets of speculators (22) _____ *(to fill / passive)* even more", critics said. In fact, a major dilemma was that banks (23) _____ *(to be)* too reluctant at first to pass cheap loans on to companies that (24) _____ *(to struggle)*, although the ECB (25) _____ *(to dish out)* cheap money all the time. Banks (26) _____ *(to keep)* parking money at the Central Bank even after the ECB (27) _____ *(to introduce)* a penalty interest for that.

practice   Mixed Tenses

H   **Protecting insurance companies or customers?** *Translate into English.*

1. Da die Zinssätze seit Beginn der Finanzkrise sehr niedrig waren, klagten die Versicherungsunternehmen im Jahr 2014 immer noch über einen starken Rückgang der Erträge.

_____

_____

_____

2. Während Vertreter der Verbraucherverbände mit den Versicherern verhandelten, verabschiedete die Regierung plötzlich ein Gesetz, das es den Versicherungen erlaubte, niedrigere Renditen (= *yields*) auszuzahlen.

_____

_____

_____

3. Die Regierung wurde umgehend kritisiert, da dies bedeutete, dass die Kunden Geld verlören, das sie für ihren Ruhestand zur Seite legten, während die Versicherungen kaum Verluste machen würden.

_____

_____

_____

4. Es gibt gute Gründe für den bedeutenden politischen Einfluss der Versicherungsbranche, der 2014 erneut deutlich geworden ist.

_____

_____

5. Seit Jahrzehnten stecken die Deutschen viel Geld in Lebensversicherungspolicen, während nur relativ wenige in Aktien investieren. Voraussagen zufolge wird sich das nicht mehr auszahlen.

_____

_____

_____

6. In den Jahren des deutschen Wirtschaftswunders zahlten viele Arbeitnehmer in das Sozialsystem ein und die Ruheständler genossen hohe Renten. Viele dachten, das würde sich niemals ändern.

_____

_____

_____

I Bretton Woods

Translate the following text into English.

Bis zum heutigen Tag wurden die meisten Währungssysteme nicht sorgfältig geplant, sondern sind entwickelten sich zufällig. Der Gold-Standard war ein erster Versuch, ein universelles Währungssystem einzuführen. Er entwickelte sich in Großbritannien, das dabei war, sich zu industrialisieren *(= to become industrialized)*. Sein wirtschaftlicher Erfolg ermutigte andere, Transaktionen gemäß seinen Regeln durchzuführen. Dennoch über°dauerte er nur eine Generation. Nach dem Ersten Weltkrieg funktionierte er nicht mehr gut und bis 1936 war er Vergangenheit (*ein Ding der Vergangenheit*).

1944 wurde ein neuer Kompromiss gefunden, während der Konferenz in Bretton Woods: Die Länder koppelten *(to peg)* ihre Währungen an den Dollar, welcher wiederum (*in turn*) ans Gold gekoppelt war. Der IWF wurde geschaffen und die Weltbank wurde gegründet. Solche Organisationen, die weltweit agieren sollten, hatten vorher nie existiert. Inzwischen ist die anfängliche Begeisterung verschwunden. Die Weltbank wird seit Jahren kritisiert; viele weniger entwickelte Länder behaupten, sie sei ein politisches Instrument der Industrieländer. Seit Beginn der Eurokrise spielt der IWF allerdings eine wichtige Rolle für Länder, deren Gesamtverschuldung zu hoch ist.

theory   mixed tenses

Sequence of tenses (Zeitenfolge):

Conjunctions are often used to introduce temporal clauses.

a, Present & Future

same time or after / gleich- oder nachzeitig

The negotiator always waits until the other side loses patience.	bis
He always waits till* prices go down.	bis
The consultant looks at his boss before he starts his presentation.	bevor
He does not start until the audience is silent.	erst wenn
The two retailers will merge as soon as the regulator approves.	sobald
As he tries to open the door, the pickets hold him back.	da / als
When he meets Mark Zuckerberg he is always nervous.	(immer) wenn
When she retires, she will go back to her home country.	(dann) wenn
(How can I go to the job interview when I look like this?)	
special shade of meaning: …. wenn ich so aussehe / so wie ich aussehe.)	

before / vorzeitig

The negotiator always waits until the other side has lost patience.	bis
He always waits till* prices have gone down.	bis
He does not start until the audience has sat down.	erst als
The consultant ignores the protests after he has stopped speaking.	nachdem
The two retailers will merge as soon as the regulator has approved.	sobald
She has had shares since she left university.	seit(dem)
When she retires, she will have lived in twenty countries.	wenn

*till: is used for until in informal written English and spoken English

Watch out:
No *will*-future in the temporal clauses after those conjunctions!

Note: Some of those *conjunctions* are also **used as** *prepositions*:

conj.	prep.
We worked until/till it got dark.	We worked until/till nightfall.
We have coffee before we work.	We have coffee before work.
After he got injured he retired.	After his injury he retired.

Some may be **used as** *adverbs*, too:
They had met the night before and met again the day after.

Note: When is **used in** *other ways*, too:

"When did you start to make profits?"	(direct) question word (wann)
He asked when I would give up.	(indirect) question word (wann)
"Stop asking when we'll be profitable."	(indirect) question word (wann)
It happened at a time when the brand was famous.	(relative) pronoun
(Es geschah zu einer Zeit, zu/in der … / da / als)	

level 2

b, Past

same time / gleichzeitig

The negotiator waited until the other side lost patience.	bis
He waited till real estate prices went down.	bis
The consultant looked at his boss before he started his presentation.	bevor
He did not start until the audience was silent.	erst als
The two retailers merged as soon as the regulator approved.	sobald
As he tried to open the door, the pickets held him back.	da / als
When he met Mark Zuckerberg he was always nervous.	(immer) wenn
When she retired, she went back to her home country.	als
(Our boss made us stay longer when we wanted to finish early.	
special shade of meaning: .... wenn / wo wir doch früh aufhören wollten.)	

before / vorzeitig

The negotiator waited until the other side had lost patience.	bis
He waited till real estate prices had gone down.	bis
He did not start until the audience had sat down.	erst als
The consultant ignored the protests after he stopped speaking.	nachdem
The two retailers merged as soon as the regulator had approved.	sobald
When she retired, she had lived in twenty countries.	als

! **Watch out:** Distinguish: *if - when*

"I will set up my own company when *(as soon as)* I get the loan   *(temporal)*
           – if *on condition)* I get it."   *(conditional)*

▶ "Ich gründe meine eigene Firma, *(dann)* wenn *(sobald)* ich   *(Zeitpunkt)*
       den Kredit kriege
       – falls ich ihn kriege."   *(Bedingung)*

Will-future

The future can be expressed in several ways.
In certain cases, the *will-future* is required:

In **If-clauses**:	If sales do not pick up, we will go online.
In **forecasts**, if something is sure:	In the end Europe will lose out to emerging markets.
Decisions made **on the spot**:	These figures are confusing? I'll show you a graph.

Die allerwichtigste Grundlage für eine richtige Anwendung der Zeiten(folge) ist die Unterscheidung der beiden Zeitschienen: gleichzeitig/nachzeitig und vorzeitig.

Merkbox:

In temporalen Nebensätzen steht kein *will-future* (*We'll pay when the shipment arrives.*). Auch im Deutschen steht i.d.R. die Gegenwart. In bestimmten anderen Fällen muss das *will*-Future stehen (s.o.), während sonst meist *to be going to* – oder andere Formen möglich oder üblich sind.
Manche Konjunktionen (*before we started*) werden auch als Präpositionen (*before lunch*) oder adverbial (*the morning after*) verwendet.
Bei wenn (dt.) ist zu unterscheiden zwischen dem temporalen wenn (dann, wenn), engl. *when*, und dem konditionalen wenn (falls), engl. *if*.

practice   Mixed Tenses

K   Keep things flowing …. Logistics in China - No future … or *will*?
Complete the following sentences by putting the verbs into the Present or the will-future.

"Despite its huge economic success China still has an inefficient logistics industry at home. **If** there is no reform, China's economy (1) _____ to suffer from that."

1 to continue

"The problem will be fixed **as soon as** the government (2) _____ bigger logistics firms."

2 to create

"This will not happen **until** local protectionism (3) _____ and corruption (4) _____ _____, or **until** regulations (5) _____."

3 to decrease
4 to rein in (passive)
5 to do away with (passive)

"**When** this (6) _____ - **if** it ever (7)_____ - it (8) _____ a big bang in the Chinese logistics industry."

6 to happen
7 to happen
8 to cause

"I (9) _____ you what: China has been so incredibly fast in change management; I am absolutely sure the country (10) _____ this problem quickly **once** the government (11) _____ _____ it priority."

9 to tell
10 to solve
11 to give

"Maybe. But innovation is needed. Reforms cannot work **as long as** most warehouses (12) _____ old and **when** goods (13) _____ many times from vehicle to vehicle. – I (14) _____ _____ you pictures next time we meet."

12 to be
13 to transfer (passive)
14 to show

"**When** the government (15) _____ cargo hubs and **as soon as** trucks (16) _____ decrepit and overloaded any more, I (17) _____ _____ you."

15 to create
16 not to be
17 to believe

188

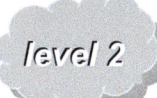

L   Prompt responses and explanations
Fill in the gaps, using the verbs in brackets in appropriate tenses.

"The board room is really stuffy now; I cannot concentrate any more."

"I (1) _____ (to open) the window. That (2) _____ (to help)."

"No, it (3) _____ (?). We (4) _____ (to take) a break. We (5) _____ (to work) twice as fast after that."

"I (6) _____ (not to think) so. We (7) _____ (to have) to start from scratch. But I (8) _____ (to go along) with it."

"There is no coffee left!"

"I (9) _____ (to tell) my secretary to make more. But I really think we (10) _____ (to have) too much already."

"Nonsense. In meetings coffee is the only thing that (11) _____ (to keep) me going."

"I (12) _____ (never to understand) that! You (13) _____ (to get) a heart condition one day."

"I (14) _____(?). Don't worry. I (15) _____ (to have) a strong heart."

M   When ..... – als *or* wenn *or* wann? *Decide, and write it down on the right.*

1. Many top executives throw away their smartphones **when** they come back from business trips to China.   _____
2. **When** the company is fully privatised it will go public.   _____
3. **When** Sony launched Vaio it created a brand that was to win dedicated followers.   _____
4. That was at a time **when** Steve Jobs was a fan of Sony.   _____
5. Many people wonder **when** Japanese electronics companies will be top performers again.   _____

Mixed Tenses

N Cyber-(in)security - *Translate the following sentences into English. Watch tenses.*

„Sie müssen ein Anti-Viren-Programm installieren, bevor Sie online gehen."

(1) _____
_____
_____

(2) _____
_____

„Das machen wir sofort – keine Sorge!"

„Gut. Ich helfe Ihnen. Sobald die Software installiert ist, werden viele Updates heruntergeladen. Danach sind Ihre Computer geschützt."

(3) _____
_____
_____
_____
_____

(4) _____
_____
_____
_____

„Wenn Berichte über gestohlene Passwörter veröffentlicht werden, überprüfen wir immer unsere gesamten Computer."

„Solange Sie keine unbekannten Dateien öffnen und ihre Firewall nicht abschalten, dürften Ihre Daten relativ sicher sein."

(5) _____
_____
_____

(6) _____
_____
_____
_____

„Ich werde daran denken. Wenn Hacker die Kontrolle übernehmen, bemerkt es ein normaler Benutzer oft erst, wenn es zu spät ist."

O **When ....** *Connect the following sentences with the help of 'when'. Be careful about what happened first - Watch the tenses!*

    e.g.: The inspectors arrived. Then the workers ran away.
        ▶ When the inspectors *arrived, the workers ran away.*

    The workers ran away. Then the inspectors arrived.
        ▶ When the inspectors arrived, *the workers had run away.*

1 The representatives of the NGO entered the sweatshop. The children were sitting in crouching positions.
   ▶ The children _____

2 The factory owner was warned. Then the police arrived.
   ▶ When the police _____

3 The workforce waited five hours. Then the CEO made an announcement.
   ▶ The workforce _____

4 Online industrial espionage was going on for a long time. Then the government eventually set up a task force.
   ▶ When the government eventually _____

5 He visited the construction site. Migrant workers were working in the sun.
   ▶ When he _____

P **When or if? – Complete.**

1 She will buy a smart fridge _____ companies have developed reliable software, not before.
2 _____ he started his laptop he realized it had been hacked.
3 The workforce would be given a pay rise _____ sales picked up.
4 The campaign will not work out _____ it is not prepared more thoroughly.
5 Wireless technology had become common _____ he started to work in R & D again.
6 _____ you didn't always open unknown files, your computer would not be infested with viruses so often.

practice　　　　　　　　　　　　　　　　　　Mixed Tenses

Q   German lessons – how to copy the German *Mittelstand*
　　　Translate the following text into English.
　　　Watch the (sequence of) tenses and the different time levels.

　　　e.g.: The truck operator **is** not reliable at all: Shipments **are** always **delayed** *(Present, Passive)*. When we **ring** them up they **claim** an unforeseen incident **has happened** or they **find** other excuses while our assembly-lines **are grinding** to a halt for lack of supplies.

　　　time level (main verb: Present)　　　same time
　　　　　　　　　　　　　　　　　　　　　　before

　　　vs.: The truck operator **was** not reliable at all: Shipments **were** always **delayed** *(Past, Passive)*. When we **rang** them up they **claimed** an unforeseen incident **had happened** or they **found** other excuses **while** our assembly-lines **were grinding** to a halt for lack of supplies.

　　　time level (main verb: Past)　　　same time
　　　　　　　　　　　　　　　　　　　　　before

---

1 Deutschlands mittelständische Unternehmen, vor allem Hersteller, sind oft Marktführer auf ihrem jeweiligen Gebiet. Man betrachtet *(to consider, personal passive)* sie als Rückgrat der deutschen Wirtschaft. Mehr als 1000 Firmen sind seit Generationen in Familienbesitz und können mit den Weltbesten konkurrieren. Aber während ausländische Unternehmen gegenwärtig versuchen, das Geschäftsmodell zu verstehen und zu kopieren, verändern sich die deutschen mittelständischen Firmen kontinuierlich. Sie werden sich allmählich [*grammatical aspect?!*] bewusst, dass sie nicht mehr nur in kleinen Städten bleiben können, und fangen an, ausländische Mitarbeiter zu rekrutieren. Bald werden auch sie global sein „in allem, was sie tun". Wir müssen von „innovativen Kunden" lernen, sagen Firmenchefs. „Wir haben aus Fehlern gelernt. Immer° wenn wir glaubten, wir hätten es geschafft, fingen wir an hinterherzuhinken."

2 Als deutsche Unternehmen in den 1960er Jahren von japanischen Firmen lernen wollten, erkannten sie sehr schnell, dass nicht alles übernommen werden konnte, da das kulturelle Umfeld in Deutschland völlig anders war. Die japanische Wirtschaft war vom Staat gelenkt und die Firmen waren sehr hierarchisch. Bevor Japan zu einem G 7-Land wurde, hatte es die Zerstörung aus dem Krieg überwinden müssen. Japan hatte es in kurzer Zeit geschafft, eine moderne Fertigungsindustrie aufzubauen. Die westlichen Industrieländer waren überrascht, wie rasch sich Japan von einer Wirtschaft mit Massenproduktion zu hohen Qualitätsstandards entwickelt hatte. Der stetige Aufstieg Japans basierte insbesondere auf dem Pflichtgefühl der Arbeiter. Es schien, als ob dies niemals enden würde, bis in den 1990er Jahren die Finanzkrise Japan traf und massive strukturelle Probleme enthüllte. Japan hat sich selbst heute nicht wirklich davon erholt.

3 Viele Aufsichtsratsvorsitzende versagen, wenn das Unternehmen plötzlich am Abgrund steht *(to face)*. Als zum Beispiel ein deutscher Stahlkonzern in eine kritische Lage geraten *(to get)* war, zögerte der Aufsichtsratsvorsitzende viel zu lange, bevor er die verantwortlichen Vorstandsmitglieder zur Rechenschaft zog. Ein Neuanfang war erst möglich, als schließlich ein neuer Geschäftsführer kam.

 **Mixed Tenses**

R Translate the following sentences into English.
   Watch tenses (and tense levels). Distinguish between 'when' and 'if'.

1. „Die Software **ist** nicht kompatibel? Ok, dann benutze ich einfach den Overhead-Projektor, auch wenn das aus der Mode ist und ich schon lange nicht mehr mit Folien gearbeitet habe. Wenn ich unter Zeitdruck arbeite, habe ich immer einen Plan B." – „Ok. Das vergesse ich nie."

2. Die Berater **hörten** nicht auf zu reden, bis sie der Firmenchef hinauswarf. Allerdings hatten sie bereits viele Mitarbeiter verärgert und demotiviert, bevor der Personalchef die Frustration merkte (to realize). Als er das erste Mal zu Gesprächen hinzukam (to join), diskutierten die Mitarbeiter der ganzen Abteilung, wann und wie sie sich verteidigen würden.

3. Seit der fehlgeschlagenen Rettung vor fünf Jahren kämpft die traditionelle Kaufhauskette ums Überleben. Wenn sie gefragt werden, sagen Führungskräfte immer, die Kunden kauften lieber online ein. Aber stimmt das wirklich? Wären die Kunden dem Kaufhaus nicht treu geblieben, wenn die Strategie nicht immer wieder geändert worden wäre, was die Kunden jedes Mal verwirrt hat? Im Augenblick sucht der Geschäftsführer wieder einen neuen Investor.

Continue:

4. Vor einigen Jahren zwang die EU-Kommission die Banken, ihre Gebühren an Geldautomaten zu senken. Vor allem bei (= *für*) Abhebungen im Ausland waren die Gebühren oft zu hoch gewesen.

5. 2014 feierte die Nürnberg-Messe *(Nuremberg Fair)* ihren 40. Geburtstag. Sie war zur sechstgrößten Messe in Deutschland geworden und es wurde erwartet *(personal passive)*, dass sie weiter wachsen würde. Allerdings gab es Bedenken, dass der kränkelnde *(ailing)* Flughafen das Wachstum der Messe beeinträchtigen könnte, wenn die Passagierzahlen nicht steigen würden.

6. Nach dem Zusammenbruch von Enron fragten sich viele Analysten, wie solcher Betrug möglich gewesen war. Hatten die Rechnungsprüfer wirklich nichts entdeckt? Wie rücksichtslos die Geschäftsführer gehandelt hatten, wurde erst klar, als ein angeklagtes Vorstandsmitglied zum Whistleblower *(whistleblower)* wurde.

7. „Wann beenden die Zeitarbeiter ihren Hungerstreik, den sie vor einer Woche begonnen haben?" – „Sie werden weitermachen, bis die Agentur bessere Bedingungen gewährt. …. Ich würde das jedenfalls tun."

theory  mixed tenses

Non-finite forms (infinite Verbformen):

Participles and infinitives are **non-finite**, depending on a main verb for tenses.

Infinite Formen werden nicht konjugiert und sind daher **unbestimmt**.
Sie hängen vom Hauptverb – und meist dem Subjekt - des Satzes ab.

Participles

Present participle (active meaning):   writing   having written *(vorzeitig)*
Past participle (passive meaning):   written   being written *(Verlauf)*

Do not mix up:

Participle   vs. Progressive Forms   and   Passive!
Signing   vs. He **is** signing the contract.   The contract **is** signed.

Participles may be used as adjectives

e.g.: a signing ceremony (Unterzeichnungsfeierlichkeit)
      a written contract (schriftlicher Vertrag)

Watch out:

Partizipialkonstruktionen *(-ing clauses)* werden sehr 'flexibel' und häufig verwendet und treten in einer **Vielzahl von Funktionen** auf, da sie formal - zeitlich, von Person und Zahl her - nicht festgelegt sind *(paying – wann? wer? wie viele?)*; sie kreisen *wie Satelliten um Subjekt und (Haupt-)Verb*.

Das ist sehr **praktisch**, aber auch nicht ganz un**tückisch**, denn es kann leicht zu völliger Beliebigkeit und damit Unverständnis oder Missverständnissen führen, wenn nicht einige **Grundregeln** beachtet werden:

1. Das **Partizip bezieht sich** normalerweise **auf das vorausgehende Substantiv**.

   The participle refers to the noun before.

   e.g.: The executive watched his colleague making a first draft.
   He handed over the business card printed out specially for the occasion.
   An employee arriving early discovered the theft.

2. In partizipialen Nebensätzen (-ing clauses) bezieht sich das Partizip oft auf das **Subjekt und Verb des** (konjugierten) **Hauptsatzes** und richtet sich in Zeit(ebene), Person und Zahl nach diesen, da es selbst unbestimmt ist.

3. Ein vollständiger **Satz** kann **nicht allein aus Partizipien** bestehen, er braucht ein **Subjekt und** ein konjugiertes **(Haupt-)Verb** als ‚**Verankerung**', damit die **Aussage bestimmt** ist.

level 3

Frequent uses of participle constructions (-ing clauses):

a, temporal clauses (*temporale Nebensätze – Varianten*)

- actions occurring **simultaneously** (*parallele Handlungen*)
  ⇒ Here the participle can come **before or after** the *main clause*.)

    She was sitting opposite the CEO, **taking** notes all the time.
    ▶ Sie saß dem Vorstand gegenüber **und machte** die ganze Zeit über Notizen.

    Sitting opposite the CEO, *she* took the minutes.
    ▶ Sie saß dem Vorstand gegenüber **und führte** Protokoll.

- an **action followed by another** (*aufeinanderfolgende Handlungen*)

    Wielding his fork like a weapon *he* continued to bargain.
    ▶ Er **schwang** seine Gabel wie eine Waffe **und** verhandelte weiter.

    Looking up from the contract *he* reached for his mobile phone.
    ▶ Er **sah** vom Vertrag auf **und** griff nach seinem Handy.

    Reading the business report *she* joined the meeting.
    ▶ Den Geschäftsbericht **lesend** ging sie in die Besprechung.

    Having read the business report (**before!**) *she* joined the meeting.
    ▶ Nachdem *sie* den Geschäftsbericht gelesen hatte, ging *sie* in die Besprechung.
    ⇒ zur Klarstellung der zeitlichen Verhältnisse, einer früheren Handlung (**Vorzeitigkeit**) wird – bei Verwechslungsgefahr - das *Past Participle* verwendet.)

- an **action following another,** possibly as a **result** of the first (*nachfolgende Handlung*, **als** *Ergebnis* oder *Folge der ersten*)

    He jumped up in anger, **knocking** over the teapot.
    ▶ Er sprang wütend auf und **stieß (dabei)** die Teekanne um.

b, indicating a **reason** (replacing a clause with *because, as, since*); esp. ***being*** (*kausaler Nebensatz*)

Being in the red *the company* was unable to buy new equipment. (*Da die Firma ...*)
Knowing that *he* would soon run out of cash *he* went public. (*Da er wußte ...*)

The day **being** *fine we* decided to meet in the open. (***Partizip* *direkt* nach dem Subjekt!**)
(*Da es ein schöner Tag war*, beschlossen wir, uns im Freien zu treffen.)
⇒ absolute Partizipialkonstruktion: **eigenes Subjekt im Partizipialsatz!** **[Avoid!]**

c, after verbs of sensation (nach *Verben der sinnlichen Wahrnehmung*)

He saw the team **arguing** and heard the secretary **whispering** into the phone.
▶ Er sah das Team **streiten** und hörte, wie die Sekretärin ins Telefon flüsterte.

(Hier kann **auch der Infinitiv – ohne *to* –** stehen, i.d.R. dann, **wenn** man die **gesamte Handlung von Anfang bis Ende wahrgenommen** hat.)

d, as relative clauses (*verkürzte Relativsätze*)

The construction firm **making** the lowest bid got the deal.   (*aktivischer Sinn!*)
(= The construction firm **that/which was making / made** the lowest bid ...)

He resold the business **acquired** a year before.   (*passivischer Sinn!*)
(= He resold the business **that/which he had acquired** a year before.)

mixed tenses

! **Distinguish:**
Present Participle (*aktivischer Sinn*) **vs. Past Participle** (*passivischer Sinn*):

aktivisch:

Convincing the shareholders that there was a market gap, *he* got them to vote for him.
► *Er* überzeugte die Aktionäre davon, dass es eine Marktlücke gab und brachte sie (so) dazu, für ihn zu stimmen.

Having convinced the whole board of his new strategy, *he* first changed the brand image.
► Nachdem *er* / Da *er* den gesamten Vorstand von seiner neuen Strategie überzeugt hatte, änderte *er* zunächst das Markenimage.

➲ *He convinced them, acted himself. (Das **Bezugswort** tut etwas, **handelt** selbst, ist **aktiv**.)*

passivisch:

Convinced that his product filled a market gap, *he* paid too much for the licence.
► Überzeugt, dass ... / Da *er* überzeugt war, dass ...

(Having been) warned about child labour, *the retailer* started an investigation.
► Da *der Einzelhändler* vor ... gewarnt worden war / Gewarnt vor ....

➲ *He was convinced or warned, i.e. something was done to him.*
 *(Das **Bezugswort** 'erleidet' etwas, etwas wird ihm / mit ihm getan, es ist **passiv**.)*

To clarify the meaning, the following words can be added:
*(in a, and b, **not** in c, and d, - see previous page)*

When / while / after / before leaving her company Sheila realized ...	temporal
Since leaving her company Sheila has realized ...	temporal
In (= *in the process of*) drafting my business plan I became aware of ...	temporal
On (= *when*) writing her application she discovered that ...	temporal
By asking the right questions team leaders can find out ... ► *Dadurch dass ... / indem* sie die richtigen Fragen stellen, ...	manner Mittel/Art & Weise
If / Even if / Whether/ Unless arriving by plane, please let us know.	Condition
The CEO will not come **unless / until / even if / (al)though** invited.	Contracted passive

---

! **Watch out: Misrelated participles**

As we know, normally a participle construction must have the same subject.
 e.g.: *He* handed over the business card, *holding* it with both hands.
 Cheated by his business partner *he* lost his entire fortune.

But not: When using this app *it* must not be forgotten .... ➲ *it uses!*

Waiting for the flight *a suitcase* fell on my foot. ➲ *a suitcase waits!*

Believing I was the only candidate *the presence* of ➲ *the presence believes!*
all the others made me nervous.

Infinitives e.g.: They seem ...

	Simple	Continuous	Passive
Present Inf.	to work hard	to be working hard	to be ignored
Past Inf.	to have worked hard	to have been working...	to have been ignored

Some major **uses** of the **infinitive** are the following:

Purpose	Let's meet **to discuss** the project.	um ... zu besprechen
relative clause after superlatives & first, second, ..., last, only	He was the first **to see** this opportunity. She was the only woman **to be invited**. His plan was the easiest **to realize**.	...der erste, der ... sah ... die einzige ..., die eingeladen wurde. ... der, der am einfachsten umzusetzen war.
certain verbs (know, wonder, find out, understand, explain) with how & wh-clauses	He did not know how **to set up** a company. She explained how **to sell** the product.	Er wusste nicht, wie man eine Firma gründet / wie er eine Firma gründen sollte. Sie erklärte, wie man das Produkt verkauft.

Satzgefüge:

Having applied for several positions **to avoid** becoming unemployed I was stunned to hear my boss **asking** me whether I would agree to stay in the company if **promoted**. Very **pleased** I said yes and turned down the offers **made** by headhunters **searching** on Xing.

*Infinite Verbformen sind im Englischen beliebt und relativ **häufig**. Gerade weil sie aber unbestimmt (infinit) sind, d.h. nicht durch Flexion (Endungen etc.) eindeutig zugeordnet, sind eine **korrekte zeitliche Verankerung** (wann?) und **korrekte Bezüge** (wer tut was?) **im Hauptsatz** umso zwingender erforderlich.*
Daher: Sparsam, gezielt und korrekt verknüpft verwenden!

Merkbox:

Partizipien erfüllen viele Zwecke, sind formal *unbestimmt* und damit sehr **flexibel** einsetzbar, aber auch trügerisch. Sie allein **bilden keinen Satz** und richten sich entweder **nach dem vorausgehenden Substantiv oder** nach dem **Subjekt des Hauptsatzes**. Das **Hauptverb** legt die **Zeitebene** fest.

Partizipien können *aktivisch* (*Present Participle*) oder *passivisch* (*Past Participle*) gebraucht werden; auch der **Verlauf** kann ausgedrückt werden (*while being unloaded*). Durch **Voranstellung** von *while, when* etc. kann die **Bedeutung präzisiert** werden.

Vorsicht vor falsch bezogenen (*misrelated*) Partizipien (**unterschiedl. Subjekt!**).

Auch der **Infinitiv** hat infinite **Formen**, die allerdings **aktivischen, passivischen** Sinn und den **Verlauf** ausdrücken können und je nachdem zu **unterscheiden** sind.

practice — Mixed Tenses

S   A case for defence
Contract the following relative clauses and indirect questions, using participles or infinitives.

1   The news about German weapons that were found in Colombia have caused a fierce political debate.

   ► The news about weapons _____ in Colombia ...

2   As Colombia is a country that is classified as unstable weapons exports there are not permitted.

   ► As Colombia is a country _____
   weapons exports there are not permitted.

3   Journalists who have been trying to disclose the hidden sales channels have found out that the weapons that were sold to the Colombian police had been bought from a well-known German manufacturer by a US company and had then been re-sold to Colombia. (2 x)

   ► Journalists _____ to disclose the hidden sales channels have found out that the weapons _____ to the Colombian police had been bought from a well-known German manufacturer by a US company and had then been re-sold to Colombia.

4   As it seems, the authorities do not know how they can prevent re-exports from friendly countries to dangerous regions effectively.

   ► As it seems, the authorities do not know _____
   re-exports from friendly countries to dangerous regions effectively.

5   There are rumours of new laws which are to be passed and tighter monitoring measures which are intended to prevent similar cases in future. (2 x)

   ► There are rumours of new laws _____
   and tighter monitoring measures _____ to prevent similar cases in future.

6   All government officials who have been interviewed again and again on television have been trying to justify the security standards in place.

   ► All government officials _____ again and again on television have been trying to justify the security standards in place.

7   They are not the first to fail to calm the public about weapons which were produced in Germany and which ended up in countries that were never meant to have access to such technology.

   (3 x) ► They are not the first to fail to calm the public about weapons _____ in Germany, and _____ in countries _____ to have access to such technology.

200

T Sanitation in India
Active or passive - Fill in the correct participle forms of the verbs in brackets.

(1) _____ (consider) an emerging economy with huge development potential, India is still struggling with typical third-world problems (2) _____ (hamper) its growth and (3) _____ (keep) living standards low, esp. in rural areas, where blackouts (4) _____ (cause) by a weak infrastructure are quite common. Another serious issue is open defecation, with nearly 600m Indians not (5) _____ (have) a toilet and (6) _____ (force) to relieve themselves behind bushes or by the roadside. (7) Deeply _____ (worry) by the lack of hygiene (8) _____ (threaten) India's public health, Mohandas Gandhi said a long time ago that good sanitation was more important than independence. Open defecation is disastrous when (9) _____ (practise) by groups in close contact with each other. India is a country with a large population (10) _____ (grow) rapidly in densely (11) _____ (populate) areas so that hygiene issues have become a major concern, with worms and bacteria from human intestines (12) _____ (spread) diseases, in large part by (13) _____ (pollute) the groundwater. (14) _____ (contaminate) water is certainly one of the major challenges (15) _____ (require) urgent solutions.
Another result of open sanitation, too often totally (16) _____ (ignore), is a problem with public safety: A few months ago, two adolescent girls (17) _____ (visit) a field (18) _____ (use) as a public toilet were raped and murdered.
While (19) _____ (upset) the public, those cases have not led to (20) _____ (increase) efforts in the fight for better hygiene; many politicians seem to believe that hygiene is a problem of the poor and less (21) _____ (educate) Indians and that the first issue to be tackled is poverty, which is the root of the evil (22) _____ (lead) to bad cultural practices, partly (23) _____ (cause) by a lack of education.

practice

Mixed Tenses

U Translate the underlined passages in the following sentences into German. Look at the main clause/verb to find an adequate translation fitting into the context.

1 Alerted by a wave of hostile takeovers from abroad the government passed new laws aimed at protecting the domestic industry.

▶ _____, verabschiedete die Regierung neue Gesetze _____

_____.

2 Although warned by business partners that the new foreign supplier did not always stick to the agreements signed solemnly at the beginning of the cooperation, the car manufacturer decided to rely fully and exclusively on that supplier, taking the risk of facing sudden problems.

▶ Obwohl _____,

dass der neue ausländische Zulieferer sich nicht immer an die

_____ hielt,

beschloss der Autohersteller, sich vollständig und exklusiv auf den

Zulieferer zu verlassen _____

_____.

3 The goods cannot be delivered franco domicile unless paid in advance.

▶ Die Waren können nicht frei Haus geliefert werden, _____

_____.

4 (When) arriving at the port he saw the containers being unloaded.

▶ _____ sah er,

_____.

5 With so many shareholders selling their shares in panic, the company was faced with an unprecedented slump of its share price.

▶ _____

war das Unternehmen mit einem noch nie dagewesenen Verfall seines

Aktienkurses konfrontiert.

6 By selling his government bonds the investor signaled a change of mind possibly causing a domino effect making borrowing pricier for the country.

_____

signalisierte der Investor einen Gesinnungswandel _____

_____.

V **Commercial correspondence** *level 3*
Fill in the gaps using the verbs in brackets. Be careful about the correct forms of the <u>participles and infinitives</u> required.

a, Dear Mr Williams

Thank you very much for our meeting last week and the samples (1) _____ (*send*) promptly to our head office. (2) _____ (*wait*) impatiently to test the new material (3) _____ (*use*) in your cartridges our engineers examined the compatibility with our technology immediately. Your cartridges have been found (4) _____ (*be*) fully compatible with all our models. Currently they are the best (5) _____ (*meet*) our requirements. Therefore I am pleased (6) _____ (*place*) a trial order for a small quantity. You will find (7) _____ (*enclose*) (8) _____ (*detail*) test results and specifications (9) _____ (*include*) our tolerance margins. (10) _____ (*enclose*) you will also find drawings of the shapes of the containers (11) _____ (*need*) for our new product line. Please send your current export price list (12) _____ (*quote*) prices FOB Singapore. (13) _____ (*give*) the high transportation costs, however, we consider the quantity discounts (14) _____ (*offer*) uncompetitive and hope you will be able to grant more favourable ones. (15) _____ (*face*) global competition we have to use every leverage on price. (16) _____ (*hope*) for a long-term business partnership we are looking forward to your reply.

Kind regards

Charles Johnson

b, Dear Charles

(1) _____ (*refer*) to your letter and your engineers' positive test results we are pleased to inform you that we will be able to carry out a small trial order within one or two weeks – if (2) _____ (*require*). Unfortunately, we do not see any possibility of granting higher discounts than the ones already (3) _____ (*offer*), as the raw material costs are rather high – as (4) _____ (*explain*) before. (5) _____ (*convince*) that you will be very satisfied with the quality of our innovative material, we are looking forward to your initial order.

Kind regards

Ian Williams

practice — Mixed Tenses

W **Beware of misrelated participles. Right (R) or wrong (W)?**

1 Believing there was a market gap the product was launched. _____

2 Seeing no chance of survival for his SME the entrepreneur finally sold his patent. _____

3 When granting generous discounts the lost revenues must not be forgotten _____

4 Before launching a marketing campaign the target group must be defined properly. _____

5 Surprised by his own success the inventor did not use his full potential. _____

6 Infested by viruses the executive had to have his operating system checked. _____

X **Translate the following sentences into English.**
Use participles and infinitives for the relative clauses wherever possible.

1 Der vom Vorstandsvorsitzenden offen zugegebene Vertrauensbruch ist ein neuer Beweis des ernsten Konfliktes zwischen den Vorstandmitgliedern.

_____

_____

2 Die Flaschen sind in Holzkisten zu liefern, wie vertraglich festgelegt. Die letzten Monat zurückgesandte fehlerhafte Ware (= Güter) kann mit der nächsten Lieferung durch neue Produkte derselben Qualität ersetzt werden.

_____

_____

_____

_____

3 Die bereits vor Wochen bestellten Textilien müssen aus demselben Stoff gefertigt (= gemacht) sein wie letztes Mal, wenn nicht anders spezifiziert.

_____

_____

4 Er war der einzige Kunde, dem klar war, dass die Bank gelogen hatte.

_____

5 Sie wollte von ihrem hoch bezahlten Berater wissen, wie sie ihr schwer verschuldetes Unternehmen retten sollte.

_____

_____

Y   **An automotive group set to reinvent itself**
Translate the following text into English.
Use participles and infinitives wherever it is appropriate.

Trotz steigender Absatzzahlen und boomender Nachfrage in China verkündete der Automobilkonzern, der jahrelang Rekordgewinne verzeichnet hatte, ein massives Kostenkürzungsprogramm, mit dessen Hilfe vor allem unrentable Sparten konsolidiert werden sollten. Obwohl weit erfolgreicher als französische Rivalen, musste der Konzern schließlich erkennen, dass er begonnen hatte, hinter technologischen Veränderungen herzuhinken. Die in aufstrebenden Märkten hergestellten billigen SUVs bedrohten die jedes Jahr geringer werdenden Gewinnspannen auch auf dem einheimischen Markt. Da *(With ….)* der Absatz in der EU aufgrund gesättigter Märkte stagniert, musste sich der traditionelle Autohersteller neu erfinden, um zu überleben.
Der erste, der das erkannte, war nicht der Vorstandsvorsitzende, sondern der Chefingenieur, der bei vielen Gelegenheiten öffentlich kritisiert worden war. Er brüskierte *(to affront)* den gesamten Vorstand mit der Erklärung *(dadurch, dass er erklärte)*, der Konzern würde in den kommenden Jahren Marktanteile verlieren. Auf der Jahreshauptversammlung überzeugte die von ihm präsentierte Lösung jedoch die Mehrzahl der Aktionäre: Es wurde beschlossen, dass der Konzern in umweltfreundliche Technologie wie Elektromotoren und Hybridantriebe investieren würde, um von der steigenden Nachfrage in Schwellenländern zu profitieren und *(while)* zugleich die Luftverschmutzung zu bekämpfen.

practice

Mixed Tenses

Z   a, Recipe for success of a German discounter
Fill in the gaps with the verbs in brackets. Do not add anything else (pronouns, and etc.). Use participles whenever possible. (It is not always the case!) - Watch the tenses, active and passive forms.

In July 2014, the secretive *Aldi* group lost its second founder, Karl Albrecht, who was a faithful Catholic (1) _____ (to make) his convictions the fundament of his business. He was known for keeping his managers on a long leash, still (2) _____ (to put) a lot of emphasis on personal reliability; he was even reported (3) _____ (to criticize) executives not (4) _____ (to live) in intact personal relationships, if that (5) _____ (to make) public. Employees (6) _____ (to want) to make a career had to agree (7) _____ (to accomplish) all kinds of tasks, from (8) _____ (to help out) at the cash register to (9) _____ (to re-fill) the shelves. Typically, outsiders hardly (10) _____ (to get) a real chance of (11) _____ (to rise) to the top management of the company while junior staff (12) _____ (to give) quite considerable responsibilities very quickly, with wages (13) _____ (to be) above the average of the industry. From the beginning to the present day, *Aldi*'s leadership structures (14) _____ (to be; always) clearly hierarchical, thus (15) _____ (to alienate) many Germans (16) who _____ (to be used) to flat hierarchies. Karl Albrecht's death (17) _____ (to announce) only five days later illustrates the systematic secrecy of the company (18) _____ (to point out) many times in business reports. The discounter revolutionized food retailing in Germany, the four basic principles of success (19) _____ (to be) the strict company culture (20) _____ (to mention) above, a clear strategy (21) _____ (to imitate) by others without much success, the market dominance and the family in the background. (22) _____ (to fall) ill with cancer several times, Karl Albrecht's son announced publicly a few years ago that he (23) _____ (never to play) an active part in the company, thus (24) _____ (to leave) room for speculations about the future of the discounter which had dominated the market for so long.

Z **b, Removing old structures at Microsoft**

Replace the underlined participles and infinitives in the following sentences by full clauses.

1   <u>Having taken over</u> from Steve Ballmer in February 2014, the new boss of Microsoft, Satya Nadella, <u>seen</u> as a sign of culture change in the company, announced a huge wave of layoffs. He had already sent out emails to all employees, <u>explaining</u> that the corporate culture had to be changed fundamentally.

▶ _____ from Steve Ballmer in February 2014, the new boss of Microsoft, Satya Nadella, _____ as a sign of culture change in the company, announced the biggest wave of layoffs in Microsoft's history so far. He had already sent out emails to all employees _____ that the corporate culture had to be changed.

2   The restructuring measures were especially targeted at the mobile phone division of Nokia, just <u>taken over</u>, <u>creating</u> double structures <u>to be done away with</u>.

▶ The restructuring measures were especially targeted at the mobile phone division of Nokia _____ double structures _____.

3   <u>While still enjoying</u> fat profits which pleased its shareholders, Microsoft was faced with enormous problems in the world of smartphones and tablets where it was lagging behind in innovation, <u>not being able</u> to compete with Apple or Samsung.

▶ While _____ fat profits which pleased its shareholders, Microsoft was faced with enormous problems in the world of smartphones and tablets where it was lagging behind in innovation _____ to compete with Apple and Samsung.

c, Translate into German.

1   By emphasizing the 'core business' of the company again and again, Nadella fuelled speculations that he would divest the loss-making tablet division, concentrating on the traditional software business instead.

_____
_____
_____

2   Analysts said: "Maybe seeing himself as the first to represent the new spirit, Nadella is determined to carry out his strategic plan – unless proved wrong by rocketing tablet sales very soon."

_____
_____
_____

VOCABULARY: English - German

e   d

abroad *adv.*	im Ausland
absent-minded *adj.*	geistesabwesend
abuse *n.*	Missbrauch
abyss *n.*	Abgrund
access *vt*	Zugang, Zutritt haben (zu *etw.*);
accession *n.* (to)	Beitritt (zu)
accordance *n.* (in ≈ with)	Übereinstimmung (in ≈ mit, gemäß)
according *adv.* (to)	gemäß
account for *vi*	ausmachen (*z.B.:* Das macht 5 % des BIP aus.)
account *n.* (hold so. to ≈)	Verantwortung; Rechenschaft (*jmdn.* zur Verantwortung ziehen); Konto
accountant *n.*	Buchhalter(in), -führer(in); Rechnungsführer(in); Bilanzbuchhalter(in); Rechnungsprüfer(in)
accusation *n.*	Anschuldigung, Beschuldigung; Anklage
achieve *vt*	erzielen
achievement *n.*	Leistung; Errungenschaft
acquisition *n.*	Erwerb, (Auf-)Kauf
act *vi*	handeln
actress / actor *n.*	Schauspielerin / Schauspieler
add to *vi* (!)	hinzufügen, vergrößern
adjust (to) *vt*	anpassen (an)
admit *vt*	einräumen, zugeben
adolescent *adj.*	jugendlich, heranwachsend
adopt *vt* (*sth.* from *so.*)	übernehmen (*etw.* von *jmdm.*)
advantageous *adj.*	vorteilhaft
advertising campaign *n.*	Werbekampagne
advice note *n.*	Versandanzeige
advisor *n.*	Berater
affect *vt*	beeinträchtigen; betreffen; beeinflussen
after all *adv.*	letztendlich; schließlich (doch)
age *n.* (for ages)	Alter; Zeitalter; (seit ewigen Zeiten)
agency *n.* (advertising ≈)	Agentur (Werbe-≈)
agenda *n.* (on the ≈)	Tagesordnung (auf der ≈)
agreement *n.*	Abkommen, Vereinbarung
aid *n.* (structural ≈)	Hilfe (Struktur-≈)
ailing *adj.*	marode, kränkelnd
aircraft (*sg.*), aircraft (*pl.*!) *n.*	Flugzeug; Flugzeuge
airline *n.*	Fluggesellschaft
alert *vt*	alarmieren
alienate *vt*	verprellen; vor den Kopf stoßen
alleged *adj.*	angeblich, mutmaßlich
alliance *n.*	Allianz, Bündnis
ally *n.*	Verbündeter; Aliierter
alternative *n.*	Alternative
alumnus (*sg.*), alumni (*pl.*) *n.*	Alumnus, Ehemaliger (*sg.*), Alumni, Ehemalige (*pl.*)
ambitious *adj.*	ehrgeizig
ancient *adj.*	antik; (ur)alt
animal testing *n.*	Tierversuche

anniversary *n.*	Geburtstag, Jahrestag
announcement *n.*	Ankündigung
annual general meeting (AGM) *n.*	(ordentliche) Hauptversammlung (HV)
anti-corruption department, compliance department *n.*	Antikorruptionsabteilung
anti-virus *adj.* software *n*	Antiviren-Software
anxious *adj.*	ängstlich, besorgt
appalling *adj.*	entsetzlich, fürchterlich, schrecklich; mies
appear *vi* (in court)	erscheinen (vor Gericht)
applicant *n.*	Bewerber(in)
application *n.*	Bewerbung
appointment *n.* (have an ≈)	Termin (haben)
approach *n.*	Ansatz, (methodische) Herangehensweise; Annäherung
approve *vt*	billigen; genehmigen
argue *vi*	argumentieren
arrest *vt*	festnehmen
assemble *vt*	zusammenbauen, montieren
assembly line *n.*	Fließband; Montageband
attend *vt* (a meeting)	teilnehmen (an einer Besprechung)
audience *n.* (*sg.*)	Zuhörerschaft; Publikum
auditor *n.*	Rechnungsprüfer(in)
austerity *n.* (measures)	Austerität; Strenge; (Sparmaßnahmen)
authorities *n. pl.!*	Behörden
autobiography *n.*	Autobiographie
automated teller machine (ATM) *n.*	Geldautomat
automotive *adj.* (group)	Automobil(konzern)
avail *n.*	Gewinn; Nutzen
to no ≈	vergeblich, umsonst
available *adj.*	erhältlich; verfügbar
award *n.*	Auszeichnung, Preis
backbone *n.*	Rückgrat
backlog *n.*	Rückstau (an Aufträgen *etc.*)
bacterium (*sg.*), bacteria (*pl.*)	Bakterium, Bakterien
bail *so.* out *vt*	*jmdm.* aus der Klemme helfen, *jmdn.* auslösen (finanziell)
balance *n.*	Gleichgewicht
balance of trade, trade balance *n.*	Handelsbilanz
ban *vt*	ausschließen; verbieten
banknote *n.*	(Geld-)Schein, Banknote
bankruptcy *n.*	Insolvenz, Bankrott
bargain (hunter) *n.*	Schnäppchen(jäger)
Bavarian *adj.*	bayerisch
be fed up (with) *vi*	satthaben (*etw.*)
be grounded (*passive*) *v.*	am Boden bleiben
bear *vt* fruit *n.*	Früchte tragen
benefit *vi*	profitieren
bid (takeover ≈) *n.*	Angebot (Übernahme-≈)
birth rate *n.*	Geburtenrate, -quote
bit by bit; little by little; gradually *adv.*	nach und nach
blackmail *vt*	erpressen
blackout *n.*	Stromausfall
blame *vt* (*so.* for *sth.*)	(*jmdm.*) die Schuld geben (für/an)

blueprint *n.*	Blaupause; Plan; Vorlage; Entwurf
blur *vt*	verwischen; verschwimmen lassen
board *n.*	Vorstand (alle ≈s-Mitglieder)
board of supervisors *n.*	Aufsichtsrat
body *n.*	Körper; Körperschaft; Gremium; Institution
bonds *n.*: government ≈	Staatsanleihen
bonus *n.* (Christmas ≈)	Leistungsprämie (Weihnachtsgeld)
book (a flight) *vt*	buchen (einen Flug)
booking *n.*	Buchung, Reservierung
boom *vi*	boomen
boost (profits) *vt*	in die Höhe treiben, befeuern
borrow *vt* (money)	(aus)leihen (Geld), (Geld) aufnehmen
borrower *n.*	Kreditnehmer; Entleiher; Borger
boss *n.*	Chef
boycott *n.*	Boykott
brain drain *n.*	Abwanderung von (hoch)qualifizierten (Fach-, Arbeits-) Kräften
brain *n.* (monkey ≈)	Gehirn; Hirn (Affen-≈)
brand image *n.*	Markenimage
brand *n.*	Marke
breach of trust *n.*	Vertrauensbruch
bribe *n.*	Bestechungsgeld
bribe *vt*	bestechen
BRIC (Brazil, Russia, India, China)	Bric(-Staaten)
bring forth *vt*, create *vt*	hervorbringen
broad *adj.*	breit, weit
brochure *n.*	Broschüre
bubble *n.*	Blase; (Spekulations-)Blase
budget flight, cheap flight *n.*	Billigflug
budget *n.*	Budget; Haushalt
bulk *n.*	Großteil
bullying *n.*	Mobbing
bumpy *adj.*	holprig
burden *n.*	Bürde, Last
bureaucrat *n.*	Bürokrat
burn down *vi/vt*	Brennen (nieder-≈)
business card *n.*	Visitenkarte
business ethics *n.*	Wirtschaftsethik
business *n.*	Geschäft
to do business (*sg.!*) uncountable *n.!*	Geschäfte (*Pl.*) tätigen, ≈ machen
to get down to business (*sg.!*) uncountable *n.!*	sich an die Arbeit machen
So. means business *(sg.!)* uncountable *n.!*	Jmd. meint es ernst.
to run a (!) business countable *n.!*	eine Firma führen
So. is in the oil business.	Jmd. ist im Ölgeschäft / in der Ölindustrie / in der Ölbranche
business people *n. pl.*	Geschäftsleute
business practices *n. pl.*	Geschäftsgepflogenheiten
bust (*coll.*)	zerbrochen; erledigt; pleite
buy up *vt*	aufkaufen
calculate *vt* (costs)	berechnen, kalkulieren (Kosten)
call off *vt*	absagen
calm *vt*	beruhigen
campaign *n.* (advertising ≈)	Kampagne (Werbe-≈)

cancel *vt*	stornieren; absagen
cancer *n.*	Krebs (*Krankheit*)
capital *n.* (start-up ≈ , initial ≈)	Kapital (Start-≈); Hauptstadt
capitalism *n.*	Kapitalismus
capture *vt*	kapern; erobern; gefangennehmen
car manufacturer *n.*	Autohersteller
career *n.* (path)	Karriere(weg); Berufslaufbahn
careful *adj.*	sorgfältig
cargo *n.* (*pl.*: cargoes)	Fracht
carpet *n.*	Teppich
carry on *vt* (a project)	fortsetzen (ein Projekt)
carry out *vt*	etwas durchführen, ausführen
cartel *n.* (drug ≈)	Kartell (Drogen-≈)
cartridge *n.*	Patrone; Kartusche (*Drucker*)
cash cow *n.*	Goldesel; Unternehmen mit hoher Liquidität
cash flow *n.*	Cashflow
cash register *n.*	Kasse; Tages-, Registrierkasse
catalogue (BE); catalog (AE) *n.*	Katalog
catch up (with) *vi*	aufholen (mit)
celebrate *vi/vt*	feiern (*etw.*)
cellphone, mobile phone *n.*	Handy
centre (BE), center (AE) *n.*	Zentrum
CFO (Chief Financial Officer) *n.*	Finanzvorstand
challenge *n.*	Herausforderung
chamber of commerce *n.*	Handelskammer
change of mind *n.*	Gesinnungswandel
change *vi/vt*	(sich) wandeln, ändern
chaos *n.* (end in ≈)	Chaos (im ≈ enden)
charge *vt*	beauftragen (*jmdn.*); belasten (Konto); beschuldigen
charge *vt* (fees)	berechnen (Gebühren); belasten (Konto)
charitable *adj.*	wohltätig
chat *n.*	Unterhaltung
cheat *vt*	betrügen
check *vt*	überprüfen
chief engineer *n.*	Chefingenieur
Chief Executive Officer (CEO) *n.*	Vorstandsvorsitzender, Geschäftsführer
child labour (BE), ≈ labor (AE) *n.*	Kinderarbeit
choice *n.* (no other ≈)	Wahl (keine andere ≈)
choke off *vt*	ersticken; abwürgen
choosy *adj.*	wählerisch
citizen *n.*	Bürger
civil rights *n.*	Bürgerrechte
civil war *n.*	Bürgerkrieg
clear (debts) *vt*	tilgen (Schulden)
client *n.*	Kunde (Geschäfts- ≈ ; Service- ≈)
climate (change)	Klima(wandel)
climb *vt*, (≈ over sth.)	(er)klettern; (≈ über etw.)
close down *vt*	schließen, still-legen
coastal *adj.* (areas)	Küsten-(Gebiete)
coin *n.*	Münze
collapse *n.*	Zusammenbruch
collapse *vi*	zusammenbrechen

colleague n.	Kollege/Kollegin
column n.	Säule; Spalte (Tabelle)
comment n. (no ≈)	Kommentar (kein ≈)
comment vt	kommentieren
commentator n.	Kommentator
commercial n. sg.; commercials n.pl.	Werbespot; Werbespots; Fernsehwerbung
committed adj.	engagiert
common adj.	allgemein; üblich; gängig
company rules n.	Unternehmensregeln
company, enterprise n.	Unternehmen
compatible adj.	kompatibel
compensate vt (losses)	ausgleichen (Verluste)
compensation (CEO ≈)	Gehalt (des Vorstandsvorsitzenden)
compensation n.	Gehalt, Entlohnung (hochrangig)
compete (with) vi	konkurrieren (mit)
competitive adj.	(Firma) konkurrenzfähig; (Markt) umkämpft
competitiveness n.	Wettbewerbsfähigkeit
competitor n.	Konkurrent, Wettbewerber
complain (about sth.)	sich beschweren (über); (etw.) beklagen, reklamieren
complaint n.	Beschwerde, Reklamation
complete vt	fertigstellen, vervollständigen
compromise n.	Kompromiss
comptroller n.; controller n.	Rechnungsprüfer(in)
computer n.	Rechner, Computer
concept n.	Konzept
concern n. (cause ≈)	Besorgnis (erregen)
condition n. (heart ≈)	Bedingung (Herzkrankheit, -leiden)
conduct vt (a survey)	durchführen (eine Umfrage)
conference n.	Konferenz
confidential adj.	vertraulich
conflict n.	Konflikt
confronted adj. (with)	konfrontiert (mit)
confuse vt	verwirren
confusing adj.	verwirrend
conquer vt	erobern
conscientious adj.	gewissenhaft
consequence n.	Konsequenz, Folge
consider vt	erwägen
consignment n.	Lieferung (Ware, nicht: Vorgang!)
consolidated adj.	konsolidiert
construction firm n.	Bauunternehmen, -firma
construction n. (of a building)	Bau (eines Gebäudes)
construction site n.	Bauplatz, Baustelle
consultant n.	Berater
consumer boycott	Verbraucherboykott
consumer n.	Verbraucher, Konsument
consumer organisation (BE), organization (AE)	Verbraucherorganisation
consumption n.	Konsum, Verbrauch
contaminate vt	verseuchen, kontaminieren
contents n.pl.; content n.sg.	Inhalt(e); Inhalt, Gehalt
continuous adj.	kontinuierlich

contract n.	Vertrag
contradict vt	widersprechen
contradictory adj.	widersprüchlich
contribution n.	Beitrag
control n. (out of ≈)	(Kontrolle (außer ≈)
control n. (take over ≈)	(die) Kontrolle (übernehmen)
convergence criterion (pl.: criteria)	Konvergenzkriterium
convert, turn (into) vt	ummünzen, umwandeln
cooperate vi	zusammenarbeiten
cope (with) vi	zurechtkommen, fertigwerden (mit)
copy vt	kopieren
copyright n.	Urheberrecht
core (business) n.	Kern(geschäft)
corporate adj. (culture)	Unternehmens-(kultur)
corporate adj. (world)	Unternehmens- (Geschäftswelt)
corporate adj. philosophy	Unternehmensphilosophie
corporate adj. structure	Unternehmensstruktur
corporate adj. tax	Unternehmenssteuer
corporation n.	Unternehmen
corruption n.	Korruption
cost savings n.pl.	Kostenersparnisse
court ruling n.	Gerichtsurteil
CR (Corporate Responsibility) n.	Unternehmensverantwortung
crash vi	abstürzen
crate n. (beer ≈; fruit ≈)	Kiste (Bierkasten; Obststeige)
creation n.	Schaffung; Schöpfung
creativity n., creativeness n.	Kreativität
credibility n.	Glaubwürdigkeit
crisis (pl.: crises) n.	Krise
critical adj. (situation)	kritisch(e Lage)
crop n.	Ernte
cross vt	durch-, überqueren
crouch vi	kauern, (sich) (zusammmen-≈)
crouching adj. (position)	hockend (Hockstellung)
crown colony n.	Kronkolonie
crude oil n.	Rohöl
crumble vi/vt	zerfallen; zerbröseln (selbst/etw.)
currency n.	Währung
current adj. (economic situation)	aktuell(e Wirtschaftslage)
customer base n.	Kundenstamm
customer base, customer portfolio	Kundenstamm
customer n. (regular ≈)	Kunde/Kundin (Stamm-≈)
customs n. pl.! (at ≈)	Zoll (beim ≈ ; Ort)
cut (≈ costs)	schneiden; kürzen; (Kosten) senken
cut down vt	verringern
cyclical adj.	konjunkturell, zyklisch
damage vt	beschädigen
damages (n. pl.)	Schadensersatz
data leak n.	Datenleck
data protection n.	Datenschutz
dazzling adj.	blendend; (hier: atemberaubend)
deal n., bargain n. (a good ≈)	Geschäft (ein gutes ≈)
dealer n. (car ≈)	Händler (Auto-≈)

debt burden *n.*	Schuldenlast
decade *n.*	Jahrzehnt
decay *n.*	Verfall
declare bankruptcy	Konkurs anmelden
decline *n.* in sales	Absatzrückgang
decline *vi*	zurückgehen, nach unten gehen
decline *vt* (an invitation)	ablehnen (Einladung)
decorate *vt*	dekorieren
decrepit *adj.*	baufällig; altersschwach; heruntergekommen
dedicated *adj.* (to *sth.*)	gewidmet; mit Leib und Seele dabei sein; sich verschrieben habend
defeat *vt*	besiegen, schlagen, bezwingen
defecation *n.*	Darmentleerung, Stuhlgang
deflation *n.*	Deflation
degree *n.* (hold a ≈)	Abschluss, akad. Grad (haben)
delay *vt*	verzögern, hinauszögern
delete *vt*	löschen (Daten)
delivery *n.*	Lieferung; Aus-, Zulieferung (*Vorgang*)
delivery time *n.*	Lieferzeit, Lieferfrist
delivery van *n.*	Lieferwagen
demand (*sth.*) back *vt*	zurückverlangen (*etw.*)
demand *n.* (domestic ≈)	Nachfrage (Binnen-≈)
demand *n.* (for *product*s)	Nachfrage (nach *Produkten*)
demand *n.* (in *an area, commodities*)	Nachfrage (auf *einem Gebiet*, nach *Rohstoffen*)
demand *vt* (that)	fordern, verlangen (dass)
demanding *adj.*	anspruchsvoll
demographic *adj.* (development)	demographisch(e Entwicklung), Bevölkerungs(entwicklung)
demonstrator *n.*	Demonstrant(in)
dense(ly populated) *adj.*	dicht (bevölkert)
department *n.* (sales ≈)	Abteilung (Verkaufs-≈)
department store (chain) *n.*	Kaufhaus(kette)
departure *n.*	Abreise, Abflug; Weggang
depend (on) *vi*	abhängen (von)
depressed *adj.*	deprimiert
deregulate *vt*	deregulieren
desalination *n.* (plant)	Entsalzung(sanlage)
desert *n.*	Wüste
despair *vi*	verzweifeln
destination *n.*	Reiseziel, Zielort
detail *n.* (in ≈)	Einzelheit, Detail (im Detail)
deter *so.* (from) *vt*	*jmdn.* Abschrecken (von)
deteriorate *vi*	sich verschlechtern
devalue *vt*	abwerten (Währung)
develop *vt/vi*	entwickeln
develop a taste (for)	Geschmack finden (an)
device *n.*	Gerät, Vorrichtung
dilemma *n.*	Dilemma
diligent *adj.*	fleißig; gewissenhaft, sorgfältig
dilute *sth.* *vt*	*etw.* verwässern
director *n.* (marketing ≈ ; sales ≈)	Leiter (Marketing-≈ ; Verkaufs-≈)
discount *n.*	Rabatt, Preisnachlass
discounter *n.*	Discounter

dispatch *vt*	abschicken, verschicken
display *n.*	Anzeige; Bildschirm
disruption *n.*	Unterbrechung, Störung
disruptive *adj.* (≈ technology)	störend (umwälzende Technologie)
distribution *n.* (network)	Vertrieb(snetz)
distributor (local ≈) *n.*	Vertriebshändler (lokaler ≈)
ditch *vt* (a plan, a strategy)	fallen lassen, aufgeben (Plan, Strategie)
divest *vt*	abstoßen (Unternehmensteile)
divide *vt*	teilen, aufteilen; aufspalten
divided *adj.* (opinions are ≈)	geteilt, gespalten (die Meinungen sind ≈)
dividend *n.*	Dividende
division *n.*	Sparte (Unternehmens-≈)
division *n.* (mobile phone ≈)	Sparte, Bereich (Mobilfunk-≈)
division of labour (BE) / labor (AE) *n.*	Teilung (Arbeits-≈)
do away (with) *v.*	abschaffen, beseitigen (*etw.*); aufräumen (mit *etw.*)
do well *vi*	erfolgreich sein
do without *sth.* *v.*	verzichten können (auf *etw.*)
document *n.*	Dokument
domestic *adj.*	heimisch, Binnen-
domino effect *n.*	Dominoeffekt
donate *vt*	spenden
dotcom *n.* *(coll.)*	Internetfirma
double *vt*	verdoppeln
doubt *n.* (be in ≈ about *sth.*)	Zweifel (*etw.* bezweifeln, an *etw.* zweifeln)
doubt *vt*	(be)zweifeln
down under (land ≈)	= Australien
down-market *adv.* (go ≈)	niedrigeres Marktsegment (in ein ≈ gehen); (in den) Massenmarkt (eintreten)
downsize *vt*	verschlanken; rationalisieren
downsizing *n.*	Verkleinerung, Abbau
draft *n.*	Entwurf
draft *vt*	entwerfen
drastic *adj.*	drastisch
drawing *n.*	Zeichnung
drinking water *n.*	Trinkwasser
drought *n.*	Dürre
due *adj.*	fällig
dump *vt*	fallenlassen, aufgeben; entsorgen
duty *n.* (sense of ≈)	Pflicht(bewusstsein)
earn *vt* (money)	verdienen (Geld)
earn *vt* (one's living)	verdienen (seinen Lebensunterhalt)
earnings (*n. pl.*)	Erträge (*pl.*)
ECB (European Central Bank) *n.*	EZB (Europäische Zentralbank)
ecological *adj.*	ökologisch
economic *adj.*	ökonomisch, (volks)wirtschaftlich
economic *adj.*	volkswirtschaftlich
economic *adj.* growth	Wirtschaftswachstum
economic *adj.* situation	Wirtschaftslage
economical (!) *adj.*	ökonomisch, sparsam
economist *n.*	Wirtschaftswissenschaftler/-in, Ökonom/-in, Volkswirt
economy *n.*, national ≈	Volkswirtschaft

education *n.*	Bildung
effect *n.*	Effekt, Wirkung
effective *adj.*	wirkungsvoll, wirksam
efficiency *n.*	Effizienz; Leistungsfähigkeit; Wirkungsgrad
electric *adj.* (engine)	elektrisch (Elektromotor)
electricity *n.* (provider)	Elektrizität; Strom (Stromanbieter)
electronics group *n.*	Elektronikkonzern
elite *n.* (schools)	Elite(schulen)
embellish *vt*	verschönern; beschönigen
emerging countries *n.*	Schwellenländer
emirate *n.*	Emirat
emphasize *vt*	betonen
employ *vt*	beschäftigen; einstellen
employee *n.*	Mitarbeiter
EMS (European Monetary System) *n.*	EWS (Europäisches Währungssystem)
enclave *n.*	Enklave
enclose *vt*	beifügen (als Anlage)
encourage *vt*	ermutigen (*jmdn.*)
encryption *n.* (software)	Verschlüsselung(ssoftware)
end up *vt* (doing sth)	schließlich/letztendlich (etwas tun)
endanger *vt*	gefährden
engineer *n.*	Ingenieur(in)
enhance *vt*	steigern
enormous *adj.*	enorm
enthusiasm *n.*	Begeisterung
entire *adj.*	gesamt
entrepreneur *n.*	Unternehmer(in)
environment-friendly *adj.*	umweltfreundlich
equipped *adj.*	ausgestattet, ausgerüstet
equip *vt*	ausstatten, ausrüsten
error *n.* (technical ≈)	Irrtum; Fehler (technischer ≈)
espionage *n.* (industrial ≈)	Spionage (Industrie-≈)
establish (a company) *vt*	gründen (ein Unternehmen)
estimate *n.*	Schätzung; Kostenvoranschlag
eternal *adj.*	ewig
European Community *n.*	Europäische Gemeinschaft
eurosceptic *n. sg.*, eurosceptics *n. pl.*	Europa-Skeptiker
evaluate *vt*	evaluieren; bewerten
evident *adj.*	offenkundig, offenbar, evident
evil *adj./n*	übel, böse; Übel
ex-banker *n.*	Ex-Banker, ehemaliger Banker
exception *n.*	Ausnahme
excessive *adj.*	exzessiv; überzogen
exclusive *adj.* (rights)	exklusiv; ausschließlich (Exklusivrechte)
excuse *n.*	Entschuldigung; Ausrede
executive *n.*	Führungskraft
exhausted *adj.*	erschöpft (*Person*); aufgebraucht (*Ressourcen*)
exhibitor *n.*	Aussteller
existential *adj.*	existentiell
exodus *n.*	Exodus; (massive) Abwanderung
expand *vi*	expandieren
expansion *n.*	Expansion
expenditure *n.*; spending *n.* (*sg.*)	Ausgaben (*Pl.*)

experience *vt*	erleben, erfahren (*etw.*)
expertise *n.*	Gutachten; Expertise; Sachverstand; Expertenwissen; fachliche Kompetenz
express freight *n.*	Eilfracht
external *adj.*	extern
extra (pay) *adj.*	zusätzlich(e Bezahlung)
extra hours *n. pl.*	Überstunden
fabric *n.*	Stoff
facilities *n. pl.* (sports ≈)	Einrichtungen (Sport-≈)
factor *n.*	Faktor
factory floor *n.*	Fertigungs-, Produktionshalle
factory *n.*	Fabrik
fail *vi*	scheitern
failed *adj.*	gescheitert
failure *n.*	Versagen, Scheitern, Fehlschlag
fair; trade fair *n.*	Messe; Handelsmesse
faked *adj.* (products)	gefälscht(e Produkte)
fall behind *vi*	zurückfallen
family business *n.*	Familienunternehmen
fare *n.*	Fahrgeld, -gebühr
farmland *n.*	Ackerland
fashion *n.* (fair)	Mode(messe)
fashion wear *n.*	Modekleidung
fate *n.*	Schicksal
faultless *adj.*	fehlerlos; makellos; tadellos
FDI (Foreign Direct Investment) *n.*	Direktinvestitionen aus dem Ausland
fear *n. sg.*, fears *n. pl.*	Angst (*Sg.*), Ängste (*Pl.*)
Federal Reserve (Fed) *n.*	US-Notenbank
fee *n.*	Gebühr
fictitious *adj.*	fiktiv; erdichtet, erfunden; fingiert
fierce *adj.*	heftig, erbittert
file *n.*	Datei
Finance Ministry *n.*/ Treasury (BE) *n.*	Finanzministerium
financial markets *n. pl.*	Finanzmärkte
financial services *n. pl.*	Finanzdienstleistungen
findings *n. pl.*	Befunde (*Pl.*)
fire *vt*	feuern, entlassen
firewall *n.*	Firewall (*PC*)
first-rate, first-class *adj.*	erstklassig
fiscal authorities *n. pl.*, fisc *n. sg.*	Steuerbehörde, Fiskus
fix (a problem) *vt*	beheben (ein Problem)
flat *n.*	Wohnung
flock *vi* (into the cities)	strömen (in die Städte)
flood *vt*	überschwemmen, überfluten
flow *vi* (keep things ≈ing)	fließen (Dinge im Fluss halten)
FOB (Free on Board)	FOB (*Incoterm*)
follow suit *vi*	auf dem Fuße folgen
follower *n.*	Anhänger; Verehrer
foreign *adj.*	ausländisch
form (registration ≈)	Formular (Anmelde-≈)
former *adj.*	früher, vorherig
former *adj.* (banker)	ehemalig(er Banker)
fortress *n.*	Festung

fortune *n.*	Vermögen
founder *n.* (company ≈)	Gründer (Unternehmens-≈)
fragile *adj.*	zerbrechlich; fragil
franco domicile *adv.*	frei Haus
fraud *n.*	Betrug
fraudulent *adj.* (practices)	betrügerisch(e Praktiken)
freight *n.*	Fracht
freight train *n.*	Güterzug
fridge *n.*	Kühlschrank
frighten *vt*	erschrecken (*jmdn.*); Angst einjagen (*jmdm.*)
fuel *n.*	Treibstoff
fuel *vt* (the economy)	antreiben (die Wirtschaft)
fundament *n.*	Fundament; Grundlage
funds *n. pl.*	Gelder, Geldmittel, finanzielle Mittel
furniture *n.* (store)	Möbel(geschäft)
gadget *n.*	technische Spielerei
gain *n.*	Gewinn
gain *vt* (ground)	gewinnen (an Boden)
gang *n.* (street ≈)	Gang, (Straßenbande)
gardener *n.*	Gärtner
gas: natural ≈ *n.*	Erdgas
gate *n.* (factory ≈)	Tor (Fabrik-≈)
gateway *n.* (to)	Tor (nach)
generate *vt*	generieren
generous *adj.*	großzügig
genuine *adj.*	echt
geopolitical *adj.*	geopolitisch
gesture *n.*	Geste
get a foothold (in the market)	Fuß fassen (im Markt)
get laid off	entlassen werden
get out of hand *vi*	ausarten; außer Kontrolle geraten
get ready (for) *vi*	sich vorbereiten (auf), einstellen (auf)
get rid (of)	loswerden (*etw.*)
get *vi* (to the coast)	gelangen (an die Küste)
get *vt*	bekommen, erhalten; werden
giant *n.* (chemical ≈)	Riese, Gigant (Chemieriese)
gift *n.*	Geschenk, Gabe, Talent
give priority (to)	bevorzugen; den Vorzug geben
give up *vi/vt*	aufgeben
glove *n.*	Handschuh
go bankrupt *vi*	bankrottgehen, Bankrott machen
go bust (*coll.*) *vi*	pleite gehen
go down *vi*	zurückgehen (=nach unten gehen)
go public *vi*	an die Börse gehen
go wrong *vi*	falsch laufen
gold standard *n.*	Goldstandard
goods *n. pl.*	Waren (*Pl.*)
government bonds *n. pl.*	Staatsanleihen
government *n.*	Regierung
government support *n.*	Regierungsunterstützung
GPS (global positioning system) *n.*	GPS
graduate (*person*) *n.*	Absolvent
graduation *n.*	Abschluss (Studien-≈)

grant *vt*	gewähren
graph *n.*	Graphik, Diagramm, Schaubild
greedy *adj.*	gierig
grind to a halt *vi*	zum Stehen kommen
gross domestic product (GDP) *n.*	Bruttoinlandsprodukt (BIP)
groundwater *n.*	Grundwasser
growth factor *n.*	Wachstumsfaktor
guarantee *vt*	garantieren, sicherstellen
habitat *n.*	Habitat; Lebensraum
hacker *n.*	Hacker (PC)
haggle *vi*	feilschen; schachern
hail *vt* (as *sth.*)	begrüßen (als *etw.*); rufen (Taxi)
halt *n.* (bring to a ≈)	Halt; Stillstand (zum ≈ bringen)
hamper *vt*	hinder, behindern
hand back *vt*	zurückgeben
hand in hand (go ≈ with)	Hand in Hand (gehen mit)
handout *n.*	verteiltes Material; ausgeteilte Unterlage
harbour (BE), harbor (AE) *n.*	Hafen
head of department *n.*	Abteilungsleiter
head office *n.*	Zentrale; Firmensitz
headhunter *n.*	Kopfjäger; Personalabwerber; Nachwuchsjäger
heap up *vt*	an-, aufhäufen
heart attack *n.*	Herzanfall, Herzschlag, Herzinfarkt
heated *adj.* (debate)	hitzig(e Debatte)
helmet *n.*	Helm
hierarchical *adj.*	hierarchisch
hijack *vt*	entführen
historian *n.*	Historiker(in)
hold so. to account	zur Verantwortung ziehen (*jmdn.*)
holiday maker	Urlauber(in)
horrendous *adj.*	horrend
hospitality	Gastfreundschaft
hostile *adj.*	feindlich; feindselig
housing bubble *n.* (bursts)	Immobilienblase (platzt)
housing *n.*	Unterkunft, Behausung; Wohnungswesen
housing prices *n.*	Immobilienpreise
HQ (headquarters) *n.*	Hauptsitz
HR (Human Resources) *n.*	HR, Personalabteilung
hub *n.* (air ≈)	Radnabe; Drehkreuz (für Flugverkehr)
huge *adj.*	riesig
hybrid drive *n.*	Hybridantrieb
hygiene *n.*	Hygiene
idea *n.* (no ≈)	Idee; Vorstellung; Ahnung (keine ≈)
idealism *n.*	Idealismus
identical *adj.*	identisch
illustrate *vt*	illustrieren; veranschaulichen; bebildern
illustration *n.*	Illustration; Abbildung
IMF (International Monetary Fund) *n.*	IWF (Internationaler Währungsfond)
imitator *n.*	Nachahmer
immigrant *n.*	Einwanderer
impact *n.*	Auswirkung; Wucht; Einschlag
implement *vt*	implementieren; einrichten
import quota *n.*	Importquote

import restriction(s) *n. sg./pl.*	Einfuhrbeschränkung(en)
import tariff *n.*	Einfuhrzoll
impose *sth.* on *so.* *vt*	auferlegen; verhängen
impose *vt*	verhängen; erheben (*Zölle*)
impose *vt*	durchsetzen
improvement *n.*	Verbesserung
impunity *n.*	Straffreiheit
in real time *adv.*	in Echtzeit
in return (for)	im Gegenzug (für)
in search of	auf der Suche nach
in the long run / term *adv.*	auf lange Sicht, langfristig (*Adv.*)
in the short term *adv.*	kurzfristig
in transit	beim Transport
incalculable *adj.*	unkalkulierbar; unabsehbar; unermesslich
incentive *n.*	(Leistungs-)Anreiz
incident *n.*	Zwischenfall
incompetence	Inkompetenz
increase *vt/vi*	steigen (intransitiv); steigern (*etw.* / *vt*)
incredible *adj.*	unglaublich
incur *vt* (losses)	(Verluste) machen
indebted *adj.*	verschuldet
indicate *vt*	auf-, anzeigen; angeben
industrialise, industrialize *vt*	industrialisieren
industry *n.*; (sector of) industry *n.*	Branche
inefficient *adj.*	ineffizient
infested *adj.* (with)	befallen (von)
inflation (rate) *n.*	Inflation(srate)
inflexible *adj.* (labor market)	unflexibel, starr, unbiegsam; unelastisch(er Arbeitsmarkt)
influence *n.*	Einfluss
inhabitant *n.*	Einwohner
initial *adj.*	anfänglich
initial public offer (IPO) *n.*	Börsengang
inject *vt* (money)	anlegen; zuführen (Geld)
innovative *adj.*	innovativ
inspect *vt*	inspizieren
inspector *n.*	Inspektor
instal(l) *vt* (anti-virus programs)	installieren (Antivirenprogramme)
instrument *n.*	Instrument
insurance company *n.*	Versicherungsunternehmen
insurance industry *n.*	Versicherungsbranche
insurance *n.* (no pl.!)	Versicherung (*Sg.*), Versicherungen (*Pl.*)
insurance policy *n.* (sg.), insurance policies (pl.)	Versicherungspolice (*Sg.*), Versicherungspolicen (*Pl.*)
integration *n.*	Integration
intellectual property *n.*	geistiges Eigentum
intelligence service, secret service *n.*	Geheimdienst
interest *n.*	Zins; Interesse
interest rate *n.*	Zinssatz
intern *n.*	Praktikant(in)
internal *adj.*	intern
internet company *n.*	Internetfirma

internship *n.*	Praktikum
interpreter *n.*	Dolmetscher(in)
interrogate *vt*	befragen; verhören
intervene *vi*	eingreifen, intervenieren
interview, job interview *n.*	Vorstellungsgespräch
intestines *n. pl.*	Eingeweide (*Pl.*)
invention *n.*	Erfindung
invest *vt* (in/into)	investieren
investigation *n.*	Untersuchung
investor *n.*	Investor
invoice *n.*	Rechnung
IPO (Initial Public Offering) *n.*	Börsengang
ironic(ally) adj. / (adv.)	ironisch(erweise)
issue *vt (Aktien; Buch)*	herausgeben, veröffentlichen
IT bubble *n.*	IT-Blase
jail *vt*	inhaftieren, einsperren, ins Gefängnis werfen
job cuts (*pl.*)	Stellenabbau, Stellenkürzungen, Streichung von Arbeitsplätzen
job interview *n.*	Bewerbungsgespräch
join *vt*, access *vt*	beitreten (Eurozone, EU etc.)
joint venture *n.*	Gemeinschaftsunternehmen
junior staff *n.sg.!*	Nachwuchskräfte (*Pl.!*)
just-in-time *adj.* (delivery)	bedarfsorientierte (Lieferung)
keen *adj.* (demand)	lebhaft(e Nachfrage)
keep out (of) *v.*	sich heraushalten (aus)
keep sth/so. alive *vt*	am Leben erhalten
keep *vt* (a promise)	halten (ein Versprechen)
kick out *vt*	rauswerfen
knee *n.* (to bring so. to his/her knees)	Knie (*jmdn.* in die Knie zwingen)
knowledge industry *n.*	Wissensindustrie
lag *vi* behind	hinterherhinken (*jmdm. / etw.*)
largely *adv.*, to a large extent	weitgehend
launch *n.*	Einführung
launch *vt* (a product)	einführen (ein Produkt)
lay off *vt*	entlassen, kündigen
layer *n.* (social ≈ ; class)	Schicht (soziale ≈ , Klasse)
layoff *n.*	Entlassung
leadership *n.* (market ≈)	Führerschaft (Markt- ≈)
leak *n.*	Leck
leak *vi*	lecken
lean *adj.* (supply chain)	schlank(e Versorgungskette)
lease *vt*	leasen
leash *n.*	Leine
give a long ≈ to, to keep *so.* on a long leash	*jmdn.* an der langen ≈ führen
legal action *n.* (take ≈)	rechtliche Schritte einleiten, klagen
lengthy *adj.*	langatmig
leverage *n.* (on) (price)	Hebel(wirkung); (Möglichkeit, den Preis zu beeinflussen)
liable *adj.*, (hold so.) liable	haftbar (machen)
licence (BE), license (AE) *n.*	Lizenz
life insurance (*sg.!*) policy	Lebensversicherung(spolice)
life-long *adj.*	lebenslang
loan agreement *n.*	Darlehensvertrag, Kreditvertrag

loan n.	Darlehen, Kredit
lobby n.	Lobby
location n.	Standort
logistics (industry) n.	Logistik(branche)
logo n.	Logo
long-term adj.	langfristig
loom vi	sich andeuten/abzeichnen; bevorstehen
loss(es) n.	Verlust(e)
low-budget (provider)	Billig(anbieter)
low-wage adj. country	Niedriglohnland
loyalty (company ≈) n.	Treue (zum Unternehmen)
lucky adj. (be ≈)	Glück (haben)
lucrative adj.	lukrativ
lure vt	anlocken
luxury (image) n.	Luxus(image)
luxury brand n.	Luxusmarke
machine tool n.	Werkzeugmaschine
magazine n.	Magazin (Zeitschrift)
magnate n.	Magnat
maintain (that) vt	behaupten (dass)
maintenance n.	Unterhalt; Instandhaltung
major adj. (investor)	bedeutend, größer(er Investor)
major order n.	Großauftrag
majority n.	Mehrheit
make ends meet	über die Runden kommen
make redundant vt	entlassen; überflüssig machen
make up v. (for) (losses)	ausgleichen (Verluste)
management n. (corporate ≈)	Leitung (Firmen-≈)
manipulate vt (accounts)	manipulieren (Konten)
manufacturer n.	Hersteller
manuscript n.	Manuskript
margin (profit ≈) n.	Rand; Spanne; Spielraum; Marge (Gewinnspanne)
marginal adj.	geringfügig, marginal
market entry n.	Markteintritt
market share n.	Marktanteil
mass production n.	Massenproduktion
material (info ≈)	Material (Info-≈)
mayor n. [≠ major !]	Bürgermeister
measure n.	Maßnahme
meeting n.	Besprechung, Treffen
megacity (sg.), megacities (pl.) n.	Megacity (sg.), Megacitys (pl.)
membership n.	Mitgliedschaft
merge vi (with)	fusionieren (mit)
merger n.	Fusion
middle class n.	Mittelschicht
migrant worker n.	Wanderarbeiter(in)
mindset n.	Mentalität
minimum wage n.	Mindestlohn
ministry n.	Ministerium
minority stake n.	Minderheitsbeteiligung
minutes (take the ≈) n. pl. [≠ protocol !]	Protokoll (≈ schreiben) [≠ zeremonielles Protokoll;

	≠ electron. Protokoll]
mobility *n.*	Mobilität
model *n.*	Modell
model range *n.*	Modellpalette
modest *adj.*	bescheiden
modify *vt*	modifizeiren, (ab-)ändern
momentum *n.* (to gain ≈)	Schwung (an ≈ gewinnen)
monetary *adj.* (Monetary Union)	Währungs- (Währungsunion)
monitor *vt*	überwachen
monopolist *n.*	Monopolist, Inhaber eines Monopols
monopoly *n.*	Monopol
mortgage *n.*	Hypothek
motorway *n.*	Autobahn
MP (Member of Parliament) *n.*	Abgeordnete(r)
municipality *n.*, city administration *n.*	Stadtverwaltung
must (a ≈) *n.*	Muss (ein ≈)
naïve *adj.*	naiv
nationalise (BE), nationalize (AE) *vt*	verstaatlichen
navy *n.*	Marine
negotiate (with) *vi*	verhandeln
negotiation *n.*	Verhandlung
news broadcast *n.*	Nachrichtensendung
niche *n.*	Nische
niche product *n.*	Nischenprodukt
nightmare *n.*	Albtraum
no-frills airline *n.*	Billigfluggesellschaft, -linie
	wörtlich: ohne Halskrausen, d.h. Luxus)
nomad *n.*	Nomade/Nomadin
non-core *adj.* (activities)	nicht zum Kerngeschäft gehörend(e Aktivitäten)
notice *n.* (until further ≈)	bis auf Weiteres
novel *n.*	Roman
nutrition *n.* (animal ≈)	Nahrung (Tier-≈)
oath *n.* (make an ≈)	Eid (schwören)
obligation *n.*	Verpflichtung
observer *n.*	Beobachter(in)
obsession *n.*	Obsession, Vernarrtheit
obtain *vt*	erlangen (*mit Anstrengung*)
occasion *n.* (on the ≈ of)	Gelegenheit (aus Anlass von)
occupy *vt*	beschäftigen; besetzen
occur *vi*	geschehen; sich ereignen
odds *n.* (against all ≈)	Risiken; (gegen alle Wahrscheinlichkeit)
offer *n.*	Angebot
office chair *n.*	Bürostuhl
office *n.*	Büro
offset *vt* (losses)	ausgleichen (Verluste)
offshore: move (sth.) offshore	(etw.) ins Ausland verlagern
offshoring *n.*	Verlagerung ins Ausland
old-fashioned *adj.*	altmodisch
oligarch *n.*	Oligarch
one-child policy *n.*	Ein-Kind-Politik
online business *n.*	Onlinegeschäft, -unternehmen
only *adj.*, single *adj.*	einzig
opening hours *n.*	Öffnungszeiten

opening *n.* (of an airport)	Eröffnung (eines Flughafens)
operate *vi*	operieren, tätig sein
operate *vt*	bedienen (*jmdn.*)
operating system *n.*	Betriebssystem
operator *n.* (truck ≈)	Betreiber (Transportunternehmer)
option *n.*	Option
order intake *n.*	Auftragseingang
ordinary *adj.* (people)	gewöhnlich(e Leute)
organized crime *n.*	organisiertes Verbrechen
organizer *n.*	Organisator
original *adj.*	ursprünglich, original
otherwise *adv.*	andernfalls
oust *vt*	absetzen, des Amtes entheben; entlassen
outcome *n.*	Ausgang (= Ergebnis)
outdated *adj.*	überholt, überaltert
outlet *n.*	Verkaufsstelle
outraged *adj.*	entsetzt, schockiert
outsource *vt*	auslagern
overcome *vt*	überwinden
overcrowded *adj.*	überfüllt
overdrawn *adj.* (account)	überzogen(es Konto)
overheads *n. pl.*	Gemeinkosten; Fixkosten
overheated *adj.*	überhitzt
overseas branch *n.*	Auslandsniederlassung
over-staffed *adj.*	zu viel Personal (habend)
overtime *adv.* (work ≈)	Mehrarbeit leisten, Überstunden machen
owner *n.*; proprietor *n.*	Eigentümer
package *vt*	verpacken
panic *vi* (*pp:* panicked)	in Panik geraten
parachute *n.* (a golden ≈)	Fallschirm (großzügige Abfindung)
pass on *vt* (information)	weitergeben (informationen)
pass through *vt*	durchfahren
pass *vt* (a law)	verabschieden (ein Gesetz)
passenger *n.*	Passagier, Fluggast
password *n.*	Passwort
patent *n.*	Patent
pay damages *n. pl.*	Schadensersatz leisten
pay off *vi*	sich auszahlen
pay rise *n.*	Lohnerhöhung, Gehaltserhöhung
payroll *n.*	Gehaltsliste
peak *n.*	Höchstwert, Höhepunkt
peg *sth.* to (a currency)	koppeln, binden an (eine Währung)
penalty *n.*	Strafe, Geldstrafe; Sanktion
pension *n.* (high ≈s)	Pension (hohe ≈en)
pension system *n.*	Rentensystem
pensioner *n.*	Ruheständler; Rentner; Pensionär
performer *n.* (top performer)	Schauspieler; Künstler; 'Diensterbringer' (Spitzenkraft)
perishable *adj.*	verderblich
persuade *vt*	überreden
petrol (BE) *n.*	Benzin
pharma(ceutical) (company)	pharma(zeutisches) (Unternehmen)
pick up *vi*	anlaufen, sich erholen (Konjunktur)

pick up *vt*; collect *vt*	abholen
picket *n*.	Streikposten
pile *n*.	Haufen; Stapel
pillar (of stability)	Säule (der Stabilität)
piracy *n*. (product ≈)	Piraterie (Produkt ≈)
pitfall *n*.	Fallgrube, Falle, Fallstrick
place *vt* (an order)	erteilen (einen Auftrag)
plague *n*.	Pest; Plage; Heimsuchung
plague *vt*	plagen, quälen
plant *n*.	Anlage; Produktionsanlage; Pflanze
pleasant *adj*.	angenehm
plie up *vt*	anhäufen; aufhäufen
plummet *vi*	abstürzen, in den Keller gehen
plummet *vi*, plunge *vi*	in den Keller gehen (= stark sinken), einbrechen, absacken
policy *n*.	Politik (= Strategie); (Versicherungs-)Police
pollute *vt*	verschmutzen
pollution *n*.	Umweltverschmutzung
popular *adj*.	beliebt
population *n*.	Bevölkerung
port *n*.	Hafen
portfolio *n*.	Portfolio
post *n*.	Posten, Position (berufliche Stellung)
postpone *vt*	verschieben
potential *n*. (market ≈)	Potential (Markt-≈)
potential(s) *n*. (cost saving ≈)	Potential(e) (Kosteneinsparungs-≈)
pothole *n*.	Schlagloch
poverty *n*.	Armut
practically *adv*.	praktisch
praise *vt*	loben
predict *vt*	vorhersagen
premises *n. pl*.	Gelände (Firmen-≈, Werks-≈)
present (a product, a person) *vt*	vorstellen (Produkt, Person)
pressure *n*. (under ≈)	Druck (unter ≈)
pretend *vt*	vorgeben; so tun, als ob ...
prevail *vi*	überwiegen; vorherrschen; sich durchsetzen
price cap *n*.	Preis-Obergrenze; gedeckelter Preis
Prime Minister *n*.	Premierminister(in)
priority *n*.	Priorität
prison sentence *n*. (serve a ≈)	Gefängnisstrafe (absitzen)
private sector *n*.	private Wirtschaft
privatisation (BE), privatization (AE) *n*.	Privatisierung
product range *n*.	Produktpalette
production industry	Fertigungsindustrie
production line *n*.	Fertigungsband
production *n*.	Produktion, Herstellung
production plant	Fertigungswerk
professional *adj*.	professionell
professionality *n*.	Professionalität
profile *n*.	Profil (*auch im Internet*)
profit margin *n*.	Gewinnspanne
profitability *n*.	Rentabilität
progress *n*. ≈)	Fortschritt (Fortschritte machen)

project *n.*	Projekt
promise *n.*	Zusage, Versprechen
promising *adj.*	vielversprechend
promote *vt*	befördern; fördern; promoten
promptly *adv.*	umgehend
property market *n.*	Immobilienmarkt
property, real estate *n.*	Immobilie
prospects *n. pl.* (career ≈)	Aussichten (Berufs-≈)
prosper *vi*	florieren; gedeihen
protection money *n.*	Schutzgeld
protectionism *n.*	Protektionismus
prototype *n.*	Prototyp
provide *vt* (jobs)	bereitzustellen (Arbeitsplätze)
provide *vt* a service	(an)bieten (eine Dienstleistung)
provider (energy ≈)	*hier:* Anbieter (Energie-≈)
public (go ≈)	an die Börse gehen
public debate *n.*	öffentliche Debatte
public funding *n.*	öffentliche Finanzierung
public sector *n.*	öffentliche Hand
public services *n. pl.*	öffentliche Dienstleistungen
public spending *n. sg.*	staatliche/öffentliche Ausgaben (*Pl.*)
publisher *n.*	Verleger, Verlag
punctual *adj.*	pünktlich
purchasing power, buying power *n.*	Kaufkraft
pursue *vt* (objectives)	verfolgen (Ziele)
pursuit *n.* (in ≈ of sth.)	Verfolgung; Streben (im ≈ nach *etw.*)
push through *vt*	durchdrücken (*etw.*)
push up *vt* (unemployment)	nach oben treiben (Arbeitslosigkeit)
put off *vt*	verschieben
put *so./sth.* at risk *vt*	*jmdn./etw.* gefährden
qualification *n.*	Qualifikation
quality standard *n.*	Qualitätsstandard
quarter *n.*	Viertel
quarter *n.* of a city	Stadtteil, Stadtviertel
quarterly *adj.* (report)	Quartals(bericht)
quarterly *adj./adv.*	vierteljährlich
question *vt*	befragen, ausfragen; infrage stellen
queue *vi*	anstehen, Schlange stehen, sich anstellen
quit *vi*	aufgeben; Stelle aufgeben
R & D (Research & Development) *n.*	F & E (Forschung & Entwicklung)
rage *n.* (all the ≈)	Wut (der Hit, der letzte Schrei)
railway (BE) / railroad (AE) company *n.*	Eisenbahngesellschaft
raise (sth.) *vt* (≈ prices)	steigern (etw.); anheben (Preise)
rampant *adj.*	wild wuchernd; zügellos
random *n/adj.*	Zufall; Zufalls-
ransom *n.*	Lösegeld
rapid *adj.*	rapide
raw material *n.*	Rohstoff
reach (objectives) *vt*	erreichen (Ziele)
reach (out) (for) *v.*	greifen (nach)
real estate agent *n.*	Grundstücksmakler
real estate prices *n.*; property prices *n.*	Immobilienpreise
real time (in ≈)	Echtzeit (in ≈)

reassuring *adj.*	beruhigend
recession *n.*	Rezession
recipe *n.* (against deflation)	Rezept (gegen die Deflation); (Koch)rezept
recognition *n.*	Anerkennung
reconsider *vt*	überdenken
record high *n.*	Rekordhoch
record *n.* (earnings)	Rekord(erträge)
record *vt*	aufzeichnen; verzeichnen
recovery *n.*	Erholung (*von Krankheit, Krise etc.*)
recruit *vt*	rekrutieren; einstellen
red *adj.* (be in the ≈)	rote Zahlen (schreiben)
referendum *n.*	Referendum, Volksentscheid
refund vt (costs)	zurückerstatten (Kosten)
regain *vt*	wieder-, zurückgewinnen
regulation *n. sg.*	Regulierung; Regelung; Vorschrift; Anordnung
regulations *n. pl.*	Bestimmungen; Vorschriften
regulator (*sg.*) / regulators (*pl.*) *n.*	Regulierungsbehörde; Aufsichtsbehörde
reject *vt*	zurückweisen, ablehnen
re-launch *vt*	wieder auf den Markt bringen
release *vt*	herausbringen, veröffentlichen; freilassen
release *vt*	freilassen
relevant *adj.*	relevant; wichtig; einschlägig
reliable *adj.*	zuverlässig
relieve *vt*	erleichtern
relieve *vt* (oneself)	sich erleichtern; seine Notdurft verrichten
relocate *vt*	verlegen, verlagern
reluctant *adj.* (be ≈ to)	zögernd; abgeneigt (*etw.* zu tun)
remedy *n.*	Heilmittel; Gegenmittel; Abhilfe
remove *vt*	entfernen
Renaissance *n.*	Renaissance
renew *vt*	erneuern
renowned *adj.*	berühmt, renommiert
rental *adj.* costs	Mietkosten
repair *n.* (in bad ≈)	Reparatur (in schlechtem Zustand)
repair *vt*	reparieren
replace *vt*	ersetzen
report *n.* (annual ≈)	Bericht (Jahres-≈)
report *vt*	berichten
representative *n.*	Vertreter
rescue plan *n.*	Rettungsplan
resent *vt*	verübeln; sich (an etw.) stoßen, stören
reservation *n.*	Reservierung
reserve *n.* (currency)	Reserve(währung)
resign *vi*	zurücktreten
resistance *n.* (to)	Widerstand (gegen)
resources *n. pl.*	Ressourcen; Rohstoffquellen etc.
respect *vt* (*rules*), comply with (rules)	einhalten (Regeln)
respective *adj.*	jeweilig
restructure *vt*	umstrukturieren, reorganisieren
result *n.* (as a ≈)	Ergebnis (infolgedessen)
results *n.*	Ergebnisse
resume *vt* (meetings)	wiederaufnehmen (Besprechungen)
retail *n.* (chain)	Einzelhandel(skette)

retailer *n.*	Einzelhändler
rethink *vt*	überdenken
retire *vi*	in den Ruhestand gehen
retirement *n.*	Ruhestand
return flight (BE), roundtrip (AE) *n.*	Hin- und Rückflug
return *n.*: in return (for)	im Gegenzug (für)
return on investment *n.*	Rendite
revenues *n. pl.*	Einnahmen
rickety *adj.*	wack(e)lig; klapprig; gebrechlich
riot *vi*	Aufstand anzetteln; randalieren; toben; Krawall machen
rise *n.*	Aufstieg; Anstieg
risk *n.*	Risiko
risk-averse *adj.*	risikofeindlich, Risiken abgeneigt
risk-friendly *adj.*	risikofreundlich
rival *n.*	Konkurrent, Rivale
road-haulier *n.*	Transportunternehmen
road-hauling industry *n.*	Transportindustrie
robust *adj.*	robust
rocket *vi*	in die Höhe schnellen, schießen
root *n.*	Wurzel
route *n.*	Route (Flug-≈)
run *n.* (in the long ≈)	auf lange Sicht, langfristig (*Adv.*)
run up *vt* losses	Verluste anhäufen
rural *adj.* (area)	ländlich(es Gebiet)
sacrifice *n.* (make a ≈)	Opfer (ein ≈ bringen)
safety check *n.*	Sicherheitsüberprüfung
sales figures *n. pl.*	Verkaufs-, Absatzzahlen
sales *n. pl.*	Verkäufe (*Pl.*), Absatz (*Sg.*)
sample *n.*	Muster (Waren-≈)
sanitation *n. sg.*	sanitäre Anlagen, Einrichtungen (*Pl.*)
saturated *adj.* (markets)	gesättigt(e Märkte)
savings *n. pl.*	Ersparnisse (*Pl.*)
schedule *n.* (behind ≈)	Fahrplan, Zeitplan (hinter dem ≈)
score (*in this meaning:*) *vi*	punkten, abschneiden
scorpion *n.*	Skorpion
scratch *n.* (from ≈)	Kratzer (von Anfang an)
search (in ≈ of)	Suche (auf der ≈ nach)
search *vt*	durchsuchen
season *n.*	Saison
seated (to be ≈)	sitzen
secrecy *n.*	Verschwiegenheit; Geheimnistuerei
secretive *adj.*	verschwiegen; heimlichtuerisch
sector *n.*	Bereich, Gebiet, Sektor, Branche
secure *adj.*	sicher
secure *vt* (revenues; jobs)	sichern (Einnahmen; Arbeitsplätze)
security (system) *n.*	Sicherheit(system)
seize *vt*	beschlagnahmen; ergreifen
self-confident *adj.*	selbstbewusst
sell off *vt*	verkaufen, abgeben, abstoßen
sell *vt*; sell well	verkaufen (sich gut ≈)
set up (a company) *vt*	gründen (ein Unternehmen)
severe *adj.*	streng; ernst

severely *adv.* (hit)	ernsthaft; streng; schwer (getroffen)
shade *n.*	Schatten; Nuance
share *n.*	Anteil; Aktie
share price *n.*	Aktienkurs
shareholder *n.*	Aktionär, Anteilsigner
shed *vt*	abstoßen (Unternehmenssparte); abwerfen (Blätter)
shelve *vt*	zurückstellen, auf die lange Bank schieben, auf Eis legen
shift *n.*	Schicht
shipment *n.*	Lieferung (Ware & Vorgang)
shipping-lane *n.*	Schiff-Fahrtsstraße
shipyard *n.*	Werft, Schiffswerft
shopkeeper *n.*	Ladenbesitzer
shoplifter *n.*	Ladendieb
shortage *n.*	Engpass; Knappheit; Mangel
shortcut *n.*	Abkürzung
short-lived *adj.*	kurzlebig
short-term *adj.*	kurzfristig
showroom *n.*	Ausstellungsraum
shrink *vi*	schrumpfen
sign *vt*	unterschreiben
signal *n.*	Signal
significant *adj.*	erheblich, signifikant
Single Market *n.* (European ≈) [vs. domestic market!]	Binnenmarkt (Europäischer ≈) [vs. Binnenmarkt eines Landes !]
skilled labour *n.*	Facharbeiter, Fachkraft
slave *n.* (work)	Sklave(narbeit)
slip *vi* (let an opportunity ≈)	ausrutschen; entgehen lassen (sich eine Gelegenheit ≈)
slope *n.* (skiing ≈)	Hang; Abhang (Skipiste)
sloppy *adj.*	schlampig, schludrig, salopp
slump *n.* (of the share price)	Einbruch, Rückgang, Absturz (des Aktienkurses); Konjunkturrückgang, Abschwung
SMEs (Small and Medium-sized Enterprises) *n.*	KMUs (kleine und mittelständische Unternehmen)
smuggle *vt*	schmuggeln
social network *n.*	soziales Netzwerk
sociologist *n.*	Soziologe/Soziologin
solar *adj.* (energy)	Solar-, Sonnen-(energie)
solder *v.*	löten
solution *n.* (of a problem)	Lösung (eines Problems)
source *n.* (of income, energy)	Quelle (Einnahme-≈ , Energie-≈)
spare part *n.*	Ersatzteil
special offer *n.*	Sonderangebot
specialise, specialize (in) *v.*	spezialisieren (sich ≈ auf)
specification *n.*	Spezifizierung, Spezifikation
speculate *vi*	spekulieren
speculation *n.* (bubble)	Spekulation(sblase)
sphere *n.* (public ≈)	Sphäre; Kugel; Raum (öffentlicher ≈)
split (*sth.*) up *vt*	sich aufteilen/trennen
spokesman *n.*	Sprecher
spot *vt*	entdecken

spread *vt*	verbreiten
spy *n.;* spy *v.*	Spion; spionieren
squeeze *vt* (out of the market)	quetschen; pressen; drängen; (aus dem Markt) (ver)drängen
stable *adj.*	stabil
stadium *n.*	Stadion (*Sport*)
stage *n.* (on the global ≈)	Bühne (auf der globalen/Welt-≈); auf globaler Ebene
stagnate *vi*	stagnieren
stall *n.*	(Markt-)Bude, (Verkaufs-)Stand
stall *vi / vt*	steckenbleiben; stehenbleiben; stocken / abwürgen (*etw.*); (*etw.*) zum Stillstand bringen
stand (about) *vi*	stehen (herum-≈)
stand *n.*	Stand (Messe)
standardized *adj.*	standardisiert
standstill *n.*	Stillstand
start *n.* (from the ≈)	Start, Beginn, Anfang (von ≈ an)
start-up phase *n.*	Anlaufphase
state (aid), state (support) *n.*	staatliche Hilfe, Unterstützung
state *n.*	Zustand
State *n.*	Staat
state-owned *adj.* enterprise	Staatsbetrieb
state-run *adj.*	staatlich geführt
status *n.* (special ≈)	Status (Sonder- ≈)
steel *n.*	Stahl
step *n.*	Schritt; Maßnahme
stick to sth. *vi*	bleiben (bei *etw.*), true bleiben; sich an etw. halten
still (stand *vi* ≈)	stehen (still≈)
sting *vt*	stechen
stock exchange *n.*	Börse
stock *n.*	(Lager-)Bestand
stock price, share price *n.*	Aktienkurs
straight (to) *adv.*	geradewegs (an/zu)
strategy *n.*	Strategie
strict *adj.*	streng
strike *n.*	Streik
strip *n.* (of land)	Streifen (Land)
struggle (for survival) *vi*	kämpfen (ums Überleben); zu kämpfen haben
stuffy *adj.*	stickig
stunned *adj.*	verblüfft; fassungslos
subscriber *n.*	Abonnent
subsidise (BE), subsidize (AE) *vt*	subventionieren; finanziell unterstützen
subsidy *n.*	Subvention
success story *n.*	Erfolgsgeschichte
successful *adj.*	erfolgreich (*Adj.*)
sue *so.* for *sth.* *vt*	*etw.* von *jmdn.* einklagen
sue *vt*	verklagen
suggestion *n.*	Vorschlag
suicide *n.* (commit ≈)	Selbstmord (begehen)
summit *n.*	Gipfel(treffen)
superior *n.*	Vorgesetzter

supervisory board *n.*	Aufsichtsrat
supplier *n.*	Zulieferer, Lieferant(in)
supplies *n.* pl. (secure *vt* ≈)	Versorgung, Nachschub (sichern, sicherstellen)
supply chain *n.*	Lieferkette/ Beschaffungskette
supply *n.* (money ≈)	Vorrat; Versorgung; Nachschub; (Geldmenge)
survey *n.*	Studie; Umfrage
survive *vi*	überleben
sustainability *n.*	Nachhaltigkeit
sustainable *adj.*	nachhaltig
SUV (Sports Utility Vehicle) *n.*	Geländewagen
sweatshop *n.*	Ausbeuterbetrieb
switch (off) *vt*	(ab)schalten
symbol *n.*	Symbol
synergy *n.*	Synergie
tackle *vt*	angehen, anpacken, in Angriff nehmen (etw.)
tailor *vt* (to)	zuschneiden (auf)
take effect *vi*	in Kraft treten, wirksam werden
take over *vt* (a company) [vs. overtake *vt* !]	übernehmen (ein Unternehmen) [vs. überholen!]
take place *vi*	stattfinden
take pride in *sth.*	auf *etw.* stolz sein
take *vt* (measures)	ergreifen (Maßnahmen)
take *vt* (*so.*) to court	verklagen (*jmdn.*)
takeover *n.*	Übernahme
target group *n.*	Zielgruppe
target *n.*	Ziel
targeted *adj.* (at)	gerichtet (auf); abzielend (auf)
task force *n.*	Arbeits-, Einsatz-, Projektgruppe; Arbeitsausschuss, -stab
task *n.*	Aufgabe
tax declaration *n.*	Steuererklärung
tax raise *n.*	Steuererhöhung
tax system *n.*	Steuersystem
taxpayer *n.*	Steuerzahler
technical inspection *n.*	technische Überprüfung
temp *n.*	Zeitarbeitskraft
temporary *adj.* jobs	Zeitarbeitsplätze
temporary *adj.*	vorübergehend
temporary *adj.* (contract)	Zeit(vertrag)
temporary *adj.* worker	Zeitarbeiter
tension(s) *n.*	Spannung(en)
tent *n.*	Zelt
Terms and Conditions of Trade *n.*	Allgemeine Geschäftsbedingungen (AGB)
testify (to) *v.*	*etw.* Bezeugen; *von etw.* zeugen
textile *adj.*	Textil-
textile *n*	Textile
theft (data ≈) *n.*	Diebstahl (Daten-≈ , -klau)
Third World *n.*, developing world	Dritte Welt
thorough *adj.*	gründlich
threat *n.*	Bedrohung
threaten *vt*	bedrohen
thrive *vi*	florieren, gedeihen

tight *adj.*	dicht; eng; streng
tighten (rules etc.) *vt*	strenger machen (Regeln etc.)
time of crisis *n.*	Krisenzeit
tool *n.*	Werkzeug; Instrument; Hilfsmittel; Tool (PC)
tourism *n.*	Tourismus
toxic *adj.*	toxisch, giftig
trade fair *n.* [≠ fair *adj.* trade!]	Handelsmesse [≠ fairer Handel!]
trading bloc *n.*	Handelsblock
train service *n.*	Zugverkehr
train *vt*	ausbilden
transaction *n.*	Transaktion; Abwicklung
transit *n.* (in ≈)	Transit; (beim Transport)
translator *n.*	Übersetzer
transmit *vt* (data *etc.*)	übertragen; übermitteln (Daten *etc.*)
transparency *n.*	Folie; Transparenz; Durchsichtigkeit
trap *vt*	Falle (*jmdn.* in die ≈ locken)
trapped (be ≈)	in der Falle sitzen; gefangen sein
treat *vt*	behandeln
treaty *n.*	Vertrag, Abkommen (*pol.*)
trigger *vt*	auslösen
trim *vt.* (workforce)	stutzen, zurechtschneiden; (Personal) abbauen
triple *vt*	verdreifachen
trojan *n.*	Trojaner (*auch: Schadsoftware*)
truck driver *n.*	LKW-Fahrer
truck *n.*	Lkw
truck operator *n.*	Transportunternehmer
trust *vt*	vertrauen
turbulent *adj.*	turbulent
turn down *vt*	ablehnen
turnover *n.*	Umsatz
tyre *n.*	Reifen
UAE (United Arab Emirates) *n. pl.*	VAE (Vereinte Arabische Emirate)
unaffordable *adj.*	unbezahlbar
unanimous *adj.*	einstimmig
underestimate *vt*	unterschätzen
underfunded *adj.*	unterfinanziert
undermine *vt*	untergraben, unterminieren
underperforming *adj.*	nicht genug erwirtschaftend; die nicht genug erwirtschaften
undertake *vt* (reforms)	unternehmen (*etw.*); (Reformen) angehen
undignified *adj.*	würdelos
unemployment *n.*	Arbeitslosigkeit
unemployment rate *n.*	Arbeitslosenquote, -rate
unfair *adj.* (competition)	unlauter(er Wettbewerb)
unfamiliar *adj.*	unvertraut
unforeseen *adj.*	unvorhergesehen
unintentional *adj.*	unabsichtlich
union (BE: trade ≈ , AE labor ≈) *n.*	Gewerkschaft
unique *adj.*	einmalig, einzigartig
universal *adj.*	universal
unpleasant *adj.*	unangenehm
unprecedented *adj.*	beispiellos; unerhört; noch nie dagewesen

unprofitable *adj.*	unrentabel
unreliability *n.*	Unzuverlässigkeit
unskilled labour *n. sg.!*	ungelernte Arbeiter (*pl.*), Hilfsarbeiter
unsolicited *adj.* (≈ application)	unaufgefordert, unverlangt (Blindbewerbung, Initiativbewerbung)
unthinkable *adj.*	(un)denkbar
until further notice *adv.*	bis auf Weiteres
unusual *adj.*	(un)gewöhnlich
update *n.*	Aktualisierung, Update
update *vt*	aktualisieren
urban *adj.*	urban, städtisch
urbanisation *n.*	Urbanisierung, Verstädterung
used car *n.*	Gebrauchtwagen
user *n.*	Benutzer
usual *adj.* (as ≈)	gewöhnlich (wie ≈)
utilization *n.* (capacity ≈)	Nutzung; Auslastung (Kapazitäts-≈)
vain: in ≈ *adv.*	vergeblich, umsonst
vehicle *n.*	Fahrzeug
vessel *n.*	Schiff; Seefahrzeug
veto *vt*	Veto einlegen (gegen *etw.*)
victim *n.* (of an accident)	Opfer (eines Unfalls)
vineyard *n.*	Weinberg
violation *n.* (of human rights)	Verletzung (von Menschenrechten)
volatile *adj.*	volatil, unbeständig, sprunghaft, unberechenbar
vote *vi* (for)	abstimmen; stimmen, votieren (für)
voyage *n.*	(See-)Reise
wages *n. pl.*	Löhne (*Pl.*)
wake *n.* (in the ≈ of)	Kielwasser (im ≈ von; infolge)
warehouse *n.*	Lager(halle)
warning *n.*	Warnung
waste *n.* (of time)	Vergeudung (Zeit-≈)
weaken *vt/vi*	schwächen; sich abschwächen
wealth *n.*	Wohlstand, Reichtum
weld *vt/vi*	schweißen
welfare *n.* (state)	Wohlfahrt(sstaat)
welfare system *n.*	Sozialsystem
wheat *n.*	Weizen
whistle-blower / whistleblower *n.*	Whistleblower
wholesaler *n.*	Großhändler
widen *vt*	verbreitern
win *vt*	gewinnen (Preis)
wipe out *vt*	auswischen; auslöschen; vernichten
wireless *adj.*	drahtlos
withdraw (from) *v.*	sich zurückziehen (von *etw.*)
withdraw *vt*	zurückziehen (*etw.*); abheben (Geld)
withdrawal *n.*	Abhebung (*Geld*)
witness *n.*	Zeuge/Zeugin
woo *vt*	umwerben
wooden box *n.*	Holzkiste
work environment *n.*	Arbeitsumfeld
workforce *n.*	Belegschaft; arbeitende Bevölkerung
working conditions *n. pl.*	Arbeitsbedingungen (*Pl.*)
work-life balance *n.*	Gleichgewicht zwischen Arbeits- und Freizeit

workload *n.*	Arbeitslast, -belastung
World Bank *n.*	Weltbank
World Trade Organisation (WTO) *n.*	Welthandelsorganisation
worm *n.*	Wurm
worried *adj.*	besorgt
worsen *vi*	sich verschlechtern, verschlimmern
yield *vt*	ergeben; einbringen; abwerfen (Rendite)
youth unemployment *n.*	Jugendarbeitslosigkeit
zero tolerance policy *n.*	Null-Toleranz-Politik

VOKABULAR: Deutsch - Englisch
d   e

Abgeordnete(r)	MP (Member of Parliament) n.
Abgrund	abyss n.
abhängen (von)	depend (on) vi
Abhebung (*Geld*)	withdrawal n.
abholen	pick up vt; collect vt
Abkommen, Vereinbarung	agreement n.
Abkürzung	shortcut n.
ablehnen	turn down vt
ablehnen (Einladung)	decline vt (an invitation)
Abonnent	subscriber n.
Abreise, Abflug; Weggang	departure n.
absagen	call off vt
Absatzrückgang	decline n. in sales
abschaffen, beseitigen (*etw.*); aufräumen (mit *etw.*)	do away (with) v.
abschalten	switch off vt
abschicken, verschicken	dispatch vt
Abschluss (Studien-≈)	graduation n.
Abschluss, akad. Abschluss, Grad (haben)	degree n. (hold a ≈)
abschrecken (*jmdn. von etw.*)	deter so. (from) vt
absetzen, des Amtes entheben; entlassen	oust vt
Absolvent (Studien-≈)	graduate (*person*) n.
abstoßen (Unternehmenssparte); abwerfen (Blätter)	shed vt
abstoßen (Unternehmensteile)	divest vt
abstürzen	crash vi
abstürzen, in den Keller gehen	plummet vi
Abteilung (Verkaufs-≈)	department n. (sales ≈)
Abteilungsleiter	head of department n.
Abwanderung von (hoch)qualifizierten (Fach-, Arbeits-) Kräften	brain drain n.
abwerten (Währung)	devalue vt
abwürgen; ersticken	choke off vt
Ackerland	farmland n.
Agentur (Werbe-≈)	agency n. (advertising ≈)
Aktie; Anteil	share n.
Aktienkurs	stock price, share price n.
Aktionär, Anteilseigner	shareholder n.
aktualisieren	update vt
Aktualisierung, Update	update n.
aktuell(e Wirtschaftslage)	current adj. (economic situation)
alarmieren	alert vt
Albtraum	nightmare n.
allgemein; üblich; gängig	common adj.
Allgemeine Geschäftsbedingungen (AGB)	Terms and Conditions of Trade n.
Allianz, Bündnis	alliance n.
alt, (ur)alt; antik	ancient adj.
Alter; Zeitalter; (seit ewigen Zeiten)	age n. (for ages)

Alternative	alternative n.
altmodisch	old-fashioned adj.
Alumnus, Ehemaliger (sg.), Alumni, Ehemalige (pl.)	alumnus (sg.), alumni (pl.) n.
an-, aufhäufen	pile up vt
an-, aufzeigen; angeben	indicate vt
Anbieter (hier: Energie- ≈)	provider (energy ≈)
andernfalls	otherwise adv.
Anerkennung	recognition n.
anfänglich	initial adj.
angeblich, mutmaßlich	alleged adj.
Angebot	offer n.
angehen, anpacken, in Angriff nehmen (etw.)	tackle vt
angenehm	pleasant adj.
Angst (Sg.), Ängste (Pl.)	fear n. sg., fears n. pl.
ängstlich, besorgt	anxious adj.
Anhänger; Verehrer	follower n.
anhäufen; aufhäufen	plie up vt
Ankündigung	announcement n.
Anlage; Produktionsanlage; Pflanze	plant n.
Anlass: aus Anlass von	on the occasion of
anlaufen, sich erholen (Konjunktur)	pick up vi
Anlaufphase	start-up phase n.
anlegen; zuführen (Geld)	inject vt (money)
anlocken	lure vt
anpassen (an)	adjust (to) vt
Anreiz, Leistungsanreiz	incentive n.
Ansatz, (methodische) Herangehensweise; Annäherung	approach n.
Anschuldigung, Beschuldigung; Anklage	accusation n.
anspruchsvoll	demanding adj.
anstehen, Schlange stehen, sich anstellen	queue vi
Anteil; Aktie	share n.
Antikorruptionsabteilung	anti-corruption department, compliance department n.
Antiviren-Software	anti-virus adj. software n
antreiben (die Wirtschaft)	fuel vt (the economy)
Anzeige (z.B. Smartphone)	display n.
Arbeits-, Einsatz-, Projektgruppe; Arbeitsausschuss, -stab	task force n.
Arbeitsbedingungen (Pl.)	working conditions n. pl.
Arbeitslast, -belastung	workload n.
Arbeitslosenquote, -rate	unemployment rate n.
Arbeitslosigkeit	unemployment n.
Arbeitsumfeld	work environment n.
Argument; Streit	argument n.
argumentieren	argue vi
Armut	poverty n.
auf lange Sicht, langfristig (Adv.)	run n. (in the long ≈)
auferlegen; verhängen	impose sth. on so. vt
Aufgabe	task n.
aufgeben	give up vi/vt
aufgeben; Stelle aufgeben	quit vi

aufgebraucht (*Ressourcen*); erschöpft (*Person*)	exhausted *adj.*
aufholen (mit)	catch up (with) *vi*
aufkaufen	buy up *vt*
aufnehmen (Geld)	borrow *vt* (money)
aufräumen (mit *etw.*); abschaffen, beseitigen (*etw.*)	do away (with) *v.*
Aufsichtsrat	board of supervisors *n.;* supervisory board *n.*
Aufstand anzetteln; randalieren; toben; Krawall machen	riot *vi*
Aufstieg; Anstieg	rise *n.*
aufteilen/trennen (*etw.*)	split (*sth.*) up *vt*
Auftragseingang	order intake *n.*
aufzeichnen; verzeichnen	record *vt*
ausarten; außer Kontrolle geraten	get out of hand *vi*
Ausbeuterbetrieb	sweatshop *n.*
ausbilden	train *vt*
Ausgaben (*Pl.*)	expenditure *n.;* spending *n.* (*sg.*)
Ausgang (= Ergebnis)	outcome *n.*
ausgestattet, ausgerüstet	equipped *adj.*
ausstatten, ausrüsten	equip *vt*
ausgestellt	on display
ausgleichen (Verluste)	compensate *vt* (losses); make up *v.* (for) (losses); offset *vt* (losses)
auslagern	outsource *vt*
Ausland: im ≈	abroad *adv.*
ausländisch	foreign *adj.*
Auslandsniederlassung	overseas branch *n.*
Auslastung (Kapazitäts-≈); Nutzung	utilization *n.* (capacity ≈)
auslösen	trigger *vt*
auslösen (*jmdn*), jmdm. aus der Klemme helfen (finanziell)	bail *so.* out *vt*
ausmachen (z.B.: Das macht 5 % des BIP aus.)	account for *vi*
Ausnahme	exception *n.*
Ausrede; Entschuldigung	excuse *n.*
ausrutschen; entgehen lassen (sich eine Gelegenheit ≈)	slip *vi* (let an opportunity ≈)
ausschließen; verbieten	ban *vt*
Aussichten (Berufs-≈)	prospects *n. pl.* (career ≈)
Aussteller	exhibitor *n.*
Ausstellungsraum	showroom *n.*
Austerität; Strenge; (Sparmaßnahmen)	austerity *n.* (measures)
Australien (*coll.*)	down under (land ≈)
Auswirkung; Wucht; Einschlag	impact *n.*
auswischen; auslöschen; vernichten	wipe out *vt*
auszahlen (sich ≈)	pay off *vi*
Auszeichnung, Preis	award *n.*
Autobahn	motorway *n.*
Autobiographie	autobiography *n.*
Autohersteller	car manufacturer *n.*
Automobil(konzern)	automotive *adj.* (group)
Bakterium, Bakterien	bacterium (*sg.*), bacteria (*pl.*)
Banknote, Geldschein	banknote *n.*
Bankrott, Insolvenz, Konkurs	bankruptcy *n.*

bankrottgehen, Bankrott machen	go bankrupt *vi*
Bau (eines Gebäudes)	construction *n.* (of a building)
baufällig; altersschwach; heruntergekommen	decrepit *adj.*
Bauplatz, Baustelle	construction site *n.*
Bauunternehmen, -firma	construction firm *n.*
bayerisch	Bavarian *adj.*
beauftragen (*jmdn.*); belasten (*Konto*); beschuldigen	charge *vt*
bedarfsorientierte (Lieferung)	just-in-time *adj.* (delivery)
bedeutend, größer(er Investor)	major *adj.* (investor)
bedienen (*jmdn.*)	operate *vt*
Bedingung (Herzkrankheit, -leiden)	condition *n.* (heart ≈)
bedrohen	threaten *vt*
Bedrohung	threat *n.*
beeinträchtigen; betreffen; beeinflussen	affect *vt*
befallen (von)	infested *adj.* (with)
befördern; fördern; promoten	promote *vt*
befragen, ausfragen; infrage stellen	question *vt*
befragen; verhören	interrogate *vt*
Befunde (*Pl.*)	findings *n. pl.*
Begeisterung	enthusiasm *n.*
begrüßen (als *etw.*); rufen (Taxi)	hail *vt* (as *sth.*)
behandeln	treat *vt*
behaupten (dass)	maintain (that) *vt*
beheben (ein Problem)	fix (a problem) *vt*
Behörden	authorities *n. pl.!*
beifügen (als Anlage)	enclose *vt*
beispiellos; unerhört; noch nie dagewesen	unprecedented *adj.*
Beitrag	contribution *n.*
beitreten (Eurozone, EU etc.)	join *vt*, access *vt*
Beitritt (zu)	accession *n.* (to)
bekommen, erhalten; werden	get *vt*
Belegschaft; arbeitende Bevölkerung	workforce *n.*
beliebt	popular *adj.*
Benutzer	user *n.*
Benzin	petrol (BE) *n.*; gas (AE) *n.*
Beobachter(in)	observer *n.*
Berater	advisor *n.*
Berater *(Beruf)*	consultant *n.*
berechnen (Gebühren); belasten (Konto)	charge *vt* (fees)
berechnen, kalkulieren (Kosten)	calculate *vt* (costs)
Bereich, Gebiet, Sektor, Branche	sector *n.* (of industry), industry *n.*
bereitstellen (Arbeitsplätze)	provide *vt* (jobs)
Bericht (Jahres-≈)	report *n.* (annual ≈)
berichten	report *vt*
beruhigen	calm *vt*
beruhigend	reassuring *adj.*
berühmt, renommiert	renowned *adj.*
beschädigen	damage *vt*
beschäftigen; besetzen	occupy *vt*
beschäftigen; einstellen	employ *vt*
bescheiden	modest *adj.*
beschlagnahmen; ergreifen	seize *vt*

Beschwerde, Reklamation	complaint *n.*
beschweren (sich ≈ über); (sich über *etw.*) beklagen; reklamieren (*etw.*)	complain (about *sth.*) *v.*
beseitigen, abschaffen (*etw.*); aufräumen (mit *etw.*)	do away (with) *v.*
besiegen, schlagen, bezwingen	defeat *vt*
Besorgnis (erregen)	concern *n.* (cause ≈)
besorgt	worried *adj.*
Besprechung, Treffen	meeting *n.*
bestechen	bribe *vt*
Bestechungsgeld	bribe *n.*
Bestimmungen; Vorschriften	regulations *n. pl.*
betonen	emphasize *vt;* point out *vt.;* stress *vt.*
Betreiber (Transportunternehmer)	operator *n.* (truck ≈)
Betriebssystem	operating system *n.*
Betrug	fraud *n.*
betrügen	cheat *vt*
betrügerisch(e Praktiken)	fraudulent *adj.* (practices)
Bevölkerung	population *n.*
bevorstehen; sich andeuten/abzeichnen	loom *vi*
bevorzugen; den Vorzug geben	give priority (to)
Bewerber(in)	applicant *n.*
Bewerbung	application *n.*
Bewerbungsgespräch	job interview *n.*
bewerten; evaluieren	evaluate *vt*
bezeugen (*etw.*); (*von etw.*) zeugen	testify (to) *v.*
bezweifeln	doubt *vt*
bieten, anbieten (eine Dienstleistung)	provide *vt* a service
Bildung	education *n.*
Billig(anbieter)	low-budget (provider)
billigen; genehmigen	approve *vt*
Billigflug	budget flight, cheap flight *n.*
Billigfluggesellschaft, -linie wörtlich: ohne Halskrausen, d.h. Luxus)	no-frills airline *n.*
Binnenmarkt (Europäischer ≈) [vs. Binnenmarkt eines Landes !]	Single Market *n.* (European ≈) [vs. domestic market!]
bis auf Weiteres	until further notice *adv.*
Blase; (Spekulations-)Blase	bubble *n.*
Blaupause; Plan; Vorlage; Entwurf	blueprint *n.*
bleiben (bei *etw.*), treu bleiben; sich an *etw.* halten	stick to sth. *vi*
blendend; (*hier:* atemberaubend)	dazzling *adj.*
Boden: am Boden bleiben	be grounded (*passive*) *v.*
boomen	boom *vi*
Börse	stock exchange *n.*
Börse: an die Börse gehen	go public *vi*
Börsengang	IPO (Initial Public Offering) *n.*
Boykott	boycott *n.*
Branche	industry *n.;* sector of industry *n.*
breit, weit	broad *adj.*
brennen (nieder-≈)	burn down *vi/vt*
Bric(-Staaten)	BRIC (Brazil, Russia, India, China)
Broschüre	brochure *n.*

Bruttoinlandsprodukt (BIP)	gross domestic product (GDP) *n.*
buchen (einen Flug)	book (a flight) *vt*
Buchhalter(in), -führer(in); Rechnungsführer(in); Bilanzbuchhalter(in); Rechnungsprüfer(in)	accountant *n.*
Buchung, Reservierung	booking *n.*
Bude, (Markt-)Bude, (Verkaufs-)Stand	stall *n.*
Budget; Haushalt	budget *n.*
Bühne (auf der globalen/Welt-≈); auf globaler Ebene	stage *n.* (on the global ≈)
Bürde, Last	burden *n.*
Bürger	citizen *n.*
Bürgerkrieg	civil war *n.*
Bürgermeister	mayor *n.* [≠ major !]
Bürgerrechte	civil rights *n.*
Büro	office *n.*
Bürokrat	bureaucrat *n.*
Bürostuhl	office chair *n.*
Cashflow	cash flow *n.*
Chaos (im ≈ enden)	chaos *n.* (end in ≈)
Chef	boss *n.*
Chefingenieur	chief engineer *n.*
Darlehen, Kredit	loan *n.*
Darlehensvertrag, Kreditvertrag	loan agreement *n.*
Datei	file *n.*
Datenleck	data leak *n.*
Datenschutz	data protection *n.*
Deflation	deflation *n.*
dekorieren	decorate *vt*
demographisch(e Entwicklung), Bevölkerungs(entwicklung)	demographic *adj.* (development)
Demonstrant(in)	demonstrator *n.*
deprimiert	depressed *adj.*
deregulieren	deregulate *vt*
dicht (bevölkert)	dense(ly populated) *adj.*
dicht; eng; streng	tight *adj.*
Diebstahl (Daten-≈ , -klau)	theft (data ≈) *n.*
Dilemma	dilemma *n.*
Direktinvestitionen aus dem Ausland	FDI (Foreign Direct Investment) *n.*
Discounter	discounter *n.*
Dividende	dividend *n.*
Dokument	document *n.*
Dolmetscher(in)	interpreter *n.*
Dominoeffekt	domino effect *n.*
drahtlos	wireless *adj.*
drastisch	drastic *adj.*
Dritte Welt	Third World *n.*, developing world
Druck (unter ≈)	pressure *n.* (under ≈)
durch-, überqueren	cross *vt*
durchdrücken (*etw.*)	push through *vt*
durchfahren	pass through *vt*
durchführen (eine Umfrage)	conduct *vt* (a survey)
durchführen, ausführen (*etw.*)	carry out *vt*
durchsetzen	impose *vt*

durchsuchen	search *vt*
Dürre	drought *n.*
echt	genuine *adj.*
Echtzeit (in ≈)	real time (in ≈)
Effekt, Wirkung	effect *n.*
Effizienz; Leistungsfähigkeit; Wirkungsgrad	efficiency *n.*
ehemalig(er Banker)	former *adj.* (banker)
Ehemaliger, Alumnus (*sg.*); Ehemalige, Alumni (*pl.*)	alumnus (*sg.*), alumni (*pl.*) *n.*
ehrgeizig	ambitious *adj.*
Eid (schwören)	oath *n.* (make an ≈)
Eigentümer	owner *n.*; proprietor *n.*
Eilfracht	express freight *n.*
einbrechen; absacken; in den Keller gehen (= stark sinken)	plummet *vi*, plunge *vi*
Einbruch, Rückgang, Absturz (des Aktienkurses); Konjunkturrückgang, Abschwung	slump *n.* (of the share price)
Einfluss	influence *n.*
Einfuhrbeschränkung(en)	import restriction(s) *n. sg./pl.*
einführen (ein Produkt)	launch *vt* (a product)
Einführung	launch *n.*
Einfuhrzoll	import tariff *n.*
eingreifen, intervenieren	intervene *vi*
einhalten (Regeln)	respect *vt (rules)*, comply with (rules)
Ein-Kind-Politik	one-child policy *n.*
einklagen (*etw.* von *jmdn.*)	sue *so.* for *sth. vt*
Einnahmen	revenues *n. pl.*
Einrichtungen (Sport-≈)	facilities *n. pl.* (sports ≈)
einschlägig; relevant; wichtig	relevant *adj.*
einsperren, inhaftieren, ins Gefängnis werfen	jail *vt*
einstimmig	unanimous *adj.*
Einwanderer	immigrant *n.*
Einwohner	inhabitant *n.*
Einzelhandel(skette)	retail *n.* (chain)
Einzelhändler	retailer *n.*
Einzelheit, Detail (im Detail)	detail *n.* (in ≈)
einzig	only *adj.*, single *adj.*
einzigartig; einmalig	unique *adj.*
Eisenbahngesellschaft	railway (BE) / railroad (AE) company *n.*
elektrisch (Elektromotor)	electric *adj.* (engine)
Elektrizität; Strom (Stromanbieter)	electricity *n.* (provider)
Elektronikkonzern	electronics group *n.*
Elite(schulen)	elite *n.* (schools)
Emirat	emirate *n.*
engagiert	committed *adj.*
Enklave	enclave *n.*
enorm	enormous *adj.*
entdecken	spot *vt*
entfernen	remove *vt*
entführen	hijack *vt*
entgehen lassen: sich eine Gelegenheit ≈	let an oppurtunity slip *v.*
entlassen werden	get laid off
entlassen, kündigen *jmdn.*	lay off *vt*

entlassen; überflüssig machen	make redundant *vt*
Entlassung	layoff *n.*
Entsalzung(sanlage)	desalination *n.* (plant)
Entschuldigung; Ausrede	excuse *n.*
entsetzlich, fürchterlich, schrecklich; mies	appalling *adj.*
entsetzt, schockiert	outraged *adj.*
entwerfen	draft *vt*
entwickeln	develop *vt/vi*
Geschmack finden (an)	develop a taste (for)
Entwurf	draft *n.*
Erdgas	gas: natural ≈ *n.*
Erfindung	invention *n.*
erfolgreich (*Adj.*)	successful *adj.*
erfolgreich sein	do well *vi*
Erfolgsgeschichte	success story *n.*
ergeben; einbringen; abwerfen (Rendite)	yield *vt*
Ergebnis (infolgedessen)	result *n.* (as a ≈)
Ergebnisse	results *n.*
ergreifen (Maßnahmen)	take *vt* (measures)
erhältlich; verfügbar	available *adj.*
erheblich, signifikant	significant *adj.*
Erholung (*von Krankheit, Krise etc.*)	recovery *n.*
erlangen (*mit Anstrengung*)	obtain *vt*
erleben (*etw.*)	experience *vt*; witness *vt*
erleichtern	relieve *vt*
erleichtern; (sich ≈), seine Notdurft verrichten	relieve *vt* (oneself)
ermutigen (*jmdn.*)	encourage *vt*
erneuern	renew *vt*
ernsthaft; streng; schwer (getroffen)	severely *adv.* (hit)
Ernte	crop *n.*
erobern	conquer *vt*
Eröffnung (eines Flughafens)	opening *n.* (of an airport)
erpressen	blackmail *vt*
erreichen (Ziele)	reach (objectives) *vt*
Ersatzteil	spare part *n.*
erscheinen (vor Gericht)	appear *vi* (in court)
erschöpft (*Person*); aufgebraucht (*Ressourcen*)	exhausted *adj.*
erschrecken (*jmdn.*); Angst einjagen (*jmdm.*)	frighten *vt*
ersetzen	replace *vt*
Ersparnisse (*Pl.*)	savings *n. pl.*
ersticken; abwürgen	stall *vt*
erstklassig	first-rate, first-class *adj.*
erteilen (einen Auftrag)	place *vt* (an order)
Erträge (*pl.*)	earnings (*n. pl.*)
erwägen	consider *vt*
Erwerb, (Auf-)Kauf	acquisition *n.*
erzielen	achieve *vt*
Europäische Gemeinschaft	European Community *n.*
Europa-Skeptiker	eurosceptic *n. sg.*, eurosceptics *n. pl.*
evaluieren; bewerten	evaluate *vt*
ewig	eternal *adj.*
EWS (Europäisches Währungssystem)	EMS (European Monetary System) *n.*
Ex-Banker, ehemaliger Banker	ex-banker *n.*

existentiell	existential *adj.*
exklusiv; ausschließlich (Exklusivrechte)	exclusive *adj.* (rights)
Exodus; (massive) Abwanderung	exodus *n.*
expandieren	expand *vi*
Expansion	expansion *n.*
extern	external *adj.*
exzessiv; überzogen	excessive *adj.*
EZB (Europäische Zentralbank)	ECB (European Central Bank) *n.*
F & E (Forschung & Entwicklung)	R & D (Research & Development) *n.*
Fabrik	factory *n.*
Facharbeiter, Fachkraft	skilled labour *n.*
Fahrgeld, -gebühr	fare *n.*
Fahrzeug	vehicle *n.*
Faktor	factor *n.*
Falle (*jmdn.* in die ≈ locken)	trap *vt*
Falle: in der ≈ sitzen; gefangen sein	trapped (be ≈)
fallen lassen, aufgeben (Plan, Strategie)	ditch *vt* (a plan, a strategy)
Fallgrube, Falle, Fallstrick	pitfall *n.*
fällig	due *adj.*
Fallschirm (großzügige Abfindung)	parachute *n.* (a golden ≈)
falsch laufen; schiefgehen	go wrong *vi*
Familienunternehmen	family business *n.*
feiern (*etw.*)	celebrate *vi/vt*
feilschen; schachern	haggle *vi*
feindlich; feindselig	hostile *adj.*
fertigstellen, vervollständigen	complete *vt*
Fertigungs-, Produktionshalle	factory floor *n.*
Fertigungsband	production line *n.*
Fertigungsindustrie	production industry
Fertigungswerk	production plant
festnehmen	arrest *vt*
Festung	fortress *n.*
feuern, entlassen	fire *vt*
fiktiv; erdichtet, erfunden; fingiert	fictitious *adj.*
Finanzdienstleistungen	financial services *n. pl.*
Finanzmärkte	financial markets *n. pl.*
Finanzministerium	Finance Ministry *n.*/ Treasury (BE) *n.*
Finanzvorstand	CFO (Chief Financial Officer) *n.*
Firewall (*PC*)	firewall *n.*
Fixkosten; Gemeinkosten	overheads *n. pl.*
fleißig; gewissenhaft, sorgfältig	diligent *adj.*
Fließband; Montageband	assembly line *n.*
fließen (Dinge im Fluss halten)	flow *vi* (keep things ≈ing)
florieren, gedeihen	thrive *vi*, prosper *vi*
Fluggesellschaft	airline *n.*
Flugzeug; Flugzeuge	aircraft (*sg.*), aircraft (*pl.!*) *n.*
FOB (*Incoterm*)	FOB (Free on Board)
folgen: auf dem Fuße ≈	follow suit *vi*
Folie; Transparenz; Durchsichtigkeit	transparency *n.*
fordern, verlangen (dass)	demand *vt* (that)
Formular (Anmelde-≈)	form (registration ≈)
Fortschritt (Fortschritte machen)	progress *n.* ≈)
fortsetzen (ein Projekt)	carry on *vt* (a project)

Deutsch	English
Fracht	cargo *n.* (*pl.*: cargoes); freight *n.*
frei Haus	franco domicile *adv.*
freilassen	release *vt*
Früchte tragen	bear *vt* fruit *n.*
früher, vorherig	former *adj.*
Führerschaft (Markt- ≈)	leadership *n.* (market ≈)
Führungskraft	executive *n.*
Fundament; Grundlage	fundament *n.*
Fusion	merger *n.*
fusionieren (mit)	merge *vi* (with)
Fuß fassen (im Markt)	get a foothold (in the market)
Gang, (Straßenbande)	gang *n.* (street ≈)
garantieren, sicherstellen	guarantee *vt*
Gärtner	gardener *n.*
Gastfreundschaft	hospitality
Gebot, Angebot (Übernahme-≈)	bid (takeover ≈) *n.*
Gebrauchtwagen	used car *n.*
Gebühr	fee *n.*
Geburtenrate, -quote	birth rate *n.*
Geburtstag, Jahrestag	anniversary *n.*
gefährden	endanger *vt*
gefährden (*jmdn./etw.*)	put *so./sth.* at risk *vt*
gefälscht(e Produkte)	faked *adj.* (products)
Gefängnisstrafe (absitzen)	prison sentence *n.* (serve a ≈)
Gegenzug (im ≈ für)	return *n.*: in return (for)
Gehalt (des Vorstandsvorsitzenden)	compensation (CEO ≈) *n.*
Gehaltsliste	payroll *n.*
Geheimdienst	intelligence service, secret service *n.*
Gehirn; Hirn	brain *n.*
geistesabwesend	absent-minded *adj.*
geistiges Eigentum	intellectual property *n.*
Gelände (Firmen-≈, Werks-≈)	premises *n. pl.*
Geländewagen; SUV	SUV (Sports Utility Vehicle) *n.*
gelangen (an die Küste)	get *vi* (to the coast)
Geldautomat	automated teller machine (ATM) *n.*
Gelder, Geldmittel, finanzielle Mittel	funds *n. pl.*
Geldschein, Banknote	banknote *n.*
Gelegenheit (aus Anlass von)	occasion *n.* (on the ≈ of)
gemäß	according *adv.* (to)
Gemeinschaftsunternehmen, Joint Venture	joint venture *n.*
genehmigen; billigen	approve *vt*
generieren; erzeugen	generate *vt*
geopolitisch	geopolitical *adj.*
geradewegs (an/zu)	straight (to) *adv.*
Gerät, Vorrichtung	device *n.*
gerichtet (auf); abzielend (auf)	targeted *adj.* (at)
Gerichtsurteil	court ruling *n.*
geringfügig, marginal	marginal *adj.*
gesamt	entire *adj.*
gesättigt(e Märkte)	saturated *adj.* (markets)
Geschäft	business *n.*
Geschäfte (*Pl.*) tätigen, ≈ machen	to do business (*sg.!*) uncountable *n.!*
sich an die Arbeit machen	to get down to business (*sg.!*) uncountable *n.!*

Jmd. meint es ernst.	So. means business *(sg.!)* uncountable *n.!*
eine Firma führen	to run a (!) business *countable n.!*
Jmd. ist im Ölgeschäft / in der Ölindustrie / in der Ölbranche	So. is in the oil business.
Geschäft (ein gutes ≈)	deal *n.*, bargain *n.* (a good ≈)
Geschäftsgepflogenheiten	business practices *n. pl.*
Geschäftsleute	business people *n. pl.*
geschehen; sich ereignen	occur *vi*
gescheitert	failed *adj.*
Geschenk; Gabe, Talent	gift *n.*
Geschmack finden (an)	develop a taste (for)
Gesinnungswandel	change of mind *n.*
Geste	gesture *n.*
geteilt, gespalten (die Meinungen sind ≈)	divided *adj.* (opinions are ≈)
gewähren	grant *vt*
Gewerkschaft	union (BE: trade ≈ , AE labor ≈) *n.*
gewidmet; mit Leib und Seele dabei sein	dedicated *adj.* (to *sth.*)
Gewinn	gain *n.*
Gewinn; Nutzen	avail *n.*
vergeblich, umsonst	to no ≈
gewinnen (an Boden)	gain *vt* (ground)
gewinnen (Preis)	win *vt*
Gewinnspanne	profit margin *n.*
gewissenhaft	conscientious *adj.*
gewöhnlich (wie ≈)	usual *adj.* (as ≈)
gewöhnlich(e Leute)	ordinary *adj.* (people)
gierig	greedy *adj.*
Gipfel(treffen)	summit *n.*
Glaubwürdigkeit	credibility *n.*
Gleichgewicht	balance *n.*
Gleichgewicht zwischen Arbeits- und Freizeit	work-life balance *n.*
Glück (haben)	lucky *adj.* (be ≈)
Goldesel; Unternehmen mit hoher Liquidität	cash cow *n.*
Goldstandard	gold standard *n.*
GPS	GPS (global positioning system) *n.*
Graphik, Diagramm, Schaubild	graph *n.*
greifen (nach)	reach (out) (for) *v.*
Großauftrag	major order *n.*
größer(er Investor); bedeutend	major *adj.* (investor)
Großhändler	wholesaler *n.*
Großteil	bulk *n.*
großzügig	generous *adj.*
gründen (ein Unternehmen)	establish, set up; found (a company) *vt*
Gründer (Unternehmens-≈)	founder *n.* (company ≈)
gründlich	thorough *adj.*
Grundstücksmakler	real estate agent *n.*
Grundwasser	groundwater *n.*
Gutachten; Expertise; Sachverstand; Expertenwissen; fachliche Kompetenz	expertise *n.*
Güterzug	freight train *n.*
Habitat; Lebensraum	habitat *n.*
Hacker (PC)	hacker *n.*
Hafen	harbour (BE), harbor (AE) *n.*; port *n.*

haftbar (machen)	liable *adj.*, (hold so.) liable
halten (ein Versprechen)	keep *vt* (a promise)
Hand in Hand (gehen mit)	hand in hand (go ≈ with)
handeln	act *vi*
Handelsbilanz	balance of trade, trade balance *n.*
Handelsblock	trading bloc *n.*
Handelskammer	chamber of commerce *n.*
Handelsmesse [≠ fairer Handel!]	trade fair *n.* [≠ fair *adj.* trade!]
Händler (Auto-≈)	dealer *n.* (car ≈)
Handschuh	glove *n.*
Handy	cellphone, mobile phone *n.*
Hang; Abhang (Skipiste)	slope *n.* (skiing ≈)
Haufen, Stapel; anhäufen, aufhäufen	pile *n.*; pile up *vt.*
Haufen; Stapel	pile *n.*
Hauptsitz	HQ (headquarters) *n.*
Hauptversammlung (HV), (ordentliche ≈); Jahreshauptversammlung	annual general meeting (AGM) *n.*
Hebel(wirkung); (Möglichkeit, den Preis zu beeinflussen)	leverage *n.* (on) (price)
heftig, erbittert	fierce *adj.*
Heilmittel; Gegenmittel; Abhilfe	remedy *n.*
heimisch, Binnen-	domestic *adj.*
Helm	helmet *n.*
herausbringen, veröffentlichen; freilassen	release *vt*
Herausforderung	challenge *n.*
herausgeben, veröffentlichen	issue *vt (Aktien; Buch)*
heraushalten (sich ≈ aus)	keep out (of) *v.*
Hersteller	manufacturer *n.*
hervorbringen	bring forth *vt*, create *vt*
Herzanfall, Herzschlag, Herzinfarkt	heart attack *n.*
hierarchisch	hierarchical *adj.*
Hilfe (Struktur-≈)	aid *n.* (structural ≈)
Hin- und Rückflug	return flight (BE), roundtrip (AE) *n.*
hindern, behindern	hamper *vt*
hinterherhinken (*jmdm. / etw.*)	lag *vi* behind
hinzufügen; vergrößern	add to *vi* (!)
Historiker(in)	historian *n.*
hitzig(e Debatte)	heated *adj.* (debate)
Höchstwert, Höhepunkt	peak *n.*
hockend (Hockstellung)	crouching *adj.* (position)
holprig	bumpy *adj.*
Holzkiste	wooden box *n.*
horrend	horrendous *adj.*
HR, Personalabteilung	HR (Human Resources) *n.*
Hybridantrieb	hybrid drive *n.*
Hygiene	hygiene *n.*
Hypothek	mortgage *n.*
Idealismus	idealism *n.*
Idee; Vorstellung; Ahnung (keine ≈)	idea *n.* (no ≈)
identisch	identical *adj.*
Illustration; Abbildung	illustration *n.*
illustrieren; veranschaulichen; bebildern	illustrate *vt*
im Gegenzug (für)	in return (for)

Immobilie	property, real estate n.
Immobilienblase (platzt)	housing bubble n. (bursts)
Immobilienmarkt	property market n.
Immobilienpreise	housing prices n.
Immobilienpreise	real estate prices n.; property prices n.; housing prices n.
implementieren; einrichten	implement vt
Importquote	import quota n.
in die Höhe schnellen, schießen	rocket vi
in die Höhe treiben, befeuern	boost (profits) vt
in Echtzeit	in real time adv.
in Kraft treten, wirksam werden	take effect vi
industrialisieren	industrialise, industrialize vt
ineffizient	inefficient adj.
Inflation(srate)	inflation (rate) n.
Ingenieur(in)	engineer n.
inhaftieren, einsperren, ins Gefängnis werfen	jail vt
Inhalt(e); Inhalt, Gehalt	contents n.pl.; content n.sg.
Inkompetenz	incompetence
innovativ	innovative adj.
Insolvenz, Bankrott	bankruptcy n.
Inspektor	inspector n.
inspizieren	inspect vt
installieren (Antivirenprogramme)	instal(l) vt (anti-virus programs)
Instrument	instrument n.
Integration	integration n.
intern	internal adj.
Internetfirma	dotcom n. (coll.); internet company n.
investieren	invest vt (in/into)
Investor	investor n.
ironisch(erweise)	ironic(ally) adj. / (adv.)
Irrtum; Fehler (technischer ≈)	error n. (technical ≈)
IT-Blase	IT bubble n.
IWF (Internationaler Währungsfond)	IMF (International Monetary Fund) n.
Jahreshauptversammlung	annual general meeting (AGM) n.
Jahrzehnt	decade n.
jeweilig	respective adj.
Jugendarbeitslosigkeit	youth unemployment n.
jugendlich, heranwachsend	adolescent adj.
Kampagne (Werbe-≈)	campaign n. (advertising ≈)
kämpfen (ums Überleben); zu kämpfen haben	struggle (for survival) vi
kapern; erobern; gefangennehmen	capture vt
Kapital (Start-≈); Hauptstadt	capital n. (start-up ≈ , initial ≈)
Kapitalismus	capitalism n.
Karriere(weg); Berufslaufbahn	career n. (path)
Kartell (Drogen-≈)	cartel n. (drug ≈)
Kasse; Tages-, Registrierkasse	cash register n.
Katalog	catalogue (BE); catalog (AE) n.
kauern, (sich) (zusammmen-≈)	crouch vi
Kaufhaus(kette)	department store (chain) n.
Kaufkraft	purchasing power, buying power n.
Kern(geschäft)	core (business) n.
Kielwasser (im ≈ von; infolge)	wake n. (in the ≈ of)

Kinderarbeit	child labour (BE), ≈ labor (AE) *n*.
Kiste (Bierkasten; Obststeige)	crate *n*. (beer ≈; fruit ≈)
klagen, rechtliche Schritte einleiten	legal action *n*. (take ≈)
klettern *vi* (≈ über etw.); erklettern *vt*	climb *vt* (≈ over sth.); climb *vt*
Klima(wandel)	climate (change)
KMUs (kleine und mittelständische Unternehmen)	SMEs (Small and Medium-sized Enterprises) *n*.
Knappheit; Mangel	shortage *n*.
Knie (*jmdn.* in die Knie zwingen)	knee *n*. (to bring so. to his/her knees)
Kollege/Kollegin	colleague *n*.
Kommentar (kein ≈)	comment *n*. (no ≈)
Kommentator	commentator *n*.
kommentieren	comment *vt*
kompatibel	compatible *adj*.
Kompromiss	compromise *n*.
Konferenz	conference *n*.
Konflikt	conflict *n*.
konfrontiert (mit)	confronted *adj*. (with)
konjunkturell, zyklisch	cyclical *adj*.
Konkurrent, Rivale	rival *n*.
Konkurrent, Wettbewerber	competitor *n*.
konkurrenzfähig(e Firma); umkämpft(er Markt)	competitive *adj*. (company); competitive *adj*. (market)
konkurrieren (mit)	compete (with) *vi*
Konkurs anmelden	declare bankruptcy
Konkurs, Insolvenz, Bankrott	bankruptcy *n*.
Konsequenz, Folge	consequence *n*.
konsolidiert	consolidated *adj*.
Konsum, Verbrauch	consumption *n*.
kontinuierlich	continuous *adj*.
Konto; Verantwortung; Rechenschaft (*jmdn.* zur Verantwortung ziehen)	account *n*. (hold so. to ≈)
Kontrolle (außer ≈)	control *n*. (out of ≈)
Kontrolle (die ≈ übernehmen)	control *n*. (take over ≈)
Konvergenzkriterium	convergence criterion (*pl*.: criteria)
Konzept	concept *n*.
Kopfjäger; Personalabwerber; Nachwuchsjäger	headhunter *n*.
kopieren	copy *vt*
koppeln, binden an (eine Währung)	peg sth. to (a currency)
Körper; Körperschaft; Gremium; Institution	body *n*.
Korruption	corruption *n*.
Kostenersparnisse	cost savings *n.pl*.
Kratzer (von Anfang an)	scratch *n*. (from ≈)
Kreativität	creativity *n*., creativeness *n*.
Krebs (*Krankheit*)	cancer *n*.
Kreditnehmer; Entleiher; Borger	borrower *n*.
Krise	crisis (*pl*.: crises) *n*.
Krisenzeit	time of crisis *n*.
kritisch(e Lage)	critical *adj*. (situation)
Kronkolonie	crown colony *n*.
Kühlschrank	fridge *n*.
Kunde (Geschäfts- ≈ ; Service- ≈)	client *n*.
Kunde/Kundin (Stamm-≈)	customer *n*. (regular ≈)

Kundenstamm	customer base *n.*, customer portfolio *n.*
kurzfristig *Adj.*	short-term *adj.*
kurzfristig *Adv.*	in the short term *adv.*
kurzlebig	short-lived *adj.*
Küsten-(Gebiete)	coastal *adj.* (areas)
Ladenbesitzer	shopkeeper *n.*
Ladendieb	shoplifter *n.*
Lager(-Bestand)	stock *n.*
Lager(halle)	warehouse *n.*
ländlich(es Gebiet)	rural *adj.* (area)
langatmig	lengthy *adj.*
langfristig *Adj.*	long-term *adj.*
langfristig *adv.*, auf lange Sicht	in the long term / run *adv.*
leasen	lease *vt*
Leben: am Leben erhalten	keep sth/so. alive *vt*
lebenslang	life-long *adj.*
Lebensversicherung(spolice)	life insurance (*sg.!*) policy
lebhaft(e Nachfrage)	keen *adj.* (demand)
Leck	leak *n.*
lecken	leak *vi*
leihen, ausleihen (Geld), (Geld) aufnehmen	borrow *vt* (money)
Leine	leash *n.*
jmdn. an der langen ≈ führen	give a long ≈ to, to keep *so.* on a long leash
Leistung; Errungenschaft	achievement *n.*
Leistungsprämie (Weihnachtsgeld)	bonus *n.* (Christmas ≈)
Leiter (Marketing-≈ ; Verkaufs-≈)	director *n.* (marketing ≈ ; sales ≈)
Leitung (Firmen-≈)	management *n.* (corporate ≈)
letztendlich; schließlich (doch)	after all *adv.*
Lieferkette/ Beschaffungskette	supply chain *n.*
Lieferung (Ware & Vorgang)	shipment *n.*
Lieferung (*Ware, nicht: Vorgang!*)	consignment *n.*
Lieferung; Aus-, Zulieferung (*Vorgang*)	delivery *n.*
Lieferwagen	delivery van *n.*
Lieferzeit, Lieferfrist	delivery time *n.*
Lizenz	licence (BE), license (AE) *n.*
Lkw	truck *n.*
LKW-Fahrer	truck driver *n.*
Lobby	lobby *n.*
loben	praise *vt*
Logistik(branche)	logistics (industry) *n.*
Logo	logo *n.*
Löhne (*Pl.*)	wages *n. pl.*
Lohnerhöhung, Gehaltserhöhung	pay rise *n.*
löschen (Daten)	delete *vt*
Lösegeld	ransom *n.*
Lösung (eines Problems)	solution *n.* (of a problem)
loswerden (*etw.*)	get rid (of)
löten	solder *v.*
lukrativ	lucrative *adj.*
Luxus(image)	luxury (image) *n.*
Luxusmarke	luxury brand *n.*
Magazin (*Zeitschrift*)	magazine *n.*
Magnat	magnate *n.*

Mangel; Knappheit	shortage *n.*
manipulieren (Konten)	manipulate *vt* (accounts)
Manuskript	manuscript *n.*
Marine	navy *n.*
Marke	brand *n.*
Markenimage	brand image *n.*
Marktanteil	market share *n.*
Markteintritt	market entry *n.*
marode, kränkelnd	ailing *adj.*
Massenproduktion	mass production *n.*
Maßnahme	measure *n.*
Material (Info-≈)	material (info ≈)
Megacity (*sg.*), Megacitys (*pl.*)	megacity (*sg.*), megacities (*pl.*) *n.*
Mehrarbeit leisten, Überstunden machen	overtime *adv.* (work ≈)
Mehrheit	majority *n.*
Mentalität	mindset *n.*
Messe; Handelsmesse	fair; trade fair *n.*
Mietkosten	rental *adj.* costs
Minderheitsbeteiligung	minority stake *n.*
Mindestlohn	minimum wage *n.*
Ministerium	ministry *n.*
Missbrauch	abuse *n.*
Mitarbeiter	employee *n.*
Mitgliedschaft	membership *n.*
Mittelschicht	middle class *n.*
Mobbing	bullying *n.*
Möbel(geschäft)	furniture *n.* (store)
Mobilität	mobility *n.*
Mode(messe)	fashion *n.* (fair)
Modekleidung	fashion wear *n.*
Modell	model *n.*
Modellpalette	model range *n.*
modifizeiren, (ab-)ändern	modify *vt*
Monopol	monopoly *n.*
Monopolist, Inhaber eines Monopols	monopolist *n.*
Montageband; Fertigungsband	assembly line *n.*
Münze	coin *n.*
Muss (ein ≈)	must (a ≈) *n.*
Muster (Waren-≈)	sample *n.*
mutmaßlich, angeblich	alleged *adj.*
nach oben treiben (Arbeitslosigkeit)	push up *vt* (unemployment)
nach und nach	bit by bit; little by little; gradually *adv.*
Nachahmer	imitator *n.*
Nachfrage (auf *einem Gebiet*, nach *Rohstoffen*)	demand *n.* (in *an area, commodities*)
Nachfrage (Binnen-≈)	demand *n.* (domestic ≈)
Nachfrage (nach *Produkten*)	demand *n.* (for *product*s)
nachhaltig	sustainable *adj.*
Nachhaltigkeit	sustainability *n.*
Nachrichtensendung	news broadcast *n.*
Nachwuchskräfte (*Pl.!*)	junior staff *n.sg.!*
Nahrung (Tier-≈)	nutrition *n.* (animal ≈)
naiv	naïve *adj.*
nicht genug erwirtschaftend; die nicht genug	underperforming *adj.*

erwirtschaften	
nicht zum Kerngeschäft gehörend(e Aktivitäten)	non-core *adj.* (activities)
niedrigeres Marktsegment (in ein ≈ gehen); (in den) Massenmarkt (eintreten)	down-market *adv.* (go ≈)
Niedriglohnland	low-wage *adj.* country
Nische	niche *n.*
Nischenprodukt	niche product *n.*
Nomade/Nomadin	nomad *n.*
Null-Toleranz-Politik	zero tolerance policy *n.*
Nutzung; Auslastung (Kapazitäts-≈)	utilization *n.* (capacity ≈)
Obsession, Vernarrtheit	obsession *n.*
offenkundig, offenbar, evident	evident *adj.*
öffentliche Debatte	public debate *n.*
öffentliche Dienstleistungen	public services *n. pl.*
öffentliche Finanzierung	public funding *n.*
öffentliche Hand	public sector *n.*
Öffnungszeiten	opening hours *n.*
ökologisch	ecological *adj.*
ökonomisch, (volks)wirtschaftlich	economic *adj.*
ökonomisch, sparsam	economical (!) *adj.*
Oligarch	oligarch *n.*
Onlinegeschäft, -unternehmen	online business *n.*
operieren, tätig sein	operate *vi*
Opfer (ein ≈ bringen)	sacrifice *n.* (make a ≈)
Opfer (eines Unfalls)	victim *n.* (of an accident)
Option	option *n.*
Organisator	organizer *n.*
organisiertes Verbrechen	organized crime *n.*
Panik: in Panik geraten	panic *vi* (*pp:* panicked)
Passagier, Fluggast	passenger *n.*
Passwort	password *n.*
Patent	patent *n.*
Patrone; Kartusche (*Drucker*)	cartridge *n.*
Pension (hohe ≈en)	pension *n.* (high ≈s)
Personal; zu viel ≈ haben	staff *n.*; be overstaffed *adj.*
Pest; Plage; Heimsuchung	plague *n.*
Pflicht(bewusstsein)	duty *n.* (sense of ≈)
pharma(zeutisches) (Unternehmen)	pharma(ceutical) (company)
Piraterie (Produkt ≈)	piracy *n.* (product ≈)
plagen, quälen	plague *vt*
pleitegehen	go bust (*coll.*) *vi*
Politik (= Strategie); (Versicherungs-)Police	policy *n.*
Portfolio	portfolio *n.*
Posten, Position (berufliche Stellung)	post *n.*
Potential (Markt-≈)	potential *n.* (market ≈)
Potential(e) (Kosteneinsparungs-≈)	potential(s) *n.* (cost saving ≈)
Praktikant(in)	intern *n.*
Praktikum	internship *n.*
praktisch	practically *adv.*; virtually *adv.*
Preis-Obergrenze; gedeckelter Preis	price cap *n.*
Premierminister(in)	Prime Minister *n.*
Priorität	priority *n.*
private Wirtschaft	private sector *n.*

Privatisierung	privatisation (BE), privatization (AE) *n.*
Produktion, Herstellung	production *n.*
Produktpalette	product range *n.*
Professionalität	professionality *n.*
professionell	professional *adj.*
Profil (*auch im Internet*)	profile *n.*
profitieren	benefit *vi*
Projekt	project *n.*
Protektionismus	protectionism *n.*
Protokoll (≈ schreiben)	minutes (take the ≈) *n. pl.*
[≠ zeremonielles Protokoll; ≠ electron. Protokoll]	[≠ protocol !]
Prototyp	prototype *n.*
punkten, abschneiden	score (*in this meaning:*) *vi*
pünktlich	punctual *adj.*
Qualifikation	qualification *n.*
Qualitätsstandard	quality standard *n.*
Quartals(bericht)	quarterly *adj.* (report)
Quelle (Einnahme-≈ , Energie-≈)	source *n.* (of income, energy)
quetschen; pressen; drängen; (aus dem Markt) (ver)drängen	squeeze *vt* (out of the market)
Rabatt, Preisnachlass	discount *n.*
Radnabe; Drehkreuz (für Flugverkehr)	hub *n.* (air ≈)
Rand; Spanne; Spielraum; Marge (Gewinnspanne)	margin (profit ≈) *n.*
rapide	rapid *adj.*
rauswerfen	kick out *vt*
Rechenschaft (*jmdn.* zur Verantwortung ziehen); Verantwortung; Konto	account *n.* (hold so. to ≈)
Rechner, Computer	computer *n.*
Rechnung	invoice *n.*
Rechnungsprüfer(in)	comptroller *n.*; controller *n.*; auditor *n.*
rechtliche Schritte einleiten, klagen	legal action *n.* (take ≈)
Referendum, Volksentscheid	referendum *n.*
Regierung	government *n.*
Regierungsunterstützung	government support *n.*
Regulierung; Regelung; Vorschrift; Anordnung	regulation *n. sg.*
Regulierungsbehörde; Aufsichtsbehörde	regulator (*sg.*) / regulators (*pl.*) *n.*
Reifen	tyre *n.*
Reise (See- ≈ , im Weltall)	voyage *n.*
Reiseziel, Zielort	destination *n.*
Rekord(erträge)	record *n.* (earnings)
Rekordhoch	record high *n.*
rekrutieren; einstellen	recruit *vt*
relevant; wichtig; einschlägig	relevant *adj.*
Renaissance	Renaissance *n.*
Rendite	return on investment *n.*
Rentabilität	profitability *n.*
Rentensystem	pension system *n.*
Reparatur (in schlechtem Zustand)	repair *n.* (in bad ≈)
reparieren	repair *vt*
Reserve(währung)	reserve *n.* (currency)
Reservierung	reservation *n.*

Ressourcen; Rohstoffquellen etc.	resources *n. pl.*
Rettungsplan	rescue plan *n.*
Rezept (gegen die Deflation); (Koch)rezept	recipe *n.* (against deflation)
Rezession	recession *n.*
Riese, Gigant (Chemieriese)	giant *n.* (chemical ≈)
riesig	huge *adj.*
Risiken; (gegen alle Wahrscheinlichkeit)	odds *n.* (against all ≈)
Risiko	risk *n.*
risikofeindlich, Risiken abgeneigt	risk-averse *adj.*
risikofreundlich	risk-friendly *adj.*
robust	robust *adj.*
Rohöl	crude oil *n.*
Rohstoff	raw material *n.*
Roman	novel *n.*
rote Zahlen (schreiben)	red *adj.* (be in the ≈)
Route (Flug-≈)	route *n.*
Rückgrat	backbone *n.*
Rückstau (an Aufträgen *etc.*)	backlog *n.*
rufen (Taxi); begrüßen (als *etw.*);	hail *vt* (as *sth.*)
Ruhestand	retirement *n.*
Ruhestand; in den ≈ gehen	retirement *n.*; retire *vi*
Ruheständler; Rentner; Pensionär	pensioner *n.*
Saison	season *n.*
sanitäre Anlagen, Einrichtungen (*Pl.*)	sanitation *n. sg.*
satthaben (*etw.*)	be fed up (with) *vi*
Säule (der Stabilität)	pillar (of stability)
Säule; Spalte (*Tabelle*)	column *n.*
Schadensersatz	damages (*n. pl.*)
Schadensersatz leisten	pay damages *n. pl.*
Schaffung; Schöpfung	creation *n.*
schalten; Schalter	switch *vt; n.*
Schatten; Nuance	shade *n.*
Schätzung; Kostenvoranschlag	estimate *n.*
Schaupsieler; Künstler; 'Diensterbringer' (Spitzenkraft)	performer *n.* (top performer)
Schauspielerin / Schauspieler	actress / actor *n.*
scheitern	fail *vi*
Schicht	shift *n.*
Schicht (soziale ≈ , Klasse)	class *n.*
Schicksal	fate *n.*
Schiff; Seefahrzeug	vessel *n.*
Schiff-Fahrtsstraße	shipping-lane *n.*
Schlagloch	pothole *n.*
schlampig, schludrig, salopp	sloppy *adj.*
schlank(e Versorgungskette)	lean *adj.* (supply chain)
schließen, still-legen	close down *vt*
schließlich/letztendlich (etwas tun)	end up *vt* (doing sth)
schmuggeln	smuggle *vt*
Schnäppchen(jäger)	bargain (hunter) *n.*
schneiden; kürzen; (Kosten) senken	cut (≈ costs)
Schritt; Maßnahme	step *n.*
schrumpfen	shrink *vi*
Schuld: (*jmdm.*) die Schuld geben (für/an)	blame *vt* (*so.* for *sth.*)

Schuldenlast	debt burden *n.*
Schutzgeld	protection money *n.*
schwächen; sich abschwächen	weaken *vt/vi*
schweißen	weld *vt/vi*
Schwellenländer	emerging countries *n.*
Schwung (an ≈ gewinnen)	momentum *n.* (to gain ≈)
selbstbewusst	self-confident *adj.*
Selbstmord (begehen)	suicide *n.* (commit ≈)
sicher	secure *adj.*
Sicherheit(system)	security (system) *n.*
Sicherheitsüberprüfung	safety check *n.*; security check *n.*
sichern (Einnahmen; Arbeitsplätze)	secure *vt* (revenues; jobs)
Sicht: auf lange Sicht, langfristig (*Adv.*)	in the long run / term *adv.*
Signal	signal *n.*
sitzen	seated (to be ≈)
Sklave(narbeit)	slave *n.* (work)
Skorpion	scorpion *n.*
Solar-, Sonnen-(energie)	solar *adj.* (energy)
Sonderangebot	special offer *n.*
sorgfältig	careful *adj.*
soziales Netzwerk	social network *n.*
Sozialsystem	welfare system *n.*
Soziologe/Soziologin	sociologist *n.*
Spannung(en)	tension(s) *n.*
Sparte (Unternehmens-≈)	division *n.*
Sparte, Bereich (Mobilfunk-≈)	division *n.* (mobile phone ≈)
Spekulation(sblase)	speculation *n.* (bubble)
spekulieren	speculate *vi*
spenden	donate *vt*
spezialisieren (sich ≈ auf)	specialise, specialize (in) *v.*
Spezifizierung, Spezifikation	specification *n.*
Sphäre; Kugel; Raum (öffentlicher ≈)	sphere *n.* (public ≈)
Spion; spionieren	spy *n.*; spy *v.*
Spionage (Industrie-≈)	espionage *n.* (industrial ≈)
Sprecher	spokesman *n.*
Staat	State *n.*
staatlich geführt	state-run *adj.*
staatliche Hilfe, Unterstützung	state (aid), state (support) *n.*
staatliche/öffentliche Ausgaben (*Pl.*)	public spending *n. sg.*
Staatsanleihen	government bonds *n. pl.*
Staatsbetrieb	state-owned *adj.* enterprise
stabil	stable *adj.*
Stadion (*Sport*)	stadium *n.*
Stadtteil, Stadtviertel	quarter *n.* of a city
Stadtverwaltung	municipality *n.*, city administration *n.*
stagnieren	stagnate *vi*
Stahl	steel *n.*
Stand (Messe)	stand *n.*
Stand, (Verkaufs-)Stand, Markt-)Bude	stall *n.*
standardisiert	standardized *adj.*
Standort	location *n.*
Start, Beginn, Anfang (von ≈ an)	start *n.* (from the ≈)
stattfinden	take place *vi*

Status (Sonder- ≈)	status *n.* (special ≈)
stechen	sting *vt*
steckenbleiben; stehenbleiben; stocken / abwürgen (*etw.*); (*etw.*) zum Stillstand bringen	stall *vi / vt*
stehen (herum-≈)	stand (about) *vi*
stehen (still≈)	still (stand *vi* ≈)
steigen *vi*; steigern (*etw. / vt*)	increase *vi/vt*
steigern (*etw.*); anheben (Preise)	raise (sth.) *vt* (≈ prices)
steigern; erhöhen *(quantitativ & qualitativ)*	enhance *vt*
Stellenabbau, Stellenkürzungen, Streichung von Arbeitsplätzen	job cuts (*pl.*)
Steuerbehörde, Fiskus	fiscal authorities *n. pl.*, fisc *n. sg.*
Steuererhöhung	tax raise *n.*
Steuererklärung	tax declaration *n.*
Steuersystem	tax system *n.*
Steuerzahler	taxpayer *n.*
stickig	stuffy *adj.*
Stillstand	standstill *n.*
Stillstand (zum ≈ bringen); Halt	halt *n.* (bring to a ≈)
stimmen, abstimmen; votieren (für)	vote *vi* (for)
Stoff	fabric *n.*
stolz	proud *adj.*;
auf *etw.* stolz sein	take pride in *sth.*
störend (umwälzende Technologie)	disruptive *adj.* (≈ technology)
stornieren; absagen	cancel *vt*
Strafe, Geldstrafe; Sanktion	penalty *n.*
Straffreiheit	impunity *n.*
Strategie	strategy *n.*
Streifen (Land)	strip *n.* (of land)
Streik	strike *n.*
Streikposten	picket *n.*
streiten	have an argument
streng	strict *adj.*
streng; ernst	severe *adj.*
strenger machen (Regeln *etc.*)	tighten (rules etc.) *vt*
Stromausfall	blackout *n.*
strömen (in die Städte)	flock *vi* (into the cities)
Studie; Umfrage	survey *n.*
Studienabschluss	graduation *n.*
stutzen, zurechtschneiden; (Personal) abbauen	trim *vt.* (workforce)
Subvention	subsidy *n.*
subventionieren; finanziell unterstützen	subsidise (BE), subsidize (AE) *vt*
Suche (auf der ≈ nach)	search (in ≈ of)
Symbol	symbol *n.*
Synergie	synergy *n.*
Tagesordnung (auf der ≈)	agenda *n.* (on the ≈)
technische Spielerei	gadget *n.*
technische Überprüfung	technical inspection *n.*
teilen, aufteilen; aufspalten	divide *vt*
teilnehmen (an einer Besprechung)	attend *vt* (a meeting)
Teilung (Arbeits-≈)	division of labour (BE) / labor (AE) *n.*
Teppich	carpet *n.*
Termin (haben)	appointment *n.* (have an ≈)

Textil-	textile *adj.*
Textilie	textile *n*
Tierversuche	animal testing *n.*
tilgen (Schulden)	clear (debts) *vt*
Tor (Fabrik-≈)	gate *n.* (factory ≈)
Tor (nach)	gateway *n.* (to)
Tourismus	tourism *n.*
toxisch, giftig	toxic *adj.*
Transaktion; Abwicklung	transaction *n.*
Transit; (beim Transport)	transit *n.* (in ≈)
Transport: beim Transport	in transit
Transportindustrie	road-hauling industry *n.*
Transportunternehmer	truck operator *n.*; road-haulier *n.*
Treibstoff	fuel *n.*
Treue (zum Unternehmen)	loyalty (company ≈) *n.*
Trinkwasser	drinking water *n.*
Trojaner (*auch: Schadsoftware*)	trojan *n.*
turbulent	turbulent *adj.*
übel, böse; Übel	evil *adj./n*
über die Runden kommen	make ends meet
überdenken	reconsider *vt*
überdenken	rethink *vt*
Übereinstimmung (in ≈ mit, gemäß)	accordance *n.* (in ≈ with)
überfüllt	overcrowded *adj.*
überhitzt	overheated *adj.*
überholt, überaltert	outdated *adj.*
überleben	survive *vi*
Übernahme	takeover *n.*
Übernahme(angebot)	takeover *n.* bid *n.*
übernehmen (ein Unternehmen) [vs. überholen!]	take over *vt* (a company) [vs. overtake *vt* !]
übernehmen (*etw.* von *jmdm.*)	adopt *vt* (*sth.* from *so.*)
überprüfen	check *vt*
überreden	persuade *vt*
überschwemmen, überfluten	flood *vt*
Übersetzer	translator *n.*
Überstunden	extra hours *n. pl.*; overtime *adv.*
übertragen; übermitteln (Daten *etc.*)	transmit *vt* (data *etc.*)
überwachen	monitor *vt*
überwiegen; vorherrschen; sich durchsetzen	prevail *vi*
überwinden	overcome *vt*
überzogen(es Konto)	overdrawn *adj.* (account)
umgehend	promptly *adv.*
ummünzen, umwandeln	convert, turn (into) *vt*
Umsatz	turnover *n.*
umsonst, vergeblich	to no avail
umstrukturieren, reorganisieren	restructure *vt*
umweltfreundlich	environment-friendly *adj.*
Umweltverschmutzung	pollution *n.*
umwerben	woo *vt*
unabsichtlich	unintentional *adj.*
unangenehm	unpleasant *adj.*
unaufgefordert, unverlangt (Blindbewerbung,	unsolicited *adj.* (≈ application)

Initiativbewerbung)	
unbezahlbar	unaffordable *adj.*
unfair(er Wettbewerb)	unfair *adj.* (competition)
unflexibel, starr, unbiegsam; unelastisch(er Arbeitsmarkt)	inflexible *adj.* (labour [BE]/ labor market [AE])
ungelernte Arbeiter (*pl.*), Hilfsarbeiter	unskilled labour *n. sg.!*
ungewöhnlich	unusual *adj.*
unglaublich	incredible *adj.*
universal	universal *adj.*
unkalkulierbar; unabsehbar; unermesslich	incalculable *adj.*
unrentabel	unprofitable *adj.*
Unterbrechung, Störung	disruption *n.*
unterfinanziert	underfunded *adj.*
untergraben, unterminieren	undermine *vt*
Unterhalt; Instandhaltung	maintenance *n.*
Unterhaltung	chat *n.*
Unterkunft, Behausung	housing *n.*
Unternehmen	company *n.*; enterprise *n.*
unternehmen (*etw.*); (Reformen) angehen	undertake *vt* (reforms)
Unternehmen (v.a. US-Großunternehmen)	corporation *n.*
Unternehmens- (Geschäftswelt)	corporate *adj.* (world)
Unternehmens-(kultur)	corporate *adj.* (culture)
Unternehmensphilosophie	corporate *adj.* philosophy
Unternehmensregeln	company rules *n.*
Unternehmenssteuer	corporate *adj.* tax
Unternehmensstruktur	corporate *adj.* structure
Unternehmensverantwortung	CR (Corporate Responsibility) *n.*
Unternehmer(in)	entrepreneur *n.*
unterschätzen	underestimate *vt*
unterschreiben	sign *vt*
Untersuchung	investigation *n.*
unvertraut	unfamiliar *adj.*
unvorhergesehen	unforeseen *adj.*
unvorstellbar	unconceivable *adj*, unimaginable *adj.*
Unzuverlässigkeit	unreliability *n.*
urban, städtisch	urban *adj.*
Urbanisierung, Verstädterung	urbanisation *n.*
Urheberrecht	copyright *n.*
Urlauber(in)	holiday maker
ursprünglich, original	original *adj.*
US-Notenbank	Federal Reserve (Fed) *n.*
VAE (Vereinte Arabische Emirate)	UAE (United Arab Emirates) *n. pl.*
verabschieden (ein Gesetz)	pass *vt* (a law)
Verantwortung; Rechenschaft (*jmdn.* zur Verantwortung ziehen); Konto	account *n.* (hold so. to ≈)
verärgern	anger *vt*, annoy *vt*, upset *vt*
Verbesserung	improvement *n.*
verblüfft; fassungslos	stunned *adj.*
Verbraucher, Konsument	consumer *n.*
Verbraucherboykott	consumer boycott
Verbraucherorganisation	consumer organisation (BE), organization (AE)
verbreiten	spread *vt*
verbreitern	widen *vt*

Verbündeter; Alliierter	ally n.
verderblich	perishable adj.
verdienen (Geld)	earn vt (money)
verdienen (seinen Lebensunterhalt)	earn vt (one's living)
verdoppeln	double vt
verdreifachen	triple vt
Verfall	decay n.
verfolgen (Ziele)	pursue vt (objectives)
Verfolgung; Streben (im ≈ nach etw.)	pursuit n. (in ≈ of sth.)
vergeblich, umsonst	to no avail adv.
Vergeudung (Zeit-≈)	waste n. (of time)
verhandeln	negotiate (with) vi
Verhandlung	negotiation n.
verhängen; erheben (Zölle)	impose vt
Verkäufe (Pl.), Absatz (Sg.)	sales n. pl.
verkaufen (sich gut ≈)	sell vt; sell well
verkaufen, abgeben, abstoßen	sell off vt
Verkaufs-, Absatzzahlen	sales figures n. pl.
Verkaufsstelle	outlet n.
verklagen (jmdn.)	sue vt; take vt (so.) to court
Verkleinerung, Abbau	downsizing n.
verlagern: (etw.) ins Ausland ≈	move (sth.) offshore
Verlagerung ins Ausland	offshoring n.
verlegen, verlagern	relocate vt
Verleger, Verlag	publisher n.
Verletzung (von Menschenrechten)	violation n. (of human rights)
Verlust(e)	loss(es) n.
Verluste anhäufen	run up vt losses
Verluste machen	incur vt losses
Vermögen	fortune n.
verpacken	package vt
Verpflichtung	obligation n.
verprellen; vor den Kopf stoßen	alienate vt
verringern	cut down vt
Versagen, Scheitern, Fehlschlag	failure n.
Versandanzeige	advice note n.
verschieben	postpone vt, put off vt
verschlanken; rationalisieren	downsize vt
verschlechtern (sich ≈)	deteriorate vi
verschlimmern; sich verschlechtern	worsen vi/vt
Verschlüsselung(ssoftware)	encryption n. (software)
verschmutzen	pollute vt
verschönern; beschönigen	embellish vt
verschuldet	indebted adj.
verschwiegen; heimlichtuerisch	secretive adj.
Verschwiegenheit; Geheimnistuerei	secrecy n.
verseuchen, kontaminieren	contaminate vt
Versicherung (Sg.), Versicherungen (Pl.)	insurance n. (no pl.!)
Versicherungsbranche	insurance industry n.
Versicherungspolice (Sg.), Versicherungspolicen (Pl.)	insurance policy n. (sg.), insurance policies (pl.)
Versicherungsunternehmen	insurance company n.
Versorgung, Nachschub (sichern, sicherstellen)	supplies n. pl. (secure vt ≈)

verstaatlichen	nationalise (BE), nationalize (AE) *vt*
verteiltes Material; ausgeteilte Unterlage	handout *n*.
Vertrag (*privatrechtlich*)	contract *n*.
Vertrag, Abkommen (*pol.*)	treaty *n*.
vertrauen	trust *vt*
Vertrauensbruch	breach of trust *n*.
vertraulich	confidential *adj*.
Vertreter	representative *n*.
Vertrieb(snetz)	distribution *n*. (network)
Vertriebshändler (lokaler ≈)	distributor (local ≈) *n*.
verübeln; sich (an etw.) stoßen, stören	resent *vt*
verwässern (*etw.*)	dilute *sth*. *vt*
verwirren	confuse *vt*
verwirrend	confusing *adj*.
verwischen; verschwimmen lassen	blur *vt*
verzichten können auf etw.	do without *sth*. *v*.
verzögern, hinauszögern	delay *vt*
verzweifeln	despair *vi*
Veto einlegen (gegen *etw.*)	veto *vt*
vielversprechend	promising *adj*.
Viertel	quarter *n*.
vierteljährlich	quarterly *adj./adv*.
Visitenkarte	business card *n*.
volatil, unbeständig, sprunghaft, unberechenbar	volatile *adj*.
Volkswirtschaft	economy *n*., national ≈
volkswirtschaftlich	economic *adj*.
vorbereiten (sich auf etw. ≈); sich einstellen auf	get ready (for)
vorbereiten: sich ≈ auf, einstellen auf *etw*.	get ready (for) *vi*
vorgeben; so tun, als ob ...	pretend *vt*
Vorgesetzter	superior *n*.
vorhersagen	predict *vt*
Vorrat; Versorgung; Nachschub; (Geldmenge)	supply *n*. (money ≈)
Vorschlag	suggestion *n*.
Vorstand (alle ≈s-Mitglieder)	board *n*.
Vorstandsvorsitzender, Geschäftsführer	Chief Executive Officer (CEO) *n*.
vorstellen (Produkt, Person)	present (a product, a person) *vt*
Vorstellungsgespräch	interview, job interview *n*.
vorteilhaft	advantageous *adj*.
vorübergehend	temporary *adj*.
Wachstumsfaktor	growth factor *n*.
wack(e)lig; klapprig; gebrechlich	rickety *adj*.
Wahl (keine andere ≈)	choice *n*. (no other ≈)
wählerisch	choosy *adj*.
Währung	currency *n*.
Währungs- (Währungsunion)	monetary *adj*. (Monetary Union)
wandeln (sich), ändern (sich); ändern	change *vi/vt*
Wanderarbeiter(in)	migrant worker *n*.
Waren (*Pl.*)	goods *n*. pl.
Warnung	warning *n*.
Weggang; Abreise, Abflug	departure *n*.
Weinberg	vineyard *n*.
weitergeben (Informationen)	pass on *vt* (information)
weitgehend	largely *adv*., to a large extent

Weizen	wheat *n.*
Weltbank	World Bank *n.*
Welthandelsorganisation	World Trade Organisation (WTO) *n.*
Werbekampagne	advertising campaign *n.*
Werbespot; Werbespots; Fernsehwerbung	commercial *n. sg.;* commercials *n.pl.*
Werft, Schiffswerft	shipyard *n.*
Werkzeug; Instrument; Hilfsmittel; Tool (PC)	tool *n.*
Werkzeugmaschine	machine tool *n.*
Wettbewerbsfähigkeit	competitiveness *n.*
Whistleblower	whistle-blower / whistleblower *n.*
widersprechen	contradict *vt*
widersprüchlich	contradictory *adj.*
Widerstand (gegen)	resistance *n.* (to)
wieder auf den Markt bringen	re-launch *vt*
wieder-, zurückgewinnen	regain *vt*
wiederaufnehmen (Besprechungen)	resume *vt* (meetings)
wild wuchernd; zügellos	rampant *adj.*
wirkungsvoll, wirksam	effective *adj.*
Wirtschaftsethik	business ethics *n.*
Wirtschaftslage	economic *adj.* situation
Wirtschaftswachstum	economic *adj.* growth
Wirtschaftswissenschaftler/-in, Ökonom/-in, Volkswirt	economist *n.*
Wissensindustrie	knowledge industry *n.*
Wohlfahrt(sstaat)	welfare *n.* (state)
Wohlstand, Reichtum	wealth *n.*
wohltätig	charitable *adj.*
Wohnung (Etagen- ≈)	flat *n.*
Wohnungswesen; Wohnungsbeschaffung; Wohnen; Unterbringung	housing *n.*
würdelos	undignified *adj.*
Wurm	worm *n.*
Wurzel	root *n.*
Wüste	desert *n.*
Wut (der Hit, der letzte Schrei)	rage *n.* (all the ≈)
Zeichnung	drawing *n.*
Zeit(vertrag)	temporary *adj.* (contract)
Zeitarbeiter	temporary *adj.* worker
Zeitarbeitskraft	temp *n.*
Zeitarbeitsplätze	temporary *adj.* jobs
Zeitplan (hinter dem ≈); Fahrplan	schedule *n.* (behind ≈)
Zelt	tent *n.*
Zentrale; Firmensitz	head office *n.*
Zentrum	centre (BE), center (AE) *n.*
zerbrechlich; fragil	fragile *adj.*
zerbrochen; erledigt; pleite	bust (*coll.*)
zerfallen; zerbröseln (*selbst/etw.*)	crumble *vi/vt*
Zeuge/Zeugin	witness *n.*
Ziel	target *n.*
Zielgruppe	target group *n.*
Zins; Interesse	interest *n.*
Zinssatz	interest rate *n.*
zögernd; abgeneigt (*etw.* zu tun)	reluctant *adj.* (be ≈ to)

Zoll (beim ≈ ; *Ort*)	customs *n. pl.!* (at ≈)
zu viel Personal (habend)	over-staffed *adj.*
Zufall; Zufalls-	random *n/adj.*
Zugang, Zutritt haben (zu *etw.*); auf *etw.* zugreifen; *etw.* abrufen	access *vt*
zugeben; einräumen	admit *vt*
Zugverkehr	train service *n.*
Zuhörerschaft; Publikum	audience *n.* (*sg.*)
Zulieferer, Lieferant(in)	supplier *n.*
zum Stehen kommen	grind to a halt *vi*
zur Verantwortung ziehen (*jmdn.*)	hold so. to account
zurechtkommen, fertigwerden (mit)	cope (with) *vi*
zurückerstatten (Kosten)	refund vt (costs)
zurückfallen	fall behind *vi*
zurückgeben	hand back *vt*
zurückgehen, nach unten gehen	decline *vi*; go down *vi*
zurückstellen, auf die lange Bank schieben, auf Eis legen	shelve *vt*
zurücktreten	resign *vi*
zurückverlangen (*etw.*)	demand (*sth.*) back *vt*
zurückweisen, ablehnen	reject *vt*
zurückziehen (etw.); abheben (Geld)	withdraw *vt*
zurückziehen; sich ≈ (von *etw.*)	withdraw (from) *v.*
Zusage, Versprechen	promise *n.*
zusammenarbeiten	cooperate *vi*
zusammenbauen, montieren	assemble *vt*
zusammenbrechen	collapse *vi*
Zusammenbruch	collapse *n.*
zusätzlich(e Bezahlung)	extra (pay) *adj.*
zuschneiden (auf)	tailor *vt* (to)
Zustand	state *n.*
zuverlässig	reliable *adj.*
Zweifel	doubt *n.*
zweifeln *vi*	be in doubt (about *sth.*)
Zwischenfall	incident *n.*

Glossar: Grammatikalische Terminologie
(glossary: grammatical terminology)

Adjektiv / adjective (*adj.*)
Eigenschaftswort, das die Eigenschaft, Beschaffenheit von etwas (Person oder Sache) angibt;
z.B.: eine *lange* Geschäftsreise (beim Substantiv), flektiert, d.h. mit angepasster Endung;
z.B.: Die Geschäftsreise ist *lang*. Nicht flektiert, unveränderliche Form.

adjunct *(englisch)* – *vs.* disjunct
wortbezogenes **Adverb**, Adverb, das sich auf ein anderes Wort (Verb, Adjektiv, Adverb) bezieht;
z.B.: He launched (*v.*) the product ***successfully***. The product launch was ***incredibly*** stressful (*adj.*).
He launched the product ***really / very*** successfully (*adv.*).

Adverb / adverb (*adv.*)
Umstandswort (Ort, Zeit, Art und Weise u.ä.), das die Umstände, z.B. einer Tätigkeit (auf das Verb bezogen), angibt (1), oder das bei einem Adjektiv (2) oder auch einem anderen Adverb (3) stehen kann und die Eigenschaft oder die Art und Weise, bzw. den Umstand quasi kommentiert,
z.B.: Die Verhandlungen liefen *glatt*. / The negotiations went *smoothly*. (1)
z.B.: Wir erlebten *unglaublich* schwierige Verhandlungen. / We experienced *incredibly* difficult negotiations. (2)
z.B.: Die Verhandlungen liefen *wirklich* glatt. / The negotiations went *really* smoothly. (3)
Ein Adverb kann sich auch auf den ganzen Satz(teil), bzw. Sachverhalt beziehen (4; vgl. *disjunct*),
z.B.: *Überraschenderweise* fiel der Aktienkurs nicht. / *Surprisingly*, the share price did not fall.

adverbial (expression)
Adverbialer Ausdruck, **gebraucht wie ein Adverb**; z.B.: the day after tomorrow / übermorgen (*Adv.*);
The other day / neulich (*Adv.*); at that time / zu jener Zeit

Agent (englisch; latein: *Agens*, also etwa: **Handelnde**, **Handlungsträger**)
Im Passiv wird der ‚Verursacher', der Handlungsträger in einer ***by***-*phrase*, d.h. mithilfe von ***by*** angegeben: z.B.: The ailing company was bought **by** a foreign investor. (Das kränkelnde Unternehmen wurde **von** einem ausländischen Investor gekauft.)
Bei der Umformung eines Aktiv-Satzes in einen Passivsatz kommt das ehemalige Subjekt des Satzes als ***agent*** nach dem ***by***; z.B.: A group of customers (**Subjekt**) sued the company. (**Aktiv**) > The company was sued **by** *a group of customers*. (**Passiv**)
Die Angabe des Agent erfolgt nur, wenn dies wirklich erforderlich ist; z.B.: The police arrested the burglar. > The burglar was arrested. (*by the police* ist unnötig,... von wem sonst?)

Aktiv / active (voice) – *vs.* Passiv / passive (voice)
Form des Verbs, die eine **Tätigkeit des Subjekts** ausdrückt;
z.B.: Er *verkaufte* seine Aktien. / He *sold* his shares.

Aspekt / aspect
Im Zeitensystem des Englischen werden i.A. folgende vier *Aspekte* (***aspects***) unterschieden: *simple*, *progressive* (auch: *continuous*), *perfect*, *perfect-progressive*. Vom deutschen Sprachsystem und –empfinden aus gesehen haben die englischen Zeitformen (*tenses*) in der Sprachpraxis jew. zwei Formen, ***simple forms*** **&** ***progressive*** (oder: *continous*) ***forms***, mit unterschiedlichen Bedeutungen, bzw. Verwendungsweisen, die eine gezielte Unterscheidung und Auswahl erforderlich machen;
z.B.: He *signed* (Simple Past Tense [**Past Tense = tense; simple = aspect**]) the contract.
vs.: While he *was signing* (Past Progressive [**Past = tense; progressive = aspect**]) the contract ...

auxiliary
Das Hilfsverb ist nicht Träger der eigentlichen Bedeutung, sondern erledigt – quasi als Stütze des (Voll-/Haupt-)Verbs – sozusagen ‚Hilfsdienste';
temporale Hilfsverben / temporal auxiliaries dienen der **Bildung der zusammengesetzten Zeiten**; z.B.: Er *hat* sein eigenes Unternehmen gegründet. / He *has* set up his own company.
Er *wird* sein eigenes Unternehmen gründen. / He *will* set up his own company.
modale Hilfsverben (Modalverben) / **modal auxiliaries** geben eine **Modalität** an;
z.B.: Sein Markteintritt *könnte* erfolgreich sein. His market entry *could* / *might* be successful.
Sein Geschäft *muss* rentabel sein. / His business *must* be profitable.
causal (s. **kausal**)

clause *(englisch)*
Nebensatz; Satzteil, der ein Verb enthält; z.B.: Having sold his patent …. As he had sold his patent …

Comparative (s. **Komparativ**)

conjunction (s. **Konjunktion**)

countable (*s.* **noun**)

disjunct *(englisch)* – *vs.* adjunct
satzbezogenes Adverb, Adverb, das sich auf einen ganzen Satz, Satzteil, bzw. gesamten Sachverhalt bezieht, im Deutschen wird in dieser Verwendung meist *–weise* an das Adverb angehängt und so als satzbezogen gekennzeichnet;
z.B.: *Seltsamerweise* hatte der Medienriese Subventionen von der EU erhalten. / *Strangely (enough),* the media giant had received subsidies from the EU.

finit(e Verbformen) / finite (clauses)
in Person und Zahl bestimmte – konjugierte – Verbformen (*vs.* **infinite Formen: Infinitive und Partizipien**);
z.B.: Der Börsengang *wurde abgesagt*. / The IPO *was cancelled*.

flektieren; flektiert(e Formen)
beugen; gebeugte Formen sind **deklinierte** Substantive (der Kunde, des Kunden etc.) und **konjugierte** Verben (ich verkaufe, du verkaufst etc.).

gerund *(englisch)*
ein **von einem Verb abgeleitetes Substantiv** (durch Anhängen von *–ing*), das sich auf eine Handlung, einen Vorgang oder einen Zustand bezieht, z.B.: speculating / Spekulieren, das Spekulieren.
Beachte: Das englische **gerund** wird **wie ein Substantiv, bzw. anstelle eines Substantivs** verwendet - z.B.: He hated **betting** [direktes Objekt], während das *Partizip Präsens* die Funktion eines Verbs in einer Verbalphrase, d.h. in einem verbalen Nebensatz oder Satzteil, hat – He made a fortune *by betting* against the Greek currency.), oder adjektivische Funktion (z.B.: a *raging* crowd / eine *tobende* Menge).

Imperativ, Befehlsform / imperative
z.B.: Verkaufe deine Aktien! Seien wir vorsichtig! / Sell your shares. Let's be cautious.

Indikativ – *vs.* Konjunktiv
Einer von drei **Modi**: Indikativ, Konjunktiv, Imperativ;
z.B.: Er *kauft* die Waren. (*vs.* … er kaufe …) / He *buys* the goods.

infinit(e Verbformen) / non-finite (clauses)
Die infiniten Verbformen sind **nicht personengebunden und nicht konjugiert** – zwei Arten: **Infinitive** und **Partizipien**;
z.B.: *Sein* oder *nicht sein ...* / *To be* or *not to be...*
Seine Gläubiger völlig *ignorierend*, betrat er die Bank. / *Ignoring* his creditors completely, he entered the bank.

Infinitiv
Grundform des Verbs; z.B.: verkaufen, verhandeln, herstellen / (to) sell, (to) negotiate, (to) produce

intransitiv / intransitive - (s. **Verb** / verb)

Inversion
Umkehrung, Umsetzung (der Wörter), **umgedrehte Wortstellung**
z.B.: Was *hatte er* (Verb-Subjekt [statt: Subjekt-Verb]) nicht alles getan, um den Konkurs abzuwenden.
Beispiele: How *can we* be profitable? *Did he* realize he was bankrupt? *Had he* known the outcome he would not have spent his whole fortune. Neither *would we*. Hardly *had he* set up his company ...

Kausal(er Nebensatz)
Nebensatz, der begründet, Gründe angibt; z.B.: Da die Belegschaft streikte, kam die Produktion zum Stillstand. / As the workforce was on strike, production ground to a halt.

Komparativ
Steigerung (bei Adjektiven und Adverbien): **1. Steigerungsstufe**;
deutsche Adjektive/Adverbien:
tüchtig – **tüchtiger** (– am tüchtig<u>sten</u> = 2. Steigerungsstufe / Superlativ),
gut – **besser** (– am besten = 2. Steigerungsstufe / Superlativ) – unregelmäßig;
englische Adjektive: tough – **tough<u>er</u>** (– tough<u>est</u> = 2. Steigerungsstufe / Superlativ),
competitive – **more competitive** (– <u>most</u> competitive = 2. Steigerungsstufe / Superlativ),
good – **better** (– <u>best</u> = 2. Steigerungsstufe / Superlativ);
englische Adverbien: brightly – **more brightly** (– <u>most</u> brightly = 2. Steigerungsstufe / Superlativ),
fast – **fast<u>er</u>** (– fast<u>est</u> = 2. Steigerungsstufe / Superlativ), (*adj. = adv.*, einsilbig),
well – **better** (– <u>best</u> = 2. Steigerungsstufe / Superlativ), unregelmäßig

Konjunktion / conjunction
Bindewort, welches einen Nebensatz einleitet, im Englischen auch einen partizipialen Nebensatz (*clause*); z.B.: Bevor alles begann. / *Before* it all started. Oder: *Before* setting up his business he took a university degree.

Konjunktiv – *(englisch: subjunctive) vs. Indikativ*
Einer von drei **Modi**: Indikativ, Konjunktiv, Imperativ;
z.B.: Der Geschäftsführer behauptete, er *habe* nichts davon *gewusst*.
Beachte: Der englische **subjunctive** wird **anders gebraucht** und **sehr wenig verwendet**.
z.B.: *Be it as it may.* / Sei es, wie es wolle. Oder: *So be it.* / So sei es, möge es sein.

misrelated participles *(englisch) (s. participle)*

modales Hilfsverb, Modalverb / modal auxiliary (s. auxiliary)

non-countable (s. noun)

non-finite (clauses) (s. infinit)

noun *(englisch)*; deutsch: Nomen, Substantiv, Hauptwort; z.B.: *Produkt / product*
Unterscheide: **countable** vs. **non-countable** (oder: **uncountable**) noun
countable noun: ‚zählbares' Substantiv, das man in Zahlen angeben kann;
z.B.: (zehn) *Mitarbeiter, Angestellte* / (ten) *employees*
non-countable noun: ‚nicht zählbares' Substantiv, welches man evtl. messen, aber nicht direkt in Zahlen angeben kann, oder ein **abstrakter Begriff** (ebenfalls nicht ‚zählbar');
z.B.: *Geld / money; Hunger / hunger*

Objekt / object
Satzglied, das von einem Verb als Ergänzung gefordert wird, als **direktes** (= Akkusativ-)Objekt;
z.B.: Er *erwarb* das Patent. / He *acquired* the patent. (**direktes Objekt** [= O_4])
z.B.: Er *erklärte* den Investoren (indirektes Objekt / Dativobjekt, O_3) seinen Geschäftsplan (O_4). / He *explained* his business plan (O_4 – direktes Objekt / wen oder was?) to the investors (O_3 – indirektes Objekt / wem?).

Partizip / participle
infinite Form / non-finite form; vom Verb abgeleitet für Partizipialsätze / partizipiale Nebensätze (participle clauses) und für adjektivischen Gebrauch; im Englischen gibt es **zwei Partizipien**: **present participle**, z.B.: buy**ing**, sign**ing**, ris**ing** / kaufend, unterzeichnend, steigend, d.h. in adjektivischem Gebrauch **in aktivischer Bedeutung**, und **past participle**, z.B.: bought, signed, risen / gekauft, unterzeichnet, gestiegen, d.h. als Adjektive **in passivischer Bedeutung**;
Unterscheide: smil**ing** (lächel**nde**) vs. disappoint**ed** (enttäusch**te**) shareholders (Aktionäre); interest**ing** offers (interessante Angebote) vs. interest**ed** parties (interessierte Parteien);
Beachte: Zu den gleichen Formen - Partizip Präsens *(-ing)* vs. Gerund *(-ing)* - s. *gerund*.

Partizipialkonstruktionen / participle constructions
Satzkonstruktionen, bzw. –teile, die als Verb ein Partizip (Present oder Past participle) haben;
z.B.: **Confronted** with the financial crisis, many car manufacturers granted generous discounts. / Mit der Finanzkrise **konfrontiert**, gewährten viele Autohersteller großzügige Rabatte.
z.B.: **Struggling** with a heavy debt burden, the company could not afford to invest in R & D. / Mit einer schweren Schuldenlast **kämpfend** *[oder:]* Da es mit einer … kämpfte, konnte es sich das Unternehmen nicht leisten, in F & E zu investieren.
Beachte: Das Partizip bezieht sich auf das Subjekt des Hauptsatzes (Beispiel 1: viele Autohersteller; Beispiel 2: das Unternehmen)

misrelated participles *(englisch)*
Partizipien, die in einer **Partizipialkonstruktion mit falschem Bezug** verwendet werden; als infinite Formen sind Partizipien nicht personenbezogen und bedürfen der Bestimmung durch den Hauptsatz, bzw. das Subjekt im Hauptsatz; daher bezieht sich das Partizip im (untenstehenden) Beispielsatz auf das Subjekt des Hauptsatzes, was wenig Sinn ergibt, bzw. der Ziegelstein würde (im Beispiel) die Straße überqueren:
z.B.: While *crossing* the street, a brick fell on his head.

Passiv / passive (voice) – vs. Aktiv / active (voice)
'Leideform', Form des Verbs, die eine **vom Subjekt** (aus gesehen) **erlittene Handlung** ausdrückt;
Beispiele: Das Unternehmen *wurde verkauft*. / The company *was sold*.
Unterscheide: **Vorgangspassiv** vs. **Zustandspassiv**
Das **Vorgangspassiv** drückt einen Vorgang, eine (dynamische) Handlung aus;
z.B.: Das Unternehmen *wurde* vom Marktführer *übernommen*. / The company *was (got [coll.]) taken over* by the market leader.

z.B.: Während der Prototyp *getestet wurde*, brach der ganze Markt zusammen. / While the prototype *was being tested*, the entire market collapsed.
Das Zustandspassiv drückt einen Zustand, ein Ergebnis aus;
z.B.: Er *ist geschlagen*. / He *is beaten*. (vs. He is being / gets / is getting beaten. [Vorgang])

phrasal verb
Das ist eine **Kombination** aus **Verb** und **Adverb** oder **Präposition** im Englischen, die zusammen eine **bestimmte Bedeutung** haben; Diese Bedeutung ergibt sich nicht aus der Summe von Verb und Adverb / Präposition;
z.B.: He *looked after* his employees very well. / Er kümmerte sich sehr gut um seine Mitarbeiter.
vs. The shareholder *jumped onto* the table to show his protest. (**kein phrasal verb**, denn *on* gehört als Ortsbestimmung zum Tisch und ergibt auch keine spezifische, andere Bedeutung in Einheit mit *jump*.)

Prädikat / (predicate)
Satzteil, der eine Aussage über das Subjekt enthält, d.h. das Verb oder die Verben, die sich auf das Subjekt beziehen; es kann aus **Hilfsverben und Voll- (oder Haupt-)verben** bestehen;
z.B.: Er **verkauft** (**Vollverb, finites Verb**, konjugierte Form = **ganzes Prädikat**) Kunstgegenstände.
z.B.: Er *hat* (**temporales Hilfsverb – 1. Prädikatsteil**) Kunstgegenstände **verkauft** (**Vollverb als Partizip Perfekt, 2. Prädikatsteil**).
z.B.: Er *will* (**modales Hilfsverb – 1. Prädikatsteil**) Kunstgegenstände **verkaufen** (**Vollverb im Infinitv – 2. Prädikatsteil**).
(*Im Englischen* wird der Begriff wenig verwendet und bezeichnet auch etwas anderes als im Deutschen, nämlich **alles, was nicht Subjekt ist**.)

Präposition / preposition
Verhältniswort, welches bei Substantiven steht; z.B.: *vor* der Besprechung / *before* the meeting

progressive form (= continuous form) – vs. simple form
Verlaufsform; z.B.: Sales *were slowing down*. The company *has been struggling* for some time.

Relativ(satz) / relative clause
Relativer Nebensatz, d.h. Nebensatz, der durch ein **Relativpronomen (rückbezügliches Fürwort)** eingeleitet wird; z.B.: die Fabrik, **die** geschlossen wurde / the factory that / which was closed down

Reported Speech *(englisch)*
indirekte Rede; z.B.: He claimed that the regulator had imposed a price cap. / Er behauptete, die Regulierungsbehörde habe eine Preisobergrenze festgesetzt.

sequence of tenses (s. Zeitenfolge)

stative verbs (deutsch: ‚statische' Verben)
Verben, die ihrem Wesen, bzw. ihrer Bedeutung nach keine (dynamische) Handlung ausdrücken, sondern einen **Zustand**, daher normalerweise nicht in der Verlaufsform (progressive / continuous form) verwendet werden, sondern in der **simple form**,
z.B.: The CEO *seemed* calm. (The CEO was seeming calm.)
Manche dieser (an sich statischen) Verben können auf verschiedene Weisen, d.h. in verschiedenen Bedeutungen, verwendet werden, die dann dynamisch sind, bzw. eine Handlung wiedergeben,
z.B.: He *had* a lot of money to spend on his business idea. *vs.* He *was having* dinner when … (active Handlung: have + dinner = zu Abend speisen)

Subjekt / subject
Satzgegenstand, der angibt, wer oder was eine Handlung vornimmt.
z.B.: *Der Vorstandsvorsitzende trat zurück. / The CEO resigned.*
Beachte: S V O = Subjekt - Verb - Objekt (normale Satzstellung);
z.B.: Neue Investoren (S) finanzierten (V) das Projekt (O_4). / New investors (S) financed (V) the project(O_4).
z.B.: Der Assistant (S) zeigte (V) ihr (O_3) viele Entwürfe (O_4). / The assistant (S) showed (V) her (O_3) many drafts (O_4).

subjunctive (s. Konjunktiv)

Substantiv (s. noun)

Superlativ / superlative
Steigerung (bei Adjektiven und Adverbien): 2. Steigerungsstufe;
deutsche Adjektive/Adverbien:
tüchtig – tüchti<u>ger</u> – **am tüchtig<u>sten</u>** = 2. Steigerungsstufe / Superlativ,
gut – besser – **am besten** = 2. Steigerungsstufe / Superlativ – unregelmäßig;
englische Adjektive: tough – toug<u>her</u> – **tough<u>est</u>** = 2. Steigerungsstufe / Superlativ,
competitive – <u>more</u> competitive – **<u>most</u> competitive** = 2. Steigerungsstufe / Superlativ,
good – better – **best** = 2. Steigerungsstufe / Superlativ;
englische Adverbien: brightly – more brightly – **<u>most</u> brightly** = 2. Steigerungsstufe / Superlativ,
fast – fast<u>er</u> – **fast<u>est</u>** = 2. Steigerungsstufe / Superlativ, (*adj. = adv.*, einsilbig),
well – better – **best** = 2. Steigerungsstufe / Superlativ, unregelmäßig

Syntax / syntax
(korrekter) Satzbau, Verknüpfung sprachlicher Einheiten im Satz

temporaler Nebensatz / temporal clause
Nebensatz, der die Funktion einer zeitlichen Einordnung hat;
z.B.: *Als ich Unternehmer war ... / When I was an entrepreneur ...*

temporales Hilfsverb / temporal auxiliary (s. **auxiliary**)

tense *(englisch)*
grammatikalische Zeitform; z.B.: Imperfekt (1. Vergangenheit), Plusquamperfekt (2. Vergangenheit) / Past Tense, Past Perfect etc.;
z.B.: *Die IT-Blase platzte, war geplatzt, wird platzen ... / The IT-bubble burst, had burst, will burst*

tense shift *(englisch)*
'Verschiebung' der Zeiten beim Wechsel von direkter zu indirekter Rede mit einleitendem Verb im Past Tense; z.B.: *The marketing assistant said: „The new campaign will boost sales." >*
The marketing assistant <u>said</u> that the new campaign would boost sales.

transitiv / transitive (s. **Verb / verb**)

uncountable (s. **noun**)

unflektiert (*vs.* **flektiert**)
nicht flektierte, ungebeugte Formen – vgl. **flektiert(e Formen)**

Verb / verb

Tätigkeitswort, das eine Handlung oder auch einen Zustand angibt und in finiten (d.h. flektierten) oder infiniten (nicht flektierten) Formen verwendet wird.

z.B.: Es *genügt* (finite Form, daher flektiert) nicht, etwas zu *sagen* (infinit, daher unflektiert als Infinitiv); man *muss* (finite Form, daher flektiert) etwas *tun* (infinite Form, daher unflektiert), nicht einfach nur unzufrieden *sein* (infinit, d.h. unflektiert).

Transitive Verben haben ein direktes Objekt;

z.B.: Er *erhielt* die Lizenz (direktes Objekt) *nicht.* / He *did not obtain* the licence (direct object).

Intransitive Verben können kein direktes Objekt haben,

z.B.: Letztes Jahr *stiegen* (selbst; kein Objekt!) die Preise deutlich. / Last year prices *rose* significantly.

Beachte: Im Englischen können zahlreiche Verben sowohl transitiv wie intransitiv gebraucht werden, z.B.: Prices *have increased* (***intransitive***) again. *vs.* The company *has increased* (***transitive***) its prices again. - <u>Vorsicht</u>: Bei manchen Verben sind die **Bedeutungen unterschiedlich**, je nachdem, ob sie **transitiv** oder **intransitiv** gebraucht werden: z.B.: Sales have declined. - Der Absatz ist zurückgegangen. (***intransitiver Gebrauch***) vs. She declined the offer. – Sie lehnte das Angebot ab. (***transitiver Gebrauch, andere Bedeutung***).

Zeitenfolge / sequence of tenses

Das (logische) Zusammenwirken verschiedener, aufeinander abgestimmter Zeitformen in einem Satzgefüge oder Text, das die Zeitebenen klarstellt,

z.B.: Als der Euro eingeführt wurde, hatten viele Investoren Immobilien erworben, da sie befürchteten, die europäische Währung würde nicht stabil sein und die ansteigende Inflation würde ihre Vermögen verringern. / When the euro *was introduced* (Past), many investors *had* already *acquired* (Past Perfect) real estate, since they *were afraid* (Past) the European currency *would not be* (Conditional) stable and rising inflation *would diminish* (Conditional) their fortunes.

Die Mechanismen sind im Englischen und Deutschen z.T. unterschiedlich,

z.B.: Wir *diskutieren* dieses Thema schon seit Stunden; ... wir *treffen* morgen eine Entscheidung. / We *have been discussing* this topic for two hours now; ... we*'ll make* a decision tomorrow.

Diagnose-Test

No.	Text	Aufgaben	Punkte
1.1	The new team leader managed the conflict in the team.	Füge folgende Wörter an geeigneten Stellen in der korrekten grammatikalischen Form in Englisch hinzu: **glücklicherweise**; **erfolgreich**. Es gibt evtl. mehrere Möglichkeiten. Bitte alle angeben.	3
1.2	Flat hierarchies are found in start-ups.	Füge **typischerweise** in korrekter englischer Form in normaler (unbetonter) Stellung hinzu.	1
1.3	The CFO pulled out of the agreement.	Füge **feige** im Englischen in korrekter Form an korrekter Stelle hinzu.	2
1.4	We could have outsourced production.	Füge **leicht** in korrekter englischer Form in korrekter Stellung hinzu.	2
1.5	The director remained … (1) although his assistant left … (2) again.	Füge folgende Wörter in korrekter Form ein: (1) **calm**, (2) **early**	2
1.6	When the applicant entered the room, he felt … (1) and looked … (2) at the interviewer.	Füge folgende Wörter in korrekter Form hinzu: (1) **uneasy**, (2) **shy**	3
1.7	The team leader hasn't attended any meetings lately.	Übersetze **lately** ins Deutsche.	1
1.8	"If you want to be promoted (1) you will have to work (2)."	Füge im If-Satz (1) in korrekter Form und in **normaler** Stellung **soon** ein; füge an der angegebenen zweiten Stelle die korrekte Form von **hard** ein.	2
1.9	She had to set up her own business.	Füge **really** (wirklich) an geeigneter Stelle hinzu.	1
1.10	The CEO didn't expect his employees to go on strike (1), as their wages had been increased (2).	Füge im ersten Satzteil an geeigneter Stelle **certainly** ein (nicht am Satzanfang!), im zweiten Satzteil **recently** und **significantly** in zwei unterschiedlichen sprachlich logischen und **normalen Stellungen** (nicht am Satzteilanfang!).	3
1.11	The CEO doubted her assistant's loyalty.	Beginne den Satz mit "Never …" und schreibe ihn in korrektem Englisch nieder.	2
1.12	With this new offer, the Japanese negotiators went … (1) than … (2) announced.	Füge die korrekten Formen ein: (1) **far**, (2) **previous**.	2

2.1	While the last few parts of the new prototype … (1), a blackout … (2) the whole plant to a standstill.	Füge folgende Verben in grammatikalisch korrekten Formen ein: (1) to assemble (Past Passive Progressive), (2) to bring (Simple Past).	2
2.2	"… we … (1) the components yet?" – "No, we … (2). Unfortunately, they … (3) yet.	Füge folgende Verben in grammatikalisch korrekten Formen ein: (1) to receive (Present Perfect Simple), (2) Kurzantwort mit erforderlicher Verbform, (3) to deliver (Present Perfect Passive).	3
2.3	The task force … (1) already, when the project … (2) by the new CEO.	Füge folgende Verben in grammatikalisch korrekten Formen ein: (1) to set up (Past Perfect Passive), (2) to cancel (Simple Past Passive)	2
2.4	"This supplier … wrong parts several times now!"	Füge folgendes Verb in grammatikalisch korrekter Form des Present Perfect (Simple oder Progressive) ein: to deliver.	1
2.5	"The government … on a tax reform for years now!"	Füge folgendes Verb in grammatikalisch korrekter Form des Present Perfect (Simple oder Progressive) ein: to work	1
2.6	Der Autohersteller ist seit Monaten in einer Krise. ▶ The car producer …. in a severe crisis … months.	Vervollständige die englische Übersetzung.	2
2.7	Before 2000, German CEOs used to … (1) a lot less. But … (2) the Daimler-Chrysler merger CEO compensation … (3) continuously in Germany, too.	Vervollständige die Sätze mit den korrekten Formen der folgenden Verben: (1) to earn und (3) to rise, sowie der korrekten Übersetzung von (2) seit.	3
2.8	Venezuela's revenues … (1) even before low oil prices … (2) the earnings of the state-run oil company again.	Füge folgende Verben in den grammatikalisch korrekten Formen (tenses!) ein: (1) to plunge, (2) to slash.	2
2.9	The German car company … (1) the construction of a new production plant in Kaliningrad, when the EU sanctions … (2) effect.	Füge folgende Verben in den jew. grammatikalisch korrekten Formen der Vergangenheit (tense / aspect!) ein: (1) to plan (still), (2) to take	2
2.10	"While the corruption scandal … (1) worse and worse, most customers still … (2) faithful to the brand."	Ergänze die korrekten Vergangenheitsformen der Verben (1) to get und (2) to remain.	2
2.11	The fate of the start-up … (1) uncertain … (2) yesterday. A week before, rivals …(3) rumours that the investors … (4) to withdraw their money.	Ergänze die korrekten Vergangenheitsformen der Verben (1) to be, (3) to spread und (4) to threaten sowie die englische	4

		Übersetzung von (2) bis.	
2.12	"We were under pressure. In order to survive we … (1) reach the break-even point … (2) December. … (3) then we … (4) well.	Ergänze die korrekten Vergangenheitsformen der Verben (1) to have to und (4) to do sowie die englischen Übersetzungen von (2) bis und (3) seit.	4
3.1	"Darf ich an der Besprechung teilnehmen? Letztes Mal durfte ich nicht." ▶ „… join the meeting? Last time I .. "	Übersetze die fehlenden Teile ins Englische.	2
3.2	The union leader … (1) play golf very well. However, when he played with the President, all of a sudden he … (2) hit the ball.	Ergänze die korrekten Übersetzungen für können.	2
3.3	"We *mustn't* only look at the quarterly results!"	Übersetze das modale Hilfsverb ins Deutsche	1
3.4	"They *must* go down-market." ▶ "They … down-market."	Setze den Satz ins Present Perfect.	1
3.5	"It is already 2 o'clock. Our business partners *should* soon be here."	Übersetze das modale Hilfsverb ins Deutsche.	1
3.6	"Thanks to many incoming orders we … to fire any employees."	Ergänze die korrekte Form von need im Past.	1
3.7	"Our sales have rocketed. But it is impossible that this is the result of our current advertising campaign alone." ▶ "Our current advertising campaign alone … sales so much."	Benutze can und to push up und formuliere den Satz so um, dass der Sinn erhalten bleibt.	1
3.8	„Die Zollabfertigung hat vielleicht zu lang gedauert." ▶ The customs clearance … too long.	Übersetze den Satz ins Englisch unter Verwendung von may und to take.	1
3.9	Vor wichtigen Entscheidungen ging der Firmenchef immer joggen. ▶ Before important decisions the company boss … go jogging.	Übersetze den Satz ins Englisch unter Verwendung eines geeigneten modalen Hilfsverbs. Gib zwei Alternativen an.	2
3.10	"We … a better offer, since they didn't really have any good alternative. But we didn't know that at the time and paid too much."	Ergänze need to make in der vom Kontext erforderten Form.	1
3.11	The whole board *was to* resign within 24 hours. ▶ Der gesamte Vorstand … innerhalb von 24 Stunden zurücktreten.	Welche zwei unterschiedlichen Bedeutungen kann das modale Hilfsverb in diesem Satz haben? Übersetze das Hilfsverb und erkläre die unterschiedlichen Bedeutungen.	3
3.12	Der Whistleblower soll angeblich eine Million Dollar erhalten haben. ▶ The whistleblower … one million	Übersetze die fehlenden Satzteile ins Englische unter Verwendung des erforderlichen modalen	2

	dollars.	*Hilfsverbs.*	
3.13	(Letztes Jahr hatten wir Engpässe in der Produktion von Weihnachtsartikeln.) a, Eigentlich sollte vor Weihnachten niemand in Urlaub gehen. b, Eigentlich hätte vor Weihnachten niemand in Urlaub gehen sollen. ▶ Actually, nobody … on a holiday before Christmas.	*Übersetze die beiden Varianten des Satzes mit dem modalen Hilfsverb sollen auf unterschiedliche Weisen, insgesamt **drei** Strukturen mit Modalverben.*	3
4.1	High-flyers often complain: "Envious managers bully us and many of our colleagues hate us." *(direct speech)* ▶ High-flyers often complain that jealous managers bullied them and many of their colleagues hated them. *(reported speech)*	*Richtig oder falsch? Korrigiere die unkorrekten Übertragungen in die indirekte Rede.*	1
4.2	HR experts claim: "Star performers partly have themselves to blame." *(direct speech)* ▶ HR experts claim that star performers partly have themselves to blame. *(reported speech)*	*Richtig oder falsch? Korrigiere die unkorrekten Übertragungen in die indirekte Rede.*	1
4.3	My boss tells me every morning: "Hold all phone calls for half an hour, will you?" *(direct speech)* ▶ My boss tells me every morning … *(reported speech)* 1. that I should hold all phone calls for half an hour. 2. to hold all phone calls for half an hour. 3. if I want to hold all phone calls for half an hour. 4. that I will hold all phone calls for half an hour. 5. that I am to hold all phone calls for half an hour.	*Kreuze alle korrekten Übertragungen in die indirekte Rede an.*	2
4.4	Last week the spokesman of the car manufacturer said: "Our assembly-lines have ground to a halt due to a strike of our most important suppliers since yesterday with the result that no cars will be produced in the next few days." *(direct speech)* ▶ Last week the spokesman of the car manufacturer said that … *(reported speech)*	*Ergänze die fehlenden Teile in indirekter Rede.*	5
4.5	The mediator asked the employee: "Have you been humiliated in front of your boss? How often has extra work been dumped	*Ergänze die fehlenden Teile in indirekter Rede.*	3

	on you?" *(direct speech)* ▶ The mediator asked the employee … *(reported speech)*		
4.6	Meine Kollegin fragte mich, wann ich meinen Jahresurlaub nehmen wolle, und riet mir gleich darauf, ich solle ihn nicht für August planen. *(direct speech)* ▶ My colleague asked me … (1) take my annual leave and advised me straight away … (2 - *zwei Möglichkeiten*) plan it in August. *(reported speech)*	*Übersetze die fehlenden Teile ins Englische.*	3
4.7	Already years ago, a representative of the Chamber of Commerce warned: "When we were looking for highly qualified graduates last month, there were only very few eligible applicants. And: talent will be even scarcer in the future." *(direct speech)* ▶ … warned that when … He added that talent … *(reported speech)*	*Ergänze die fehlenden Teile in indirekter Rede.*	4
4.8	The sheikh told the press: "My country would be forced to step up the production of crude oil if the oil price decreased further." *(direct speech)* ▶ The sheikh told the press that … (1) to step up the production of crude oil if the oil price … (2). *(reported speech)*	*Ergänze die fehlenden Teile in indirekter Rede.*	3
4.9	The government official said: "We had better cut public spending since tax revenues may decline even further." *(direct speech)* ▶ The government official said … (1) public spending since tax revenues … (2) *(reported speech)*	*Ergänze die fehlenden Teile in indirekter Rede.*	2
4.10	In the search for ideas on how to be more competitive the sales director said: "What about selling online?" *(direct speech)* ▶ … the sales director …. online. *(reported speech)*	*Finde ein geeignetes (einleitendes) Verb und ergänze die indirekte Rede möglichst idiomatisch.*	2
5.1	In the takeover battle, several small start-ups … (1). The founder of a small private bank remembered … (2), too, long ago.	*Ergänze die Verben im Passiv in der angegeben Zeit: (1)* **to swallow** *(Past); (2)* **to take over** *(gem. grammatikalischer Notwendigkeit in der Struktur); ersetze das Hilfsverb in einem Fall durch ein alternatives.*	2
5.2	He had to admit it: he was beaten – again. ▶ Er musste es eingestehen: Er … - wieder einmal.	*Übersetze ins Deutsche.*	1

5.3	It is clear now: the factory ... (1) Little remains ... (2).	Ergänze die Verben im Passiv in der angegeben Zeit: (1) **to close down** (Future); **to do** (Zeitform gem. gramm. Struktur)	2
5.4	Einige unserer besten Leistungsträger scheinen von einem Headhunter überredet worden zu sein, eine gut-bezahlte Position bei einem Konkurrenten anzunehmen. ▶ Some of our star performers ... by a headhunter to accept a well-paid position with a competitor.	Übersetze (die fehlenden Teile) ins Englische.	2
5.5	Shareholders were 'grilling' the CEO (with critical questions) at the AGM, while speculators bought significant blocks of shares. ▶ .... (1) (with critical questions) at the AGM, while ... (2) again and again.	Setze die Sätze ins Passiv.	3
5.6	It turned out that children ... (1), although the factory ... (2) not long before.	Ergänze folgende Verben in geeigneten Passivformen in den angegebenen Zeiten: (1) **to make work** (Past), (2) **to inspect** (Past Perfect).	2
5.7	The company gave fresh water to the workers. ▶ ...	Setze den Satz ins Passiv (in zwei Varianten). Lass den Agent (the company) weg.	2
5.8	Everybody expected him to leave the company. ▶ ...	Setze den Satz ins Passiv (in zwei Varianten). Lass den Agent (also: everybody) weg.	3
5.9	Man sagt, der Autohersteller sucht zurzeit nach einer Lösung für seine technischen Probleme. ▶The car producer ... for a solution for their technical problems at the moment.	Übersetze die fehlenden Teile ins Englische.	2
6.1	1. The shipment had arrived on time if there had been no strike. 2. If the maintenance service would be more reliable we might prolong the contract. 3. If the consignment does not arrive by Friday, we cancel all orders. 4. Our costs would have been much lower, if the government had issued the import licence earlier.	Richtig oder falsch? Hake die korrekten Sätze ab und korrigiere die fehlerhaften.	4
6.2	If the Chinese government did not back its own ex-monopolists, the economy ... (1)	Vervollständige die Sätze grammatikalisch korrekt mit	2

	healthier. We might have conquered the market, if our patent … (2)	*folgenden Verben: (1)* to be, *(2)* not to be stolen.	
6.3	1. If the company is state-owned, there may well be corruption. 2. Don't save money if the interest rate is around zero. Invest or buy real estate. 3. You should not become part of a sharia fund if you are in the sex industry. 4. "We could go out for a drink after the meeting, if you'd like to."	*Richtig oder falsch? Hake die korrekten Sätze ab und korrigiere die fehlerhaften.*	4
6.4	You can get a reasonable share of the market. But you have to find a suitable regional distributor. ▶ If you find a suitable regional distribution partner you … a reasonable share of the market.	*Verbinde die beiden Sätze zu einem Haupt- und Nebensatz (mit* if*).*	1
6.5	1. If the protectionist measures have been abolished it truly is a free market. 2. If you have no anonymous bank account in Delaware, you're fine. 3. If you continue to ignore CSR (Corporate Social Responsibility), you would have met with a lot of resistance from NGOs. 4. If the textile managers were really sorry, they would pay factory workers in Bangladesh a little more. 5. If he had adapted his product range to new trends he could be the market leader now.	*Richtig oder falsch? Hake die korrekten Sätze ab und korrigiere die fehlerhaften.*	5
6.6	1. "If the government had played fair, we would have had the first mover advantage." ▶ "… , we would have had the first mover advantage." 2. "We would have to re-think our strategy, if the authorities changed their procedures unexpectedly." ▶ "We would have to re-think our strategy, …"	*Formuliere die Sätze um, so dass* if *wegfällt.*	2
7.1	1. As the project manager left, the project was delayed. 2. As the project manager had left, the project was delayed.	*Richtig oder falsch? Hake alle grammatikalisch möglichen, zeitlogischen korrekten Sätze ab und streiche die falschen (Zeitformen) durch.*	3

	3. As the project manager has left, the project was delayed.		
	4. As the project manager has left, the project will be delayed.		
	5. As the project manager had left, the project would be delayed.		
	6. When the project manager has been leaving, the project was being delayed.		
7.2	The new express service promises: 1. Every book that is ordered in the morning arrives on the same day. 2. Every book that is ordered in the morning will arrive on the same day. 3. If a book is ordered in the morning, it will arrive on the same day. 4. If a book is ordered in the morning, it arrives on the same day.	*Richtig oder falsch? Hake alle grammatikalisch möglichen, zeitlogischen korrekten Sätze ab und streiche die falschen (Zeitformen) durch.*	2
7.3	The loan was approved … 1. as soon as the credit enquiry agency … the green light. 2. although the valuation of the flat …missing. 3. faster than the borrower … 4. because the bank … new borrowers.	*Vervollständige die Sätze grammatikalisch korrekt mit folgenden Verben: 1.* **to give**, *2.* **to be, still**, *3.* **to expect**, *4.* **to need**; *when two tenses are possible, write down both forms.*	2
7.4	He said he would not cut jobs if the union … (1) demanding higher wages. He said that if the wages had not increased significantly he … (2) to cut jobs.	*Vervollständige die Sätze grammatikalisch korrekt mit folgenden Verben: 1.* **to stop**, *2.* **not to have to**.	2
7.5	She said she … (1) her shares of the cosmetics group as long as it … (2) to be involved in animal testing.	*Vervollständige die Sätze zeitlogisch und grammatikalisch korrekt mit folgenden Verben: 1.* **not to sell**, *2.* **not to find** *(passive).*	2
7.6	I wish the interest rate … so low now.	*Füge* **not to be** *in der grammatikalisch korrekten Form hinzu.*	1
7.7	"The investors keep asking when our new venture … (1). They don't seem to be convinced that our technology … (2) profitable as soon as the new law … (3)."	*Vervollständige die Sätze zeitlogisch und grammatikalisch korrekt mit folgenden Verben: 1.* **to break even**, *2.* **to become**, *3.* **to pass** *(passive).*	3
7.8	"We had a fierce argument before we … (1) a unanimous decision. But I still believe that we must carry out several surveys until we … (2) sufficient statistical evidence."	*Vervollständige die Sätze zeitlogisch und grammatikalisch korrekt mit folgenden Verben: 1.* **to reach**, *2.* **to get**.	2

7.9	She ... (1) several temporary jobs since she ... (2) from university. During her studies she ... (3) work part-time. Now she ... (4) for a permanent position in the media industry.	Vervollständige die Sätze zeitlogisch und grammatikalisch korrekt mit folgenden Verben: 1. to have, 2. to graduate, 3. used to, 4. to look for.	2
7.10	Renault will have a huge problem when the current charismatic CEO, Carlos Ghosn, ...	Füge to retire in der grammatikalisch korrekten Form hinzu.	1
7.11	1. By offering attractive discounts you can push up sales, but also lose money. 2. The CEO left the boardroom to take an urgent call. Speaking too long on the phone, an important decision was made without him. 3. With the sanctions taking effect tomorrow, we must quickly find domestic suppliers. 4. While staring at the display of her mobile phone all the time, the plane took off without her, because she was totally distracted and arrived too late at the check-in.	Richtig oder falsch? Welche Sätze sind korrekt?	2
7.12	... (1) with too many bureaucratic obstacles the retail chain gave up its plans to enter the Indian market soon. However, ... (2) its market leadership at home already, it had to find new potential for growth.	Ergänze die korrekten Formen von 1. to confront, 2. to lose.	2

Diagnose-Test
Lösungen

No.	Lösung	Level	Punkte
1.1	**Luckily / Fortunately,** the new team leader managed the conflict in his team **successfully**. / The new team leader **luckily / fortunately** managed the conflict in his team **successfully**.	1 / 3	3
1.2	Flat hierarchies are **typically** found in start-ups.	1 / 4	1
1.3	The CFO pulled out of the agreement **in a cowardly fashion**.	1	2
1.4	We could **easily** have outsourced production.	1 / 4	2
1.5	The director remained **calm** although his assistant left **early** again.	2	2
1.6	When the applicant entered the room, he felt **uneasy** and looked **shyly** at the interviewer.	2 / 4 1 / 2	3
1.7	**in letzter Zeit**	3	1
1.8	If you want to be promoted **soon** you will have to work **hard**.	1 / 3 / 4	2
1.9	She **really** had to set up her own business.	4	1
1.10	The CEO **certainly** didn't expect his employees to go on strike, as their wages had **recently** been increased **significantly**.	4	3
1.11	**Never did** the CEO **doubt** her assistant's loyalty.	4	2
1.12	With this new offer, the Japanese negotiators went **further** than **previously** announced.	4	2
2.1	While the last few parts of the new prototype **were being assembled**, a blackout **brought** the whole plant to a standstill.	1	2
2.2	"**Have** we **received** the components yet?" – "No, we **haven't**. Unfortunately they **have not / haven't been delivered** yet."	1	3
2.3	The task force **had been set up** already, when the project **was cancelled** by the new CEO.	1	2
2.4	"This supplier **has delivered** wrong parts several times now!"	2	1
2.5	„The government **has been working** on a tax reform for years now!"	2	1
2.6	The car producer **has been** in a severe crisis **for** months.	2	2
2.7	Before 2000, German CEOs used to **earn** a lot less. But **since** the Daimler-Chrysler merger CEO compensation **has been rising** continuously in Germany, too.	3 / 2	3

2.8	Venezuela's revenues **had plunged** even before low oil prices **slashed** the earnings of the state-run oil company again.	3	2
2.9	The German car company **was still planning** the construction of a new production plant in Kaliningrad, when the EU sanctions **took** effect.	3	2
2.10	"While the corruption scandal **got / was getting** worse and worse, most customers still **remained** faithful to the brand."	3	2
2.11	The fate of the start-up **was** uncertain **until** yesterday. A week before, rivals **had spread** rumours that the investors **were threatening** to withdraw their money.	4	4
2.12	"We were under pressure. In order to survive we **had to** reach the break-even point **by** December. **Since** then we **have been doing** well."	4	4
3.1	"**May I** join the meeting? Last time I **wasn't allowed to**."	1	2
3.2	The union leader **could** play golf very well. However, when he played with the President, all of a sudden, he **was unable / not able to** hit the ball.	1	2
3.3	„Wir **dürfen nicht** nur auf die Quartalsergebnisse schauen!"	1	1
3.4	"They **have had to go** down-market."	1	1
3.5	… **dürften** (bald hier sein)."	2	1
3.6	"Thanks to many incoming orders we **didn't need to** fire any employees."	2	1
3.7	„Our current advertising campaign alone **cannot have pushed up** sales so much."	2	1
3.8	The customs clearance **may have taken** too long.	2	1
3.9	… the company boss **would go / used to** go jogging.	2	2
3.10	„We **needn't have made** a better offer …"	3	1
3.11	… **sollte** …. 1. Es wurde vom ihm erwartet. (Zwang von außen) 2. So sollte es kommen. (Schicksalhafte Fügung)	3	3
3.12	The whistleblower **is said to have received** one million dollars.	3	2
3.13	(Last year we had bottlenecks in the production of Christmas items.) Actually … a, 1. nobody **was supposed to go** … b, 2. nobody **should have gone** … b, 3. nobody **ought to have gone** …	3	3
4.1	High-flyers often complain that envious managers ~~bullied~~ **bully** them and many of their colleagues ~~hated~~ **hate** them.	1	1
4.2	*correct*	1	1

4.3	*wrong: 3, 4*	1	2
4.4	Last week the spokesman of the car manufacturer said that **their** assembly-lines **had ground** to a halt due to a strike of **their** most important suppliers since **the day before** with the result that no car **would be produced in the following days**.	2	5
4.5	The mediator asked the employee **if he / she had been humiliated** in front of **his / her** boss and **how often** extra work **had been dumped** on **him / her**. *(normal word order!)*	2	3
4.6	My colleague asked me **when I wanted to** take my annual leave and advised me straight away **not to** plan it in August / that **I shouldn't** plan it in August.	2 / 3	3
4.7	Already years ago, a representative of the Chamber of Commerce warned that when **they were looking for** highly qualified graduates **the month before, there were** only / **had been** only very few eligible applicants. He added that talent **would be even scarcer in the future**.	3	4
4.8	The sheikh told the press that **his** country **would be forced** to step up the production of crude oil if the oil price **decreased** further.	3	3
4.9	The government official said **they had better cut** public spending since tax revenues **might decline** even further.	3	2
4.10	… the sales director **suggested selling** online.	3	2
5.1	… several small start-ups **were** / **(got) swallowed**. The founder of a small private bank remembered **being** / **getting taken over**, too, long ago.	1	2
5.2	… **war geschlagen**.	1	1
5.3	It is clear now: The factory **will be closed down**. Little remains **to be done**.	1	2
5.4	Some of our top performers **seem to have been persuaded** to accept a well-paid position with a competitor.	1	2
5.5	**The CEO was being 'grilled' by the shareholders** at the AGM, while **significant blocks of shares were bought by speculators**.	1 / 2	3
5.6	It turned out that children **were made to work** there, although the textile factory **had been inspected** not long before.	2	2
5.7	Fresh water **was given** to the workers. The workers **were given** fresh water.	2	2
5.8	**It was expected** that he would leave the company. **He was expected** to leave the company.	2	3
5.9	The car producer **is said to be looking** for a solution for their technical problems at the moment.	2	2
6.1	1. The shipment ~~had~~ **would have arrived** on time if there had been no strike. 2. If the maintenance service ~~would be~~ **was** / (**were** – *Level 3*) more reliable we could prolong the contract.	1	4

	3. If the consignment does not arrive by Friday, we ~~cancel~~ **will cancel** all orders. 4. *korrekt*		
6.2	(1) ... **would be** ... (2) ... **had not been stolen**.	1/2	2
6.3	1. *korrekt* 2. *korrekt* 3. *korrekt* 4. *korrekt (alternativ ist „... if you like" auch korrekt.)*	2	4
6.4	... **will be able to get** a reasonable share of the market.	2	1
6.5	1. *korrekt* 2. *korrekt* 3. ... you ~~would have met~~ **will meet** / **may meet** / *etc.* with a lot of resistance from NGOs. 4. *korrekt* 5. *korrekt*	2/3	5
6.6	1. "**Had** the government **played** fair, we ..." 2. "... **should** the authorities **change** their procedures (unexpectedly).	3	2
7.1	*korrekt: 1, 2, 4;* *falsch: 3, 5, 6.*	1	3
7.2	*alle korrekt*	1	2
7.3	1. ... **gave** / **had given** ... 2. **expected** / **had expected** 3. **was still** 4. **needed**	1	2
7.4	(1) ... **stopped** ... (2) ... **would not have had to** ...	1	2
7.5	(1) ... **would not sell** ... (2) ... **was not found** ...	1	2
7.6	... **were not** ...	2	1
7.7	(1) ... **will break even**, (2) ... **will become** ..., (3) ... **is passed**.	2	3
7.8	(1) ... **reached** ... (2) ...(we)**'ve got** / **have got** ...	2	2
7.9	(1) ... **has had** ... (2) ... **graduated** ... (3) ... **used to** ... (4) ... **is looking for** ...	2	2
7.10	... **retires**.	2	1
7.11	*korrekt: 1, 3;* *falsch: 2, 4.*	3	2
7.12	(1) **Confronted** with .... (2) ... **having lost** ...	3	2

Summen: ch. 1:   24 Punkte   ch.5:   19 Punkte
         ch. 2:   28 Punkte   ch.6:   18 Punkte
         ch. 3:   21 Punkte   ch.7:   24 Punkte
         ch. 4:   26 Punkte

Summe: 1-7:   **160 Punkte**

'Benotung' / Grading:

A   160 – 145
B   144 – 129
C   128 – 104
D   103 – 81
E (fail) 80 –   0

Business and Grammar

Grammar Rules and Exercises with Business English

Arbeitsbuch zum Selbstlernen

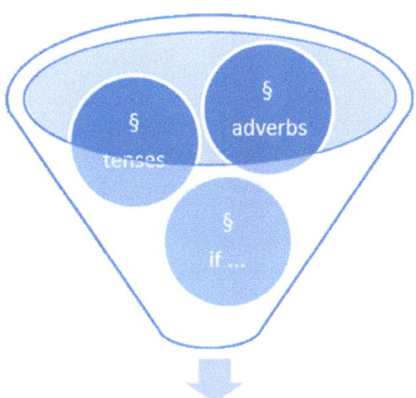

Lösungen und Übersetzungsempfehlungen

Lösungen & Übersetzungsvorschläge

Ch 1 (Adverbs), L 1:

Tasks

a, here, quite, far, very, often **b,** fast, early, daily, weekly, only **c,** pretty, well, late

A

1. As the factory is <u>too</u> old, it will <u>soon</u> be closed down.
2. We will dispatch our new summer catalogue <u>already</u> tomorrow.
3. Have you <u>already</u> visited our stand at the fair?
4. We are <u>still</u> waiting for your offer!
5. We have <u>already</u> sold a lot of mobile phones <u>here</u>.
6. This brand is <u>even</u> popular in China. / ... is popular <u>even</u> in China. / ... in China <u>even</u>.

B

1. thoroughly 2. wisely 3. punctually 4. patiently 5. immediately 6. publicly [exception! not: ~~publically~~!] 7. hastily 8. cynically or drily

C

1. impressively 2. successfully 3. sincerely and in a friendly manner 4. easily

D

1. Unemployment / The unemployment rate went down <u>slightly</u> last month.
2. The CEO / Chairman of the Board reacted <u>extremely</u> <u>slowly</u> to the crisis.
3. You could <u>easily</u> increase / raise (your) sales if you improved your service <u>significantly</u>.
4. Our employees are <u>fully</u> committed and <u>regularly</u> get bonuses.
5. Think <u>logically</u>: It is a good business. Sign <u>immediately</u> / <u>instantly</u> / <u>right away</u> / <u>straight away</u> / <u>on the spot</u>!
6. <u>Eventually</u> / <u>Finally</u> he succeeded <u>remarkably</u> <u>well</u> in gaining market share / he managed <u>remarkably</u> <u>well</u> to gain market share.
7. The CEO <u>publicly</u> complained about mobbing.
8. Our boss informed us <u>politely</u> that the factory would be closed down.
9. Many customers <u>furiously</u> / <u>angrily</u> demanded their money back.
10. This success story is <u>historically</u> unique.
11. The employee <u>openly</u> admitted his mistake and felt <u>visibly</u> sorry (about it).
12. Now the company is <u>completely</u> ruined. The workforce is <u>totally</u> shocked.
13. China <u>urgently</u> needs steel and oil, therefore the Chinese government is looking <u>intensively</u> / <u>intensely</u> for partners in Africa.
14. The new models will <u>probably</u> be presented at the fashion fair. (... are likely to be presented ...)
15. The share prices have dropped <u>dramatically</u> in the last few weeks.

CH 1 (Adverbs), L 2:

E

1. international (partners) ... (is) international
2. modestly ... modest (pay rises)
3. embarrassingly .... (being) embarrassing
4. easy (task) ... easily

5. (sounds [!]) good ... well
6. (are) inhumane ... inhumanely
7. differently ... (look [!]) different
8. (seems [!] attractive ... (isn't) attractive
9. simply ... (find it) simple
10. furiously ... furious (e-mails) .... furious

F

1. early ... early 2. far ... far 3. quarterly 4. dramatically 5. annually 6. weekly 7. friendly 8. in an unfriendly way

G

1. Initially 2. sceptical 3. newly 4. gradually 5. irresistible 6. formerly 7. critical 8. prosperous 9. early 10. Consequently 11. fast [Form mit –ly existiert nicht: fastly] 12. far 13. original 14. new 15. enthusiastically 16. surprisingly 17. deeply 18. controversial 19. firmly [seems ... determined, wie entschlossen? Fest!] 20. different 21. culturally 22. religiously 23. demographic 24. final 25. badly 26. inevitably 27. clearly

H

1. Your new office chairs look modern and comfortable. Could you send us a few samples immediately? If the economic situation remains stable, we can certainly double our sales figures. That would be advantageous for you, too. / That would also be advantageous for you.
2. Product piracy causes enormous harm/damage globally / on a global scale. As counterfeited products increasingly look absolutely genuine it is getting more and more difficult to protect intellectual property effectively. Manufacturers and counterfeiters work / are working almost equally fast / quickly and professionally.

CH 1 (Adverbs), L 3:

I

1. lately [in letzter Zeit] ... hard [hardly bedeutet: kaum!] ... hardly [= kaum] shortly [in Kürze] ... hard ... hard .... badly ... late
2. hardly [kaum / gerade erst] ... high ... cold-heartedly ... widely ... commonly ... Unsurprisingly [nicht überraschenderweise / es überrascht nicht ...] nearly ... current ... fairly ... understandably [verständlicherweise]
3. near [nahe (am Bankrott)] ... Repeatedly ... literally ... dangerous ... Fortunately .... Lately [jüngst] ... largely [großteils] sufficiently (consolidated [wie konsolidiert? Genügend]) ... near [nahe an] ... usual
4. Strangely ... sudden ... pretty [pretty als Adverb = ziemlich; prettily = hübsch]... late ... (found it) hard ... angrily ... low ... promptly ... shortly [in Kürze]

K

1. Traditionally [Traditionellerweise] / Traditional [Traditionelle (Politiker)] 2. Chiefly 3. growing 4. permanent 5. Politically 6. economically 7. Increasingly 8. unfamiliar 9. painful 10. hardly [kaum] 11. already [ursprüngliches Adverb, daher unverändlich] 12. monthly 13. generally 14. late [Bedeutung: spät, nicht: in letzter Zeit / lately!] 15. fast 16. high 17. Sadly 18. pretty [ziemlich] 19. hard [= schwer / hardly = kaum!]

L

Dear colleagues,
Until a short time ago we all believed that corruption was a problem of the Third World. Unfortunately we are now faced / confronted with an unpleasant case in our own company, ironically in our anti-corruption department. And possibly we are not far from a consumer boycott after local newspapers recently published precise / exact details. We will examine the case conscientiously and strictly comply with our company rules. I have already underlined our zero tolerance policy in public / publicly [not: publically] Now we have to be extremely careful with comments so that we do not unintentionally keep the debate alive / so that we do not keep the debate alive unintentionally. Admittedly, the situation was temporarily critical.

M

1. Soon even more cheap Chinese cars will be competing with European brands in Europe. Paradoxically the Chinese have profited / benefited from alliances with European car manufacturers and suppliers. This massive technological support has helped the Chinese (to) develop competitive vehicles for the European market relatively fast / quickly. Customers will soon discover new cars with unfamiliar names and unusual appearance, but unusually low prices. Purchasing cars / The purchasing of cars remains largely emotional. Thus / So customers can hardly be persuaded by purely rational arguments.
2. Many business people have accepted cheap flights with little service. Even big airlines with traditionally good service and relatively high ticket prices are increasingly forced / compelled to offer cheap flights. According to experts, that is exactly the problem. They fear that technical inspections / checks are no longer carried out reliably and carefully. The airlines point out that there is "absolutely no compromise regarding / concerning technical safety". Travelers will be able to plan their flights economically in (the) future, too, especially / particularly / in particular if / when they book the same return flights weekly or monthly / on a weekly or monthly basis.
3. The electronics group is completely dissatisfied with the latest sales figures in the euro zone and is currently preparing an advertising campaign with special offers. "Our quarterly results in the EU are comparatively bad although / though demand has significantly / substantially risen / gone up", a company spokesman admitted publicly yesterday.
With these words he indirectly criticized the policy of the former CEO, who had resigned / stepped down unexpectedly after the unusually turbulent AGM (Annual General Meeting). "The late son of the company founder would have been terribly angry," he added surprisingly.
4. Economically, Australia's future looks bright. The / Its geopolitical position in the Pacific area, which once seemed isolated, strengthens / is strengthening the Australian trade balance significantly / substantially. For many companies the land 'down under' has become extraordinarily important for trade with South East Asia. Especially China's incredible economic growth has made Australia highly attractive, as it offers Western companies familiar business practices. Geographically far away, the country still seems relatively near / close to European mentalities emotionally and culturally.
5. London's importance / significance for the British GDP (Gross Domestic Product) has rather increased than decreased recently. The City is an impressively sustainable growth factor; the country sticks to its currency, strictly rejects the euro and is slowly getting used to the *Brexit* (British exit from the EU).

CH 1 (Adverbs), L 4:

N

1 harder (and) harder 2 earlier 3 later 4 absolutely 5 well 6 faster 7 conscientiously 8 efficiently 9 earlier 10 easily 11 truly 12 precisely 13 best 14 clearly 15 more self-confidently 16 noticeably 17 better 18 faster 19 further 20 gratefully 21 perfectly 22 well 23 most loyally 24 most naïvely 25 worse 26 marginally 27 less 28 Regrettably 29 earlier

30 better 31 least 32 more realistically 33 strongly 34 objectively 35 rationally 36 more easily / easier (*coll.*) 37 firmly 38 most.

O

1. The company could * have ~~easily~~ gained more market share in China. [nach Modalverb]
2. The foreign delegation * didn't ~~simply~~ want to strike a deal at that time. [verneintes Hilfsverb]
3. It ~~really~~ was * obvious that the government official expected a bribe. [nach *to be*! Diese Stellung, nach dem Subjekt und vor to be ist sehr, bzw. hier allzu betont]
4. The product launch has ~~carefully~~ been * planned. [Passiv, adverb of manner / Art und Weise]
5. *correct!*
6. They * send ~~normally~~ a letter of credit. [vor einfacher Zeit / Past]
7. We ~~soon~~ would * send out a reminder. [normale Stellung nach Modalverb; auch möglich: *We would send out a reminder soon.*]
8. We * have to ~~still~~ cut costs. [vor *have to*]
9. Our application for the licence is * being ~~still~~ examined by the authorities. [Verlaufsform, kein Adverb der Art und Weise, beim Passiv]
10. The pharma group * accepted ~~readily~~ the deal. [einfache Zeit / past; auch möglich: *The pharma group accepted the deal readily.*]
11. The consignment ~~safely~~ arrived *. [*vi*, kein Objekt, daher nach dem Verb]
12. *correct!*
13. Our suppliers ~~yet~~ don't understand * what we really [ok] need. [*noch nicht: yet* am Satzteilende (vs. *Yet* am Satzanfang: *Doch*)]

P

1. a, + c, Erstaunlicherweise waren die Waren in gutem Zustand.
   b, Die Waren waren in erstaunlich gutem Zustand.
2. a, Nur Stammkunden ... b, wurden nur Rabatte gewährt (≈) c, nur Rabatte d, [wird in dieser Stellung anders verstanden, nämlich als] erst [!] letzten Monat
3. a, Tatsächlich bekommt / bezieht ... b, bekommt / bezieht ... tatsächlich aus Niedriglohnländern
4. a, Überraschenderweise ... b, überraschend stabil
5. a, normale unbetonte Stellung b, hervorgehoben, betont, als Teil der Hauptaussage
6. a, Traurigerweise / Bedauerlicherweise ... b, Der Vorstandsvorsitzende reichte traurig seinen Rücktritt ein.
7. a, ... beklagte sich wiederholt ... b, ... das Produkte wiederholt gefälscht worden waren.
8. a, + b, normaler Gebrauch (unbetont) c, sehr betont, hervorgehoben d, (ebenfalls:) normale Stellung

Q

a, [example]
b, **But (n)** the drama had **already (n)** become inevitable ... / **But (n)** the drama had become inevitable **already (e)** two years earlier. **But (n)** the drama .... two years earlier **already (e)**.
c, **Meanwhile (e)**, in order to satisfy their shareholders **again (n)** / In order to .... banks have **meanwhile (n)** cut costs **significantly (e)** [have significantly cut costs ist in diesem Sinnzusammenhang zu unbetont, zu schwach] and introduced **completely (n)** [gehört zum folgenden Adjektiv, ist also wortbezogen] new administration charges
d, US banks are **still (n) widely (n)** despised [am besten hier] / ... are **still (n)** despised **widely (e)** / ... are **widely (n)** despised **still (e** – [allzu]sehr betont!**)**
... **but (n)** they are **now (n)** in reasonable shape / ... **but (n)** they are in reasonable shape **now (n / e** [nur wenn in der Aussprache hervorgehoben]**)**
e, **highly (n)** capitalized and **fairly (n)** profitable [eine umgekehrte Zuordnung der Adverbien – *fairly capitalized and highly profitable* ist weniger wahrscheinlich, ergibt weniger Sinn wegen der nicht so logisch-semantischen Kombination *fairly* und *capitalized*]
f, [**Only** am Satzanfang ist enorm betont und würde so etwas wie eine Einschränkung bedeuten: Nur (e) / Allein / Aber – das Problem ist ...; außerdem erfordert *only* am Satzteilanfang Inversion, d.h.

Umstellung von Subjekt und Verb / Prädikat]; [The problem is **only (n)** that ... passt nicht so recht in den Sinnzusammenhang, denn es ergibt mit dem Rest des Satzes kaum Sinn.]; [... only in the USA ... wäre wortbezogen und bezöge sich nur auf die USA (*nur in den USA*), was ebenfalls sinnwidrig wäre]; ... the banks are **only (n)** part of the game [die einzig sinnvolle Stellung in diesem Satz; ganz am Ende wäre eher unwahrscheinlich und zudem mündlicher informeller Stil]
g, ... a second, **highly (n)** independent structure ... which is **very badly (n)** capitalized / ... which is capitalized **very badly (e)**
h, This parallel system is **barely (n** – Sinn im Kontext) profitable and **largely (n)** nationalized / [.... nationalized largely (e) ist unmöglich, da *largely* hier wortbezogen – auf *nationalized* - ist]
i, **Still, (e)** it is .... Ist sehr betont und sinngemäß nur denkbar als Gegensatz zum Vorherigen (*dennoch, immer noch*), aber eher weniger wahrscheinlich in dieser Satzlogik, wo ein einfaches *noch* logischer erscheint; It is **still (n) closely (n)** linked to .... / It is **still (n)** linked **closely (e)** to ... – weniger wahrscheinlich, da unnötig betont) / ... and **probably (n)** represents the biggest concentration ...
k, **Altogether (n)**, it remains **fundamentally (n)** dangerous.

R

a, **Recently,** carmakers and tech firms have **clearly** been dominating the headlines, in the race to develop autonomous vehicles **as soon as possible**.
b, A **whole** range of firms have been working **very intensively** on **driverless** lorries.
c, **However,** fears that steering wheels will disappear **completely any time soon** seem **largely** exaggerated.
d, **But** what employees in the road haulage industry **really** fear **most** is the risk of losing their jobs to **new automatic** lorries that can **easily** do without drivers.
e, **In general, / Generally, most autonomous** systems are **currently** being designed for motorways **rather** than for small roads.
f, **Most likely, / Most probably,** drivers will continue to be necessary, **at least in the short term** – until **further** innovation makes humans **completely** redundant.
g, **On the other hand,** self-driving lorries may attract **new** drivers to this **hard** job and require other, **better paid** skills.
h, Road haulage in rich countries is a~~n~~ **fairly / rather** old-fashioned business, **chiefly** dominated by small firms, which means that such **fully autonomous** lorries will **certainly** not be ready before 2030.

S

a, 1 some / roughly / approximately 2 widely 3 absolutely 4 nearly / almost 5 wrongly
6 Surprisingly, 7 Even more surprisingly, 8 happily 9 quite 10 simply (11) charitably
12 wiser 13 convenient 14 (even) more conveniently 15 lowest 16 traditionally 17 purely
18 religiously 19 totally / completely / ... 20 more easily 21 simply 22 keen 23 brutally
b, 1. A / One month ago some *Dalits*, formerly called *Untouchables*, were suddenly attacked by a group of religious fanatics, who wrongly believed the Dalits had killed a cow.
2. Never before had the Indian businessman seriously thought of earning money with cows. Later, however, / However, later he increasingly began to sell milk.

T

1. Strategically, the decision of the furniture group to adapt the product names better to the individual markets followed a worldwide trend. In this case, marketing experts see particularly / especially high risks for the brand identity, which could / might be significantly / substantially changed by this unexpected measure. Completely different product ranges could slash profit margins / reduce profit margins drastically, which [bezieht sich zurück auf den vorigen Sachverhalt, daher nicht *what*] would make things even worse.
2. The CEO certainly did not intend to announce publicly that the expansion to India would not take place so soon. But a journalist had happened to overhear a telephone conversation

at the airport / had overheard a telephone conversation by chance at the airport and promptly made the confidential information public.
3. The head of R & D explained details of the newly developed product vividly. While he was gesticulating wildly, a representative of the sales department asked critically if / whether there was actually genuine demand for the product.
4. Obviously, the past financial year had been extraordinarily / exceptionally difficult for the insurance industry. A representative of the industry tried shyly to explain the losses logically: "Natural disasters are definitely becoming almost / nearly biblical in regions that / which are extremely exposed to climate change. Seldom have we witnessed / experienced as many floods and fires as in the last few months."
5. Deeply moved / (touched) the director remained seated / sitting for minutes, unusually silent, before he got up / rose from his chair smiling ['natürlicher' als das Adverb *smilingly*]. He looked relieved and thanked his workforce sincerely / honestly. The firm had recovered from the severe crisis better and earlier than expected / better and earlier than expected from the severe crisis.

Ch 2 (Past Tenses), L 1:

Tasks (a-b)

Present Perfect:
has been (under attack) – for months [signal!]; have not been fulfilled – so far [signal!]; ... have left / have been thinking – since [signal!]; has lost – now ... [signal!]
Past Tense:
went / seemed (while) were buying – ago [signal!]
Past Perfect:
had ... recorded - before [signal!]; had been doing – [context / meaning - vorzeitig!]; had ... given [vorzeitig]
Present Tense:
Are ... enjoying / is – [context: now!]

A

had .... was trying ... rang .... had been expecting ... wasn't ... felt ... didn't ... got ... had never met ... were made up ... lived ... were told ... was lost ... knew ... was closing ... remembered ... had been asked ... had Liu started ... arrived ... had been waiting ... (had) become [Past Perfect! Hilfsverb muss nicht wiederholt werden] ... was being transmitted ... decided ... needed ... had been asked ... was ready ... needed ... That was it ...opened ... had forgotten

B

Many simple tasks **have been moved** *(Present Perfect Simple, Passive)* offshore or **(have been) taken over** *(Present Perfect Simple, Passive)* by machines. This trend **has been worrying** *(Present Perfect Progressive)* the entire workforce for some time now. Payrolls **have been trimmed** *(Present Perfect Simple, Passive)* by 30 per cent in the meantime. Some parts of the company which **had become** *(Past Perfect Simple)* totally unprofitable **were sold off** *(Past Simple Passive)* months ago. Some employees **had been expecting** *(Past Perfect Progressive)* all those measures before they **were announced** *(Past Simple, Passive)* by the board, but when they actually **came** *(Past Simple)*, everybody **was** *(Past Simple)* still shocked. Against their better judgement, employees **had been hoping** *(Past Perfect Progressive)* job cuts could be avoided. With underperforming company divisions gone profits **began** to increase *(Past Simple)* almost instantly. Since then things **have been looking up** *(Present Perfect Progressive)* again.

C

1. When the EU imposed import restrictions on textiles from Asia, Chinese companies shifted / moved / relocated their production to Africa.
2. In Nigeria textile factories were built. They created new jobs.
3. The country had already produced cheap clothes / garments.
4. Since new import quota were imposed the new factories have been closing (down) one by one / one after the other.

Ch 2 (Past Tenses), L 2:

D

1 have prices reached 2 have been working 3 have never experienced 4 have always been 5 has got 6 has been going on 7 have lost 8 have been struggling 9 has been trying 10 has even bailed out 11 has been saved 12 have succeeded

E

1 are reminding 2 is approaching 3 have received 4 need 5 has confirmed 6 have been trying 7 have not called 8 have not dispatched 9 are urging 10 have not arrived 11 have advertised 12 expect 13 have not given up 14 are seriously worried 15 depend 16 does

F

(1.) 1 are flown 2 are 3 open / (have opened)
(2.) 4 have implemented 5 has largely been made redundant 6 have become
(3.) 7 are indicated
(4.) 8 have cut down 9 are affected 10 have been downsizing 11 may
(5.) 12 have been using 13 has become 14 has decided 15 has started
(6.) 16 has failed 17 rots

G

1. Since the takeover of Nissan by Renault the Japanese car manufacturer / producer has continuously been developing new models to be able to offer an attractive range of models / model range again.
2. The mobile phone / cellphone producer / manufacturer has been falling behind competitors for years. So far it has not succeeded in using / has not managed yet to use the new trends to regain market share(s).
3. The airline is struggling again with increased fuel costs. For months it has been making losses and losing passengers. So far this has been the worst year in its history. At present it is luring travelers with special offers in order to generate revenues.
4. The luxury brand is still number one in/on the Chinese market. Since its market entry it has succeeded in increasing / has been managing to increase its sales steadily in spite of / despite cheap counterfeits. Several other foreign manufacturers / producers have given up in the meantime / have meanwhile given up.
5. The energy market is changing dramatically at the moment. While some companies stick to their old strategies others are looking for new sources of energy.
6. Electronic products have been getting cheaper and cheaper for years while consumers have constantly had to pay more for fruit and vegetables. Do you know the reasons?

Ch 2 (Past Tenses), L 3:

H

1. The company **was forced to sell off** its mobile phone division, because it **had ignored / had been ignoring** market trends for years.
2. Many house owners who **went bankrupt and lost** everything **had signed** unaffordable loan agreements.
3. By the time the whole market **collapsed** investors **had already left** the country.
4. Two years ago the new law finally **took effect**. Retailers **had been waiting** impatiently for that to happen.
5. Before the government **imposed** high import tariffs the market **had been flooded** with cheap products from low-wage countries.

I

1. had rescued ... announced ... were ... had made ... did not seem ... had written ... had to admit ... was beginning ... was slowly developing ... wondered / (were still wondering) ... was going
2. had promised ... had the two car producers merged [Nach negativen (No) oder einschränkenden (Hardly) Adverbien am Satzanfang erfolgt Inversion, d.h. Umstellung von Subjekt und Verb wie in der Fragestellung.] ... was ousted ... kept ... split up / was eventually split up ... had lost ... had paid ... had massively underestimated
3. announced ... were ... welcomed ... did not work out ... gave up ... had been sold out
4. was suffering ... was hit ... had failed ... had already become

K

1. According to market research beer consumption in China rose / increased (by) around / ca. / approximately / about / some 5 per cent in 2000. Several / Some / A few years later Foster's tried to get a foothold in/on the Chinese market. Before 2000, the Australian group had already built ... / Already before 2000 the Australian group had built an expensive brewery in China, but (had) withdrawn from the Chinese market due to high losses. Apparently the Australians had chosen the wrong market entry strategy.
2. At the beginning of 2012 / In early 2012 Argentina nationalized its oil industry. Although / Though many shareholders were surprised, the Argentinian government had apparently been considering this step for a long time already. It followed the example of other Latin American countries. Venezuela had also nationalized its oil industry several years before (that).
3. In 2011 the lobby of Indian retailers managed to prevent a new law which was (meant / supposed) to open (up) the Indian market to/for foreign retail chains. *Carrefour* and other companies promptly complained about the "unreliability" of the Indian government. Finally / After all [*schließlich* ist hier nicht zeitlich gemeint, bedeutet nicht "am Ende", sondern gibt quasi einen bekannten Grund an.] they had relied / had been relying on / they had trusted / had been trusting the promises of politicians and (had [Wiederholung des temporalen Hilfsverbs nicht nötig, stilistisch nicht optimal]) invested a lot of money.
4. In the early 1990s the property prices / real estate prices went down slightly / decreased slightly in Munich. Between 1972 and 1990 they had risen / increased / gone up drastically.

L

1. When was the euro introduced / launched?
2. On the 1st of January 2002 the Europeans withdrew euro notes from ATMs (= Automated Telling Machines) / cash machines for the first time. Many had been waiting impatiently for this moment and celebrated it the whole night.
3. Had the Germans not loved their Deutschmark? Why did they give up their strong currency so easily?

4. Many had been fighting fiercely against the introduction of the euro until the last minute. Others had simply been relying / had simply relied on politicians.
5. Hadn't convergence criteria been fixed which guaranteed the stability of the euro?
6. The rules were not respected / complied with by all countries right at the beginning of the monetary union. When Greece almost went bankrupt it became clear that the country had been cheating for years.

M

a, 1 presented 2 had been working on 3 came up 4 had added 5 were offering 6 had yielded 7 displayed / were displaying 8 claimed 9 came 10 re-launched 11 had done 12 had been solved 13 were desperately trying 14 had (been) changed 15 gave up
b, 16 did not look 17 were 18 were still waiting 19 being repaired 20 was running 21 wanted 22 threatened 23 was not banned 24 was

N

1 had been acquired 2 expressed 3 had been sold 4 pointed out 5 took 6 was 7 were being assembled 8 were soldering 9 welding 10 were lifting [7-10: (bereits) im Verlauf befindliche Handlungen und Vorgänge!] 11 noticed [daraufhin, nach Eintreten der Gruppe] 12 was walking [,war (bereits) am Herumlaufen', lief nicht daraufhin los] 13 stopped [daraufhin] 14 looked up 15 seemed [stative verb! → keine Verlaufsform, da keine Handlung] 16 responded 17 was 18 had been made 19 remained 20 knew 21 had discussed 22 was finished 23 were still examining [waren immer noch dabei] 24 was sweating [die ganze Zeit über, nicht plötzlich daraufhin] 25 was still answering [war noch dabei]

O

1. The share price of the company had just reached a new record high when the CEO admitted massive technical problems in production. Immediately the share price plummeted / plunged.
2. Nobody had anticipated the collapse of the group. When the managing director declared bankruptcy / filed for bankruptcy many investors panicked. [*to panic*: Ausnahme bei Anfügung von –ed] They had apparently not seen the structural weaknesses and were now trying desperately / desperately trying to save as much money as possible. But for many it was too late.
3. While the politician was stepping / walking [im Verlauf befindliche Handlung, die unterbrochen wird] to the micro(phone) to open the fair the light went out suddenly / suddenly went out. Workers had cut through a cable yet again. Blackouts had also occurred / happened during earlier / former fairs and had raised questions about concerning the professionalism of the organizers.
4. While an advertising campaign was trying to create an environment-friendly image of the group many litres of oil were flowing from a leaking pipeline. It had been damaged during the civil war and was now contaminating the few fertile fields.
5. Although the report had been completed / finished weeks ago, it was not printed / it did not get printed.

P

1 stay 2 be 3 getting 4 take 5 changing 6 working 7 surviving 8 worry 9 worrying 10 be

Q

With his niche products the company founder used to have a worldwide monopoly. He was used to getting / receiving orders from all continents and having no direct competitors. Even in times of crisis demand remained brisk / buoyant. China seemed to become / turn into the most lucrative market; therefore he was already considering relocating the entire production to Chonqing, when a Chinese company launched an almost identical product range (on the market). He had not been aware of that / (this) danger. He had been used to relying on his patents.

Ch 2 (Past Tenses), L 4:

Tasks

a, & c,

was established: *Simple Past Tense – signal word*: when ... ago [(2 x) Zeitpunkt einer (punktuellen) Handlung in der Vergangenheit], looked [selbe Zeit wie Nebensatz! *looked* = Fakt, nicht (vorübergehender) Vorgang];
had indicated ... (and) had ... granted: *Past Perfect Simple – signal word*: before [vor einem anderen Zeitpunkt, der bereits in der Vergangenheit liegt, also **vorzeitig;** punktuelle Handlung & punktueller Fakt → Simple Form];
had built up: *Past Perfect Simple – signal word*: by (the end ...) [bis zu diesem Zeitpunkt in der Vergangenheit bereits abgeschlossen, beendet, Ergebnis → Simple Form];
continued: *Past Tense – signal word*: until [einfache(r Vorgang in der) Vergangenheit; hier Fokus auf Fakt, Tatsache, nicht Vorgang];
has been running up: *Present Perfect Progressive – signal words*: in the meantime & (v.a.) for some time [Fokus liegt auf Vorgang, nicht Ergebnis (ist nicht genannt, quantifiziert!) –deutsch: Präsens: häuft seit einiger Zeit schwere Verluste auf];
has had: *Present Perfect Simple – signal word*: for the last few weeks [*have* = stative verb (kein Vorgangsverb), daher Simple Form];
were grounded: *Simple Past Passive* [– tückisch: recently = häufig signal word für Present Perfect, kann aber auch Past sein, wenn der Zustand nicht mehr besteht];
announced: *Simple Past – signal word*: yesterday [Tatsache, nicht Vorgang gemeint];
has ... managed & has lost: *Present Perfect Simple – signal word*: now [aktuelles Ergebnis einer abgeschlossenen Handlung wird angegeben].

R

1 applied 2 had sent 3 have received 4 were 5 have been enhancing 6 have been considered 7 have become 8 did you attend 9 have you gained 10 Have you ever lived and worked 11 took part 12 obtained 13 started 14 had done 15 have been trying 16 left

S

1. "**Since** this company was set up in 2008 it has been growing at dazzling speed. **For** the last two years it has continuously been expanding across Asia and Africa. **Since** the new CEO took over it has tripled its revenues. And **since** then it has regained and successfully defended its market leadership at home. It will be thriving **for** a long time to come!"
2. "I joined this company to write my thesis - and stayed on after my graduation **for** fifteen years! **Since** last year, however, I have developed a taste for a new challenge. I now feel I shouldn't go on working like this **for** the next fifteen years."
3. "The influence of the UN Global Compact has been growing steadily **since** 2000, when it was set up. At the beginning, **for** several years, it was struggling for recognition. But **since** the rules were tightened a few years later it has been gaining ground. It will probably define global ethics **for** years to come.

T

Until/Till 1997 Hong Kong was a British crown colony. Then it was handed back to the People's Republic of China. Some of its inhabitants had obtained a British passport **by** then, because they did not trust the special status which was to be granted to Hong Kong for another 50 years, **until/till** 2047.

U

A month **ago**, five days **before** the retail chain's IPO, top executives were arrested for fraud. Sales figures plummeted **before** [hier keine Präposition, sondern Konjunktion, d.h. *before* leitet einen Nebensatz ein – was *ago* nie tut, da es nur Adverb ist, nie Konjunktion] company representatives were able to comment. Quickly, the IPO was called off "until further notice". The company would not go public until [im Sinn von *erst wenn*] all accusations were cleared up! Remember: A few years **ago** another retail chain did not cancel its IPO despite a scandal. The share price lost half its value **before** the closing of the stock exchange!

V

1. The pharmaceutical company **stopped** all animal testing two days **ago** due to a consumer boycott which had been going on **for** weeks.
2. The company **has not declared** bankruptcy yet, but it **has piled up** too much debt **since** last year, when it was restructured.
3. **For** several days now, many truck drivers **have been** on strike for better working conditions and higher pay. The strike is to continue at least **until / till** the end of this week, unless an agreement is reached **before** then.
4. Two weeks **ago** the government lifted all import tariffs it had imposed on imported cars only a month **before** that. The domestic market has to be deregulated **by** the beginning of next year, when the country Is to join the WTO.
5. While the inflation rate **rose** only marginally last year and **had not risen for** two years before that, it **has risen** quite significantly **since** January this year.
6. Train services **were disrupted for** 2 hours yesterday.

W

Have you heard? Many internet companies / dotcoms have been cooperating for years with governments and secret services!
Before its IPO (Initial Public Offering) my social network stood for freedom and civil rights. That lasted only until its founder was able to turn / convert the value of the collected data into profits. Then his idealism was gone!
I was reading the General Terms and Conditions of Trade when a news programme / program on television / TV started to report on a scandal.
I had already read about it in a newspaper (before). Since then I have been using the network much less. And I have deleted my data.
The internet never forgets! Companies whose websites you have visited regularly have known your profile for a long time.
I have never uploaded photos and never revealed / disclosed my real identity. I was suspicious already years ago.

X

a, 1 Since the 1980s the oil prices have exploded.
2 In recent years capitalism has been criticized increasingly.
3 Until 1566 England was threatened by / was under threat from the Spanish Armada.
4 There have been a lot of inventions in this country lately.
5 Last time the demonstrations ended in chaos.
6 By the 1960s Germany had largely been rebuilt.
7 For years now the fair has not been such a big/great success.
8 Decades ago Deng Xiao Ping opened (up) China.
b, 9 Since Mao's death China has changed totally.
10 Before 2008 the financial sector was totally / completely out of control.

11 Recently there have been more and more temporary workers / temps.
12 From World War II / WWII until/till 1990 Germany was divided.
13 In 1914 the Panama Canal was opened. By 2008 more than 800,000 ships / sea vessels had passed through it. Decades earlier, the Suez Canal had been opened.

Y

1. This company was set up / established/founded five years ago by Jonathan Seagull. He had invented a secure method of protecting data on a PC and wanted to sell it himself. At first the company increased / raised its sales very fast / quickly, the number of subscribers rocketed for five years – until a data scandal ruined the credibility of the software. The customer portfolio shrank rapidly and by the end of the / that same year the business was bankrupt/bust.
2. The Chinese technology group has been conquering one foreign market after another for two decades. It had originally been created as a joint venture with a German company and was seen as a symbol of successful international cooperation until 1988. In that year China ended / terminated the partnership and made / converted / turned / changed it into a state(-owned) company. Until / Till 2000 the German and the Chinese group were operating in/on separate markets. Since the privatization of the Chinese group the two technology giants have been competing with / against each other worldwide. Due to the current decline in sales the German group has had to fire / dismiss / lay off 2000 employees in the meantime.
3. Since the 1990s Japan has been struggling with high public / government debt(s) and deflation.

Ch 3 (Modal Auxiliaries), L 1:

Tasks

a-c,
temporal: has (built up - *Present Perfect*); ... be reduced (*Passive infinitive;* ... have had (*Present Perfect*); had cut (*Past Perfect*); will come (*Future I*)
modal: ... is to (*sollen – Present*); (have) had to (*müssen – Present Perfect*);
incomplete modals: might; could; should; can

A

1 had to 2 would have to 3 needed to 4 had already been allowed to 5 were not allowed to 6 were not able to 7 need to 8 cannot / are not able to 9 should 10 must not / mustn't 11 did not have to

B

1. For a few years the police **have** [*police* immer mit Plural-Verb!] **been able to** arrest more shoplifters.
2. In (the) future the discounter **will have to** accept unions.
3. Without state support the airline **would not have been able to** survive.
4. For years Walmart **has been allowed to** operate (officially) as a wholesaler in India.
5. The company **did not have to** fire / dismiss / lay off anybody / anyone because it **had been able to** clear the/its debt(s).
6. Banks **must not be able to** rely on state bailouts any longer.

C

1 Last week the old industrial town/city **was** no longer **able to** pay its bills and **had to** file for bankruptcy.

2 **Couldn't** it **have been** bailed out in time? **Can** the government be persuaded to take over the debts? It simply **has to** do that!
3 No, it **mustn't** do that! The taxpayers **have had to** pay for incompetence and corruption so often already / already so often / ... taxpayers have already had to ....
4 **May** I contradict? The taxpayers **will have to** pay anyway / anyhow.
The government **should** act immediately.
5 **Is** it **able to** do that? **Is** it **allowed to** do that? **Mustn't** it keep out of this?
6 With government support / the support of the government the city/town **would not have had to** cut public services.

Ch 3 (Modal Auxiliaries), L 2:

D

1 will 2 would / used to 3 a, would b, used to c, was used to 4 used to

E

1 must have been frightened 2 could be held 3 should have passed 4 will be ... should have got 5 can't have

F

1 must have known 2 can't have had an idea 3 a, must have been hijacked b, should know it 4 could be 5 a, may have seen it b, might boycott

G

1 may be right after all 2 a, must have alienated b, may explain 3 might 4 will have doubled

H

1 must have known 2 can't imagine 3 can't have seen 4 must have bribed 5 must be 6 may / might come out

I

1 must have known 2 can't have arrived 3 should

K

1. German employees used to stay their whole lives in the same company, as they were used to getting regular pay rises as they got older.
2. "Couldn't we cut / lower our prices in Africa? (In) that / (this) way we might be able to increase our market share."
3. "No, we cannot make an exception! We would spoil / ruin our luxury image. Our competitors could / might / (would be able to) conquer our market niche.
4. The country should have reduced/cut its debts significantly / substantially in ten years / in ten years' time. The austerity measures were decided yesterday and will already have had an impact by the end of the / this year.
5. Italy used to devalue its currency to stay / remain competitive in tourism. With the euro the government can no longer use this instrument and has to take other economic measures.

L

would = Conditional: no. <u>2</u>   **would** = past habit: no. <u>1</u>

Ch 3 (Modal Auxiliaries), L 3:

M

1 a, need not / needn't have done b, did not need / have to close down 2 did not need / have to take 3 need not / needn't have imposed 4 need not / needn't have changed 5 did not need / have to put

N

1 could have been 2 was able to make up 3 a, could have cut b, was able to retain 4a, was able to keep b, could have developed 5 could have ousted

O

1 needn't have bought (a) ... could have leased (b)
2 was able to enter (b) ... did not need /have to build up (a) ... could have known (b)
3 need not have interviewed (a) ... could have used (b) [but they did not do that: they didn't want to rely on other people's findings and started from scratch!]
4 needn't have [Vollverb wird nicht wiederholt, um schwerfällige Wiederholungen zu vermeiden.] (a) ... could have applied (b)
5 did not need / have to raise (a) ... was even able to pay off (b) ... could have done (b)

P

1. "Youth unemployment has risen / increased / gone up again. The government should have reacted much earlier. Then the measures may / might have had an effect / impact."
2. "We needn't have implemented new software. We could simply have trained our employees better."
3. "The property prices / real estate prices in our region have significantly / substantially fallen / gone down / decreased /... We needn't have made debts. We could simply have waited."
4. "As the government lowered/cut the corporate tax some time ago, we did not need / have to move / shift / relocate our HQ / headquarters / main office to Ireland to save taxes."

Q

1 c 2 a 3 b 4 e 5 f / (e) 6 a 7 e 8 e 9 d 10 b 11 a

R

1 He is said to have stolen the patent.
2 "Shouldn't we try to get more customers?"
3 Every employee is to wear gloves at this machine.
4 The factory burned down completely. The owner is said to have disappeared.
5 The railway company ought to have been privatized this year. Is the IPO to be postponed / put off?
6 The (company) Management had decided: all offices were to be searched the next day. But the stolen documents were never to be found.

S

1 The data theft has shown that we will have to invest more in security systems in (the) future. [in the future → Future Tense!]
2 We should have done that ten years ago already. Now we mustn't waste any more time.
3 The CEO is said to have engaged / commissioned an external company already. He could have asked **us**.

T

(1) For a long time the shipyard had been able to defend itself with innovative technology and first-class quality against/from the/its Asian competitors / the / its competition / competitors from Asia.
Last year it had to give up and was taken over by a Chinese group.
The takeover had to be approved by the shareholders.
As they were allowed to vote online, they did not have to travel to Hamburg.
The shipyard may / might have been able to survive with state subsidies.
But the state would not have been allowed to subsidize the shipyard. The EU Commission would have sued Germany for unfair competition. For months the union representatives have had to negotiate with the Chinese Board of Managers to prevent job cuts.
Will they be able to achieve that?

(2) Before EU countries were allowed to join the euro zone they had to fulfil the convergence criteria.
Since the introduction of the euro on the 1st of January 2002 politicians have had to rescue / save countries that had not been able – or willing - to fulfil the criteria concerning state deficits.
Italy was allowed to introduce the euro although/though it had only been a member of the European Monetary System (EMS) for one year (instead of two years).
And then there is Greece...
What will become of the European Monetary Union?
Will it be able to serve as a stable reserve currency on a global scale/globally/worldwide?
Or will we have to say some time in the future: "Once upon a time there was a European currency which was (supposed) to become the symbol of the European Union. But that was not to happen."

(3) Medium-sized companies whose competitiveness depends on a single patent have to protect their knowhow.
They must not rely on being lucky all the time / on always being lucky.
What [*which* bedeutet: aus einer bekannten Liste / Auswahl an Gefahren, daher hier: *what* – da es alles mögliche sein kann, ohne Vorauswahl] dangers may be underestimated?
How can SMEs (= small and medium-sized enterprises) protect themselves?
They do not have to panic.
But they should be a little more careful.
'The Chinese intern could hardly speak German; it cannot have been him, can it?' – 'It might have been him after all.'
Data might / could also have been transmitted to an external computer by a trojan on your PCs.
You would hardly have noticed/realized anything.
You urgently need [Kombination mit *urgently* → *need*] to install a professional anti-virus program on your system.
Regular updates are an absolute must.

U

1 As I was not able to find / couldn't find any investors I had to sell my real estate before I had enough start-up capital to build up my online business alone.
2 Couldn't you simply have got a bank loan?
3 I might have been able to convince a bank of my business idea. / Maybe I would have been able to convince a bank of my business idea. But I told myself: "I must not depend / be dependent on banks. They could / would be able to influence my decisions."
4 You shouldn't have specialized in carpets alone.
5 You may be right. But the trend must have changed suddenly. For a few weeks now I have not been able to pay suppliers any more. I will have to file for bankruptcy.
You needn't / (don't have to) worry. You can work for me as a gardener.

Ch 4 (Reported Speech), L 1: *no tense shift!*

Tasks

a-b, Im Englischen und im Deutschen ändern sich Bezüge wie Personal- und Possessivpronomen, temporale Angaben u.ä.; im Deutschen wird der Konjunktiv benutzt, im Englischen die sog. Zeitenverschiebung.

A

a, 1 The founder of the traditional family business often tells his children (that) when **he** set up **his** first company the whole area **had not been developed** yet.
The motorway **hadn't been built** and the delivery of goods **took** much longer. **They** [his children!] **are** in a comfortable situation today. **They don't need** big warehouses as **he has made** the supply chain lean.
2 He tells them **to be** modest and patient, **not to go** for quick profits, but **to plan** for the long term and, above all, **not to ruin their** business.

b, 3 She says (that) **they are** very proud of **his** company and the employment opportunities **he has** created.
4 She asks if it was difficult for **him** to get enough initial capital to set up **his** own business, why **he** did it on **his** own, how long it took **him** to become profitable and if **he was** sure his business idea would work.
5 He tells her **to read his** autobiography. **She** can find all the answers there in detail.

Remember: If the <u>introductory verb</u> is in the <u>present</u> tense, the tenses remain unchanged – <u>no tense shift</u>!

B

1 The owner of the vineyard looks sad and admits (that) he is not happy about his decision to sell his vineyard to a Chinese actress, but he had no other choice / alternative / option. He has been making losses for months because the prices are too low due to the competiton from overseas. He has too many debts.
2 Local politicians are criticizing his decision publicly and ask if he knows what it means for the region and why he does not cooperate with colleagues. They ask him to rethink / reconsider his decision and advise him to sell his wine online or to merge.
3 The young Chinese actress says (that) it has always been her dream to live in France and points out that French wine is getting more and more popular in China. She adds (that) she is planning to train Chinese employees who could produce wine in China later.

Remember: If the <u>introductory verb</u> is in the <u>present</u> tense, the tenses remain unchanged – <u>no tense shift</u>!

Ch 4 (Reported Speech), L 2:   *+ tense shift!*

C

1 **were working**
2 **their** strategy centers **had** the broadest portfolio in the animal-nutrition industry. **They had** two factories in Brazil and **exported** to Venezuela, Guatemala and even Cuba. In the area of animal nutrition, Mexico **was** secure due to several factors.
3 **they had** the capacity to attract companies like General Electric and Siemens, and that **they were moving** from a manufacturing state to a state of innovation and high technology.

4 Querétaro **had witnessed** the largest amount of jobs development since 2009 and **was hailed** as a success story of NAFTA (= North American Free Trade Area). It **had** significantly **increased** local supply.

D

1a, In an interview in 2013, Mr. Draghi was asked if **he was** sure the euro crisis **was** over and **if** the taxpayer **would be spared** a heavy burden as some critics **assumed**.
1b, He replied (that) he **could not give** any guarantees; that **would be** foolish but **their** measures **had stabilized** the euro.

2a, The journalist asked how long **it would be** stable this [noch aktuell!] time So far, all the measures **had been** very short-lived.
2b, Draghi replied (that) a series of steps **was needed** of course, and that **was** what they **had done**. The euro **would prevail**.

3a, The journalist asked Draghi what **he thought** of critics who **would like** to ditch the euro and **if he had** ever **had** any doubts.
3b, Draghi replied (that) it **was his** duty to defend the euro. And
(that) **that was** what **he would** do. A few years **before**, the task **had been** much easier. Then he told the journalist **to be** patient.

E

a, 1. Als der Aufsichtsrat von Siemens im Juli 2013 Löscher loswerden wollte, sagte der gefeuerte Vorstand: „Ich werde gehen, aber Aufsichtsratsvorsitzender Cromme muss auch zurücktreten. Sonst trete ich gar nicht zurück, sondern werde gemäß meinem Vertrag die nächsten vier Jahre bleiben."
2. Bereits zwei Tage später jedoch sagte Löscher der Presse: „Das Schicksal des Unternehmens ist wichtiger als die Interessen Einzelner."
3. Es wurde behauptet: „Die Entscheidung ist einstimmig gewesen und alles ist ganz schnell gegangen."
4. Der neue Vorstandschef Kaeser erklärte: „Ich werde nicht versuchen, Siemens neu zu erfinden, denn das ist nicht nötig. Ich will der Firma ihr Gleichgewicht zurückgeben."
5. Während Cromme sagte: „Siemens hat unter Löschers Führung zwei der erfolgreichsten Jahre in der Unternehmensgeschichte erfahren." Gewerkschaftsvertreter kritisierten: „Löscher hat auch durch seine Jobabbau-Politik Ängste erzeugt."

b, 1. "**I will go**, but the chairman of the Supervisory Board, **must / has to go**, too. Otherwise **I will not resign** at all, but **stay** for the next four years in accordance with **my** contract."
2. "The fate of the company **is** more important than the interests of individuals."
3. "The decision **was** unanimous and everything **went** very quickly."
4. "**I will not try / I am not going to try** to reinvent Siemens. I **want** to give the company its balance back."
5. "Under Löscher's leadership, Siemens **(has) experienced** two of the most successful years in its company history." ... "Löscher **(has)** also **caused** fears through **his** policy of jobs cuts."

c, 1. he **would go** ... **would have to go**, too. ... he **would not resign** at all, but **stay** for the next four years according to **his** contract.
2. **was** more important than the interests of individuals.
3. **had been** unanimous and everything **had gone** very quickly.
4. he **would not try / was not going to try** ... **that was** not necessary. ... **he wanted** to give ...
5. **had experienced** ... **had** also **caused** fears through **his** ...

F

1. ... had been postponed .... would be the following / the next year
2. ... was to start the next / following day ... would have been heard by the end of the following / next week ... could be expected early the following / next year.
3. ... ten years before they had dominated ... then they had had to compete ... they were ... that year

G

1. ... why he had decided to sell his ... if he would stay
2. what other options he had considered before eventually accepting the offer ... if he had expected ...
3. what his plans were, if he was working ...
4. ... to stop asking ... (to) wait ...

H

1. The company boss informed his employees/workforce that the company would merge with its biggest competitor. The negotiations had been successful and the merger could take place within the next six months.
2. Already five months ago the workforce was informed that the factory had been making losses for years and (that) the bank was no longer willing / ready / prepared to grant more / further loans. Unprofitable divisions would have to be divested / shed. The company boss was negotiating already with investors who had shown interest.

3. ... *Galbraith said* he did not understand *why* Greece wanted to sell *the state-owned energy group, as* the business/industry yielded / was yielding *fat profits and* would secure *high public revenues in the long term. For him,* that was *a signal that the Greek government* did not seriously believe *it* would ever be able *to reduce the debt burden. He added that* that did not astonish him *as the old oligarchs* had not really lost *their influence and* even benefited / profited / were even benefiting / profiting *from the crisis and* (were) increasing *their wealth while European tax payers* were constantly paying. *He concluded* (that) that was not *sustainable and* could lead to *existential conflicts within the EU.*

Ch 4 (Reported Speech), L 3: *all mixed!*

I

1 ... he had been ... accepted ... 2 ... would not have signed the contract ... had offered him ... 3 had been thinking ... had decided ... 4 ... had* (doubts) ...talked* ... 5 wanted* ... would have to* ... 6 ... wished ... told* ... 7 ... had had ... he was employed (there)*

* In these sentences a shift to the Past Perfect would change the meaning, esp. in if-clauses and temporal clauses (when, until etc.)! So the Past Tense has to be kept.

K

1a, ... his ... had been known ... he went [temporal clause: *before*!] ... he had taken
1b, ... was (going down)... his ... were selling [temporal clause: *while*!] ... they would have done
2a, ... if [= *ob, nicht wenn/falls*! Kein *if-clause*, sondern indirekte Satzfrage] he was [not completed at the time when!] piling up ... he took [*when*!] that ... [remember: usually, after an introductory verb in the Past: *this* > *that, here* > *there* etc.]
2b, ... was not ... were [both: not completed at the time when, in 2a,!]

301

3a, ... he would do ... failed [*if*-clause!] ... could survive [*if* = *ob*]
3b, ... could ... should withdraw [auxiliaries!] ... would also take to [normal shift from *will* / Future to *would* / Conditional] ... would go [meaning! Zum Zeitpunkt der Aussage keine vollzogene Handlung, daher Cond. I, nicht Cond. II]

L

1. The hotel owner reported (that) he was seriously considering giving up his hotel when the bookings plummeted during the financial crisis.
2. He quickly added (that) he decided* not to do that when he saw a TV report about tourism in Morocco, as there was a huge potential for hotels for European guests.
[zum selben Zeitpunkt, nämlich des Fernsehberichts (*when*!), nicht davor bzw. *vorzeitig* - daher würde das *Past Perfect* den Sinn verzerren, den Zeitbezug verfälschen.]
3. He said (that) he had immediately flown to Marrakesh and (had) [*had* muss nicht wiederholt werden, wäre stilistisch weniger gut] begun the construction of a hotel for European holidaymakers, as he hoped / as he was hoping / hoping (that) he would soon be able to make up for his losses / compensate his losses if the hotel in Morocco was built quickly and (if) he started to make profits there.
4. He admitted (that) he had been a little / bit too optimistic at first / initially, but eventually he had been able to save his hotel at home.
5. He said (that) he had to thank the reporter for the TV report; he wished he could remember her name.
6. He smiled and added (that) he ought to invite her actually to spend a week in his hotel; that might be the best way of thanking her.

M

1. emphasizing / asked if they could not emphasize the trendy design
2. to get him the file / asked her boss if she should get him the file
3. for the minutes / to show him the minutes / if she could show him the minutes
4. offered to fetch the product specification from the CEO's desk / if she should fetch ... his
5. for support / give him his support
6. if they should / if they were to
7. offered / suggested / if they should
8. if they should send / if they were to send / offered

N

1 was held ... worked 2 had ... kept ... had ... did* not 3 should not* be underestimated ... were ... needed to know the right people and (to) be ... 4 is slowly improving ... are becoming more international ... have got used to spending ... are often considered ... appears ...
5 ... are ... lack ... are not ... could be ... were ... are usually believed ...
6 ... to leave ... be afraid ... them to be ... (to) learn ... (to) understand ... they will be ...
7 ... were successful ... had usually worked ... lost out ... they did* not have ...
8. ... to study and work / they should study and work ... (to / they should) build up ... not to shy away / they should not shy away ... they receive

* short forms are common in direct speech, not so much in reported speech (language levels: oral vs written)

O

1. Historians often point out (that) education and progress go hand in hand with the rise of cities. Urbanization in Greek and medieval cities led to the division of labour and specialization, art and philosophy would hardly have been possible without urban structures.
2. Even critical economists recognize (that) the rich cities of the Italian Renaissance massively furthered the 'knowledge industry', they add, however, (that) the early Industrial

revolution in England generated/spawned/created a new social class and quickly led to mass poverty.
3. Already years ago scientists pointed out / Scientists already pointed out years ago (that) the demographic development in poor countries could / might lead to chaos in the megacities.
4. At that time sociologists warned (that) overcrowded cities could / might lead to civil wars.
5. Last year an African politician said (that) cities like / such as Lagos were the new centres / hubs of innovation, as poor people who had flocked into the cities, full of hope, needed creativity in the daily struggle for survival.
6. He added (that) people in rich countries had become too lazy and relied / were relying too much on the welfare state. That did not further / encourage innovation.
7. Car manufacturers confirm (that) the emerging economies are more important for them than the saturated markets in the European Union, as the emerging middle class there is developing enormous purchasing power.
8. During a press conference in the German-Chinese Chamber of Commerce in Shanghai a journalist asked if the Chinese cities did not already have too many traffic jams and criticized that smog was already causing / already caused serious health problems. A representative of the car industry replied (that) it was the task of politicians to find sustainable economic and social solutions. He asked the journalists to read the info material before asking / they asked further / more questions.
9. Before his election the mayor had promised (that) he would cut/lower the corporate tax and make the city safer / to cut/lower the corporate tax and (to) make the city safer. Before he was re-elected last year the opposition complained (that) organized crime had conquered entire quarters of the city and (that) it was practically impossible to get orders without bribing / bribes.
10. The city administration announced last week (that) from January companies would no longer be allowed to pay migrant workers below the minimum wage (level).

P

1. For more than a decade consumer organizations have been complaining (that) the British banks are charging / charge far too high fees and interest for overdrawn accounts. In 2000 already / Already in 2000 a government agency found out that the banks were able to impose excessive prices and profits, because there was no real competition. A spokesperson said: "Enough is enough. We urgently need more competition."
2. A former investment banker / An ex-investment banker admitted (that) nothing had happened in the following years and banks had even cheated the tax office. "The *Libor* scandal could have been prevented," he said, but no measures were taken to monitor the banks. Nothing would change as long as nobody / no one was punished.
3. Members of the European Parliament claim (that) the British government has done everything to prevent stricter rules. They say openly: "The tax payers continue to pay for the excesses of banks, because the British government protects / is protecting its financial industry."
4. Worried economists already explained before the financial crisis what had to be done and what had already gone wrong. "The EU must/has to take action," they demanded.

Q

1. Benjamin Barber argumentiert, dass die Zivilisation in städtischen Gebieten geboren sei. Sie / Diese sind „die öffentlichen Sphären / Räume, in denen wir uns als Bürger kundtun," fügt er hinzu.
2. Er weist darauf hin / hebt hervor / betont, dass mehr als die Hälfte der Weltbevölkerung jetzt in Städten lebt.
3. Herr Barber stellt auch fest: „Die Demokratie ist in Gefahr" und argumentiert weiter, dass die Demokratie in Städten der Antike geboren sei und daher in der globalen Weltstadt wiedergeboren werden könne.

4. In *TedGlobal* 2013 verlieh Herr Barber seiner Überzeugung Ausdruck, dass Bürgermeister daher die besten Herrscher seien / wären, da sie mit täglichen Problemen konfrontiert seien und sie / diese lösen, nicht nur theoretisch / in der Theorie diskutieren müssten / sie / diese zu lösen und nicht nur theoretisch / in der Theorie zu diskutieren hätten.
5. Vor Jahrzehnten warnten Experten (davor), dass Städte außer Kontrolle geraten könnten, wenn / falls sie zu groß würden, besonders in armen Ländern, während die demographische / Bevölkerungsentwicklung in reichen Ländern Städte schrumpfen lassen würde.
6. Ein Fernsehbericht verwies vor ein paar Jahren darauf, dass der Bürgermeister von London mehr Einfluss gewonnen habe, da die britische Hauptstadt ein Fünftel des englischen BIP ausmachte und (da) ihr Reichtum/Wohlstand ärmeren Regionen als / in Form von Strukturhilfe zugutekäme.
7. Ein ehemaliger / früherer Bürgermeister von London verlangte / forderte, dass London mehr von seinem Geld behalten dürfen solle, da die Infrastruktur schlimm unterfinanziert sei. „Wir zahlen für das ganze Land, während London mit dem Verfall konfrontiert ist / vor dem Verfall steht," warnte er.

R

1. Before the election the party complained (that) the tax burden was too high and had to be reduced / cut / lowered / *etc*. There were hardly any incentives for unemployed people to accept a job with a low salary. The government had not kept its promise. Instead of carrying out a reform it had worsened / aggravated the situation / it had made the situation worse.
2. After its victory this party now says (that) it does not see any possibility of lowering / cutting / *etc*. taxes in the current economic situation. All public spending has been examined, the budget will only allow cuts in spending in three years/in three years' time. Of course, that is the fault of the former government, as it made wrong strategic decisions, the party says.
3. The opposition had promised before the election to simplify the tax system radically, as it was unjust. There would hardly have to be any exceptions if all subsidies were done away with. Then the tax system would be simple and fair and every citizen would be able to complete his tax declaration within half a day.
4. Now it is part of the government and declares (that) it is naïve to believe (that) in a complex national economy a simple system could be fair. Years ago experts proved that. The Finance Ministry will follow this insight.

S

1. Während des Wahlkampfes beklagte die Partei, dass die Mittelschicht unter einer schweren Steuerlast leiden würde, während multinationale Unternehmen ihre Gewinne ins Ausland verlagern würden / verlagerten und sehr wenig zum Haushalt beitrügen/beitragen würden. Wenn sie gewählt (werden) würden, würden sie das beenden, was sie unfairen Missbrauch öffentlicher Mittel nannten. Große Unternehmen / Großunternehmen würden dazu gebracht werden, ihre Beiträge zu leisten, zum Beispiel zur Infrastruktur und zur Bildung.
2. Einen Tag nach der Wahl behaupten die Politiker nun, dass internationale Unternehmen einfach das Land verlassen würden, was zu massiven Arbeitsplatzverlusten führen würde, wenn die Regierung versuchen würde, einen größeren Anteil ihrer Gewinne zu bekommen. Sie behaupten jetzt, dass die Steuerpolitik des Landes nicht geändert werden dürfe, internationale Regelungen seien nötig, um das Problem zu lösen. Sie fügen hinzu, dass es das sei, was sie immer versucht hätten, den Wählern zu erklären / dass sie genau das den Wählern immer versucht hätten zu erklären. Sie sagen, sie würden / werden das Thema auf die Tagesordnung des nächsten EU-Gipfeltreffens setzen.
3. Bevor der Regierungschef zurücktrat, fragten die Oppositionsführer, warum Unternehmer nicht durch Steuervergünstigungen und andere Maßnahmen unterstützt würden, da das Land dringend mehr Innovation brauche / bräuchte. Sie behaupteten, dass die Schaffung von *Start-ups* stattdessen abgewürgt worden sei / wäre, und forderten die Regierung auf, ihre Politik zu ändern / sagten der Regierung, sie solle ihre Politik ändern.

4. Der neue Premierminister erklärt nun, dass echte Unternehmer in der Lage sein müssten, ohne öffentliche Gelder / Gelder der öffentlichen Hand / (öffentliches Geld) zu überleben / ohne öffentliche Gelder überleben können müssten, sonst wäre ihr Erfolg nie nachhaltig / würde ihr Erfolg nie nachhaltig sein.

Ch 5 (Passive), L 1:

Tasks

b,

... a business magazine published ...; have been searched ... seized ... interrogated [**difficult**, because the agent is not clear – probably: .... *The police have searched the offices, seized computers and interrogated witnesses*]; ... is reported to ... [**difficult**: who reports? agent unclear!]; is said to have destroyed [**difficult**: who says that? agent unclear!]; Who had warned the CFO; who had helped him; ... is being checked [**difficult**: who checks? agent unclear!]; will anything be found [**difficult**: it is not important who finds anything ...]; Can anybody convince ...; *Can (anybody)* [who? agent unclear!]; Can they be made to witness [**difficult!** Who is supposed to make them witness? agent unclear!]; if [who? agent unclear!] grants them impunity .....; somebody [**difficult!** who? agent unclear!] has sued them for damages; ... and [**difficult!** Who should refund?] the money to the victims

c, ... (the members of the board) are granted (impunity)

d, ... is being checked

e, lost: with all data lost = *verkürzter Nebensatz (wobei alle Daten verlorengegangen sind; d.h. sie sind jetzt weg)*;
convinced: Can ... be convinced = *Passiv Infinitiv nach modalem Hilfsverb* (can)

A

a, While **the anti-virus software was being updated** the whole system broke down. What had to be done?
b, **The demonstrators were stopped** at the factory gate by the police.
c, **The merger had been prevented** several times by the government.
d, **Our delivery vans have been held up** for hours by the mob. When **will the mob be stopped** from rioting by the police?
e, **Discounts** of up to 20 per cent **were granted** by the furniture store, before **bankruptcy had to be declared** (by it). [In the second part of the sentence the passive construction does not sound elegant.]
f, Currently **our premises cannot be accessed*** because **a gas leak is being repaired.*** When **will this job be finished**? A lot remains to be done.
g, **Our employee seems to have been bribed** by a competitor. He has been questioned [here the Progressive Form – *been being questioned* - is not used in the Passive, as it would be too clumsy!] for hours now by the police. When **will he be released?***
h, If **pink washing-machines were produced, would they be bought?***

* *by + agent* kann in diesen Fällen wegfallen, da keine zusätzliche Information gegeben wird oder *they* zum Beispiel ohnehin für ein neutrales *man* steht, also kein spezifischer Urheber genannt wird.

B

1 ... mussten viele Lizenzen / Genehmigungen von den lokalen Behörden eingeholt werden / waren viele ... einzuholen.
2 ... wurden wir aufgefordert, Bestechungsgelder zu zahlen.
3 ... nachdem unsere Läden eröffnet (worden) waren ...
4 ... die von Staatsbediensteten verursacht zu sein schienen ...
5 ... wir wollten nicht erpresst werden ...

6 Einer unserer Führungskräfte wurde bedroht …
7 „Du wirst zusammengeschlagen (werden), wenn wir nicht auf die Gehaltsliste deiner Firma kommen / gesetzt werden."
8 Ich erinnere mich nicht daran, jemals so massiv erpresst worden zu sein.
9 … waren wir geschlagen / besiegt ….
10 … muss das verhindert werden / ist das zu verhindern
11 … wenn sie von der Regierung geschützt (werden) würden
12 … eingeladen zu werden
13 sie sollten unterstützt werden …
14 Wenig scheint getan worden zu sein …
15 Unsere Mitarbeiter …. hätten erwartet, ernst genommen zu werden …
16 alle ihre Bitten wurden ignoriert

C

1 Ich wurde von der deutschen Handelskammer kontaktiert
2 … meine Werkzeugmaschine könne/könnte leicht verkauft werden / sei / wäre leicht zu verkaufen
3 sie wurde als einzigartig angesehen
4 .. wurde ich viele Male von der Presse gefragt …
5 … das müsse geheim gehalten werden / bleiben
6 … saß ich neben einer Chinesin
7 … die sagte, sie sei / wäre … von einer deutschen Versicherungsgesellschaft eingestellt worden …
8 Sie schien sehr gut informiert zu sein …
9 … die sie beantwortet haben wollte …
10 … ich fühlte mich geschmeichelt.
11 während unser erstes Produktionsband gebaut wurde …
12 … bevor die Werbekampagne gestartet wurde …
13 .. eine einzigartige Werkzeugmaschine hoch gelobt wurde …
14 … (da) sie in China hergestellt wurde
15 … war schockiert
16 Meine Technologie war nachgemacht worden …
17 … unser Gespräch war aufgezeichnet worden …
18 meine Geschäftsträume waren zerbrochen …
19 … ich war pleite und fühlte mich betrogen

D

1. At the AGM (Annual General Meeting) the CEO / Chairman of the Board was criticized and asked why his compensation had been doubled. While he was being interviewed by reporters, he was even hit in the face by a shareholder.
2. For months the IPO (Initial Public Offering) has been known, but so far no shares have been issued. When will the company really be privatized?
3. Our logo should have been modernized years ago. It is considered as old-fashioned by many. Our brand would be more easily accepted by young customers if our image was better tailored to this target group.
4. Part of our product range seems to have been copied by companies in Asia. I would be surprised if the counterfeits there were seized by the authorities. Our business partners must be informed immediately.
5. How can drug cartels in Latin America be fought effectively? Politicians seem to have been bought; the battle seems to be lost. Furthermore, weapons are continuously being smuggled into the country.
6. For years the opening of the new airport has been postponed / put off again and again.

Ch 5 (Passive), L 2:

E

a, **Our fiercest competitor was given** the licence despite all our efforts.
b, This year again, **the shareholders were not paid** any dividend.
c, **The whole team was given** huge bonuses for their repeated success.
d, Most workers consider the pay rises **they will be given** to be far too low. Also, due to the crisis **they have been paid** a smaller Christmas bonus.
e, Before **the journalists were shown** the latest prototype all cameras ....
f, **Banks were helped** by the government during the financial crisis. Now **the government would need to be given** financial support by the banks.
g, For a period of time, **the East India Trading Company was granted** a monopoly of trade by the British government.
h, If **we had been given** exclusive rights by the manufacturer ... **He has been shown** the evidence many times – in vain.

F

1. The company **is known to have made** a bid for the IT division of its French rival.
2. ... the solar project **has been believed to be** a cash cow.
3. The retail chain **is expected to start** an online shop soon.
4. The entrepreneur **is said to have lost** a lot of money before he was successful.
5. The politician **was thought to have signed** a secret agreement with an energy group.

G

1 It is expected that the Central Bank will find a recipe against deflation.
   The Central Bank is expected to find a recipe against deflation.
2. Financial support was given to the country as long as there were reforms.
   The country was given financial support as long as there were reforms.
3. The Controlling Department is said to have discovered/disclosed the fraud.
   The fraud is said to have been discovered by the Controlling Department.
4. It is reported that the oil company has been nationalized in the meantime.
   The oil company is reported to have been nationalized in the meantime.
5. Yesterday it was reported that the energy company would soon be privatized again.
   Yesterday the energy company was reported to be / get privatized again soon.

H

1. Obwohl der Führungskraft eine weitere Lohnerhöhung angeboten wurde, blieb sie nicht.
2. Es wird erwartet, dass sich die Binnennachfrage abschwächt, aber nicht einbricht.
3. Bevor das Projekt gestartet werden kann, müssen alle Risiken bewertet werden. Viele Fragen sind noch zu beantworten.
4. Was bleibt sonst noch zu tun? Den Investoren sind bereits alle relevanten / wichtigen Fakten und Zahlen gegeben worden. Nun sollen sie innerhalb einer Woche entscheiden, damit das Projekt weitergeführt werden kann.
5. Oman soll in den letzten Jahrzehnten modernisiert worden sein. Ist die Tradition gegen Wohlstand eingetauscht worden? Tatsächlich wurde die Modernisierung durch die Öleinnahmen unterstützt.
6. Viele Gastarbeiter werden/sind gezwungen / werden dazu gebracht, stundenlang ohne Essen und Trinken / ohne zu essen und zu trinken in der Sonne zu arbeiten. Das wird von Menschenrechtsorganisationen als Verstoß gegen die Menschenrechte betrachtet. Es wird kritisiert, dass das Sportereignis durch Sklavenarbeit ermöglicht wird.
7. Man glaubt, dass die Regierung erwägt, auf Gebrauchtwagen Einfuhrzölle zu erheben.

8. Unsere Stammkunden wollen, dass man sich intensiver um sie kümmert. Es wird erwartet, dass wir auf ihre Beschwerden und Vorschläge hören, um die Qualität unserer Produkte zu verbessern.
9. Die Entwicklung soll von Gier getrieben gewesen/worden sein.

I

1 was discovered 2 has been changed 3 has been turned 4 has been created 5 protected [*has been* wird aus stilistischen Gründen nicht wiederholt] 6 have been used 7 have been paid for / are paid for 8 is not expected 9 is said 10 to have been bailed out 11 was blamed 12 are forbidden 13 have been diversified 14 to be turned 15 is being developed 16 are reported 17 are expected 18 are needed 19 are not wanted 20 be influenced 21 (be) made 22 is plagued 23 to be solved 24 to be supplied 25 has been wooed 26 has been hampered 27 is fueled / is being fueled

K

1. In this press article it is pointed out that the foreign shareholders were not looked after at all last time. They were totally ignored. They were given no help to understand the contracts, they were not even given a translation of the annual report.
2. "By whom had the report been translated? Who should we meet with to discuss the contents? Who did the report have to be approved by? It [= the report] was expected to be published in several languages."
3. "In the graph (which / that was) submitted by you at our last meeting no cost saving potentials are to be found. I would have expected to be offered a few alternatives before negotiating/negotiations."
4. "Technical errors can never be totally avoided, that is accepted. But: Are you prepared for the negotiations? Our Asian partners are being picked up / collected at the hotel at this very moment; on their way here they will already be shown pictures of the prototypes. The showroom is being decorated.
5. "During the business dinner we were served monkey brain. We had not been told how to eat it. It was obviously to be taken/understood as a gesture of hospitality."

L

1. "What is to be done? Our services have to / must be tailored more to our customers' needs / requirements."
2. "Who was expected to save / rescue the company? We had not been helped by anybody / anyone years ago either."
3. "The battle is lost – the war is not / isn't! A new takeover bid has just been made."
4. We have just been given the licence – from now on we'll produce and sell!"
5. First we'll inspect the factory, / "First the factory will be inspected, then we'll talk to the employees.
6. The expenses are represented by the red column. Where are the revenues to be found?"
7. The catalogues should be dispatched by Monday. The brochures should have been dispatched already."
8. The figures are to be updated before the meeting."

Ch 6 (If-Clauses), L 1:

Tasks

If (I) had done [Past Perfect - pat 3], ... (I) would not have developed [Cond.II - pat 3];
(we) would ... be living [Cond. I Progressive - pat 3 & 2];
if (you) have (a talent) [Present Tense – pat 1], go ahead / don't let [imperative – pat 1];

would not have been [Cond. II – pat 3], if (my parents) were (rich) [Past Tense – pat 2], had sent [Past Perfect – pat 3];
Should [Cond. 1 – pat 2 (inversion!)], (I) would not hesitate [Cond. I – pat 2]; even if (that) meant [Past Tense – pat 2], (I) would not finish [Cond. I – pat 2];
… if … goes [Present Tense – pat 1], (I) will look [Future I – pat 1];
… (I) will set up … [future I – pat 1], if (I) have not received … [Present Perfect – pat 1]
If … are (Present Tense – pat 1], (they) are … [Present tense – pat 1];
Don't think [imperative – pat 1], if (you) see … [Present tense – pat 1], take it [imperative – pat 1]

A

a, will be ousted (PAT 1); PAT 2: was delayed … would be (ousted); PAT 3: had been delayed … would have been (ousted)
b, would have sued (PAT 3); PAT 1: causes … will sue; PAT 2: caused … would sue
c, would not take place (PAT 2); PAT 1: will not take place … vetoes; PAT 3: would not have taken place … had vetoed
d, had not been improved (PAT 3); PAT 1: are not improved … will close ; PAT 2: were not improved … would close
e, refused (PAT 2) – [also possible here: *had refused* – in case the investor has already done it – see level 3]; PAT 1: will have … refuses; PAT 3: would have had … had refused

B

1 will lose 2 will go down 3 does not reduce 4 was 5 stopped 6 would not have plunged 7 had been given up 8 fails 9 had been deregulated 10 would have paid off 11 stayed 12 will jump in 13 (will [repetition not necessary, stylistically rather clumsy) fill

C

1 raise 2 will accept 3 were enhanced 4 would 5 had been 6 would have recruited 7 would have worked out 8 were 9 cancel

D

1 go 2 will happen 3 would have become 4 would have to 5 will damage 6 did 7 had not / hadn't done 8 do not / don't find 9 would be 10 acquired 11 would have been 12 had accepted 13 will plummet

E

1. "Many qualified employees would not leave their country, if they earned enough money at home. If this trend continues, there will soon be a massive shortage of skilled labour and graduates."
2. "If the four freedoms of the European Single Market had not taken effect in 1993, many young Southern Europeans would not have had the opportunity to find a job in other countries of the EU / EU-countries."
3. "Would you leave your country, your family and your friends to live in another country whose language you do not speak if you did not have a job?"
4. "I would not hesitate to emigrate, for example to Australia, if I had better job opportunities there. Would you not do / Wouldn't you do that, at least if you spoke good English / English well?"
5. "If the government had fought corruption more effectively, the economy would have developed much better, that is certain. If the EU Commission does not increase the pressure, nothing will change."
6. "If 'social tourism' continues to increase, the government will have to do something."

Ch 6 (If-Clauses), L 2:

F

a, ☒ If no publisher wants your manuscript, publish it yourself.
☒ If your new book is rejected by all publishing houses you can publish it online.
☒ If no one wants your manuscript you might consider having it printed at your own cost.
☒ Your novel is really great! If no publisher wants it you should publish it yourself.
☒ If your new book is rejected by all publishers, why don't you upload it for sale on your website?
☒ What will you do if your publisher refuses to publish your next book?
☒ If no one buys your book, don't despair. Try publishing it as an e-book.
☒ If the bookshops did not display your latest novel it was because you did not give them any incentive to do so.
○ If you sent this manuscript to your publisher he will reject it.
○ If your publisher will reject your manuscript, you will send it to others.

b, ☒ If you have already finished drafting your business plan I will read it right away.
☒ If you had provided more detailed information the investors would have accepted your business idea.
☒ The investors would certainly consider injecting money into your business idea if your business plan was more detailed.
○ Your business plan will be accepted by the bank if it was more detailed.
☒ If the potential investors require a detailed business plan it is because they do not want to lose money.
☒ You must raise your own funds or take a loan if no investor can be found for your project – it is a brilliant idea!
○ If the bank had really been willing to grant you the loan it had asked you to hand in a business plan.
○ Your business model might work if you would not have been so sloppy with the implementation.

c, ☒ If you are sure they have cheated you sue them!
○ You sue them if they will cheat you.
☒ You should change your suppliers if they are not reliable.
☒ If you kick out an unreliable supplier the others will be more careful.
☒ If you engage an NGO you may finally get rid of child labour in your supply chain.
☒ If you do not inspect the factories in Bangladesh you can never be sure that safety regulations are respected. *[a general fact, truth]*
☒ Child labour must be avoided if you do not risk a consumer boycott.
○ If child labour will be discovered by the press, you have a problem!

G

1 must / (should) 2 may 3 will / can(not) 4 should 5 will 6 will / can

H

1 are 2 want 3 sold off 4 boost 5 have 6 wait 7 had had 8 did not / didn't postpone / (*also*: had not postponed) 9 don't ... go 10 announced 11 will follow 12 do not / don't want 13 want 14 would miss

I

1. "If the Central Bank cuts the interest rate once again, there will soon be a real estate bubble."
2. "If investors fear deflation and the interest rate is low, they will buy real estate. That is quite normal."
3. "But if inflation does not go up soon, many citizens will lose their savings."
4. "If you want my advice: Buy shares or real estate if you have money to spare."
5. "If I had money to invest, I would do that."
6. "If the real estate prices continue to rocket, that will soon lead to a dangerous bubble."

K

1. If the birth rate in japan does not go up soon, the pension system will collapse / break down in a few years / in a few years' time. The government could improve the situation if it allowed more young immigrants into the country.
2. "Why don't you shift / move / relocate your production to Viet Nam, if wages in China have risen so much that your production there is no longer profitable?"
3. The demographic development in China would be much worse still, if the government had not given up the one-child-policy several/a few years ago.
4. If the banks do not grant more loans to entrepreneurs, economic growth will soon dwindle / go down / decrease. The government should re-consider / re-think / re-examine its economic policy if nothing changes.
5. If the secret service knew about the systematic industrial espionage, why did it not inform / why did it fail to inform the government? Many problems could have been avoided, if the companies had been warned. What would you do if your patent was stolen? If you have a niche product, be careful / watch out!
6. If intellectual property rights are not protected sufficiently, there are fewer incentives for innovation. If this is the case, the government has to act!

Ch 6 (If-Clauses), L 3:

L

a,
- ○ If the car dealer would not have offered cheaper cars he had lost customers.
- ○ If the new model will not have lower petrol consumption it does not sell.
- ☒ If the SUV did not have a rear camera it would be difficult for inexperienced drivers to park it.
- ☒ If the fuel efficiency of the SUV had not been improved few Europeans would have bought the new model last year due to high petrol prices.
- ☒ The new SUV would not sell well if it had not been made more economical.
- ☒ If the car company does not spend more on R& D it may soon lag behind its competitors.
- ☒ If the automotive group had not invested massively in new designs it might have lost even more market share.

b,
- ☒ If the software company did not enjoy a near-monopoly it could not have imposed its third price increase in a row now.
- ☒ If no new functions had been added to the standard software it would be hopelessly outdated by now.
- ○ The IT giant would have acquired the start-up if there would be no public protest against the acquisition.
- ☒ The software company might have withdrawn from that market if the government had not clamped down on software piracy more severely.

M

1. Should the immigrant workers go on strike in Qatar, the stadium could not be completed in time.
2. Had more migrant workers committed suicide, the Chinese government would have had to intervene.
3. Were the government to decide against deregulation, all our plans would be thwarted.
4. [here: **not possible**, because *had* is used as a full verb (Vollverb), not an auxiliary (nicht als Hilfsverb)]

N

1. Should the project not be approved by the government, we would urgently need a new major order.
2. Had our research department worked better, we would not have to pay such high damages.
3. Should we close the factory (down), if the reports about terrible working conditions turn out / prove to be true?
4. Had the product been introduced / launched last year already, we would now be market leader.
5. If we had better relations with the government, we would not have to wait so long for licences.

O

1 will plunge 2 keeps 3 could have saved 4 would (now) be 5 If we had concentrated / Had we concentrated 6 would have stayed 7 Should 8 would be

P

1. „Wenn der Chef uns absolut nicht mehr für diese gefährliche Arbeit/Aufgabe zahlen will, streiken wir alle / (werden wir alle streiken)."
2. „Wenn du ihn unbedingt erpressen willst, solltest du nicht überrascht sein, wenn er ablehnt."
3. „Wir wären dankbar, wenn Sie / du aufhören würden/würdest uns zu kritisieren / wenn Sie / du uns nicht mehr kritisieren würden / würdest."
4. „Wenn der Verhandlungsführer seinen Willen bekommen sollte, wäre dieses Unternehmen nicht mehr wettbewerbsfähig/konkurrenzfähig."

Q

a, 1 would not have been freed 2 would not have been released [schon geschehen] / would not be released [noch nicht geschehen, wird aber geschehen] 3 may have been killed
b, 4 would be richer 5 would have boomed earlier
c, 6 were lower 7 had been suffering

R

1. If Mexico does not defeat / fails to defeat the drug cartels, the killing will never stop. Above all, the North of Mexico would be helped, if no illegal weapons came / were coming into the country.
2. Should the tensions in the region increase, the energy supply chain could / might collapse / break down. This would have serious/grave/severe consequences for the economy of the EU / the EU economy.
3. Had oil not been so cheap in the USA for decades, the car manufacturers would have been forced much earlier to develop vehicles with lower fuel consumption. Then they would be more competitive today.

4. If you won't cooperate / work together with us, we will look for another partner. That would mean (that) we could form an alliance with one of your competitors. If you would examine our offer once again, we would be very grateful / obliged.
5. We would hire / employ you / take you on immediately, if you were better trained and spoke Arabic. If something is missing in your CV / C.V. (BE) / résumé (AE), it is experience abroad / foreign experience.
6. If you have already filled in / filled out / completed the form, please wait here. We can start / begin the (job) interview immediately if you want.

Ch 7 (Mixed Tenses), L 1:

Tasks

e, feeling *(relative clause; past level)*; rising *(causal; past level)*; weakening *(effect, consequence; past level)*

A

1 has 2 takes place 3 have cut 4 are 5 have had 6 had not been cut 7 would not have deteriorated 8 are 9 look 10 will pose 11 has extended 12 are / (have been) 13 have not kept up 14 was opened 15 has become / (is becoming) 16 saw 17 were built 18 was developed 19 has declined 20 will ... improve

B

1.a 2.a 3.d 4.d 5.c 6.a,b,c,d 7.c,d 8.a 9.a,b,c 10.a,b,c 11.a,b,c

C

1. "Since the oil crisis in the 1970s it has been clear (that) there are limits to growth, as we will run out raw materials / commodities."
2. "For years everybody has been talking of sustainability. But what has been done? Do we have a solution?"
3. "The EU is currently financing a project in the Sahara (desert) to use solar energy. It was launched / initiated quickly when investors had been found."
4. "Will it supply enough / sufficient energy for the European industry? Wouldn't it / Would it not be cheaper to use the solar energy in Spain?"
5. "The costs are a problem, indeed. While they were going up in the first few years, important investors withdrew from the project."

D

1 (that) it had been clear since the oil crisis in the 1970s (that) there were [allgemeine Feststellung, die immer noch zutrifft] limits to growth, as we [nicht *they*, denn es geht um uns alle, die gesamte Menschheit] would run out of raw materials / commodities.
2 (that) for years everybody had been talking of sustainability ... what had been done, if we [wir alle, gesamte Menschheit, s.o.] had a solution.
3 (that) the EU was currently [falls es gegenwärtig immer noch zutrifft] / at that time [falls nicht mehr] financing a project in the Sahara (desert) to use solar energy. It had been launched / initiated quickly when investors had been found.
4. if it would supply enough / sufficient energy for the European industry and if it would not be cheaper to use the solar energy in Spain.
5. (that) the costs were a problem indeed. While they had been going up in the first few years, important investors had withdrawn from the project [written English] / While they were going up in the first few years, important investors withdrew from the project. [spoken English]

E

1. Bevor Hongkong an China zurückgegeben wurde, war die Stadt eine britische Kronkolonie gewesen. Seit 1997 sind die Menschen beunruhigt/besorgt über den Einfluss aus Beijing (der Hauptstadt der Volksrepublik China, also der chinesischen Regierung).
2. (Im Jahr) 2014 nahmen viele Einwohner an einem Referendum zur Verteidigung des Sonderstatus von Hongkong teil, der offensichtlich von Beijing (d.h. von der chinesischen Regierung) nicht voll/in vollem Umfang anerkannt wurde. Es war unsicher, wie die chinesische Regierung reagieren würde.

F

For years young Africans from countries to [= *südlich von* ... vs. *in* the South = *im Süden der Sahara*, also *in der südlichen Sahara*] the South of the Sahara have been trying to cross the desert (and) to get to the coast. Their true destination [= *Zielort*!] is Europe. Last year again many people climbed over the fence around Melilla, as they had heard that they would be brought from the small / little Spanish enclave in the North of Africa / in Northern Africa to Europe. Others paid for a place in an overcrowded boat and failed to / did not reach Europe. Italy has asked the EU for help several times already. But the problem will not be solved as long as Africa suffers [*as long as* = temporale Konjunktion!] from poverty and wars. Will Europe really become a fortress? Would it not be good for the demographic development in several / some / a few EU countries, if more people immigrated?
What will happen if there is really a shortage of skilled labour? What will companies do? Then they may try to / Then maybe / perhaps they will try to lure young labour from abroad, as was the case in the 1950s and 1960s, during the German economic miracle. Would it not be better to train young immigrants now already?

G

1 would be held 2 would be published 3 became 4 would continue 5 had been criticized 6 were (divided) 7 are (divided) 8 are fighting 9 believe 10 will get 11 keep [stative verb / statisches Verb! daher keine Verlaufsform] 12 is 13 has been attacked 14 has been 15 be changed 16 remain 17 will strike 18 has not been solved 19 worry / are worrying 20 celebrate / are celebrating 21 fuels / will fuel 22 will be filled 23 were 24 were struggling 25 was dishing out 26 kept 27 introduced / had introduced

H

1. As the interest rates were [bezieht sich auf die Klagen im Jahr 2014, also vergangen / Past] very low since the beginning of the financial crisis, the insurance companies still complained / were still complaining about a strong decline in revenues in 2014.
2. While representatives of the consumer associations were negotiating with the insurers, the government suddenly passed a law allowing/permitting / which/that allowed / permitted insurances to pay out lower yields.
3. The government was promptly criticized, since [= *da (ja)*] / as this meant (that) clients would lose money (that) they were putting aside for their retirement, while the insurance companies would hardly make any losses.
4. There are good reasons for the significant political influence of the insurance sector / industry, which became clear again in 2014.
5. For decades the Germans have been putting a lot of money into life insurance policies, while only relatively few have been investing [immer noch: *for decades*!] in shares. According to forecasts this will not pay off any longer.
6. In / During the years of the German economic miracle many employees paid/were paying into the welfare system / social security system and pensioners enjoyed high pensions. Many thought (that) that would never change.

I

Up to the present day most monetary systems have not been planned carefully, but (have) evolved randomly. The gold standard was a first attempt to introduce a universal monetary system. It developed in Britain, which was becoming industrialized. Its economic success encouraged others to do transactions in accordance/line with its rules. It still lasted only one generation. After World War I / the first world war it did not work / function well and by 1936 it was a thing of the past.
In 1944 a new compromise was found during the conference in Bretton Woods: The countries pegged their currencies to the dollar, which, in turn, was pegged to gold. The IMF (International Monetary Fund) was created and the World Bank was set up. Such organizations which were to act worldwide / globally had never existed before. Meanwhile / In the meantime the initial enthusiasm has disappeared / vanished. The World Bank has been criticized for years; many less developed countries claim (that) it is a political instrument of the industrialized countries. However, since the beginning of the euro crisis the IMF has been playing an important role for countries whose overall indebtedness is too high.

Ch 7 (Mixed Tenses), L 2:

K

1 will continue 2 creates 3 decreases 4 is reined in 5 are done away with 6 happens 7 happens 8 will cause 9 (I')ll / will tell 10 will solve 11 gives 12 are 13 are transferred 14 'll / will show 15 creates 16 are not 17 'll / will believe

L

1 'll / will open 2 'll / will help 3 won't 4 'll / will take 5 'll / will work 6 don't / do not think 7 'll / will have 8 'll / will go along 9 'll / will tell 10 have had 11 keeps 12 'll / will 13 'll / will 14 won't / will not 15 have

M

1 wenn 2 Wenn 3 Als 4 als / ([*zu einer Zeit*] zu der) 5 wann

N

1 "You have to install an anti-virus program / antivirus software before you go online."
2. "We'll do that at once / immediately – don't worry."
3. "Good. I'll help you. As soon as the software is installed many updates will be downloaded. After that your computers will be protected."
4. "When reports about stolen passwords are published we always check all our computers."
5. "As long as you don't / do not open any files and don't / do not switch off your firewall, your data should be relatively safe."
6. I'll / will think of that. If hackers take over control, a normal user only realizes / notices that when / doesn't / does not realize / notice that until it is / it's too late."

O

1 were sitting in crouching positions when the representatives of the NGO (Non-Governmental Organization) entered the sweatshop.
2 arrived, the factory owner had been warned.
3 had waited / had been waiting five hours when the CEO made an announcement.
4 set up a task force, online industrial espionage had been going on for a long time.
5 visited the construction site, migrant workers were working in the sun.

P

1 when 2 When 3 if 4 if 5 when 6 If

Q

1 Germany's medium-sized companies, above all manufacturers, are often market leaders in their respective fields [jeder hat sein Gebiet, also sind es mehrere, d.h. es muss Plural stehen]. They are considered to be the backbone of the German economy. More than 1,000 companies have been family-owned for generations and are able to / can compete with the world's best. But while foreign companies are currently trying to understand and copy the business model, (the) German medium-sized companies are changing continuously. They are starting to realize / They are becoming aware that they can no longer just stay in small towns and are beginning to recruit foreign employees. Soon they will be global, too, "in everything (that) they do". We must / have to learn from "innovative clients", company bosses say. "We have learned from mistakes. When(ever) we believed we'd made it we started to lag behind."

2 When German firms wanted to learn from Japanese companies they realized very fast (that) not everything could be adopted, as the cultural environment in Germany was completely different. The Japanese economy was directed by the State and the companies were very hierarchical. Before Japan became a G 7 country it had had to overcome the destruction from the war. Japan had managed, in a short (period of) time, to build up a modern production industry / Japan had succeeded ... in building up .... The Western industrialized countries were surprised (at) how quickly Japan had developed from an economy with mass production to high quality standards. The steady rise of Japan / Japan's steady rise was based in particular on the employees' sense of duty. It seemed as if that was never going to end / would never end until the financial crisis hit Japan in the 1990s and revealed massive structural problems. Japan has not really recovered from that even today.

3 Many chairpersons of supervisory boards fail when the company is suddenly facing the abyss. When, for example, a German steel concern had got into a critical situation, the chairman of the supervisory board hesitated far too long before he held the responsible members of the (executive) board accountable. A new beginning was not possible until / ... was only possible when a new managing director came.

R

1. "The software is not compatible? Ok, then I'll / will simply use the overhead projector, even if that is a bit out of fashion and I haven't / have not worked with transparencies for a long time now. When I work under pressure / When I'm / When I am working under pressure I always have a plan B." – "Ok. I'll/will never forget that.
2. The consultants did not stop talking until the company boss threw them out. However, they had already angered and demotivated many employees, before the head of HR / Personnel realized / became aware of the frustration. When he joined talks for the first time, the whole department was discussing when and how they would defend themselves.
3. Since the failed rescue five years ago the traditional department store chain has been struggling / fighting for survival. When (they are) asked, executives always say (that) customers prefer to shop online. But is that really true? Would the customers not have remained loyal to the department store if the strategy had not been changed again and again, which confused customers every time? At the moment the managing director / CEO is looking for a new investor again.
4. A few years ago the EU Commission forced the banks to cut/lower / made the banks cut / lower their fees / charges at ATMs. Above all for withdrawals abroad the fees / charges had been too high.
5. In 2014 Nuremberg Fair celebrated its 40th anniversary. It had become the sixth-biggest fair in Germany and was expected to continue to grow / was expected to grow further. There

were concerns, however, that the ailing airport could/might affect / impair the growth of the fair if the passenger figures did not increase.
6. After the collapse of Enron many analysts wondered how such fraud had been possible. Had the auditors really discovered/detected nothing? How recklessly the top executives had acted / had been acting only became clear when an accused member of the board turned into / became a whistleblower.
7. "When will the temps / temporary workers end their hunger strike, which they began a week ago? – "They will go on / continue until/till the agency grants better conditions. ... That's what I would do, at any rate."

Ch 7 (Mixed Tenses), L 3:

S

1 ... found ...
2 ... classified as unstable ...
3 ... trying ... sold ...
4 ... how to prevent ...
5 ... to be passed ... intended
6 ... interviewed ...
7 ... produced ... ending up ... never meant ...

T

1 Considered 2 hampering 3 keeping 4 caused 5 having 6 being forced 7 worried
8 threatening 9 practised 10 growing 11 populated 12 spreading 13 polluting
14 Contaminated 15 requiring 16 ignored 17 visiting 18 used 19 upsetting 20 increased
21 educated 22 leading 23 caused

U

1 Alarmiert durch eine Welle von feindlichen Übernahmen aus dem Ausland ... , die darauf abzielen / mit dem Ziel, die heimische Industrie zu schützen.
2 ... er von Geschäftspartnern gewarnt wurde, ... feierlich zu Beginn der Zusammenarbeit unterzeichneten/unterschriebenen Abkommen / Verträge ... und ging (damit) das Risiko ein, plötzlichen Problemen gegenüberzustehen / mit plötzlichen Problemen konfrontiert zu werden / sein.
3 ... wenn sie nicht im Voraus bezahlt werden / außer, sie werden im Voraus bezahlt.
4 Als er im Hafen ankam ... wie die Container abgeladen wurden.
5 Da so viele Aktionäre ihre Aktien in Panik verkauften, ...
6 Dadurch, dass er seine Staatsanleihen verkaufte, ... , der möglicherweise einen Dominoeffekt auslösen würde, welcher Kreditaufnahme für das Land teurer machen würde.

V

a,
1 sent 2 Waiting 3 used 4 to be 5 to meet 6 to place 7 enclosed 8 detailed 9 including
10 Enclosed 11 needed 12 quoting 13 Given 14 offered 15 Facing 16 Hoping
b, 1 Referring 2 required 3 offered 4 explained 5 Convinced

W

1 W 2 R 3 W 4 W 5 R 6 W

X

1. The breach of trust openly admitted by the CEO / chairman of the board is (a) new proof of the serious conflict between the members of the board.
2. The bottles are to be delivered in wooden cases as stipulated / agreed (upon) in the contract. The defective goods returned last month can be replaced by new products of the same quality with the next shipment / consignment.
3. The textiles ordered already weeks ago have to be made of the same fabric as last time unless specified differently.
4. He was the only client to be aware/to realize / (who was aware/realized) that the bank had lied / been lying.
5. She wanted to know from her highly paid consultant / advisor how to save / (how she should save) her heavily indebted company.

Y

In spite of / Despite increasing / rising sales figures and booming demand in China the automotive / automobile group which had been posting record profits / gains for years announced a massive cost savings program with the help of which chiefly / above all unprofitable divisions were to be consolidated. Although far more successful than French rivals, the group had to recognize eventually / finally / at last that it had started lagging / to lag behind technological changes. The cheap SUVs produced / manufactured in emerging markets were threatening the profit margins, which [kein Partizip, da *nicht notwendiger Relativsatz*; außerdem würde der Satz zu unübersichtlich und unverständlich] were getting thinner / smaller every year also / even in the domestic / home market.

With sales in the EU stagnating due to saturated markets the car manufacturer / producer had to reinvent itself to survive. The first (person) to recognize that / (who recognized that) was not the CEO / chairman of the board but the chief engineer, who had been criticized publicly on many occasions. He affronted the whole executive board by declaring that the group would lose market share(s) in the coming years. At the AGM (Annual General Meeting), however, the solution he presented [Passivkonstruktion 'unschön' im Englischen!] convinced the majority of the shareholders: It was decided that the group would invest in environment-friendly technology like / such as electric engines and hybrid drives in order to benefit from increasing demand in emerging economies while, at the same time, fighting (against) air pollution.

Z

a, 1 making 2 putting 3 to criticize 4 living 5 was made public 6 wanting 7 to accomplish 8 helping out 9 re-filling 10 got 11 rising 12 was given 13 being 14 have always been 15 alienating 16 are used 17 announced 18 pointed out 19 being 20 mentioned 21 imitated 22 Falling 23 had never played 24 leaving

b, 1 After / When he had taken over … who was seen … and explained …
2 … which had just been taken over and created … which / that had to be done away with.
3 While it was still enjoying … and not able …

c, 1 **Dadurch, dass er** das 'Kerngeschäft' des Unternehmens immer wieder **betonte**, gab Nadella Spekulationen Nahrung, dass er die verlustreiche (Verluste machende) Tablet-Sparte abstoßen würde **und sich stattdessen auf** das traditionelle Software-Geschäft **konzentrieren würde**.
2 Analysten sagten: „**Da er sich** vielleicht als den ersten **sieht**, der den neuen Geist verkörpert, ist Nadella entschlossen, seinen strategischen Plan auszuführen – **wenn er nicht / außer wenn er** sehr bald durch steil ansteigende Tablet-Verkäufe **widerlegt wird**."